W9-DDD-098

A

JUST A SIMPLE PHARMACIST

FRANK RASKY

Just a Simple Pharmacist

The Story of Murray Koffler

Builder of the Shoppers Drug Mart Empire

M&S

Canadian Cataloguing in Publication Data

Rasky, Frank, 1923 –
Just a simple pharmacist

Includes index.
ISBN 0-7710-7294-5

1. Koffler, Murray, 1924 –   . 2. Pharmacists –
Ontario – Toronto – Biography. 3. Businessmen –
Ontario – Toronto – Biography. 4. Philanthropists –
Ontario – Toronto – Biography. I. Title.

RS73.K63R38 1988   615'.4'0924   C87-095035-5

Printed and bound in Canada

McClelland and Stewart
The Canadian Publishers
481 University Avenue
Toronto, Ontario
M5G 2E9

Contents

Foreword

MY FAVOURITE MEMORY of Murray Koffler is an incident during a June, 1979, reception given by Pat and Gordon Gray (then chairman of the LePage real estate empire) at Drynoch Farms, their country seat northwest of Richmond Hill, Ontario. The invitations had suggested that couples dress-to-match and most did, in guises such as paired sailors, duplicate clowns, Caesars and Cleopatras, and so on.

Murray and his wife Marvelle, fitted out in Great Gatsby white linen suits, looked elegant in their Fitzgeraldian finery. When Toronto-Dominion Bank chairman Dick Thomson and his wife Heather arrived wearing the plaid, there was much commotion because their entrance was heralded by a piper from the 48th Highlanders in full parade regalia. The guests were still craning their necks when Koffler approached first Thomson, then the piper, asking to borrow their swords. Signalling the piper he wanted the bagpipes at full skirl, Koffler in his white 1920s suit then performed a faultless Scottish sword dance.

Somebody remarked afterward it was not a gesture you'd expect from that year's chairman of the United Jewish Appeal – yet it was, somehow, typically Koffler. That sense of occasion, and the surprising skill, displayed the man's class and versatility.

This book documents a bewildering array of Murray Koffler's accomplishments, and it would be superfluous to pass judgement on his amazing performance. One short formula to weigh the character of a man of business is to analyse his attitude toward the money he makes. Most successful businessmen must eventually choose whether to allow the capitalist system to use them (and wear them down) or to harness that system to create something of permanent value. There's a subtle philosophical bridge over which they cross at the moment they decide whether or not to put time and effort into changing the world or to focus simply on enriching themselves.

Koffler has never stopped trying to change the world he lives in, whether the project is creating a scientific infrastructure for Israel, helping confused youngsters to kick hard drugs, or counselling Canadian native entrepreneurs toward financial success. He is soft-hearted toward every cause except defence of the status quo – and as someone once remarked, "Murray is the ideal chairman; he could organize even an Italian infantry attack."

I remember discussing Koffler's unusually high energy quotient with Professor Emil Fackenheim of the University of Toronto. After we had affably agreed that the man could be taken only in small doses because his drives are just too exhausting for the average mortal, Fackenheim commented that he thought Koffler's greatest strengths are that he "works by example, and has a real sense of values." A wise summary from the savant, and one that rings true.

Koffler's sense of values was displayed forcefully and effectively during the 1973 Arab war that threatened Israel. When the need was apparent, he promptly choreographed a flash fund-raising campaign that amassed the largest per-capita donations of any Jewish community anywhere. At one memorable half-hour meeting at the Skyline Hotel in Toronto, he personally collected $6.5 million.

Whether he is fund-raising, sailing, or riding one of his championship horses, Koffler concentrates fully on his enthusiasms of the moment. His thoughts and ideas flow so fast sometimes that he is the only man I know who interrupts himself.

It's a rarefied world he lives in. He and his wife Marvelle were two of the few Canadians invited to the wedding of Princess Anne and Mark Phillips. Murray has entertained several of our prime ministers with great style at Jokers Hill Farm, source of some of the most delicious privately produced maple syrup in the country. He knows everybody, but what matters is that he gets them all to want to *do* things – writing prefaces for biographies, for example.

Murray's greatest asset is Marvelle, who once hinted at the secret of their happy family life when she told me: "Our children have been encouraged to move in any positive direction they wish, and they haven't abused that privilege. Of course – nobody has ever gone to bed in our house without being kissed good night."

In his personal and professional realms, Koffler lives as a good and caring man. This book is a record of his life thus far – and a gauge of the momentum this *mensch* has developed for the rest of it.

CHAPTER ONE

Prince Charming Kicks the Can

Murray Koffler felt two ways about the occasion. A week before the event, he expressed his feelings to a friend. "I have this crazy vision," he confided, with a characteristic touch of whimsy. "It's a vision of my swollen ego floating right up in the stratosphere like a hot air balloon. Then it explodes from all the excess helium of flattery. And I come tumbling down."

At the same time, he recognized it would be a dazzling culmination of his career. "It'll be my last big kick at the can," he said. Then, with equally characteristic *joie de vivre*, he exclaimed, "And what a way to go!"

Others who came to attend the tribute dinner, held on February 24, 1986, likened it to an international gathering of close to 2,000 members of a family who had congregated to pay homage to the living icon of the clan. Kofflerian devotees all, they came from every province of Canada and from the United States, England, and Israel to attend a hundred-dollar-a-plate black-tie dinner in the Metropolitan Ballroom of Toronto's Hilton Harbour Castle Hotel. And they came to roast and toast the man they variously called "Mr. Wonderful," the "Jewish Cary Grant," "Cecil B. De Mille of retail pharmacy," and "Midas with a humanitarian touch."

The focus of their paeans was Murray Bernard Koffler, justly revered by his admirers as "Prince Charming," for he is one of the most charming entrepreneurs in Canada. He is also one of the rarest amalgams one can find in the multinational financial world: an immensely successful magnate who combines the heart of a socially responsive idealist with a very practical business head.

When being verbally enshrined at the tribute dinner, he had just turned sixty-two and was known to some as the co-founder of the international Four Seasons Hotel chain. But he was much better known as the innovator who carved out the Shoppers Drug Mart empire across Canada and consequently changed the face and persona of the corner drugstore throughout the nation.

He prefers to be known as "just a simple pharmacist." Somebody took him up on that statement and remarked jocularly – and simplistically – during the evening that the reason for Koffler's success could be summed up in six simple words: "Dress British, look Irish, think Yiddish." It was evident, though, from the evening's outpouring of affection that they were not merely saluting the conventional success story of a simple pharmacist who was born over the drugstore of his Romanian immigrant father in what was then Toronto's Jewish neighbourhood.

After all, the celebrants hymning his praises that night, either in person or via videotape, comprised a veritable Valhalla of personages who transcended the boundaries of commerce. Among those honouring Koffler were three prime ministers (Israel's Shimon Peres, Canada's present Conservative PM Brian Mulroney, and Canada's past Liberal PM Pierre Trudeau); a nation's president (Israel's Chaim Herzog); two provincial premiers (Ontario's present Liberal Premier David Peterson and past Conservative Premier William Davis); a Canadian Roman Catholic cardinal (Emmett Cardinal Carter of Toronto); and a British aristocrat (Lord Sieff of Brimpton). The luminaries also included a good many of Canada's reigning merchant princes and industrial barons, as well as the *crème de la crème* of local politics, broadcasting, publishing, the arts, and high society.

Their names all added glitter to next morning's social column in *The Globe and Mail* written by Zena Cherry, the daily

Almanach de Gotha recordkeeper of the Canadian Establishment. Lacking only were greetings from two members of royalty. One was Prince Philip, who had been a weekend guest at Koffler's manorial, thousand-acre Jokers Hill equestrian farm near Toronto. The other was Queen Elizabeth, who had returned his hospitality by inviting Koffler and his wife Marvelle to attend the wedding of Princess Anne and Mark Phillips at Westminster Abbey and had played hostess to the Kofflers at Buckingham Palace.

The guests had come to this affair to pay their respects to Koffler for manifold reasons. The mercantile-minded were honouring his golden merchandising touch. The Four Seasons Hotel chain he had co-founded twenty-five years ago with two partners, Toronto furrier Edmond (Eddie) Creed and Toronto apartment builder Isadore (Issy) Sharp, has since become the Rolls-Royce of hotel chains. It is a network of twenty-two luxury hostelries in principal cities in Canada, the United States, and England, with a staff of more than 8,000 employees and gross revenues of $550 million. The Shoppers empire he had likewise launched twenty-five years previously, beginning with a nucleus of two Toronto neighbourhood drugstores, has flourished even more luxuriantly. It now embraces more than 550 stores, with 12,000 employees and a gross of close to $2 billion. In terms of dollar sales volume, this makes it the largest drugstore chain in Canada and the fifth largest in North America; in terms of setting trends, it can boast of a self-serve supermarket pharmacy concept that revolutionized the industry in Canada.

A platoon of drugstore suppliers – the heads of Canadian corporations ranging from Fabergé to Clairol, Coca-Cola to Nabisco, Procter & Gamble to Johnson & Johnson, Parke-Davis to Chesebrough-Pond's – had come because Koffler had chosen the occasion of his chain's twenty-fifth anniversary to step down as board chairman. He thereby left in total command David Bloom, the dynamic forty-two-year-old Toronto pharmacist disciple he had groomed to assume office as president and chief executive officer. Bloom was pleased to announce officially that his mentor would continue to serve as honorary chairman of Shoppers Drug Mart Limited, as well as a multi-functioning director of its parent company.

This is Imasco Limited, a multinational consumer products and financial services conglomerate headquartered in Montreal. It operates Canada's biggest tobacco company, Imperial Tobacco Limited; Canada's largest trust company, Canada Trustco Mortgage Company; the Canadian chain of about 500 United Cigar Stores; the United States chain of more than 2,700 Hardee's, Burger Chef, and Grisanti's restaurants under the umbrella of Hardee's Food Systems; and the United States chain of 850 Peoples Drug Stores. It grosses more than $10 billion annually in revenue, and Koffler's 2 million shares in the company make him one of Imasco's largest individual shareholders – and a very rich man.

But while Koffler is a millionaire many times over, he is not a super-rich Canadian Croesus. For example, the titans who rule two Canadian dynasties are infinitely wealthier: Edward and Peter Bronfman, whose Edper Investments Ltd. controls assets worth an estimated $40 billion; and the brothers Paul, Albert, and Ralph Reichmann, whose Olympia and York has become the largest property development firm in the world, worth more than an estimated $30 billion. Furthermore, Koffler's wealth is picayune compared to the fortunes amassed by such Canadian billionaires as Lord Thomson of Fleet, Steve Roman, Galen Weston, K.C. Irving, E.P. Taylor, and the Eaton and Molson families.

It's not the amount of his wealth, but what he does with it that has gained *yiches* (prestige, glory) and *mitzvoth* (good deeds, meritorious acts) for Koffler. He had attracted so many admirers from all walks of life to his tribute dinner because he is such a virtuoso in the art of performing good deeds joyfully. He has consistently adhered to the philosophy of the seventeenth-century essayist Francis Bacon that money is like manure – worthless unless you spread it to make things grow. And the number of worthy projects that have flourished, thanks to being fertilized by Kofflerian largess, shows that as a man and a philanthropist he has indeed a green thumb. He is a confirmed life-enhancer who dispenses his time and his money prodigiously to what he regards as an extension of his family – the Jewish and non-Jewish communities of his native Toronto, the community of Canada, and the community of Israel.

The beneficiaries of his generosity are myriad. To pick at random from a page-long list of more than forty, his contributions to the betterment of humankind range from the $1 million he donated to found the Koffler Centre of the Arts in Toronto's Jewish Community Centre to the $2 million he provided to help establish the eighteen-storey "atom smasher" called the Koffler Accelerator Tower built to aid peacetime nuclear research at Israel's Weizmann Institute of Science.

His continuing good deeds illustrate why the Canadian government honoured Koffler in 1977 by awarding him the nation's highest honour, the Order of Canada. One project was the formation in 1984 of the Canadian Council for Native Business. He called on more than 300 corporate leaders to initiate a unique nation-wide board of trade, in which both native and non-native entrepreneurs would strive to bring Canada's first citizens into the mainstream of Canada's business community.

The tribute dinner was designed in part to celebrate the successful outcome of another Koffler project. He was the prime donor among close to 700 company representatives and friends present who had contributed more than $3 million toward the founding of the $6 million Koffler Institute of Pharmacy Management. To be affiliated with the University of Toronto's Faculty of Pharmacy, the institute will upgrade the business skills of undergraduates and graduates of pharmacy colleges across Canada. When completed, it will be the only facility of its kind in the world, and Koffler had planned it to be his ultimate good deed on behalf of the profession that has been so good to him.

Koffler and his colleagues at Shoppers made of the tribute dinner a genuine rejoicing, and as one would expect from the former drummer boy with the 48th Highlanders of Canada, the affair was staged with showmanlike panache. Indeed, a troupe of eight pipers and drummers, wearing the scarlet and green tunics and tartans of the 48th Highlanders, skirled on their bagpipes and beat a cheerful drum tattoo as they led the march of dignitaries to the two massive headtables.

The cover of the royal blue menu displayed in silver a caricature of Koffler that highlighted his most prominent features: his Irishy pug nose and wide grin. And as the guests dined on the Lucullan repast, they were entertained by lampoon images flashed on three giant screens. Most amusing was the smiling face of Koffler beaming out of a cutout portrait of Mona Lisa. A comic voice announced that the portrait, painted by the well-known artist Moishe da Vinci, would be sold at the Shoppers Drug Mart discount price of $14.99.

Also shown on the screens was a thirty-five-minute, audio-video tribute to Koffler. It was narrated by Lorne Greene, the Canadian actor who had won global renown by playing Ben Cartwright in the *Bonanza* television series and was a one-time drama counsellor at the Ontario summer camp where young Koffler had first exhibited his performing skills by starring in *The Mikado*. The accolades of those interviewed for this presentation were both gently joshing and deeply moving.

George Cohon, president of the Canadian McDonald's hamburger chain, wisecracked about his fellow franchisor in the pharmacy field: "For years, I've been attending Murray's fund-raising dinners. Yet I've never been asked to cater for any one of them. Please, Murray, can I cater to the next one?"

Bea Arthur, the TV comedienne who stars as one of the husband-hunters of *The Golden Girls* and is the commercial spokeswoman for Shoppers Drug Mart, asked wistfully: "What can I say of a man who is successful and debonair and generous and worldly ... ? Is he single? Has he got a brother? A cousin?"

Former Prime Minister Trudeau, who has gone skiing with Koffler and been his house guest on several occasions, said with impressive simplicity: "I admire Murray for the way he has reached out to mankind, helping individuals to fulfil themselves to the best of their ability. But the best tribute I can give to him is this: he is a good citizen ... and he is a good man."

Ron Satok, the blind painter who now heads the Satok School of the Arts, typified those who attested to Koffler's talent for inspiring others to self-fulfilment. He recalled how the Toronto Outdoor Art Exhibit, an annual City Hall art show Koffler initiated twenty-five years ago, had served as a catalyst for a new career for him when he most needed it. "I'd hit the bottom of the pits," he said. "I'd run out of hope and money. I was being evicted from my studio. My wife had left me. I didn't know what to do. Then Murray picked me up from this low in my life. He did more than commission a mural. He became my patron. He helped me lecture before groups of the handicapped and start my school. He encouraged me to act as a role model for the disabled in the community. I bless him for doing all this without once ever offering pity and saying he felt sorry for me."

The tributes paid by the headtable guests were likewise eloquent in lauding Koffler's gift for infectious friendship. Rabbi Arthur Bielfeld, Koffler's spiritual guide and good friend for the past nineteen years at the Reform Temple Emanu-El, asserted when saying grace: "We thank you, God, for Murray Koffler, whose passion for life animates our presence here. He is one of those rare souls who finds pleasure in living every day without waiting for the days to be gone before finding charm in them.... It is Murray's belief that our life belongs to the whole community, that as long as we live it is our privilege to do for it whatever we can, for the harder we work the more we live."

Cardinal Carter, when his turn came, said he was pleased to honour a civilized man in the precise sense of the term *civitas*, meaning the ability to live together and communicate together in a community spirit. "Murray represents the best of our Canadian community spirit that allows us to live and let live together," he said. He could not resist adding in jest: "I must admit that when I see this large group in community here, the parish priest in me comes forward, and I'd like to take up a collection."

Federal Indian Affairs Minister David Crombie praised Koffler for founding the Canadian Council for Native Business. He went on to say that "the secret of Murray Koffler" could be summed up in this phrase: "You know that when you give you get, and when you get you give." On behalf of Canada's native people he presented to Koffler the Ojibway Indian word, *lagwech*. "It means thank you for your thousand kindnesses," he said.

The most touching presentation was made by Koffler's five children. After they gathered in front of the headtables, his oldest son, Leon, said, "Tonight we heard him called 'Mr. Wonderful,' 'Mr. Civilized,' and a lot of other fine and fancy nicknames. But we as his children just call him 'Good Old Dad.'" He then unveiled a portrait of their father by the world's most illustrious photographer of prime ministers and presidents and kings, Yousuf Karsh of Ottawa. "Good Old Dad," he said, "your portrait will hang in the central foyer of the Koffler Institute of Pharmacy Management, where it will serve as an inspiration to all young pharmacists who enter its doors."

The heartfelt tributes moved Koffler close to tears. In his closing speech in response, he made the evening's most telling statement by quoting from the philosopher, William James: "The great use of life is to spend it for something that outlasts it."

Altogether, it had been a magnificent kick at the can.

CHAPTER TWO

Mahatma Koffler,
Creative Gamesman

"What's it like to be part of Murray Koffler's life?" his wife Marvelle asked rhetorically at his tribute dinner. "It's like being part of a whirlwind attached to the eye of a tornado." Indeed, he radiates an electric bonhomie that reminds his friends of Salvador Dali's description of the artist's limitless vitality: "I don't take drugs; I *am* drugs."

Just as flowers turn to the sun, so do people seem to gravitate toward Murray Koffler, who projects a charismatic magnetism. It's an elusive, quicksilver quality as difficult to pin down as Jello on a wall, but he certainly has it, and it is a magical gift. As J.M. Barrie, the author of *Peter Pan*, once said of charm in certain women: "If you have it, you don't need to have anything else; and if you don't have it, it doesn't much matter what else you have." Part of his charm stems from his natural geniality and solicitude, his contagious goodwill and good humour.

Paul Paré, the board chairman of Imasco Limited, himself a considerable charmer, thinks it's based on an essential sweetness of character virtually unknown among powerful men of business. "When Murray walks into a room, whether it's a trade convention or a cocktail party," says Paré, "suddenly the whole place sparkles. He claps people on the back. He gives the impression he knows their first name even if he doesn't. And he has this absolutely marvellous positive outlook of the bottle being half full instead of half empty. You can be faced with the worst bloody problem, and he'll find a way of identifying its silver lining."

The Koffler mystique is palpable even to a blind man, according to Ron Satok, the Toronto artist who became sightless in mid-career. "You can *feel* it when he makes an entrance," says Satok. "He has a flair for making you feel you're somebody special."

The magical spell he casts on Shoppers' employees is truly hypnotic. He is regarded by them as a kind of benign *pater familias*. Their admiration of him is described with wry and affectionate amusement by Gordon Stromberg, Shoppers' vice-president of advertising, who has known Koffler for almost twenty years. "Because of the incredible number of things he's done, a lot of staffers in the field are initially intimidated by Murray's reputation," says Stromberg. "They ... put him up on a pedestal. They come up to me and say, 'You really talked to him? Does he know your name? Can you relate to him as a person?' I tell them, 'He's really a hell of a great guy gifted with the common touch; also a great kibitzer who can take your kidding.' But I can understand their awe. I felt the same way the first time I met him. Your mouth just drops to the floor and you think, 'My gawd! I'm meeting the saint in the flesh, Mahatma Koffler!'"

Koffler is no saint, nor is he "just a simple pharmacist," as he constantly reiterates; rather, he is a complex personality. A penetrating portrait of a corporate high achiever bearing the imprint of the Kofflerian psyche has been limned by Dr. Michael Maccoby, author of the business study *The Gamesman*. Maccoby, a psychoanalyst who teaches at the Washington School of Psychiatry, in effect put the modern big business executive on the couch. In a seven-year study sponsored by Harvard, he interviewed in depth 250 managers in twelve large North American companies.

Maccoby delineates the chief archetypal personalities in the corporate hierarchy who play the game of business management. The Jungle Fighter, for example, is a power-hungry predator. Wily, ruthless, manipulative, he frequently dreams of being locked in combat with enemies out to destroy him. This personality, according to Maccoby, is typified by former Presidents Richard Nixon and Lyndon Johnson. The Company Man is a loyal careerist totally committed to the company way of life. Suspicious of change, a cautious writer of memos, he often dreams of being chased through a tunnel and is typified by Presidents Dwight Eisenhower and Gerald Ford.

The Creative Gamesman, the superstar of the corporate species, seems to embody to a remarkable degree many of the attributes that his colleagues claim for Murray Koffler. Epitomized by President John F. Kennedy, he is described by Maccoby as being a stylish, boyish, playful risk-taker who revels in playing the managerial game. His main goal is to be known as a winner and his deepest fear is to be labelled a loser; hence, he is prone to have anxiety dreams of spinning like a top, falling down, failing to pass an examination. It's not money that drives him (a sizable salary is merely the means of keeping score), but he loves competing for the sheer exhilaration of winning the contest and its attendant glory.

He is a flexible gambler, always fascinated by new methods, and a fluent speaker, able to dramatize new ideas with verve. He has an extraordinary talent for getting to the meat of a matter, a radar-like sensitivity for scanning the emotional horizon, and a Tom Sawyer zest for motivating others to tackle a dreary chore as though it were a barrel of fun.

He is as much a liveaholic as he is a workaholic. He enjoys a rich, almost childlike, fantasy life, has a desire to do what is noble, a strong need to be accepted, and tends to favour sports such as skiing and sailing, individually oriented activities, where he can be alone and compete against the elements but escape from the pressure of competing against people. He takes an interest in people who work for him and is sensitive about hurting their feelings. He lacks the Jungle Fighter's willingness to destroy competitors or even to fire incompetents; he would rather strive to give a spark to deadwood. Yet in a crisis he does have a "surgeon's touch."

Maccoby defines the Creative Gamesman as an ambivalent bundle of paradoxes: "He is idealistic, yet shrewd and pragmatic; a team leader, yet often a rebel against bureaucratic hierarchy; gregarious, yet a bit of a loner; dominating, yet not destructive; graceful, yet impatiently restless; energetic, yet itchy. Serious on the one hand, he is also puckish and playful, with a twinkle in the eye." On the negative side, Maccoby says his worst flaw is that, in his reach for the top, he tends to harden his heart and is impassive to social concerns outside his corporate world. He bottles up his feelings of love and develops a hard-boiled shell for fear of being deemed a softy. "Like the mythical King Midas, who turned his daughter into gold, the corporate manager can no longer choose when to be intimately related and when to be detached."

Only a rare few, Maccoby found in his survey, have developed a heart that listens to the anguish of the weak in the outside world. The Creative Gamesman who attains that peak, he concludes, is a "grave-merry" life-affirmer who "kicks the world away from him with the airy grace of a dancer, and yet at the same time, presses it to his heart."

But generalized panegyrics of this kind still make Koffler seem like some sort of sugary Pollyanna. A more intimate insight is provided by his two closest friends, who have been yachting with him, got drunk with him, and gone disco-dancing with him until three in the morning. Both acknowledge he can be vain, infuriatingly opinionated, and an excessively domineering grandstander. But they cheerfully tolerate his faults because of his many redeeming virtues.

They are also best equipped to pinpoint his motivating force most succinctly. Furrier Eddie Creed, who served as best man at Koffler's wedding just as Koffler did at his, says his friend has a compelling need for approval: "What drives Murray is that he likes people, and he likes people to like him, and he works damned hard at it." George Zuckerman, president of the international textile firm, Doubletex Inc., an intimate since their college fraternity days when Koffler was nicknamed "Mr. Clean," says a Micawberish optimism is the key to his success: "Everybody wants to be a millionaire, but they just talk about it and don't go after it. Murray went after it with the zeal and sunny conviction that life is a bowl of cherries waiting for you to pick them up."

Koffler himself denies that he ever set out to become a millionaire and had ever planned a formula for financial success. He makes his accomplishments all seem absurdly simple. "They *were* simple," he kept insisting ingenuously when a friend asked him to sum up his many achievements. "Remember, I'm just a simple pharmacist, and I simply took advantage of opportunities as they came. There's been no set pattern, no grand design, no scheme whatsoever. They just evolved. Everything I've ever done, whether in business or community affairs, has been one happenstance following logically on the tail of another happenstance."

A doer rather than a navel-gazer, he is not given to introspection and has a disarming way of belittling the hyperboles of praise heaped on him by his admirers. He debunks, for instance, the claim that he is a natural geyser of unflagging energy. It stems in good part, he has stated publicly, from the Life brand multi-vitamin pills produced by Shoppers Drug Mart that he pops down every morning. This sounds suspiciously, though, like a piece of advertising hucksterism. The fact is that Koffler seems to walk with a springy step from the time he gets up in the morning and the rest of the day appears to vibrate with vigour like a walking tuning fork.

He disclaims emphatically the accuracy of the label pinned on him that his success is founded on dressing British, looking Irish, and thinking Yiddish. "Frankly, I detest that pat phrase," he confides. "It really makes me wince. I detest it almost as much as I hate being stereotyped a 'tycoon' or a 'mogul.'"

He maintains, first of all, that he is hardly a tailor's beau ideal of sartorial *savoir-faire* because he lacks the patience to have his suits custom-made. He concedes he admires men who look immaculately groomed and admits, "I feel *very* uncomfortable at the thought of wearing just a sweater when I go to a restaurant; I have to wear a sports jacket at least. At home, when we have dinner with the family, we put jackets on, and my kids enjoy that, too. But how can people say I dress British," he asks triumphantly, "when I prefer shopping for suits in Toronto when they have sales—and I buy everything off the rack?"

Woody Woodcroft diplomatically begs to differ. For the past ten years, Woodcroft has fitted Koffler at Lou Myles Disegnatore. It is one of the three posh tailoring establishments in Toronto that help Koffler, an inveterate table-hopper, party-hopper, and country-hopper, maintain his rotating wardrobe of several dozen suits and winter and summer tuxedos, which always make him appear so buffed, bandboxed, and dandified. Woodcroft says it's true that Koffler buys off the rack, but that's because his trim figure (5'10½", 180 pounds) is a tailor's dream. "Mr. Koffler has such a good physique and natural flair for wearing clothes that he can make almost any off-the-rack suit look elegant," says Woodcroft.

Koffler does not entirely dispute the notion that his broad, retroussé, potatoey nose does make him look somewhat Irish. He acknowledges that he has "atypical" wide nostrils, but prefers to think of them as rather imperial "significant" nostrils. "I'm never short of air," he jokes. In fact, he has an attractive, jovial, bon vivant face, with sparkly brown eyes, glossy dark hair flecked with grey, and a head-thrown-back, full-bellied laugh.

"I love the melodious sound of his laugh," says John Bassett, the former publisher of the Toronto *Telegram* and the present CTV television titan, who is celebrated for his own clarion-call voice and the camaraderie of his Irish merriment. "He's one hell of a fella the way he laughs heartily after you spin him a yarn. Murray may not look like an Irishman, but he certainly *laughs* Irish."

As for thinking Yiddish, if that means having the Jewish *kopf* of a financier, Koffler blithely denies it. True, he says, he may have mastered the art of assessing financial statements and has a keen grasp of the bottom line of his own enterprises. But Koffler contends he has no head for the abstractions of economic theory and no memory at all for the minutiae of bookkeeping figures. Indeed, as an idea man rather than a detail man, he claims he has the memory of a dunce. "There are three major things I can't remember," he likes saying. "I can't remember names. I can't remember faces. And I can't remember the third thing."

Perhaps his most endearing trait is his ability to laugh at his own foibles. One of them is his forgetfulness about carrying spare cash in his pocket. He is a congenital borrower of quarters to make phone calls. He is often forced to borrow when he runs out of the six-for-a-dollar Anthony and Cleopatra cigars he enjoys smoking after dinner. When borrowing small change, he has been known to make the contrite excuse that it's not uncommon for three supermagnates of his acquaintanceship to be similarly strapped. Jacob Rothschild, a scion of the banking dynasty, once had to borrow cab fare from Koffler in New York City. John Craig Eaton, of the Canadian department store dynasty, had to borrow money for gas when driving Koffler from Toronto to London, Ontario, for a speaking engagement in Eaton's $150,000 Ferrari. And Allan Bronfman, of the distillery dynasty, was compelled to borrow twenty-five pounds from Koffler when both were travelling in Israel to an international economic conference.

The reluctance to keep walking-around-money on hand appears to have become a Koffler family shortcoming. Adam, his twenty-eight-year-old son, who is president of the $30 million King Ranch Health Spa and Fitness Resort to open near Toronto in 1989, delights in telling a story that illustrates the seemingly inherited family idiosyncrasy.

He and his father sat down for a business meeting in downtown Toronto to figure out the family assets available so that Adam could go ahead comfortably with building the spa, the most lavish of its kind in Canada. "We added up a figure of X number of dollars and were both overwhelmed," recalls Adam. "Dad leaned back and said 'Can you believe that amount? Do you realize how privileged we are as a family to be able to undertake such a project?'

"We left the office wearing these big smiles on our faces and I say, 'Come on, Dad. Let's grab a quick bite of lunch at the deli across the street.'

"Then we're standing in line waiting with the other customers and I say, 'Dad, I hope you have some cash with you because I've run out. I've just got two bucks in my wallet.'

"Dad says, 'Well, I've got just enough to get out of the parking lot, plus one buck left over.'

"I had to take out a line of credit with the cashier, telling her I'd be back later in the afternoon to pay for our ten-dollar lunch. And over our salad and coffee, we both break up laughing at the irony of the situation."

Koffler père is notorious for another failing that provokes his dismay rather than his amusement. Like the bustling Rabbit in Walt Disney's cartoon version of *Alice In Wonderland*, Koffler seems to be forever moaning to himself the rhymed couplet: "I'm late! I'm late! For a very important date!" Koffler is invariably late for meetings. Peering frantically at his watch, he can often be identified as the tardy passenger racing across the tarmac at the last minute to catch a plane. When he was the chief executive officer of Shoppers, he was compelled to have a phone installed in his car. "There was only one reason for having the phone," he says with a sigh. "I needed it to call up the next person on my appointment list to apologize, 'Sorry, I'm going to be late a little.'"

It's a habit he deplores and yet it continues to embarrass him. He thinks it stems from his Toronto high school days when a certain Major Dunkley, the martinet of a vice-principal at Oakwood Collegiate, used to bawl him out regularly for coming late to classes. "Koffler, you'll be nothing but a bum all your life," Dunkley would upbraid him, "unless you smarten up and get to appointments on time."

Koffler now rationalizes that he fell into the lateness habit because he was such a poor student. "I only really got down to studying by eleven o'clock at night and I'd study right through until two or three," he says. "Then I'd go to sleep and wake up thoroughly exhausted, sometimes unable to finish an exam because I forgot much of what I learned the night before."

His erratic sleeping pattern persists until this day. "My best ideas come to me in the middle of the night," he says. "Unfortunately, I've never been able to talk my ideas into a dictaphone. I often wished I did, because my brain is usually buzzing with some of my brightest ideas at two or three in the morning."

It's also the time when he rehearses his best "ad-lib" speeches. Koffler is considered a genius by his colleagues for his inspirational speeches, delivered in an easy conversational style, which ignite them with an almost religious fervour to beat last year's company sales. "I don't take it lightly," he says of his speech-making. "I work very hard at it. I sweat over it."

Hilda Wilson, the long-time public relations consultant for Shoppers, expertly drafts the bare bones of a speech. Koffler may retain key phrases, but more often than not he will rewrite it completely. He usually begins scribbling his ideas furiously on unlined note paper at close to midnight; by two o'clock in the morning he is pacing up and down, practising his delivery.

He loves the nuances and cadences of words, according to his wife Marvelle, and every word must sound exactly right to his ears. "When he's struggling over a speech in his den, no matter how late at night, I go from the bedroom to the kitchen to prepare hot cereal and milk and that keeps him going," she says. "I must hear his speech five, six, or seven times. We go over and over it for sentence structure. Then he's finally ready to verbalize what seems to be so easy for him."

"I'm gratified" and "I'm privileged" and "I'm enamoured" and "I'm enthused" are among the frequently used exclamations that ginger up his speeches. A problem is never called a problem but instead is presented as an invigorating "challenge" or "opportunity." And by his sheer necromancy of words coupled with exuberance, he manages to add a lustrous patina to his profession. Under his spell, pharmacy is not merely a fusion of the mercantile and medicinal; it emerges instead as a holy crusade.

Hearing Koffler's uplifting rhetoric, a listener is apt to be reminded of the story of two labourers whacking away at rocks on a building site. When a stranger asked what they were doing, the unimaginative labourer said, "I make a living by cracking rocks." But the Koffleresque workman said, "I'm helping Christopher Wren to build a cathedral."

Koffler is well stocked with a thesaurus of cracker-barrel homilies that serve as boosters to himself and his audiences. He has borrowed them from two unlikely sources. One is an evangelist who delivers homespun sermons on a Sunday morning radio religious program. The other is the late Dale Carnegie's pop bible for Babbitts and other Rotarians in the 1920s, *How To Stop Worrying and Start Living*. Koffler's five children are so accustomed to hearing him recycle his repertoire of pick-me-up bromides that they can parrot them by rote.

"It's corny, but it works," says his youngest daughter Tiana, as she recites her favourite Kofflerian maxim: "I'm going to be happy today. Whether it's blue or grey, no matter what comes my way, I'm going to be happy today." Theo, his oldest daughter, is rejuvenated by: "Today is the first day of the rest of my life." His sons, Adam, Tom, and Leon, echo as in a trio: "It is as important to do the thing right as to do the right thing." Koffler himself often repeats while he shaves the credo pasted on his mirror: "The greatest success is to be able to lead your life in your own way."

Despite the palliatives of Dale Carnegie, under Koffler's façade of perpetual ebullience, he is occasionally gnawed by the inner doubts that Winston Churchill termed his own interior "black devils" of depression. Ulcer cases are often diagnosed by physicians as repressed worrywarts; and it is perhaps significant that Koffler, until he underwent surgery six years ago, endured a duodenal ulcer. Though Koffler says, "I'm generally happy inside my skin," he acknowledges that he is indeed sometimes bedeviled by problems that cannot be disguised glibly as opportunities.

"Nobody likes to reveal his weaknesses, so I try not to air my troubles in public," he says. "I can be very critical of myself in my own quiet hours. But I do my complaining at home to my wife. I do it at our ritual cocktail hour before we have dinner. It's the only time we have a chance to sit down for a real chat. She'll have hors d'oeuvres ready and she'll have white wine and I'll have my customary Chivas Regal. Marv is a marvellous listener and I'll discuss absolutely everything with her, including business matters. We may disagree strongly, but I respect her opinions about the things that trouble me. It's a wonderful way to relieve tensions! After I've had my Scotch and soda with Marv, I feel like another person. And that person enjoys a Scotch as well."

Marvelle, a serene and elegant beauty, enjoys playing the role of listener to her mercurial and sometimes moody husband whom she calls adoringly the *"uno numero* man in my life." After being married to him for thirty-seven years, she claims she never gets bored listening to his oft-repeated stories. She considers him a superb raconteur, with Jack Benny's sense of timing and a gift for mimicry and whimsical drollery. "His storytelling is so infectious and brings such joy to people," she says, "that I just sit back and share in their pleasure."

When friends come to their home for a dinner party, he can be a one-man theatre, Falstaffian in his humour. "He can be a very funny man," she says. "Once you wind him up, you can't wind him down. He can go so far in his antics that he may drape himself in the living-room curtains and imitate a stripteaser. He'll have us gasping for breath and begging him to stop making us laugh so hard."

But that is when he's in a clowning mood. "Sometimes he comes home very uptight," she says. "That's when he must be handled with care. You have to sense intuitively that he's having his pressures and you must work around them. There's no sense locking horns at that point. That's when he needs his calming-down time. I sometimes wait until about two in the morning. Again I may go into the kitchen and make his hot cereal and milk, give it to him, and that settles him down. Or I may stay up reading upstairs and wait until he's ready to come up and talk."

Koffler rarely loses his temper, and, publicly at least, he has never been known to lose his cool in an outburst of rage. He concedes, however, that he frequently loses his patience and, when pressed, will grudgingly admit he even harbours a couple of healthy hates. Asked by a friend to list them, the incorrigibly benign Koffler paused for a long while and then finally blurted, "Well, I hate phonies—you know, the type of people who posture and say things just to impress. And I hate bores—I don't suffer gladly fools who twitter on about trivia over card games."

"Only *two* hates?" the friend asked incredulously.

"Well, I do lose my patience with other types of people," Koffler answered sheepishly. "But they are only peeves, not hates."

One of his pet peeves reflects his old-fashioned sense of courtesy. "I dislike people with bad manners," he says. "If I see young people eating with their elbows on the table, I'll let them know.

"Once I walked into a room when my daughter Theo was entertaining a boyfriend she was dating. Theo said, 'Dad, I'd like you to meet So-and-So.'

"The kid was sitting on one of our low couches and he just puts his hand up. So I grab his hand and yank him up. 'Nice of you to stand up,' I said.

"The kid was so shocked that from then on he stood up smartly every time I came into the room. On the other hand, I'm very impressed by young fellows who are gentlemen and will open a door for a lady."

A major peeve is to be given an overblown introduction before he delivers a speech. "It irks me when people overstate my case," he says. "I'm honest enough with myself to know I don't measure up to their grandiose perception. Often they'll give me credit for things I haven't done. I like being well thought of in the community, but if their kudos aren't credible it bothers the hell out of me. I break into a cold sweat! I'm nauseated! I can't stand it! On a scale of one to ten, I think I have a medium to large ego. But I don't have a really top ego that needs to be constantly fuelled and massaged."

Members of his family call it a healthy ego, but not an overweening one. Lucy Samuels, his eighty-one-year-old cousin and one-time babysitter for the infant Murray, says fondly, "Sure, he's got an ego, but he doesn't have the kind of *mammoth* ego that makes you feel like wanting to swat him." His daughter Tiana considers it a vulnerable ego that sometimes needs coddling. His need for reassurance after he

has delivered a speech on a formal occasion she finds especially engaging.

"Dad may have wowed them in a talk with plenty of umph
followed by stand-up applause, but he still looks to the family
for our reaction," she says. "When the meeting's over, he'll
glance at me with a sort of unspoken look that asks, 'Well, how
did I do?' I'll respond with a thumbs-up sign that says, 'Dad,
you did real good.' Then he'll give that impish grin of his and
walk away feeling satisfied."

Koffler's self-esteem is peeved no end if he is interrupted
when delivering a speech. It irritates his usually unruffled
composure because he stage manages a formal address so
painstakingly. Some colleagues call him the "Cicero of his
profession," and Goldie Brass, the Shoppers Drug Mart meeting planner for almost two decades, has justly nicknamed him
the "Cecil B. De Mille of retail pharmacy." When Koffler is
preparing to give a talk before a couple of hundred people at a
staff meeting, she says he issues her two edicts: "Number one,
he doesn't want the podium set on a platform but on an equal
floor level with the audience, so he doesn't seem to be talking
down to them. Number two, he insists that the lights be turned
on, so he can look at their faces."

And when he delivers a speech in his mellifluous, resonant
voice and seeming off-the-cuff manner, he makes a point of
following the advice of two experts. One is his folksy mentor in
the art of influencing people, Dale Carnegie, founder of the international chain of public-speaking courses, who once said:
"Always speak as if there's only one person in the hall you
have to convince. Plead with him, argue with him, arouse him,
touch him, but feel that your audience is one human whose
confidence and affection you want to win." His other guide is
President Franklin D. Roosevelt, who summed up the oratori-
cal secret of his famous radio fireside chats in six terse words:
"Be sincere. Be brief. Be seated."

Koffler, who can be a Roman candle of loquacity, concedes
that he sometimes is carried away into verbosity. He was at his
windiest when he once made the mistake of paying a ghost

writer to produce a formal address on the need to clean up the littered environment of Israel. Funds were being raised to create the new Foundation for Ecological Action, a program equivalent to Pollution Probe.

"It was a Jewish National Fund Negev Dinner in my honour, with John Bassett introducing me," he recalls, chuckling at the ghastly memory. "Bassett gave a brilliant speech. I stood up and spoke about *garbage*. It was the lousiest speech in my life! Ever since I've tried to write my own."

He is not always so chucklesome. Since he takes seriously the message conveyed in his speeches, he loses his patience with rude "anti-semantics" who don't have patience to listen to the words he has prepared with such lapidary care. He still bristles at the recollection of the rudeness he once encountered in Winnipeg. A female chatterbox at the head table kept nattering away to the woman beside her while Koffler was giving a speech on the need to lend a helping hand to the Indians of Manitoba.

"I was really thrown by her idiotic babbling," he later said. "It bothered me to such a degree I couldn't articulate what I wanted to say. When I finished, I went over to the woman and I said crisply, 'Madam, I must congratulate you. You were successful in talking all the way through my address!'

"She got flustered and I walked away in a huff."

At less formal gatherings he is far less brusque about being interrupted. Like most raconteurs, he likes to hold centre stage and dislikes an intrusion when he is in full throttle. If somebody butts in, he holds up his hand like a standup comic being heckled and protests good-humouredly, "Hey, I'm doing a single!"

At board meetings, he uses humour adroitly if he feels he has not captured the full attention of his fellow board members. Jack Gwartz, the cigar-puffing former president of Shoppers, remembers with amusement one device that Koffler employed effectively during the company's pioneer days in the 1960s. They both shared a twelve-by-fifteen-foot hutch of an office behind a Shoppers store at Dufferin and Lawrence in north Toronto. The boardroom table consisted of their two desks on wheels, which they pushed together to accommodate meetings. In this smoke-filled cubbyhole, with several of the non-smoking druggists coughing and hacking away like seals, it was not particularly easy to chair a meeting. Consequently, if Koffler felt they weren't listening to his every word, he would turn his back on the lot of them. "Well, since you fellows won't pay attention to me," he would mutter in mock exasperation, "I might as well talk to the wall." And he did.

One time, an executive brainstorming session at his Jokers Hill Farm north of Toronto seemed to run on interminably. Goldie Brass recalls how Koffler terminated the proceedings with *lèse majesté* informality. He excused himself and then returned wearing his dressing gown over his pajamas. "I don't mean to give you a hint," he said, yawning elaborately, "but *I'm* going to bed."

It was somewhat out of character for Koffler, says Brass, in the sense that he is a seemingly inexhaustible, take-charge showman who thrives, literally, on the excitement of leading the band. She recalls once organizing a Shoppers outdoor athletic festival on behalf of the Jerry Lewis fund-raising campaign to combat muscular dystrophy. She arranged to have bleachers set up in a Toronto park for Shoppers employees and their families, and the festivities were scheduled to begin with the arrival of the kilted, bagpipe-skirling Metro Police Band.

"We were sitting in the bleachers and waiting for the parade," she said. "So guess who comes marching in at the head of the band, twirling a baton? It was Murray Koffler! The spectacle just blew everybody away. It was all impromptu, definitely not planned by me. He loves doing that sort of thing. If you're going to put on a show, he'll be the first to put on a straw hat and strut right into the spirit of the thing."

When a friend reminded Koffler of his theatrical ex-hibitionism at the event, Koffler grinned affably and said, "Yes, there are times when I get a kick out of hamming it up a bit."

He is far from amiable, though, about his cardinal peeve. He has a mania for spit-and-polish cleanliness and for years has waged a campaign urging the employees of Shoppers to make sure their stores are what he terms *alles in ordnung*–German for everything neat and orderly. It has become a fetish with him, and Koffler goes about it as relentlessly as Xerxes scourging the Hellespont, as unremittingly as the legendary Mrs. Partington who fought a tidal wave with a mop. On his inspection tours of the empire he built, Koffler is somewhat like a punctilious Napoleon ready to rip the tarnished braid off his less fastidious generals in the field. At one slipshod outpost, he is celebrated for having grabbed a broom and zealously swept the entire floor of the drugstore–right to the curb of the front pavement. He made his point.

But ordinarily Koffler, being a diplomat rather than a dictator, exercises more tact when setting an example for the troops. "I'll tell you what Murray's style is like in that situation," says David Bloom, the chief executive officer groomed by Koffler to take over total command of the Shoppers empire. "First, he's Henry Kissinger, handing out the praise to brace you. Then–pow!–you get a well-deserved kick right in the pants."

Bloom illustrates by describing the drama that occurred in 1968 when he was a neophyte who had just taken over management of the Shoppers store at Yorkdale Plaza in Toronto's suburbia. Bloom makes it seem like comedy, and describes the scene with Kofflerian gusto. As reconstructed by Bloom, the scenario of dialogue between himself and Koffler in the role of Mr. Clean went something like this:

KOFFLER: "Gee whiz, David! Your Yorkdale Shoppers is the most exciting promotion-wise store I've ever seen!"

BLOOM: "Thank you, Mr. Koffler."

KOFFLER: "No, no, it's Murray. Gee, your staff seems so enthusiastic! Look at the tremendous cosmetic sales spiel going on there between your beauty adviser and that customer."

BLOOM: "Thank you very much, Mr. Koffler."

KOFFLER: "No, it's Murray. You know, David, I've got to tell you the selection of merchandise in this store is outstanding! Absolutely outstanding!"

BLOOM: "Thank you very much, Murray."

KOFFLER: "There, you've got it. It's Murray. How are your sales, David?"

BLOOM: "Sales are up thirty-eight per cent."

KOFFLER: "Gee, that's terrific! I'm so gratified and enthused. You know, David, never in my wildest dreams did I ever expect this store would be so successful! It's a tribute to you and your personnel . . ."

(At this point, according to Bloom's stage directions, he feels at least ten feet off the ground: "I'm flying up there with the angels. But then, after a pause, he whams me with the thunderbolt.")

KOFFLER: "Now tell me, David, why in the hell is this store so damn dirty? Look at the terrible dust here. Look at the unpolished railings there. Look at the fingermarks everywhere! You know, David, cleanliness in a store is just as important as all those other things you've achieved. You've got to check it day by day. You've got to walk up and down the aisles, keeping on top of your merchandise manager."

BLOOM: "But . . . but . . . Mr. Koffler, we just did a cleanup yesterday."

KOFFLER: "You know, David, I've developed an interesting habit. I find I have to change my shirt every morning. That's because, when I go to bed at night, I find there's a ring around the collar of my soiled shirt. Don't you change into a fresh shirt every morning?"

BLOOM: "Yes, Mr. Koffler."

Bloom concludes the re-enactment of his playlet dolorously: "All of a sudden I've gone from the angels to the subterranean depths. I'm digging a new subway on Yonge Street. After sort of picking myself up from the ground, I set the wheels in motion to make sure our store is always spic and span. It's a lesson I learned on setting store priorities, and believe me, it's a Murray-style lesson I never forgot."

Koffler was able to perform as such a galvanizing catalytic agent because he had a prophetic conception of what a pharmacy should be. He was virtually the father of the modern pharmacy, and his pioneering stemmed from a curious love-hate relationship with his profession.

To Koffler, a pharmacy was not just an emporium with a pill pusher in a white jacket behind the back counter of the store. He preferred to regard it as a kind of magic land. He saw a certain poetry in his profession, part mercantile and part medical, which the romantic visionary tried to communicate to others. He understood and loved the mortar and pestle and other instruments of his craft, genuinely loved the smell and the language and the rituals of the dispensary.

"I've always loved the art of pharmacy," says Koffler, looking back on his forty-five years in the field. "I've loved filling prescriptions written in Latin by doctors and loved speaking to both doctors and their patients. I always felt it was a thrill and privilege to talk to doctors on their own level. I've always enjoyed phoning a physician to get a prescription repeated, or informing him about a possible incompatibility in the medicine he has prescribed, and the gratification of having him treat you as a fellow professional. You feel proud to be part of the health team in the healing arts.

"I've also loved the salesmanship side of it. I've always enjoyed putting merchandise on the shelf, making beautiful displays, hatching ideas for promotions, writing my own ads, giving guidance to customers. And, yes, I even got a sense of accomplishment from washing the windows and mopping the floor until the place sparkled."

What he hated were the needless and demeaning drudgeries of the corner drugstore. He abhorred especially its penny-ante bicycle delivery practices, its nickel-and-dime soda jerking, its fusty bargain-basement image. He resolved to change these and other backwardnesses and began selling his own vision of what his profession could aspire to be, and in doing so, Koffler the Creative Gamesman revolutionized the pharmacy game.

Pioneering Personality Kids

T he earliest – and most delightful – image of Murray Koffler in action was unfortunately never photographed. Happily, though, it has remained etched in the memory of his cousin, Lucy Samuels. Now eighty-one, she is better known to him as Aunt Lucy because she was the first baby-sitter for the infant Murray.

Picture then a scene on a Sunday afternoon in the 1920s at Scarborough Park in the east end of Toronto. A military band is playing jaunty Gilbert and Sullivan tunes to an audience stretched out on the grass. Suddenly Lucy and Murray's parents hear the people nearby burst out laughing.

"Look at that kid!" one of them exclaims, pointing. "Isn't he cute as a button?"

There, standing behind the conductor, wearing his hand-knitted white short pants and blouse, was curly-haired, three-year-old Murray Bernard Koffler (also known in his boyhood as Mush) ecstatically waving his upstretched arms and conducting the band.

"Murray was a personality kid right from the beginning – always full of pep," Aunt Lucy now says.

It is also an apt description of his forebears, who were not only vivacious personalities but resilient survivors. His mother, Tiana Reinhorn Koffler, and his father, Leon, were both *fusgeyers* (Yiddish for footloose immigrants) born in rural communities in Romania. And both were of pioneer stock, the father of one of them pursuing in Canada the Jewish immigrants' traditional trade derisively described by Sir John A. Macdonald, the country's first Prime Minister, as "Old Clo' peddling."

But it was an opportunity seized gladly. For his ancestors were among the more than one-third of the Jews from Eastern Europe who left their homes in a mass exodus between 1870 and 1905 bound for North America. Usually dirt-poor, clannish, culturally energetic, they were a hardy breed toughened by centuries of anti-Semitic torment. Outcasts all, they yearned for the religous and economic freedom that beckoned to them in the semi-mythical Golden Land spelled out in the magical word "America."

Murray Koffler's maternal grandfather, Harry Reinhorn, was a born trailblazer. By all accounts, he had bounce, ebullience, and lots of audacity. The son of a Bucharest merchant, he chafed under Romanian racial restrictions that prevented Jews from owning land and obtaining a higher education. Consequently, at the age of thirteen, he made his way alone to Paris bent on attending high school, but he was frustrated in his hopes.

According to his only living son, Dr. Abraham Reinhorn, an eighty-two-year-old eye surgeon now retired in West End, New Jersey, Koffler's grandfather, with just a smattering of English, somehow wangled passage to New York City, where he walked up and down Riverside Drive, knocking on doors and asking in Yiddish for a job. By a fluke, the German-speaking steward at Delta Kappa Epsilon, the fraternity house of the Rockefellers and other American gentry, answered the rap at the door and asked, "Can you speak German?" Because Yiddish is basically a mongrel Germanic dialect, Reinhorn answered brazenly that he was fluent in the language and was hired as the steward's assistant. The wealthy fraternity members were beguiled by the lad's engaging personality and virtually adopted him.

After about six years on the job, the short, stubby, elegantly moustachioed Reinhorn returned to Romania in search of a nice Jewish bride. In Bucharest, he met and married Topalicu

Gropper, a plump, tiny, exceptionally pretty tailor's daughter known to everybody as Toby. Not long after the birth of their daughter, Tiana, Reinhorn served as a leader of a group of forty-nine Romanian families seeking a new life in the wilds of what was then called the North-West Territory of the new Dominion of Canada. Thanks to Baron Maurice de Hirsch, a German financier-philanthropist, the Jewish Colonization Association was offering each family of homesteaders transportation plus an advance of $200 to farm their tracts of 160 acres of virgin land. The land itself was given free, allocated by Canada's Minister of the Interior, Clifford Sifton.

The Romanian wayfarers set out on their odyssey in 1901. They took with them their precious brass Sabbath candlesticks and their separate sets of copper pots and pans for meat and dairy dishes so they would be able to adhere to the dietary laws. They left in buoyant spirits, with Reinhorn leading them in singing the cheery Yiddish "Song of the Fusgeyer": *Geyt, Yidelech, in der vayter velt: in Kanade vet ir ferdinen gelt* ("Go, dear Jews, into the wide world; in Canada you will make your fortune").

Alas, they were not singing cheerfully when they eventually reached their destination that chill spring. They were dismayed to find themselves in the bald and wind-whipped Saskatchewan prairie, seventy miles northeast of what had originally been called "Pile O' Buffalo Bones" and had been majestically renamed Regina after Queen Victoria. The *fusgeyers* had to slog by foot across marshy sloughs twenty miles north of the Canadian Pacific Railway's end of steel at Qu'Appelle.

There, under the kindly guidance of Cree Indians and mixed-blood Métis who took pity on them, the inexperienced Jewish farmers learned how to swing axes and scythes to erect poplar log huts chinked with mud and roofed with sod. They ploughed up a few acres each for potatoes and put up some hay. And that winter they shivered through the forty-below-zero weather in their primitive hovels like prairie gophers, huddled together for warmth as they slept on straw-and-mud floors.

Their little encampment was stricken with an epidemic of diphtheria. Drought and hail and grasshopper plagues further compounded their woes. But the pioneers endured. They acquired oxen. They learned what it meant to "sow seed and stook and stack, using nothing but elbow grease." They subsisted on saskatoon berries they picked and the wild goose eggs they plucked from nests. And they got together for community "*matzo*-baking bees" to prepare from flour and water unleavened bread for Passover, as had the ancestral children of Israel in the Bible.

When agricultural disasters plagued them, they took heart from the other courageous Jewish colonies which then sprouted in Saskatchewan. Immediately east of them was the settlement of Wapella, headed by Ekiel Bronfman, the black-bearded patriarch who fathered what was to become the patrician Bronfman industrial clan. South of them near Moosomin was the settlement optimistically named New Jerusalem. And north of them beside the Carrot River was the flourishing colony whose name concealed a private Jewish joke.

When the Canadian government asked the settlers to give their colony a name because of the post office being established there, they had suggested either "Jew Town" or "Israel Villa." Both were rejected because they sounded too ethnic. "Edenbridge" was the name finally accepted; it sounded pleasantly Anglophone to civil service ears as well as spiritually elevating, suggestive of a paradisial bridge arching over the Carrot River. The jest was that the word "Eden" is a pun on "*Yidden*," which designates "Jews." And so the settlers laughed to see how they had triumphed over petty officialdom by winning, after all, the colony name of "Jews' Bridge."

Ultimately the colony at Qu'Appelle was named Lipton, after one of its co-founders. But by then, Reinhorn's wanderlust had stimulated him to adventure far north of Saskatoon to an even more remote community bearing an historically significant name. It was Duck Lake, the locale of the outbreak of the 1885 North-West Rebellion where Louis Riel's Indian and Métis supporters had fought a victorious battle, defeating the Mounties and land-hungry British settlers invading their territory.

Reinhorn, by now fluent in French, English, and German as well as Romanian and Yiddish, had no trouble communicating with the some 400 Indian and Métis inhabitants of Duck Lake. Over the next six years there he became a legendary figure: a Jewish peddler in fringed buckskin and moccasins. His winning ways were said to be irresistible, whether he was buying beaver peltry or vending dry goods and metal trinkets. He went through the four conventional stages of peddling in Duck Lake: first trudging on foot, while hefting a heavy backpack with tinware items garlanded around his neck; then trundling a pushcart; followed by a horse and wagon; and finally rising to the pinnacle of the trade, which meant ownership of his own little general store.

"He was a master salesman," says Aunt Lucy of her Uncle Harry Reinhorn. "He had a smile and a joke for everybody. A jolly, outgoing man, with strong leadership qualities. That was Uncle Harry." Lucy recalls how her Bucharest-born father, a Talmudic scholar and poet named Herman Lazaresco, joined his brother-in-law Harry Reinhorn as an itinerant peddler and then assistant manager in his Duck Lake general store. The Lazarescos and Reinhorns were the only two Jewish families in Duck Lake, and her chief childhood recollection is of the cordiality shown them by the Indians and Métis. She adds: "We were observant Orthodox families in the sense that we never cleaned the house or lit a fire to cook on the Sabbath. But since there weren't enough Jewish men to form a quorum of ten, we had no synagogue prayer services."

This was a key reason why the two families eventually moved to Saskatoon, which had a Jewish community of about thirty families. Reinhorn, the more enterprising of the two men, opened Reinhorn's Furniture Store on Second Avenue, and the poetry-writing Herman Lazaresco worked as his manager. Soon the store's merchandising promotions gained it a reputation almost as flamboyant as Harry Steinberg's tiny

"Montreal Great Bargain Store" in the nearby town of Manitou, which advertised: "Small store, big name! Think big!"

Possibly in the same spirit of exaggeration, Lucy refers to her cousin Tiana as "the prettiest girl in Saskatoon." A photo she has preserved of Murray Koffler's mother at the age of sixteen shows she was a Botticelli beauty as lovely as the rose she is posed holding in her right hand.

Lucy Samuels recalls that Tiana was gentle and seemingly shy, yet extremely popular with the boys. "Despite her apparent bashfulness, she was a strong character and had both feet on the ground," says Lucy. She grew up to be a well-read, artistically cultivated woman. She was an accomplished pianist; loved to sing semiclassical songs in a sweet soprano voice; had a cook's gifted touch; and, rather unusual for Jewish girls in that period, she was allowed to attend the University of Saskatchewan, where she graduated in a liberal arts course.

Tiana's comeliness in the eyes of Gentile suitors she met at college social affairs alarmed her parents. "There were not enough Jewish boys around for dating," says Lucy. "And our parents were dead set against intermarriage – dead set!" Consequently, on his next furniture-buying trip to Toronto in 1921, Harry Reinhorn made discreet inquiries about the availability of a prospective Jewish husband for his daughter. He was informed about a bright and handsome fellow named Leon Koffler, also an immigrant from Romania; he seemed a good catch, because he was a professional planning to open a drugstore on College Street, one of the main commercial arteries of Toronto's Jewish neighbourhood.

In a ploy that smacks of *Fiddler On The Roof* matchmaking, it was carefully arranged that the couple should meet casually at a social gathering. In the words of Lucy Samuels: "They clicked."

In 1922, Harry and Toby Reinhorn moved to Toronto along with their entire family of three daughters and two sons, of whom Tiana was the eldest. The Lazarescos followed soon after in time to attend the wedding of the pair of Romanian-born immigrants.

Little is known with certainty about the family roots of Leon Koffler, except that he was born in a Romanian village with the unpronounceable name of Piatraniamz. A good deal is known, however, about the pharmacy profession he was about to enter and shake up and which his son, in turn, was destined to transform.

There is a family tradition that Leon Koffler's father, Baruch Koffler, worked in Piatraniamz as a "chemist" or "apothecary." In other words, he was practising what fourteenth-century Venetians called the *arte nobile* of compounding and dispensing drugs. It was an art with a gaudy past, laced with magic and religion and romance. The practitioner was commonly called an *apotheke*, the Greek word for both the shop and the shop-keeper who operated a storehouse of medication. Over the centuries, the apothecary was also known as a spicer and pepperer, a barber-surgeon and priest-herbalist, an alchemist and pharmacopolist, a wizard and witch-doctor, a midwife and witch.

It was not until 1617 that this motley crew was incorporated under a London charter as "The Worshipful Society of the Art and Mystery of the Apothecaries." The Royal College of Physicians, already established since 1518, did not accept them worshipfully. They derided the intruders as a mongrel fraternity of "Chymists mixing and selling all manner of Druggs" and, incidentally, threatening their own august authority. Since the physicians had access to the royal ear, a regal decree was granted empowering the doctors to fine or have pilloried "Poticaries who sell evil and faulty stuff."

The potions and elixirs and purgatives dispensed by both embryonic professions were truly dubious stuff, if one examines today Jean de Renou's then popular *Medicinal Dispensatory*, subtitled *The Whole Body of Physick: Pharmacopea of Apothecaries Shop*. Medicinal ingredients listed include bear's grease, fox lungs, unicorn horns, frogs, crabs, vipers, worms, scorpions, "Spanish-flies ants," and dog's dung. It is little wonder that Ben Jonson's satirical comedies, *The Alchemist* and *Volpone*, ridiculed Elizabethan drug dispensers as quacks and charlatans.

41

William Shakespeare was even more mordant in his plays. The witches mixing their devilish brew in *Macbeth* were merely reciting the ingredients common in "bills," as medical prescriptions were then called:

> Eye of newt and toe of frog,
> Wool of bat and tongue of dog,
> Adder's fork and blind-worm's sting,
> Lizard's leg and howlet's wing.

In *Romeo and Juliet*, Shakespeare's caricature of the apothecary, who provides Romeo with poison, preserved for posterity a poisonous image. He depicts the Elizabethan drugstore as a slovenly disgrace:

> In his needy shop a tortoise hung,
> An alligator stuff'd and other skins
> Of ill-shaped fishes; and about his shelves
> A beggarly account of empty boxes,
> Green earthen pots, bladders and musty seeds,
> Remnants of packthread and old cakes of roses,
> Were thinly scattered, to make up a show.

The apothecary himself, who compounds the illicit poison for forty ducats, is portrayed as an impoverished wretch:

> In tatter'd weeds, with overwhelming brows,
> Culling of simples; meagre were his looks;
> Sharp misery had worn him to the bones.

Romeo addresses him disdainfully as though the pill-roller were at the bottom of the social and economic heap:

> Need and oppression starveth in thy eyes,
> Contempt and beggary hangs upon thy back,
> The world is not thy friend, nor the world's law:
> The world affords no law to make thee rich.

No pioneer pharmacists got rich in the New World by concocting medications. But their status was ranked somewhat higher there than that of the penurious wretches who toiled in a European "spicery" or "druggery."

Unquestionably, the first pharmacists in North America were the Indian medicine men. Jacques Cartier was indebted to them on his 1534 voyage up the St. Lawrence River to Stadacona, the site of Quebec City. The Iroquois there showed him how the boiled bark and leaves of a spruce tree were an effective anti-scorbutic for the scurvy that had afflicted his crew. Cartier was astonished by the six-day cure, but offered precious little gratitude to the native folk healers. "Had all the doctors of Lourain and Montpellier been present, with all the drugs of Alexandria, they could not have effected as much in a year as this tree did in six days," Cartier wrote in his journal. "For it was so beneficial that all those who were willing to use it were cured and recovered their health, thanks be to God."

Louis Hébert, the first paleface pharmacist to practise in North America, was more generous in giving credit to the Indian herbalists. Hébert was a former court apothecary to King Henry IV of France; the adventurer accompanied Samuel de Champlain in his 1604 expedition to establish a colony at Acadia in the Canadian Maritimes. A tablet in the history museum at Annapolis Royal, Nova Scotia, honours him for his medical services to his fellow colonists and the healing lore he picked up from the Micmac Indians.

Two pharmacists were among Canada's Fathers of Confederation in 1867: Sir Charles Tupper, Premier of Nova Scotia, and Sir Leonard Tilley, Lieutenant-Governor of New Brunswick. Another historic pharmacist was William Lyon Mackenzie, leader of the 1837 Upper Canada Rebellion against the ruling Family Compact. He was the first mayor of Toronto and grandfather of Canadian Prime Minister William Lyon Mackenzie King. An advertisement he placed in the *Upper Canada Gazette* in 1823 reflects the mishmash of items carried in his Dundas drugstore. It stated that his shop was selling "on moderate terms for Cash or produce, Dry Goods, Hardware,

Groceries, Drugs and Medicines, Glassware, Crockery, Books, Stationery, Teas, Fancy Goods, Oils and Paints, but has declined to continue to retail spirituous liquors."

Apothecaries generally in the nineteenth century were a mixed bag. A few were so-called "ethical" chemist shops. The British diarist Anna Jameson described one in her supercilious 1836 journal, *Winter Studies and Summer Rambles in Canada*. She mocked the pretensions of a Toronto apothecary on King Street for flaunting "panes of plate glass with brass divisions between them." It had thus assumed an "English watering-place kind of tone . . . worthy of Regent Street in its appearance."

Most of them, though, followed the pattern of two pioneer shops in the Maritime provinces, each called Apothecaries Hall. The hall opened by Thomas and Albert Desbrisay in Charlottetown, Prince Edward Island, in 1810 advertised a large stock of "Cow-Pox vaccine, Jamaica Spirits, moist sugars, soap, cotton stockings, pantaloons, short drawers, cutlery, horse fleams and spurs." The hall opened by William Simpson in Chatham, New Brunswick, in 1830 suggests in its advertising the manifold functions of an apothecary. It read: "A general assortment of trusses, both on the old and latest approved principles, drugs, patent medicines, perfumery, etc. as usual . . . Practitioner of Physic . . . Consulted at any hour . . . Advice to the poor gratis."

By 1920, pharmacists in North America were called druggists and their spiceries, druggeries, and chymist dispensaries were known as drugstores. Their profession, however, was not particularly an exalted one. The corner druggist was the friendly fellow who probably knew everyone in your family by first name. His formal medical education was limited to one year at a college of pharmacy. And he ran a folksy but musty raggle-taggle sort of general store. Hidden in the back was a little dispensary, and in the middle was an assortment of glass showcases, but his pride and joy was a marble-topped soda fountain resplendent in front. His notions of merchandising, promotion, and advertising were primitive. Typically in that era, according to the authoritative *Kilmers and Urdang's History of Pharmacy*, L.K. Liggett, the burgeoning North

American drugstore chain, displayed in its front window "festoons of dusty sponges, exhibits of cochineal bugs, rock sulphur, and flyspecked cards announcing the 'Old Folks Supper' at the Methodist Church."

Into this quaintly old-fashioned atmosphere swept Leon Koffler, like a cyclone, and after him the typhoonic Murray.

CHAPTER FOUR

"Doc" Koffler

Whether they worked for him as apprentices at five dollars a week or as graduate pharmacists at twelve dollars a week in the Depression years, they all remember his speed. "He walked fast and he talked fast and he thought fast," recalls one of them, seventy-five-year-old Harry Kalb. "One! Two! Three! Always on the go-go-go! That was Mr. Koffler."

Invariably, even though they may be greybeards today and operate their own corner drugstores, as does sixty-eight-year-old Albert Abrams, they still refer to Murray's father, Leon, as *Mr.* Koffler. "You called him that," says Abrams, "because Mr. Koffler was a perfectionist who automatically commanded your respect."

Mr. Koffler is remembered as a lean, tense, handsome, almost austere workaholic, with large, piercing brown eyes and a very persuasive voice; he chainsmoked Sweet Caporals, looked like a dapper version of Al Jolson, and was finnicky about keeping things spotlessly clean, just as his son Murray would be. Abrams recalls how his meticulous boss would line up the staff at the College Street store for a dress inspection each morning. He would examine their ties, shirts, and brown uniform jackets to make sure they were immaculate. If a pair of shoes wasn't shined, he would crisply advise the laggard to get them polished.

He would then run his finger down the length of a cosmetic and perfume showcase. If there was a hint of dust, he would shake his head in dismay. *That* would be enough of a warning, says Abrams.

Altogether there were five glass showcases in the store, with one inch of space between each case. Abrams was once reprimanded for allowing dust to accumulate in those spaces. "Mr. Koffler, how are we supposed to clean them?" he asked. "They're nothing more than big cracks and they're deep."

Mr. Koffler promptly took a broomstick and wrapped it in a rag and vigorously showed him. In other words, Mr. Koffler took exception to the old proverb mocking the unequal division of labour, whereby the employee does all the hard work while the employer does all the grunting. "No, Mr. Koffler would pitch right in and teach us by example," says Abrams.

He can think of only one memorable occasion when his usually unflappable mentor came close to losing his temper. Mr. Koffler pulled out one of the fourteen drawers where pills and razor blades were kept and was embarrassed because he couldn't find the item requested by the customer he was serving.

"So Mr. Koffler," Abrams recalls, "yanked out all fourteen drawers and dropped the contents on a counter and said, 'Okay, fellas. Pick it all up and put it all back in the drawers, nice and neat and exact, the way it should be.'"

Others schooled by Mr. Koffler remember him as a promotion-wise pacesetter. He was a consummate marketing man years ahead of his time, according to Lou Starkman, who served his apprenticeship at the College Street store. Now in his seventies and the president of Starkman's Surgical Supply Ltd. on Bathurst Street in midtown Toronto, the former pharmacist recalls how Mr. Koffler kept himself up to date with the latest United States trends in merchandise display.

"On a Saturday night it would be nothing for him to phone Moe Haberman, a fellow pharmacist who had a lot of promotional savvy," said Starkman. "He would drive Moe across the border to look at windows of drugstores on the main street of Buffalo. Then he would come in Monday morning and say to me and anybody else working the shift, 'I don't want this here and I don't want that there. I want this changed. I want that changed. And I don't want any more of *this* stuff to go in the window. I want *that* stuff to go in the window.'

"He would change things around faster than any other drugstore would today. He would change more in a year than any other drugstore would change in a lifetime. A marvellous dynamo with merchandise, Mr. Koffler was."

In the pre-TV era, his store window displays provided the liveliest entertainment on College Street, according to another former apprentice, sixty-seven-year-old Lawrence Shankman. They were gimmicky crowd-pullers, a combination of a bazaar and a zoo, with lots of live action. One of his most successful front-window shows was staged on behalf of Lentheric and Helena Rubinstein fragrances. Twitching menacingly amid the piles of products while squatting in an open-topped glass case was a deodorized skunk borrowed from the University of Toronto. A placard announced: "Don't be a stinker! Buy our colognes!"

Shankman recalls arriving at the store each morning to find that the skunk was hiding in one of the wall cupboards. The prima donna had to be enticed back to its audiences in the front window spotlight with sticks of celery and chunks of ham obtained from Tibando's Fruit & Grocery Store next door.

More docile were the goldfish wiggling in a fish tank to promote the sale of Coutts-Hallmark greeting cards. A miniature fishing rod was hooked over the side of the tank and a placard invited the oglers outside: "Why don't you drop me a line?"

The bait to attract attention in another window display consisted of a cage of white mice running around on a treadmill. The sign atop this one stated: "We do pregnancy tests." It indicated that specimens of a woman's urine would be injected into a hamster at a lab to determine within a week whether the woman was pregnant.

Truly mammoth crowds were lured to the sidewalk fronting the Koffler's store to participate in a yo-yo competition for teenagers. Evidently a friend of his named Charles Dubiner had seen a variation of the plaything in Africa and brought it to Toronto to be developed into the yo-yo commercial phenomenon. It enabled Leon Koffler to stage what is believed to be Canada's first yo-yo tournament. The prize was a brand-new CCM bicycle exhibited in the front window. For weeks hundreds of youngsters divided their time between pressing their noses against Koffler's window and practising their rock-the-baby and loop-the-loop yo-yo stunts.

One of Koffler's show-window spectaculars deviated from the course of his stage management and had an unexpected conclusion. His store sold so many bags of Neilson's chocolate maple buds that he had a bright idea. He struck a deal with George Metcalfe, the president of Neilsons Ltd., who was a pious church choirmaster with a sweet tooth. At a mutually agreed-upon price he bought two barrels of the twisted little milk chocolate buds. Then he turned the barrels sideways to fill the entire show window. Customers were invited to come in and buy their maple buds directly from the window display, which would be weighed on a scoop scale.

That Saturday a snowstorm blanketed the city. When Koffler opened the store Sunday morning, he was aghast at what had happened to his window extravaganza. The bright sun, reflected off the snowbanks and magnified by the plate glass, had melted the display into a sea of gooey milk chocolate.

Leon Koffler was undaunted. He phoned up the church to persuade choirmaster Metcalfe to let him discount the price of the maple buds, which, after all, had suffered from what was clearly an act of God. Then, after the stuff had solidified, he broke it into pieces with a hammer and sold it in irregular blocks at a bargain basement price. It was a smashing success with the public, and that's how the mass merchandising of Neilson's block chocolate began.

Not all of his merchandising stunts were smash hits. At that time, Gillette razor blades were bestsellers in a package of five blades featuring a blue-coloured picture of King Gillette. Leon Koffler copied the Gillette package exactly, but with his own picture depicted on the package of King Koffler blades. They flopped. "Why buy five of these unknown Koffler blades for a quarter," customers said to themselves, "when we can buy five of the internationally advertised Gillette blades for a quarter?"

His son learned a lesson from that mistake years later when introducing his own house brand of Life vitamins, which were sold at prices far lower than the heavily promoted standard brands. As for Leon's deposed King Koffler blades, Murray Koffler has since said, "We had a stockpile on hand for years, and they just wouldn't sell. We finally had to give the darned things away."

Generally, though, everybody agreed that Leon Koffler's originality was matchless when outsmarting his rivals. His store, located on the northeast corner of Borden Street, competed fiercely with druggists whose stores were on virtually every other corner of College: Issy Rothbart at Major Street, Irving (Red) Kates at Lippincott, Frank Reingold at Bathurst, and Wilfred Isaacson at Grace, not to forget Tamblyn's and Liggett's as well. "Leon was smart as a fox and certainly kept us on our toes," acknowledges his Grace Street competitor, Wilfred Isaacson, now retired at eighty-eight in Venice, Florida.

Leon Koffler outfoxed them with a barrage of cunning marketing tactics. He was the first in the neighbourhood to distribute advertising fliers, the first to advertise his store on match flaps, the first to install a post office, the first to hire a platoon of bicycle delivery boys, and the first to coin catchy slogans to boost his free delivery service. His ads in the 1920s featured such brash mottos as "Rain or shine, we deliver in a jiffy!" and "Telephone us with confidence – we answer like a flash!" and "We'll rush you a dime's worth of postage stamps – without charging a penny!"

He went to extreme lengths to supply his customers with incomparably cheap delivery service, which was responsible for 25 per cent of his trade. Lou Kesten, a pharmacist and one-time Koffler delivery boy, remembers delivering *The Toronto Star*, which then sold for two pennies, or a nickel ice cream cone, or a large bottle of the twelve-cent soda pop called Kik.

To this day, Lou Starkman, the septuagenarian ex-pharmacist, swears a blue streak as he recollects the dreadful frustration of taking phone orders for bricks of Neilson's ice cream.

"Oh, it was miserable!" he says, wincing at the memory. "From four o'clock on people would phone to order an ice cream brick they wanted to have delivered precisely at twenty minutes to six in time for their dessert.

"They'd ask: 'What's your ice cream special today?'

"You'd tell them: 'Peach melba.'

"'What's that?'

"'That's vanilla, with little pieces of fresh peach throughout it.'

"'What other kind have you got?'

"'Neapolitan.'

"'What's that?'

"'Chocolate, vanilla, and strawberry.'

"'And what else have you got?'

"'Buttered pecan.'

"'What's that?'

"'Well, that's maple walnut with pecan nuts . . .'

"It would take anywhere from seven to ten minutes to describe all the different bricks of ice cream. Then I'd hang up and blaspheme in disgust: 'This is one hell of a blankety-blank disgrace! A slap in the face to a university graduate with a degree in pharmacy!'"

This daily exasperation eventually led him and his brother to start the successful Starkman's Chemist dispensary on Bloor Street, which was open around the clock devoted exclusively to prescription service (and later was taken over by Murray Koffler as part of the Shoppers Drug Mart chain).

Leon Koffler did not share Starkman's attitude. He had a passion for all aspects of his profession. He treasured his customers and loved serving them in every way possible, whether with ice cream bricks or medications for their pains and aches. He didn't merely dispense pills and fill prescriptions and hand out products to them. He wanted to know what ailed them, truly cared about helping them, and regarded them not as customers but as patients and neighbours and friends.

They in turn called him "Doc" Koffler, and the many green-horns in the area would refer to him in all sincerity as a *felcher*. It was the term for "folk healer," which originated in the village ghettos of Eastern Europe, where physicians were rare and Jews were not able to study or practise medicine. It is conceivable that Leon Koffler's father Baruch, who is believed to have been a chemist or apothecary in the Romanian village of Piatra-niamz, may also have been called a *felcher*.

We do not know for sure, just as we do not know the circumstances that brought Leon Koffler to Toronto at the age of about fifteen. What is certain is that Leon and his three older sisters and their mother arrived to set up a small grocery store in the Jewish neighbourhood known as "the Ward," extending from Queen Street north to College Street. A photograph survives of the youthful Leon driving the horse and wagon he used for delivering groceries. It is believed he later performed similar chores for a neighbourhood drugstore and thus aspired to enter the profession.

Ambitious Jewish youths with a scientific or medical bent began pursuing the pharmacy profession in the early 1920s for a number of reasons. Many of them were frustrated would-be physicians; they were thwarted by the infamous WASP gentlemen's agreement of silent anti-Semitism then prevalent in Toronto, as in the rest of Canada. Quotas were imposed on the number of Jewish students permitted to study medicine at the University of Toronto. Furthermore, the major hospitals followed the lead of Toronto General Hospital in disgraceful discrimination; until World War II, they accepted only one or two Jewish medical graduates each year as token interns. Pharmacy was more accessible. It was certainly cheaper than the $200 tuition fee required to study medicine. You could earn money working in the field during your four years of apprenticeship; moreover, you could continue to work nights and weekends at a store during your one year of studies at the Ontario College of Pharmacy.

Leon Koffler graduated from the Toronto-based college in 1921. Within two years he scraped together enough money to open a small drugstore at 376 College Street. But recognizing the value of a corner location, he soon moved two doors west to 380 College at Borden. In a cosy, two-bedroom flat above that store Murray Bernard Koffler was born on January 22, 1924, and there he spent the first seven years of his life.

The 1,200-square-foot store in a red-brick building, directly opposite the historic Number Eight fire station with its clock tower, eventually grossed close to $100,000 a year; this was considered astounding for the period. Its success, of course, was due to the scrupulous care that Leon Koffler lavished on the narrow, fifty-eight-foot-long store; it was beautifully panelled with stained oak, elegant with enormous glass showcases, and ornamented with yards of wooden fixtures. Its ceiling consisted of sheets of art deco design aluminum, patterned as a mélange of intricate diamonds with rose petals. It is a stunning piece of art work. The store's proprietor for the past two decades, Mario Iannace from Callabria, Italy, still retains the ceiling fresco in the basement of his Mario & Son Food Market as though it were a treasured relic of the Sistine Chapel.

People passing by could instantly identify the drugstore from the two huge pear-shaped globes of red and green liquid glistening in the window. Since ancient times, these have been the traditional symbols of the apothecary-chemist's profession, just as the striped red-and-white poles signified the entrance to the shop of a barber-surgeon.

On entering the Koffler establishment, customers were engulfed by heady whiffs of the then characteristic "drugstore smell." It was a pleasant blend of Shalimar perfume and Yardley lavender, the peppermint smell of rock candy, the lemon of English fruit drops, the cinnamon of senna and cassia leaves used for brewing a laxative tea, the sweet, sharp pungency of iodoform, the sour, rotten-egg odour of hydrogen sulphide, the astringent aroma of belladonna (the deadly nightshade extract mixed with carbonates to quiet a queasy stomach), the subtle smell of buchabead herbs for "flushing and cleansing out" the kidneys, and the all-pervasive, exotic fragrances of cloves and balsa and other spices imported from far-off lands.

The dispensary at the back of the store imparted an atmosphere suggestive of the arcane "art and mystery" of the profession. Neatly arrayed on shelves were glass-stoppered bottles of liquids and powders. Like prescriptions, their labels were handwritten in Latin. The dead language was not used to mystify patients. Rather, it was a lingua franca universally understood by physicians and pharmacists in case the patient travelled from one country to another.

Apprentices learned by rote the Latin morse code of abbreviations: q.i.d. being short form for *quater in die*, meaning "four times a day"; a.c. for *ante cibum*, meaning "before meals"; p.c. for *post cibos*, "after meals"; and h.s. for *hora somni* or *somne*, that is "at bedtime."

They learned how to handle the tools of their trade. Paramount among them were the paired mortar and pestle. The mortar was the strong vessel in which materials were pounded or ground by the club-shaped pestle, and both might be fashioned from cast iron or earthenware or polished Wedgwood glass. There was an art to rotating the pestle smoothly, and it required similar finesse to wield the spatula. It was the thin, flat, elongated instrument made of wood or metal and used for stirring, scooping, and spreading mixtures and ointments.

The apprentice was expected to become adept at shaping and rolling pills and compounding capsules and unguents as specified by physicians. Those were the days before the big pharmaceutical drug companies had standardized the manufacture of tablets and ointments and various patent medicines that could be turned out by the thousands. More than 70 per cent of prescriptions were composed of six to ten ingredients that might require a half hour to compound, a labour-intensive chore that would be economically prohibitive today.

Food and Drug Act regulations were also far more lax in those days. The best that could be said about some of the non-prescription remedies then current was that they were innocuous placebos. They couldn't hurt you, the psychology went, and if you truly believed in a cure-all, it made you *feel* better.

Most outrageous were the claims made by the hucksters of various Indian snake-oil tonics. In the trenchant phrase of one of Leon Koffler's former assistant pharmacists, Al Sabsay, their nostrums were touted as cures for "everything from halitosis to ingrown toenails." Thanks to a hyperbolic radio advertising campaign, the best-seller during the Great Depression was a tonic called Mus-Kee-Kee (ballyhooed as the Cree Indian term for "big medicine"). Two other popular tonics were Ki-Wah-Na and Al-O-Phama. Each bottle bore a picture of an Indian chief. They were hawked at fairs and drugstores by befeathered braves in full regalia claiming to be Alberta medicine men. And they purported to "clean out your system and boost your blood and make you feel like a million dollars."

In fact, according to Lou Starkman, most of them were laxatives containing a stiff dose of cascara. "They were at least good for your morale," Starkman says wryly. "After you belted them down, you had the satisfaction of seeing that *something* was working."

Some patients swore by certain remedies because the images on the outer package appeared so reassuring. For women suffering from menstrual cramps, hot menopause flashes, and other female disorders, nothing was more comforting than the sight of the Victorian dowagers pictured on the fancy, pinkish brown package, which announced in Old English type that contained inside was Lydia Pinkham's Vegetable Compound. Others were soothed by the lilting sound of the name of Carter's Little Starters or Carter's Little Liver Pills (actually a laxative that had nothing to do with one's liver) or Crazy Crystals (nothing more than epsom salts) or the so-called blood-builder concocted in Brockville, Ontario, and euphonically named Dr. Williams Pink Pills For Pale People (known to doctors more simply as a stomacher).

Still other potions won a following based on the masochistic principle that the worse a medicine tasted the better it was for the rusted iron in your tired blood. Tincture Nux Vomica, for instance, tasted as nasty as it sounded. Its bitter taste was a result of its strychnine basis, and its devotees had total faith in its ability to recharge, so to speak, their internal sparkplugs.

More permanent was the popularity of the patent medicine created by William K. Buckley, a pharmacist from Cape Breton, Nova Scotia. He came to Toronto to dispense an admittedly vile-tasting cough syrup that evidently proved effective during the great flu epidemic of 1918-19. His sixty-five-year-old son Frank Buckley boasts in ads today that its ammonium carbonate base still makes Buckley's Mixture taste awful. In confessional style, a recent advertisement read: "I CAME BY MY BAD TASTE HONESTLY. I INHERITED IT FROM MY FATHER."

Leon Koffler developed his own fans for the non-prescription medications that he packaged and sold under the Koffler label or that carried the imprint of local physicians. Koffler's Fever Powders For Babies, Koffler's Cough Syrup, Koffler's Headache Powders, and Koffler's Boracic Acid were all top sellers at low prices. He sold batches of Dr. Harold Taube's Stomach Powder, a mixture of sodium bicarbonate and magnesium oxide that was prescribed by the Bloor Street stomach specialist and caught the fancy of his patients.

"Leon was wonderfully inventive when you asked him to improve on a medicine," says Dr. William Garbe, a pioneer skin specialist in Toronto and still practising today in his late seventies. Dr. Garbe was impressed by a hot mustard plaster-like pack to combat acne he found in Europe. Unfortunately, though, when the pack was applied, it smelled, as Dr. Garbe phrases it, "like a neglected cow stable." He asked Koffler to try his hand at developing a substitute less redolent of the barnyard. "Leon obliged me," he says, "by coming up with a cream preparation perfumed like a rose."

Indeed, Leon won the respect of just about every physician in the College Street area, according to Dr. Ralph Weinstein, who is still a general practitioner also in his late seventies. Dr. Weinstein recalls how Leon used his business ingenuity to win the vital prescription trade of local physicians. "He was a clever entrepreneur," says Dr. Weinstein. "First he'd say, 'You don't have to bother writing a prescription. Just phone me and give your instructions.' In case that wasn't convenient, he went to the trouble of having printed your own special physician's prescription pad. The doctor's name, address, and phone number were printed on each prescription card. And printed prominently on the back of each card in capital letters were the same particulars about the Koffler store."

He capped that astute promotional practice by becoming chummy in his off hours with physicians. Rather unusual for a workaholic like Koffler, who was said to be "100 per cent all business," he even disciplined himself to play poker so that he could socialize with them on equal terms. Dr. Weinstein recalls playing poker with him at a stag party held at the King Edward Hotel for a physician about to be married.

When asked what sort of card player he was, Dr. Weinstein paused and deliberated for a moment. "Definitely no big-time gambler," he replied. "Though the stakes were only five pennies a card, Leon played a *very* cautious game."

In some ways, according to his former associates, he was a pennypincher of the waste-not, want-not school. "Mr. Koffler was a funny-peculiar guy when it came to money," says Lawrence Shankman. "No way he'd go for using brown paper bags. Not dignified enough. He insisted on using the best green wrapping paper and the best red Sea Island string. He was very picky about how you tied packages. If you tore off too much paper or used too much string, he'd give you hell."

"Yes, Mr. Koffler was a strict taskmaster, who didn't believe in fraternizing with his staff, but he could be oddly generous," agrees Al Sabsay. "One minute he'd scold you for wasting paper. The next he'd graciously share his bottle of Pepsi with you."

And when it was a matter of giving to charity, says Sabsay, he was noted for being a soft touch. He never refused fund-raisers for the societies aiding the elderly and needy. He would slip them a few dollars each. And at the end of the year he felt guilty if he had no extra cash to spare. Sabsay recalls how he would take his bank book from a drawer and show it to the canvasser.

"Look," he would say in embarrassment. "There's nothing left in my account. Come back in the second week of January and I'll give you my usual contribution plus more."

In wintertime, he was particularly generous about helping needy customers with big families to feed, clothe, and keep warm. Customarily, they would cash their cheques and pay what they owed him on Fridays. But if they were short of funds and needed ten sacks of coal, he would not only extend credit but give them money to pay for the coal order. In those days, legend has it, the old stuccoed frame cottages in the area would sometimes have coal piled up in the hallway that was called "Koffler coal."

St. John's Ward, to give the district its official name, was regarded as Toronto's "foreign quarter." It was a polyglot village of some 45,000 immigrants, including Italians, Chinese, Poles, Ukrainians, Finns, and Macedonians, who co-existed amicably with the Jewish majority and provided the staid city with a vibrant street life. On weekdays the hub of the area sprawled between the garment trade on Spadina Avenue to that tumultuous outdoor bazaar spanning College and Dundas known as the Kensington Market. On Saturdays and Sundays the greenhorns promenaded in their spiffiest finery along College Street.

The favourite rendezvous spot for many was the soda fountain extending down the left side of Koffler's Drugstore. It was a sumptuous affair, perhaps second only to the lavish soda fountain in the Sherbourne Street drugstore of J.J. McLaughlin (brother of the pioneer auto magnate Colonel Sam McLaughlin) who in 1907 invented the soda fountain formula for the ginger ale he named Canada Dry. The Koffler soda fountain consisted of twelve cushioned step-up brass stools mounted on a tile platform, a mottled grey marble-like counter backed by a large mirror and aglitter with nickel-and-chrome taps and soda-making machines, and three booths, or "settees" as they were called, on the side.

The apprentices took pride in being versatile soda jerkers. They were taught to make Koffler's own chocolate syrup and serve extremely generous scoops of ice cream for five cents. A soda frothing with strawberry concentrate and marshmallow sold for a dime. A sundae, gooey with banana, crushed walnut, and ice cream topped with a maraschino cherry, sold for fifteen cents. The price of a maltshake varied, depending on how many eggs, at five cents each, were mixed in.

"Mr. Koffler," recalls Lawrence Shankman, "trained us *not* to ask, 'Do you want it with an egg?' Instead you were supposed to accentuate the positive. You always suggested with your biggest smile, 'One egg or two?'"

In addition, Mr. Koffler taught his apprentices to respect the niceties of sexual taboos then current in polite society. It was an era when women were so prudish they refrained from exhibiting themselves on the street once pregnancy began to show. They even felt queasy about asking a fresh-faced young apprentice for a box of Kotex or Modess. Indeed, ex-apprentice Al Sabsay recalls how some women were so reticent they would send in a five-year-old son to purchase one of the "women's personal products," as sanitary napkins were then euphemistically called. To avoid offending the sensibilities of such genteel folk, Leon Koffler arranged to have the boxes of sanitary napkins prewrapped in green paper, stamped "K" and "M," and stacked on open display where a woman could discreetly help herself.

This was a breach of convention, because self-service in a drugstore was then unheard of; just about everything was kept behind glass or in a cupboard. Even Leon Koffler, the avant-garde merchandiser, did not have the audacity to display openly prophylactics for men. Known as "safes" or "rubbers" or nicknamed "Agnes" and "Mary," the Ramses and Sheik products were kept circumspectly in a wooden drawer behind the counter as though they were lethal drugs. The apprentices were to remember it as low comedy when they were approached by pimply-faced adolescents shuffling their feet in front of the counter and too bashful to ask directly for their first pack of condoms.

"The Victorian prudery was thoroughly pervasive and hush-hush then," recalls Leon Koffler's contemporary, Norman Hughes, the retired dean of the Ontario College of Pharmacy.

Chuckling at the memory, he says, "Why, even older men would sidle up quietly and *whisper* when they asked you for a little tin of Sheiks or Ramses."

His regular customers, however, kept no medical secrets from Leon Koffler. He was revered as a combination of sage, healer, pastor, and family confidant. He knew by first name virtually everybody who lived in the district. He knew without being told whether a family was strapped for cash merely by noting they were reduced to ordering a small rather than a large tube of toothpaste.

And for various reasons he was the first person who *was* told when somebody in the family was ailing. The immigrants trusted him because he was their neighbour. They tended to fear hospital physicians because they symbolized the official-dom that had tyrannized them in the Old Country. And they preferred to accept his expertise because it cost them nothing.

In contrast, a so-called "society doctor" for the Jewish mutual aid societies and fraternal lodges charged immigrants from fifty cents to two dollars for a hasty house call. So it is little wonder that immigrants stricken with illness would first consult the much-beloved "Doc" Koffler. His "counter pre-scribing," which his profession prohibited in later years, was given with heartfelt dedication, and he did not mind visiting his "patients" at home, without charging a fee, of course, in-tent only on helping them get well.

A story often recounted concerns a certain Eva Seligman of Borden Street who consulted Leon Koffler about her infant son Sam tossing and turning in his crib with a fever. The druggist was not content with personally delivering the prescribed rec-tal thermometer after midnight; he also demonstrated how it worked and explained how to interpret the baby's fever symptoms.

Then he looked at the child and said, "Some day I hope to have a little boy like that."

"I'm sure you will," said Eva Seligman.

Soon after, Murray Koffler was born. Twenty-six years later he married her daughter, Marvelle Seligman.

"Sam Seligman thus became my brother-in-law and I was then told this story," says Murray Koffler today. "It illustrates how caring and concerned my father was about the people who came into his store. He won their hearts and they really loved the man."

It seemed to some people that Leon Koffler was more devoted to satisfying his customers than his family. His College Street store – as well as a second one he acquired in 1930 at 1584 Bathurst Street in then thinly populated north Toronto – were open seven days a week, from eight o'clock in the morning often until well past midnight. It was not unusual for him to work more than ninety hours a week.

The sole recreation time he shared with his wife Tiana was on Monday evening. They would go to a movie theatre that offered a double bill of feature films and two or three cartoons to patrons seeking escapism from the Great Depression.

Murray Koffler remembers his father taking his family on only one vacation – a seven-day cruise on the *Empress of Britain* to Cuba. The Kofflers had a cottage in Toronto's east end Beaches district and later one at Hanlan's Point on the Toronto Islands, but rarely was his hypertense father able to relax there. Likewise, Murray and his mother enjoyed their subscription to the Toronto Symphony Orchestra pop concerts every Thursday evening at the Varsity Stadium, but his father never attended. Like other ambitious immigrants of the period, he seemed to be a go-getter obsessed with getting ahead and becoming thoroughly "Canadianized." Yet, the more successful Leon Koffler became, the more obsessed he was with work.

By 1941, the one-time horse-and-wagon delivery boy had left behind the rough-and-tumble life of College Street and had risen to upper-middle-class respectability. He had built up from scratch two flourishing drugstores; each displayed the sign Koffler's Pure Drugs, with the word "Pure" proudly imprinted on his profession's symbolic utensils, the mortar and pestle. He owned an apartment building at 2 Connaught Circle in Toronto's northern suburbs. Nearby his family lived in a handsome, two-storey, greystone house at 315 Rosemary Road in affluent Forest Hill Village.

But when all seemed to be rosy, his work addiction and his high blood pressure caught up with him. On January 16, 1941, that restless, single-minded, never satisfied perfectionist, Leon Koffler, died of a heart attack. He was only forty-seven years old and his son was seventeen.

"His death was a traumatic experience to me, but not a painful one," recalls Murray Koffler. "He had always been remote as a father. My lasting image of him was of a man in a spotlessly clean pharmacist's jacket, busy on the phone or in the dispensary. I respected him and I admired him and I loved him dearly, but I was never close to him. He was closer to his work.

"The doctors kept warning him about his cardiac condition and telling him to ease up on the job. But he simply wouldn't listen because he couldn't live that way. He had to be active in the work he loved, and I believe he was happy to finally go with his boots on, conferring with doctors, counselling patients, his hands on his mortar and pestle."

CHAPTER FIVE

The Maturing of Murray

Occasionally he still dreams the same recurring dream. But when it first began, shortly after the death of his father Leon in 1941, the dream was a horrifying nightmare to Murray Koffler. The scene never changes. He is in his last year at Oakwood Collegiate, and he dreams he is entering the examination room. He picks up the chemistry exam paper and he panics. The questions are too tough for him, his mind is a blank, and he is petrified with fear at the thought of failing. It means he won't be able to shoulder the burden of somehow managing the two drugstores left to him by his father, while simultaneously pursuing his studies at the Ontario College of Pharmacy. He wakes up in a cold sweat.

Fortunately, he passed his chemistry exam with a mark in the mid-seventies and went on to graduate from the college in 1946 with two degrees – as a Bachelor of Pharmacy and as a Pharmaceutical Chemist. The double responsibility of studying while operating two stores was the making of seventeen-year-old Murray. According to his boyhood friends, it transformed him from being a pampered only child into a *mensch*, a person of substance to admire and emulate.

Two former pharmacists employed by Leon Koffler use stronger words than "pampered" to describe Murray as a child. "He was a brat," says the peppery Lou Starkman. He remembers how Murray as a tot once brought a couple of his little playmates into the College Street store. Then he climbed on top of the old-fashioned ice cream cabinet, removed one of the round covers, and reached down to take out three frozen Eskimo pies for himself and his friends.

Starkman pulled him down and said, "Go on outside and play. You can't do that here."

"I can so," pouted Murray.

"You *can't* do that. Now get the hell out of here."

Twenty minutes later, Murray returned, climbed up on the ice cream dispenser again, and attempted to repeat his purloining of Eskimo pies.

"This time," recalls Starkman, "I went over to him and I gave him a little slap on the rump and I said, 'Now you get the hell outside and don't you dare come back in!'"

"You can't do that to me!" Murray retorted defiantly. "This is my father's store."

"Next time you come in and do that," Starkman warned him, "I'll wallop you!"

Murray ran upstairs crying. His father and mother, who lived in a flat above the store, came downstairs and Leon Koffler demanded, "What did you do to our Murray?"

"I just told him he can't go on top of the ice cream cabinet and I gave him a little pat on the behind."

"You shouldn't hit him," said Leon.

"I didn't really hit him," said Starkman. "But next time I'll wallop him real good. He's a smart little boy and he's a smart little brat. And if you don't watch out, I predict he's a little smart aleck who'll come to no good."

Today Starkman laughs as he tells the story. "Just shows you what a lousy fortuneteller I am," he says. "That little brat turned out to be the greatest philanthropist and best pharmacist we've ever had."

Somewhat similar is the recollection of Harry Kalb, a former pharmacist who worked for both Murray and his father Leon off and on over a period of almost half a century. Now semi-retired, he works mornings as a broker of odd-lot products, plays the card game of klubyash in the afternoon with his elderly cronies at Toronto's Primrose Club, and at night alleviates twinges of pain from that professional hazard of all

FAMILY ALBUM

Murray Koffler's Romanian-born parents, Tiana Reinhorn (who added an "a" to her first name "just to be different") and Leon Koffler, were married in Toronto in 1921.

A Botticelli beauty at sixteen, Murray's mother Tiana was ranked "the prettiest girl in Saskatoon."

An industrious immigrant at eighteen determined to be "Canadianized," Murray's father Leon delivered groceries and vegetables in Toronto via horse and wagon.

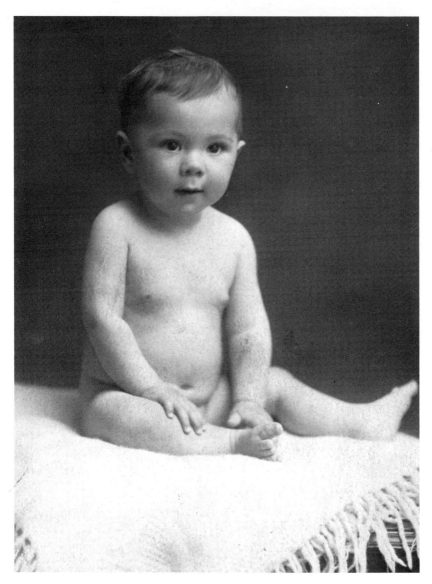

Murray Bernard Koffler, nicknamed "Mush," was born in a four-room flat over his father's drugstore on College Street on January 22, 1924. Here he is four months old.

A pampered only child, Murray
was often garbed in fancy sailor
suits.

Murray with Aunt Anne outside his
father's College Street store. Note mortar
and pestle sign.

Murray at four, wearing a white wool outfit knitted by his mother, won the "Most Beautiful Child" contest staged by Toronto Hadassah.

Murray, third from left, wore a fake moustache to play a lead role in Gilbert and Sullivan's comic operetta *The Gondoliers* at Camp Winnebago.

Kilted Koffler can be seen third from right in this 1942 regimental snapshot.

Murray at eighteen was a drummer in the 48th Highlanders Pipe and Drum Band of Canada.

The Kofflers, both father and son, enjoyed working behind the prescription counter. Leon, top, is seen at the College Street store in 1939 and Murray at Bathurst Street store in 1950.

At their wedding on January 20, 1950, Marvelle Seligman, a freckle-faced beauty, looked radiant in a Molyneux gown of white silk taffeta, while Murray was all smiles in a pearl-grey vest and cutaway coat.

On their honeymoon, the newlyweds went out on the town nightclubbing at the Château Madrid in Manhattan.

Marvelle and Murray ogle each other lovingly on a ship cruise.

Murray and Marvelle visited the Sphinx on a trip to Egypt.

Owners of ski chalets in Collingwood, Ontario, and Sun Valley, Idaho, the Kofflers are skiing zealots.

All sunburned from skiing, the Kofflers play host to Prime Minister Pierre Trudeau at their Sun Valley chalet, 1986.

The Kofflers with their golden retrievers at Jokers Hill Farm, in King, Ontario, 1973.

On Father's Day, June 14, 1963, proud Papa Murray posed in this charming photo with his then four children (from right): Leon, eleven, Theo, ten, Tom, six, Adam, four.

The Koffleresque pug-nosed profile is evident
in this 1966 photo of all five of his children
(clockwise): Leon, Theo, Tom, Adam, and Tiana.

All five Koffler kids became fine equestrians. That's ten-year-old
Tiana aback Splashdown at a 1973 Pony Club rally.

Murray and Marvelle at opening of the Koffler Student Services Centre with their children and spouses (from left): Murray, Theo, Yoav Stern, Shayla, Tiana, Adam, Marvelle, Anna, Tom, Irit, and Leon.

Murray and Marvelle with their eight grandchildren, all boys (from left): Itimar, Logan, Omri, Corey, Zachary, Shawn, Brandon, and Dustin.

At Leon's fabulous torch-lit wedding with Irit Strauss before 1,200 guests in an ancient fortress at Acre, Israel, on May 9, 1985 (from left): Theo, Israeli Prime Minister Shimon Peres, Murray, Leon, the bride's mother Ella, and Irit.

Murray and Marvelle with the two couples who are among their best friends (from left): George and Sharon Zuckerman, Eddie and Edie Creed.

pharmacists – flat feet – by propping them up on a pile of pillows.

"When Murray was about ten, we would refer to him among ourselves as a spoiled-rotten brat," says Kalb. "We called him that because he'd take certain privileges that grated on us. After school, he'd bring in three or four kids to the Bathurst Street store. He'd sit them down at the soda fountain and order ice creams for them all and raise a terrible rumpus.

"I once phoned his father to lay it on the line: 'Either he leaves or I leave!'

"Mr. Koffler asked to speak to his son. I don't know what the conversation was. But Murray hung up and said to his friends, 'Let's scram out of here.' So Mr. Koffler took my threat seriously."

As it happened, the formerly obstreperous young whelp begged Kalb to run the College Street store for him when his father died and was grateful for everything that Kalb could teach him. "Murray turned out to be a perfect gent," says Kalb. "Over the years, you couldn't ask for a more appreciative boss. You never worked *for* Murray. You worked *with* him."

Aunt Lucy Samuels readily concedes that Murray was pampered ever since he was a toddler. Her snapshots reveal an appealing little boy: pudgy and bright-eyed, his wavy brown hair neatly combed, buckled shoes polished and gleaming, always immaculate in short pants and shirts personally sewn for him by his mother. His clothes may well have been considered too sissified by the street-smart youngsters of the Ward, and it appears likely that they taunted him in the schoolyard.

Murray himself prefers to forget how traumatic it was for him to attend King Edward Public School from the ages of five to seven. "I hated that school and I was frightened when I was almost dragged there every day. I have a memory lapse about what caused it, but I so dreaded going there that I used to throw up every morning."

A key factor that prompted his parents to move to Rosemary Road was Forest Hill Village Public School. His mother, a well-read, cultured woman, had heard that it was the city's most progressive elementary school, which included

French lessons from kindergarten on. His move to that elite new area of suburbia – so new that most of the roads were unpaved and students at a riding academy galloped through empty fields – resulted in Murray having a foot in two cultures, one poor and one affluent.

Morris Kerzner, a contemporary who later was his classmate at the Ontario College of Pharmacy and business associate, used to think of Murray as an exotic rich kid. It is little wonder. Kerzner was one of seven children of an immigrant Polish Talmudic scholar turned sweatshop pants presser; his impoverished family wore second-hand clothes bought from a bargain-basement on Queen Street and slept on benches in cramped quarters above the Kielcer Synagogue on Dundas Street. When he first met nine-year-old Murray, Kerzner recalls, "he was dressed like Little Lord Fauntleroy." The difference in their economic status became apparent to Kerzner when Murray later invited him to a Friday night Sabbath dinner at 315 Rosemary Road. The exquisite two-storey house, with sunken living room, beamed ceiling, and stone fireplace, seemed to him "like a palace."

Murray today makes light of living "up on the hill." That exalted label then meant moving north of the big hill that began sloping at Davenport Road and ascending above St. Clair Avenue. Murray denies that the term had a snobbish connotation.

Others strongly differ. Among them are Johnny Wayne and Frank Shuster, the Canadian comedy team, proud of being born and bred in the Jewish area south of College Street. They wrote a satirical music revue in the 1930s, which was performed at the University of Toronto's Hart House Theatre and produced by the so-called poor man's fraternity, Beta Sigma Rho. Its most popular song, "We're Sophisticated Tonight," lampooned the *nouveaux riches* living it up "up on the hill." Twenty men in top hats, white ties, and tails strutted across the stage with their canes and sang:

We're sophisticated tonight,
At every cocktail party

And social affair
In Forest Hill Village
We'll always be there
We only breathe the air
That's north of St. Clair
Because we're sophisticated tonight.

Another in disagreement with Murray's poor-mouthing of his *haute bourgeoisie* past is Dr. Oscar Kofman, his former school chum and still a dear friend, who is now a neurologist. The son of an Austrian immigrant grocer, Kofman, like Koffler, moved at the age of seven from the Ward up to Forest Hill Village. "Of course, 'moving up to the hill' was a status symbol to both our parents," says Kofman. "It signified that you were a success and your children could expect certain privileges."

He says Murray was never a snob, but certainly never lacked the niceties of life. At the age of ten, for instance, Kofman remembers buying his first bicycle. It was a spiffy, green-and-gold, top-of-the-line CCM model which, albeit second-hand, cost him $38.50 – a considerable sum for a boy in the Depression era. "A couple of days later," he says, "Murray showed up with exactly the same bike."

As a boy, he found Murray a likable, sociable, voluble fellow who could talk your ear off. "He was no jock, but neither was he run of the mill," says Kofman. "He was good at organizing things and was a very creative idea person even then. But nobody ever expected him to be the most meteoric success story in Our Gang."

The capitalized Our Gang, which kept shifting and growing over the years, consisted initially of ten boys aged about eleven or twelve organized by Murray under the swashbuckling name of the Forest Hill Rangers. Their most adventuresome exploit, though, consisted of playing poker at the home of Normy Simpson – without letting Normy's parents know about their gambling escapades. Norman D. Simpson, prior to his death in 1987 at the age of sixty-five, recalled with amusement: "Murray was no hotshot poker player, maybe because our stakes were a measly one or two cents. If any member would have walked away from a game losing thirty cents, it would have constituted a federal case." Their Sunday meetings, he adds, were not altogether devoted to illicit vice of that sort. His father, Morris I. Simpson, a pious shoe wholesaler, arranged to bring in speakers who addressed them on good conduct, morality, and other lofty topics.

The circle of Murray's Our Gang expanded when he attended boys' camps in northern Ontario, alternating each summer between Camp Arowhon in Algonquin Park and Camp Winnebago in Muskoka. He became an accomplished horseback rider and canoeist. And he was a better than average actor performing alongside the likes of Lorne Greene, Lloyd Bochner, and composer Lou Applebaum in Gilbert and Sullivan operettas that included *The Mikado*, H.M.S. *Pinafore*, and *The Gondoliers*.

The comedian Frank Shuster, then a camp counsellor at Camp Arowhon, recalls casting and directing him in the role of the Pirate King in *The Pirates of Penzance*. "He was a robust kid with a robust baritone voice and every other note was in tune," Shuster assesses his theatrical talents jocularly. "The kid was smart. He quickly realized there was no business in show business and so he decided to go into a business that *was* a business."

Young Murray showed no inclination toward any business. An exception perhaps could be counted when he joined another boys' club called the Grads and emerged as a champion Monopoly player. (It has long since become a joke of one of the club members that Murray was the only one in Our Gang who took Monopoly seriously.)

Apart from the two-dollar weekly allowance he got from his mother, which was an extraordinarily large sum for the Depression period, Murray's Toronto boyhood was not exceptional. Once called "a sanctimonious icebox" by a visiting novelist, Toronto was then nicknamed both "Hogtown" and "Toronto the Good." It was a provincial city, then dominated by Protestant Orangemen and ridden with Scot Presbyterian Sundays and liquor blue laws. But that didn't mean that Jewish boys couldn't have plenty of fun growing up there.

He wasn't much of a moviegoer, though he enjoyed the Cecil B. De Mille biblical spectaculars. And he wasn't much of a book reader, though he enjoyed biographies of achievers. "I've always loved reading about people who've led fascinating lives and made a significant impact," he says. "That's one reason why, beginning as a kid, I devoured *Time* magazine from cover to cover. The Americans seemed to breed so many doers and the ideas they generated helped me immensely later in building up my own career."

He was not devoutly religious as a boy, though he enjoyed the clannishness, the feeling of belonging, produced by Jewish ritual and worship. Some of that feeling was engendered when his parents switched from the ultra-conservative Romanian Synagogue on Centre Avenue to the more liberal Goel Tzedec (Hebrew for Righteous Redeemer) Synagogue on University Avenue. He enjoyed what he calls the "feeling of community" when his mother took him to the special children's prayer services on Saturday mornings. But he definitely did not enjoy Sunday school, which he quit after six sessions, or the Hebrew instruction he was given in preparation for his *bar mitzvah*, the traditional celebration of a boy's attainment of manhood on his thirteenth birthday.

"Religious education then was taught boringly," he says. "Even worse was the teacher who came to my house twice a week to prepare me for my *bar mitzvah*. Really, it was the most idiotic thing. I was primed to repeat phonetically by rote, in Hebrew that I did not understand, a portion of the Bible. You got no sense of history or background that would enlighten you about the meaning of Judaism. That's why I helped co-found years later the Reform Temple Emanu-El."

By the time of his *bar mitzvah*, he'd already had crushes on the pretty, dark-eyed Jewish girls in Our Gang, and soon Murray would be taking them dancing to the jitterbug music at the open-air Sea Breeze dance floor at Sunnyside where you were charged a dime a dance, or to the nearby Palais Royale Ballroom on Lakeshore Boulevard where you could "cut a rug" to the groovy music of Trump Davidson. Murray would take his dates to the big tent at the Canadian National Exhibition where they would listen to the big band swing music of Benny Goodman and Lionel Hampton and the Dorsey Brothers, Tommy and Jimmy. He would take them to the best chopsuey joints on Elizabeth Street, when it was the hub of Chinatown and where there was a twenty-five-cent charge for a table cloth and where you never dared ask what mysterious ingredients were mixed into your chow mein. Then there were those chichi Saturday nights of "brown-bagging" an illicit bottle of booze, which was hidden beneath the table when you took your date to the Royal York Hotel's Imperial Room.

Murray might easily have become just another shallow playboy, a rich man's pampered son cocooned in what one sociologist called the "gilded ghetto" of Forest Hill Village. Several circumstances, however, helped him break out of that insularity. The first and most far-reaching event that shook up his glossy world and abruptly terminated his youth was the death of his father in 1941. As a coddled youth who never before had been asked to work behind the counter in either of the stores, he was understandably at first in a state of turmoil.

"There I was, a high school boy, in the middle of the war, and in the middle of my final fifth-form year at Oakwood Collegiate, and with no business knowledge of how to even run a peanut stand," he now says, recalling his internal anxieties. "I was the sole support of my mother. She had no business feeling whatsoever. I had no training in figures or finance at all. I didn't know what a balance sheet looked like. I didn't know what a profit-and-loss statement looked like. I got a year-end report and even that was too complex for me."

Fortunately, he was able to turn to a mentor who became what he calls "my surrogate father, bookkeeping teacher, and financial confidant to this very day – I never make a business move without first consulting Bill."

Bill was William Eisenberg, Leon Koffler's long-time accountant. He used to work downtown out of a dinky little office on Simcoe Street, so cramped for space that he kept his accountancy files between the spokes of an old-fashioned wire radiator. Now in his eighties, looking like an avuncular Mark Twain with his glacier-white moustache and dazzling Panama suits, the former rug peddler from Hungary maintains a staff of 200 in the opulent offices of Wm. Eisenberg & Co. occupying no less than six floors of an uptown skyscraper.

"I don't think I've taught him anything lately," said Eisenberg with a smile when asked about being the *éminence gris* responsible for Murray's financial education. Then he points to a plaque on his office wall whose advice, he says, has governed his career. It concludes: "Don't let your knowledge turn you into a snob. Find out what the other guy knows before you show off what you know."

Murray appears to have followed that guideline over the next five years, listening and absorbing assiduously while he worked toward his pharmacy degrees. Though his father's lawyer, the late Edward Laxton, helped him enormously in that transition period, the first three years were particularly difficult for him. He was in the ticklish situation of operating his two stores while serving his apprenticeship under the guidance of graduate pharmacists older than himself who also happened to be his employees.

"Suddenly Murray had to learn humility and he did so in an amazing turnabout," says his former pharmacy mentor-cum-employee, Lawrence Shankman. He recalls how Murray as a youngster once commanded him peremptorily at the College Street store: "Look here. *I* want *you* to sweep the floor."

Shankman now says, "I simply ignored him and walked away. I could have answered back, 'I take orders only from your father and not from some know-nothing punk of a kid.' But it's not my style to start fights and I just let it go by."

After serving in the Army, Shankman returned in 1945 to work at the College Street store and was astonished by the change in the once arrogant young whippersnapper. "From a brash kid," says Shankman, "he'd turned into an adult, and it was a delight to work with him."

His maturation stemmed in large part from his experiences while studying during 1945 and 1946 at the Ontario College of Pharmacy. Murray looks back on them as two exhilarating years devoted to mastering the art and science of his profession. They were spent in the stately, Gothic-style stone building at 44 Gerrard Street in midtown Toronto, the oldest pharmacy college in Canada, established in 1871 a scant four years after Confederation and long since designated an historic site. And they were years crowded with hectic activity, according to his classmate, Morris Kerzner, who shared his notes with Murray and got a lift with him every morning to classes.

He remembers how Murray would pick him up at downtown Division Street in the two-toned blue 1940 Buick Torpedo he had inherited from Leon Koffler. "Our classes began at nine o'clock and, true to form, Murray was late even then," he says with amusement. "I'd usually get into his car at five or ten minutes before nine and with a burst of speed we'd somehow just barely make it in the nick of time. Our classes often lasted until four o'clock and Murray would have to leap into his Torpedo and whiz off to check up on his two drugstores."

Because of the pressures on him, Murray managed to squeak by with average marks in the sixties and seventies rather than top honour grades. He gives credit to Kerzner for his diligent note-taking for both of them. "Without his notes, I'd never have got through," he says.

Of his pharmacy professors, he remembers most vividly the college's late Dean Robert Oscar Hurst, a portly raconteur with Irish wit and a Shakespearean stage presence. "He was like an actor in his demonstrations," says Koffler, imitating him in pantomime. "First he'd show us how a sloppy pharmacist would dump pills in his hand and count them with his fingers. Then he'd say, 'The precise, hygienic way of doing it is to put the pills on a tray and very carefully handle them with a spatula. Remember, if you're measuring out a liquid, don't ever pour it like a bottle of beer. Always hold the beaker *exactly* at eye level. And when approaching a customer, you must always wear a white smock buttoned right up to the neck – never, ever exposing whatever colourful tie you're wearing. Remember, you're a *professional!*'"

In addition, Koffler was impressed by the scholarship of the erudite Professor Norman Hughes, later appointed dean and now retired at seventy-nine. Hughes remembers Koffler as "a personable, good-looking young man, not an outstanding student, but one who minded his Ps and Qs." Koffler in turn remembers how Hughes kept stressing the social utility and values of the profession. "A pharmacist may not know all that a physician knows, but he sometimes knows things about patients and potions that physicians don't know," Hughes liked saying. "And pharmacy is a noble profession only as long as you possess the dedication, coupled with the knowledge, that you're making people feel better."

But while he absorbed the lore and the philosophy and methodology of the profession, Murray was acute enough to perceive the deficiencies of a college that was essentially a glorified trade school. Its curriculum was restricted to the medicinal aspects of the dispensary, which incorporated such basic subjects as chemistry, biology, and physiology; over-looked entirely were the business aspects of merchandising and managing the store. Murray brooded about this vacuum for forty years; his remedy, of course, is the current creation of the $6 million Koffler Institute of Pharmacy Management to be affiliated with the University of Toronto's Faculty of Pharmacy.

Another void that Murray felt keenly was the lack of a cosmopolitan atmosphere that one expects in an institution of higher learning. Not only did the college neglect to teach courses related to the humanities and the arts; the building itself was physically separated about one mile from the university proper. "Except for two lectures a week we took in the labs at the university's chemistry building," he recalls, "we were cut off from the University of Toronto and didn't feel we were a part of the campus."

To overcome that sense of isolation, he joined Pi Lambda Phi, an interdisciplinary fraternity that embraced law, medical, engineering, and liberal arts students. He recalls that this step aroused a certain amount of peevish resentment from his fellow Jewish students. Most of them had elected to join Rho Pi Phi. It was the pharmacy fraternity, which was the result of a merger with the exclusively Jewish Rokeah Club that Leon Koffler had co-founded. But Murray considers his pledging to Pi Lambda Phi the wisest move he could have made to enrich his life as a college student.

"I never personally experienced overt anti-Semitism as a student," he says. "I knew it existed. But I always felt comfortable being completely homogeneous in the broad crowd. And I sometimes feel my fellow Jews bring on their own antagonisms by refusing to reach out and mingle. I know that the core of my pharmacy class consisted of Jewish apprentices from the College Street area. They kept absolutely separate. They didn't mix at all.

"In fact, they were so cliquish and wary of mixing they used to think of me as the fifth column. I was the guy who went over to the other side. For lunch, they'd stick together at Bassel's, a restaurant near the college at Gerrard and Yonge Street. But I'd jump into my car and whip over to the frat house on the campus on St. George Street. I mixed it up with guys from every profession, got a feel for public speaking and debate, played a leading role in organizing the fraternity's annual charity ball, and had myself a ball making lifelong friendships."

Murray's changing attitude toward his Jewishness is a complex matter. An interesting observation is put forward by George Zuckerman, still the closest of the lifelong friends he made at Pi Lambda Phi. The son of a Russian immigrant garment embroidery tailor, Zuckerman is president of the international Doubletex Inc. textile corporation, Murray's former partner in the co-ownership of an ocean-going luxury yacht, and a liberal arts student at University College when the pair first met at the fraternity.

"Murray was hypersensitive in those days about being Jewish in the sense that he didn't want to convey a poor image of Jews," says Zuckerman. "If we were at a Varsity football game and were yelling and screaming, he'd caution us: 'Take it easy. Not so loud. Let's not stand out as loudmouths.' The same thing was true if we went to one of those rinkydink dives in Chinatown on Elizabeth Street. If one of the couples in Our Gang would give the order for our food noisily, Murray would say: 'Hey, let's not behave like stereotypes.' It was only years later, when he first visited Israel, that Murray became really proud of his Jewishness."

Friends from his student days all agree that Murray was adventuresome in breaking down the barriers of Jewish clannishness. His passkey to a hitherto undiscovered world was the drum he played as a cadet in the bugle band at Oakwood Collegiate. A minor medical problem and the fact that he was the sole support of his widowed mother prevented him from enlisting for active service during wartime. But his experience as a drummer boy served him well when he joined the reserve unit of the 48th Highlanders. He thus became a kilted drummer parading with a bagpipe band, and he particularly enjoyed it because it gave him an understanding of the Scottish people.

"They were among the happiest years of my life," he says. "I belonged to the St. Andrew's Society, and I used to take out lovely Scot girls to the Robert Burns dinners who taught me how to dance Highland flings and reels. Most of the pipers came from Glasgow and I can still pick out a Glaswegian accent and mimic it fairly well myself. They're marvellous sensitive people, the Scots, once you get to know them, and I feel like one of them whenever I hear that thrilling skirl of the bagpipes."

Indeed, he recalls with amusement attending a traditional Sabbath dinner in the home of a Jewish girlfriend after a 48th Highlanders parade one Friday night. "I arrived in my kilt, which was quite a shock for her parents, because they'd never had kilts in their home before," he says. "That was a bit of a laugh. But it reminded me once again how insulated we Jews can sometimes be living in our closed world."

He also matured in other ways. His intimates believe that Murray, a person not given to public exhibition of his deeply felt emotions as though it were a weakness, developed his own sensitivity and unusual intuitiveness as a result of his close relationship with his widowed mother. Tiana had always been a loner rather than a joiner. She is remembered as a quiet, thoughtful, aesthetically cultivated, fastidiously tidy homemaker with a regal bearing. She read a lot and had definite liberal views on current events. But she was not an outgoing woman.

When Leon was alive, she had belonged to the Kadima chapter of Hadassah, whose members were the wives of physicians, dentists, and pharmacists. On her husband's death, she became increasingly reclusive, not bedridden but house-ridden, and more emotionally dependent on her son. There was a tenderness between them that was most poignant, especially when she was afflicted in the last eight years of her life with chronic ulcerative colitis. She became one of the first patients in Canada to use a colostomy bag, the bypass tube of which was frequently clogged.

"I had to become an expert on colostomies," says Murray matter-of-factly. "They were very primitive in those days. For years I had to change my mother's colostomy bag four or five times a day. It was an embarrassing experience for her, but I accepted it." Her condition worsened, and eventually she was in the hospital for a long period under life-support systems. Murray sometimes wondered whether it would have been more humane to remove the life-supporting equipment and thus end the pain and indignity she was suffering. In 1956, she finally succumbed and died in her sleep at the age of fifty-six.

Lucy Samuels remembers that Murray did not cry at his father's funeral. Neither did he cry at his mother's funeral. "But after Tiana was buried," she says, "he went home that night and wept as though his heart would break." Murray, she feels, by exhibiting the strength to thus express his so-called weakness freely, had truly become a *mensch*.

CHAPTER SIX

Murray Minds the Store

Picture Murray Koffler at twenty-two with, as he phrases it, "my sleeves rolled up and ready to go to work." The scene is set at his Bathurst Street store. The time is a Monday morning in the summer of 1946. And, as usual, the newly graduated druggist is late. It's at least five minutes past nine o'clock by the time he arrives in his blue Buick Torpedo and unlocks the front door of his 2,000-square-foot store in the suburbs north of St. Clair Avenue. He invariably begins the day with two chores. One he enjoys; the other he despises.

He enjoys the morning ritual of making sure the store is sparkling clean. First he pours ammonia fortis, the strongest cleaning agent there is, into a pail of hot water. He brushes the solution on the two big front windows and dries them down with a squeegee. He sweeps the outside pavement with a corn bristle broom. He washes the floor inside with a mop. He dusts and polishes the oak-and-glass showcases until they shine. Then he stands back, arms akimbo, to admire his handiwork.

"I never thought that scrubbing a store clean was a mundane thing," he now says. "On the contrary, I've always found it extremely pleasant. It's something I probably inherited from my father. That's the satisfaction and pride of welcoming your customers in a store that you know is perfectly spotless."

He hated, however, the morning routine of preparing breakfast for the bachelors who lived in the area. He would stand behind the soda fountain that extended three-quarters down the length of the store. Then for a half hour or more he would fry bacon and eggs, pop bread in the toaster, squeeze orange juice, serve hot soups, and soak and dry the dirty dishes.

"I detested the greasy smell of the food pervading my store all day," he says. "And I couldn't stand the filth of the soda fountain. That used to kill me. I'd moan to myself, 'Why did I spend five years getting a college degree? Did I do it to become a waiter, bottle-washer, and short-order cook?'"

But his *bête noire*, he says, was the menial pettiness of the nickel-and-dime delivery service that his father had inaugurated at the Bathurst Street store with a squad of ten bicycle delivery boys. Murray himself never delivered via a bike, but he did so in his father's 1940 Buick. When Murray was sixteen, Leon Koffler had conceived the idea of importing the *New York Sunday Times* and promoting it as a loss leader. And so every Sunday morning at ten minutes before twelve, Murray would pull up at the Canadian National Railway's express office at Union Station and load up his dad's new Buick with fifty or sixty copies. He would assemble the various sections at the store and deliver them at cost price of nineteen cents a copy, along with perhaps a carton of Coca-Cola and two packages of either Export or Players or Sweet Caporal cigarettes.

"A delivery boy would accompany me in the car and together we'd deliver a whole bloody order that amounted to less than a dollar," he says. "That Sunday chore was really my only business experience. So I didn't mind doing it as a teenager because it gave me a feel for customer relationships, and I could drive the car."

But what was fun at sixteen became onerous at twenty-two. It rankled increasingly because customers began to take unfair advantage of the fierce rivalry between drugstores. It was common for a customer to place an order with both the Koffler store and Crosstown Pharmacy for a carton of Cokes and a brick of ice cream. Whichever delivery boy reached there first had his order accepted. The latecomer would be told, "You're out of luck. You were beaten by your competition."

Arthur Resnick, a pharmacy graduate who used to assist Koffler at the Bathurst Street store, remembers one deadbeat customer who would phone up daily. "Send me for ten cents a Turret with a cork," the man would say, meaning a package of cork-tipped Turret brand cigarettes. Then he would have the *chutzpah* to say, "Put it on charge." Another nervy customer would order a bottle of Canada Dry ginger ale. When it arrived, he would feel the bottle and scowl. "That's not cold, sonny," he would tell the delivery boy. "Take it back."

Adjoining the Bathurst Street store was a small Dominion supermarket. Murray would fume inwardly when a customer would phone up to say, "Murray, dear. Please have your delivery boy pick up the following list of groceries next door and put it on my charge order for toilet paper and soda pop."

But there was one "Murray, dear" request that exasperated him most of all. After he had delivered the *Sunday Times*, along with a couple of cartons of Coca-Cola, some customers had the gall to say, "Murray, dear. Would you mind taking all our accumulated empties back?" It involved cleaning out the customer's basement full of empty pop bottles, paying a refund on all the empties whether purchased from Koffler's or not, and returning to the store with the Buick's back seat loaded with literally dozens of grimy bottles. Koffler became increasingly disenchanted with this burdensome task; it eventually darkened his dreams like a hellish scene out of Dante's *Inferno*.

"We used to stack the empties in the cellar near where I'd shovel coal into the furnace," he recalls. "I'd wake up at night with this nightmare image of myself shovelling coal amid mountains of pop bottles that hadn't yet been sorted out. I'd dream of shovelling and then trying endlessly to put bottles of Coke in the Coke cases, and Pepsi in the Pepsi cases, and Canada Dry in the Canada Dry cases, and 7-up and root beer in the other cases."

He remembers waking up with the shakes and asking himself, "'What the hell am I doing in this drugstore that's more like a grocery store? I love being behind the counter and I love serving customers in need of medication and guidance. In fact, I get goose pimples of satisfaction from helping people with their health care. But am I going to spend the rest of my life just selling chewing gum and jerking sodas and delivering soda pop?'

"No, I didn't call it professionally demeaning, because I didn't know then what that word meant. But I felt it, and I knew it was rotten, and I told myself, 'There's got to be a better way.'"

Koffler then vowed to himself to revamp the needless drudgery that plagued his profession or to get out of it. He later called his innovations a series of "adventures," but others at the time called them sheer madness.

The first thing he did was to throw out the soda fountain. He remembers summoning a drugstore interior designer, a Mr. Wakely who had been his father's friend. "Mr. Wakely, I want you to remove the dispensary from the back of the store and put it in the front of the store, right in the window," he instructed him. "As for the soda fountain that's been occupying that valuable front space, I want you to dispose of it altogether."

Wakely was shocked. "Mr. Koffler, your father would *never* do such a thing. It's dead wrong. You do that and you won't be able to pay your bills."

"Well, my father might not have done it, but I'm going to," said Koffler. "I want you to build me a real super dispensary with sliding glass panels. And I want it to fit right into the front window. So then people driving by will see a dispensary instead of a soda fountain and they'll know instantly we're not a drugstore but a pharmacy."

Koffler designed a bold new dispensary unit with Wakely and it worked. At that time, Starkman's Chemists, which was open all night on Bloor Street in downtown Toronto, was widely regarded as *the* dispensing pharmacy. People would often buy their cigarettes, Cokes, and toothpaste at Koffler's, but they would go to Starkman's to have their prescriptions filled. Before the change, Koffler's store would fill five to ten prescriptions in an average day. But as a result of putting the focus on the dispensary, the store began to fill fifty to sixty and sometimes as many as 100 prescriptions a day.

As physicians responded to Koffler's calculated showmanship, he added another touch of professionalism. He insisted that the staff wear smartly starched white smock coats buttoned right up to the collar. He thus heightened the store's image as the area's foremost prescription pharmacy.

His next move was more startling: to get rid of free delivery service. It took a great deal of spunk, for the we-deliver-anything service promoted so zealously by his father accounted for 25 per cent of the business. But Koffler figured it was a penny-ante business that had been abused to the point where it was no longer profitable. Consequently, he devised a strategy for phasing it out that would encourage his competitors to help establish an enlightened, industry-wide trend. He phoned his fellow pharmacists and also talked to them in small groups at the Rokeah Club and the Toronto Pharmacists Association.

"Look, gentlemen," he remembers advising them. "As of Monday morning, I'm not delivering soft drinks and cigarettes without a drug order, and that minimum order has to be worth a dollar. Then I intend charging twenty-five cents to deliver an order. Then it'll be fifty cents and then one dollar. And then ultimately I'll only deliver prescription orders."

He let that sink in and then, to avoid suspicion of collusion, he said further: "You fellows can do what you want. You can grab all the delivery business we lose. But that's what *we're* doing. If you're smart, you'll all do the same."

Murray expected his old-time customers to protest vehemently that Leon Koffler, blessed be his name, must be turning over in his grave horrified at his son's break with the old man's way of doing things. Indeed, they did and still do compare Murray, not always favourably, with the revered Leon. Murray maintains it doesn't bother him. He goes further than that; he claims he has never been influenced, except subliminally perhaps, by his father and does not try to emulate him. Yet he savours the praise heaped on him by elderly customers he encounters at Jewish social functions.

Some of his friends speculate that Murray may be boxing unconscious childhood shadows, trying to surpass the achievements of Leon. However, any glib Freudian suggestion that he either resents the father who was so detached from him or that Murray posthumously strives to seek his approval is dismissed lightly with a joke. "For years I was Leon Koffler's son," says Murray. "Customers would complain, 'You're not like your father' and 'Leon would have done this' and 'Leon would have done that' and 'Why can't you be like Leon?' Then along came Leon Koffler, my eldest son named after my father. He became a top ski athlete. His name was always in the newspapers. And so I became known as Leon Koffler's father. I've never been *me*!"

Murray enjoys recounting, with great gusto and mimicry, what has become his classic story of being rebuffed repeatedly by an unswervingly loyal fan of the late Leon Koffler. He knew her over the phone simply as Mrs. Feinsod, who lived across the road at 1539 Bathurst Street in Apartment 202. She was said to be the retired owner of Feinsod's Delicatessen; and from her British-accented voice and speaking manner, she seemed to be an ample woman of ample spirit and acrid sarcasm.

Murray's father had regarded her admiringly as a feisty character; he liked exchanging banter with her when she phoned up every day for her three-penny *Toronto Star* and three-penny *Toronto Evening Telegram* to be delivered along with a couple of other minor items such as a nickel package of chewing gum and a nine-cent bottle of ASA aspirin.

Murray also appreciated her salty wit – that is, until she phoned up one rainy day, gave her usual order, and demanded, "Send it over right away."

"I'm sorry, Mrs. Feinsod," he told her. "There's a flu epidemic going around and we're busy delivering prescribed medicines. Besides, as you know from the notice we sent out, we've set a fifty-cent minimum on delivery orders."

"Young man, you're not like your father!" she bellowed. "I'm a sick old lady and I just can't stand it. I *knew* you'd ruin your father's drug business."

When she banged the receiver down on his ear, Murray winced and thought, "Well, if I lose her, I can't help it, I lose her. You can't please them all."

But it was the opening ploy in a daily barrage of phone calls. "You're a no-goodnik compared to your father!" she would bluster, and Murray was equally obdurate about refusing to send her the daily newspapers.

A week later, during a Rexall product two-for-the-price-of-one sale, Murray had persuaded a young woman to buy Rexall cough syrup for her sore throat, Rexall nose drops for her sniffles, and successfully urged her to try Rexall vitamin C pills as well. Just as he was concluding the sale, a capacious woman of about 300 pounds came lumbering up to the counter and stood there listening, supported by two canes.

She tapped the young woman on the shoulder, and Murray heard her say in what was by now a familiar, haughty British tone, "Why are you listening to this boy? Listen to me instead. Forget about these useless products he's peddling. Go home and take a glass of hot tea with lemon and add a little bit of sherry and I guarantee you'll wake up tomorrow with your cold all better."

"Thank you, ma'am, for your sound advice," said the young woman. She walked out, leaving all the Rexall products on the counter and Murray miffed yet amused by the audacity of the intruder.

It was, of course, Mrs. Feinsod. She turned to Murray and, with a combination of a gloat and a threat, she said, "See, I came out here to prove my point. Don't you think it would be worth your while to help out a helpless old lady by continuing to send me my two papers every day?"

Privately, Murray suspected that the doughty old battleaxe was as helpless as an express train in full throttle. Publicly, he bowed in defeat and said, "Mrs. Feinsod, I'll send you your *Star* and *Tely* at least for another month."

After the thirty days were over, and he had discontinued her newspaper delivery, Murray was challenged once again in the middle of a sales spiel. A customer had come in seeking relief for his aching flat feet and the accompanying pain in his back. Murray took off his shoe and showed the man his own inserted Scholl's leather-covered metal arch support. "Look, I stand on my feet all day and my aching feet and back used to kill me," said Murray. "Ever since I started using these insoles, I've never had a back ache and my feet feel terrific."

The indomitable Mrs. Feinsod came waddling in like a walrus, and, with outlandish theatricality that Murray will never forget, she pulled out her false teeth.

"If you wear these arch supports, I bet you'll find them as uncomfortable as these false teeth of mine," she said, with a malicious, toothless grin. "This young squirt once advised me to buy a certain tube of toothpaste. If I were you, I wouldn't listen to his advice, sir, because look at what happened to me."

She popped her teeth back in and waddled out in vengeful victory, leaving Murray with his mouth agape and utterly wordless.

Eventually he stopped hiring delivery boys and replaced the bicycle squadron with a delivery van. And gradually he reduced use of the truck, too. Special bargain prices on items – he never used the word "discount" – did not apply if the goods were delivered by van. Furthermore, the bill would make a pointed reminder: "This item would have cost you eighty cents less if you had picked it up cash and carry."

This is not to imply that Murray discouraged people from phoning his store. On the contrary, like his father, he was a yeasty entrepreneur who kept bubbling over with ideas to promote the name, location, and phone number of Koffler's. One of his brightest innovations was the distribution of a black laminated cover advertising his store that slipped like a bulky jacket over a telephone book. It cost him about seventy-five cents to produce it, but he offset the expense by selling ads to the hardware store, the bakery, and other local shops. He had about 2,000 of the covers made. Then he handed them out door to door to potential customers in the Bathurst-St. Clair area.

After introducing himself, he would offer it as a gift with a pitch that ran: "I'm gratified to meet you personally because I want you to be our customer. This is to remind you that we are as close to you as your telephone."

He now says, "You really had to hustle to fight for business in those early days." And yet, though the fight for survival may have been fierce, it was tempered with an old-fashioned camaraderie. That neighbourly spirit is remembered with nostalgic fondness by many of Murray's former competitors who later became his executive colleagues in the Shoppers Drug Mart family.

One of them is Irving Horowitz, inevitably nicknamed "Tiny" because of his hefty girth and considerable height (6'3", 240 pounds). "There was a certain closeness in the profession that I miss today," he says. "We were rivals and yet we were buddies. If a guy was opening a store, you can be sure that five or ten of us fellows would drop around to help him set up the merchandise and even lend a hand with the cash register on opening day.

"What I don't miss are the terrible economic pressures that forced us to stay open until past midnight. Before closing our store in what was then the suburbs on Yonge Street and Lawrence, we were so hungry for business I'd first look outside up and down the block. If I saw a guy on the street, I'd say, 'Let's wait and see if he walks by or comes in before we shut up shop for the night.'"

Max Glazer, now in his seventies, another Shoppers old-timer, also likes thinking back on the sharing that went on. "If you ran short of a certain item for a prescription, you'd behave like a housewife borrowing an egg or a cup of flour from a friendly next-door neighbour," he recalls. "We pharmacists were all in the same boat, and we stuck together for survival's sake, especially during the darkest days of the Depression, when you had to scramble hard for a buck or get into the breadline."

Murray's Bathurst Street customers were better off financially than patrons of his College Street store, which he left under the management of Lawrence Shankman. Consequently, he only occasionally dealt with customers "on the pogie." And he recalls having very few problems with deadbeats who did not pay for goods delivered on credit. "No matter how bad business was, you never turned away anybody in need of medication," he says. "That's always been the unwritten law of pharmacists."

Murray's college classmate, Arthur Resnick, who worked for him at the Bathurst Street store, recalls how Murray became increasingly restless and was constantly percolating ideas for making money in sideline enterprises. "Murray was a visionary, always reading the American retail trade magazines and looking for something else," he says. "Some of his brainwaves were brilliant. But quite a few were real lulus that went haywire. I give Murray credit for admitting to his mistakes and learning from them."

Slapping his palm to his forehead in mock agony, Koffler grins and acknowledges, "Oh, boy! How could I ever forget those cockamamy ideas of mine that bombed? You see, I was trying hard to get out of the drug business then and into something more challenging. And so I was sometimes grabbing at straws."

Some of his ventures were simply several years ahead of their time. The incorrigibly positive-minded Koffler prefers to call them "managerial exercises" or "entrepreneurial sojourns" rather than outright failures. One was proposed by the sales representative of Arrow Photo Company, who supplied his store with cameras, film, and flashbulbs. The man lugged in a huge machine equipped with two circular reels and a microphone.

"I know you're interested in newfangled inventions," the salesman said. "So I felt I've just got to show you this one. It's a prototype model of the latest dictating machine. They've just started manufacturing them in England, Japan, and the U.S. And we've just acquired the licensing rights for Canada. Isn't it phenomenal, Murray?"

"Sure is," Murray agreed, after the demonstration.

"What's it called?"

"A tape recorder."

"I'd love to get into that."

"You've got it! Your store has a camera department. So you can be our sales agent."

Koffler rashly ordered twenty of the monstrous machines. Then he hired two salesmen to hawk them, at a price of $650 each, to physicians and company executives.

"The tape recorders were lined up in the store, and the salesmen were coming and going, and we even sold a few," he says. "Several years later tape recorders became as common as ballpoint pens. But these were too cumbersome, and we lost everything. I marked it off as my first introduction to getting into something beyond the drugstore."

His next entrepreneurial sojourn was equally disastrous. This time he was approached by a Damon Runyonesque character named Henry Males, described by Murray as a rough-diamond-in-the-rough promoter. Males proposed that Murray buy from a distributor at a half cent each 100,000 comic books that had been returned unsold by store retailers.

"You put up the dough and I'll put up the time selling them in a booth at the Canadian National Exhibition," said Males. "It's a terrific idea and a terrific deal. I'm sure the kids will be ecstatic about it."

The kids were not. They had already read or spurned the Superman and Batman comic books, with their primitive Wham! Bang! Aargh! lines of dialogue, the first time around. Murray attempted to recoup his losses by paying Males to try peddling them at fairs in Ottawa and in Ontario small towns. After a year, Murray concluded there was nothing funny – or lucrative – in the second-hand comic book business. He decided to call it quits before being Whammed! Banged! and Aarghed! penniless.

Males was also a confederate in Koffler's next sojourn, into the perfume-squirting business. The initial promoter in this exercise was a boyhood friend named Julie Gross. His father owned the Silver Rail, Toronto's first restaurant licensed to operate a cocktail bar in the post-war liberalization of Ontario liquor laws. Gross asked Koffler to be his partner in selling a new dime-a-squirt vending machine called Perfumatic, which would be affixed to the walls of women's washrooms in the city's burgeoning cocktail lounges.

"A super idea," said Koffler. "Why do you need me in the deal?"

"The manufacturer of the machines needs a guy like you with the contacts to get four different kinds of bulk perfume for the Perfumatics," said Gross. "Can you handle it?"

"Count me in."

The machines cost $250 each if paid for in thirty days, and the two partners installed an experimental model at the Silver Rail. The machine paid for itself in three weeks.

"It was crammed so full of dimes we could hardly take the machine off the wall," recalls Koffler. "By God, I thought, *this* is the way to become a millionaire! *This* is what I've been looking for. So I said, 'Okay, Julie, let's go ahead with this thing.'"

Koffler persuaded Fabergé, Chanel, and Yardley to provide bulk lots of Tabu and Tigress and other colognes; they co-operated on the theory that the machine squirts would help introduce their new fragrances to the Toronto market. With financing from the Dominion Bank, he ordered 100 machines to be delivered in stages over a certain period. The plunge into perfumery paid off handsomely at first. "The money kept dropping into the machines at such a rate we had trouble counting it all," he recalls. "The first ten were fantastic. The next five were pretty good. But then, as we started to get into some of the low-class taverns around town, it used to take three months to pay off, and then six months."

At that stage, Koffler brought in as a junior partner that rough-diamond-in-the-rough, Henry Males, who knew his way around the rough drinking spots in town. He was an excellent salesman and collection agent at those antiquated dank dives then known as beer parlors. He even did a brisk trade by installing a dispenser of feminine fragrances in the men's washroom of a gay bar, followed by the introduction of Yardley's after shave and Brute. But generally, the profits kept dropping as the novelty faded and the market became saturated.

Things reached a melodramatic climax on New Year's Eve of 1950. Koffler had married that year the former Marvelle

Seligman, and he had agreed to let her make the rounds of the taverns with Males so that she could collect the cash from the machines in the women's washrooms. Meanwhile, Koffler was working the late shift at the Bathurst Street store.

"It got to be past midnight and she's not back and then one o'clock and then I panic," he recalls. "I phone the police departments and the hospitals and I say to myself, 'What an idiot I am! What the hell am I doing here working in the store while my own wife's out in a car with this rough diamond of a fellow going from one sleazy bar to another on New Year's Eve with all those drunks?'

"They finally come back and I hug her and I kiss her and I say, 'Marvelle, that's it. We're selling the perfume business tomorrow.'"

His ad in the newspapers was answered by a female evangelist. He remembers her telling him she had received a divine "message from on high" to buy the entire Perfumatic business, lock, stock, and squirters, and to devote the dimes amassed from tavern frequenters to her church group's good works. Koffler did not question Divinity.

"She paid us hard cash on the barrel," he says. "We made five or six thousand dollars on the whole deal. And Marvelle and I went and blew it all on one vacation trip."

Koffler's next sojourn was into the realm of manufacturing and packaging. In the immediate post-war years there was a shortage of men's toiletries, which were customarily boxed and sold in Koffler's stores as Christmas gift items. Wartime restrictions had curtailed the Canadian importation of these gift boxes. They had come from England (where Yardley, for example, produced its well-known shaving bowl), or from the U.S. (where Guardsman produced its popular after-shave lotion in bottles cunningly shaped like a soldier and topped with a wooden cap).

With these sources temporarily cut off, the entrepreneurial Koffler remembers thinking, "Well, if I have no Christmas gift toiletries to sell to men, why don't I create my own?"

Dominion Bottlers designed for him a round bottle rather similar in shape to Fabergé's. He obtained from a fragrance supplier quantities of a certain blend of cologne, an after-shave lotion, and a coloured talc. He packaged them in a standup gift box with a cardboard base and an acetate top. Then, seeking a brand name that might be catchy, he literally lifted the name Life from *Life* magazine.

"I figured *Life* was the biggest magazine at that time, and the products would look as though they were being advertised in *Life*," he says. "But to avoid trademark problems, I reversed the colours on the logotype, using orange letters on white instead of *Life*'s white on orange."

Time-Life Inc. did not protest, because *Life* magazine temporarily discontinued to circulate as a weekly after the war. The only problems arose as a result of the nit-picking complaint of Judy LaMarsh, Canada's federal Minister of Health. She brooded over the possibility that the word Life on a package might connote that it was prolonging a person's life. Koffler changed the name to "Life Products" to disabuse the most obtuse person who might think he was selling an elixir of perpetual life.

But that came later. In the immediate post-war years, his Life Products lived a short-lived life. The men's toiletries sold well when he was pushing them at his own two stores. But they flopped when he tried to sell them to his competitors via the industry's co-operative wholesaler, Drug Trading Company. "The Life gift boxes were all sent back to Drug Trading and they were all dumped back on me," he says. Happily, the venture proved to be a failure only in short-range terms. Koffler gained practical experience from his exercise in manufacturing. Eventually, after he founded Shoppers Drug Mart, the chain's exclusive line of 800 Life brand products, ranging from vitamins to pantyhose, developed into a healthy business of more than $100 million a year.

Throughout this sojourning period of dabbling in alien fields, from the late 1940s to the early 1950s, Koffler's fortune waxed and waned. It waned down to its worst when he assumed the role of a Bay Street plunger and gambled on penny stocks. Businessmen who strive to become professional promoters are notorious for being susceptible to the honeyed words of experts who are supersmooth talkers. And so Koffler naively succumbed to the hucksterism of a former Oakwood Collegiate classmate who had become a super-slick stock salesman.

Mr. Slick, as we'll call him, persuaded Koffler to gamble on a manganese stock. Slick and his fellow hypesters had already promoted it from twenty cents to forty cents to one dollar and it had received considerable publicity in the financial press.

"Murray, old pal, you'd better buy it while it's hot," Koffler remembers being told by Slick. "I'm taking a whole planeful of journalists to the manganese mine on an island in the High Arctic. I'm flying up the editor of the *Financial Post*, the editor of the *Northern Miner*, the editor of the Canadian edition of *Time* magazine, and a lot of other press VIPs. I want them to see with their own eyes the mine in operation. We're going to break a big news release worldwide. So buy it today, because I predict the stock will shoot up as high as three dollars."

"Are you sure?"

"We've been old pals since high school. Would I fool you?"

Koffler was so excited he wrote out a cheque for $12,000. Then, in a frenzy, he borrowed another $12,000 so he could buy on margin.

The day the stock reached two dollars and forty cents, Koffler was at the Toronto airport about to join the group of journalists on their Arctic junket. They were ready to take off when Slick took Koffler aside and said, "Old pal, I just got another business writer who wants to come on this flight. Because it's so important to the deal, would you mind giving up your seat?"

"I don't mind," said Koffler.

But he minded terribly when he read their jeering news reports. On their arrival, the so-called mine turned out to be a fiasco on the frozen tundra producing ore that was worth zilch. Meanwhile, Slick's promoter accomplices on Bay Street had unloaded their shares, and overnight the market price tumbled from $2.40 to twenty cents.

For Koffler, it was a financial catastrophe that cost him his College Street drugstore. To pay for his losses, he sold it to the store's manager, Lawrence Shankman, for $26,500. His misplaced judgement taught Koffler several hard-earned lessons. "It taught me not to gamble on penny stocks, not to go on margin, and not to trust somebody else to make you a fortune," he says. "I learned to invest in myself and in enterprises where I'm in charge of my own destiny."

He turned his attention mainly to cultivating and improving the field he knew best, and thus be came to terms with his love-hate relationship with the pharmacy profession. He decided to follow the folksy advice of Dale Carnegie: "If fate hands you a lemon, make lemonade out of it."

Young Koffler had served his sojourning apprenticeship and was on his way to squeezing a lemon ultimately worth, in terms of total sales, close to $2 billion.

CHAPTER SEVEN

Invasion of the Suburbs

Murray Koffler began his climb toward bigness by getting involved in Toronto's post-war real estate boom. The decade between 1945 and 1955 was a giddy period of growth for bustling Toronto the Good. From the city of churches and banks, it burgeoned into the city of suburbs and shopping plazas, bursting at the seams with 1.25 million people. War veterans tramped home and marched into a drastic housing shortage. The homes available for their brides and budding families consisted of nothing but glorified chicken coops and ticky-tacky boxes. European immigrants poured into the city at the rate of 50,000 a year. Many of the newcomers were eager to acquire their own patch of land at almost any price.

Like gold-seekers rushing to a new Klondike, land developers of every stripe clamoured to take their money. Real estate advertisements in the Toronto newspapers jumped from four columns to as much as twenty pages. Radio commercials promoting properties in glowing terms became as commonplace as soap operas. Circusy stunts were used to lure prospects to the rows of bungalows sprouting up in the meadows, as some architectural critics claimed, like "instant slums before the paint dried . . . look-a-like blobs in the burbs of boredom."

An ex-milkman named Riley Brethour and an ex-playwright named Gerry Morris teamed up to found the

Brethour & Morris real estate agency. They grossed $30 million a year by driving customers to properties while being serenaded by musicians in a private bus. A former clothes cleaner named Dave Mann and a former bank clerk named Paul Martel joined forces to form the Mann & Martel real estate company. They grossed $40 million a year by using promotional hoopla borrowed from the break-the-bank quiz shows then the rage on the newly emerging medium of television. The partners attracted more than 3,000 prospects to the Weber Park subdivision in the Etobicoke suburbs by giving away twenty new Nash sedans to the first twenty home buyers.

The most showmanlike premieres were staged by Principal Investments Ltd., which was hailed by *The Toronto Star* in a 1954 banner headline as: "TORONTO FIRM CANADA'S BIGGEST COMMERCIAL LANDLORD." Despite that splashy designation, the three Bennett brothers who headed the $100 million corporation (Archie B., David E., and Jacob M. Bennett) were usually so publicity-shy that they attempted to keep their names anonymous.

But when opening a shopping mall, the Bennetts behaved like Barnums. The debut of Golden Mile Plaza in Scarborough was heralded by a twenty-page supplement of the *Toronto Evening Telegram* and given national newsreel and television coverage. For the first three days a special police detail was needed to unscramble mile-long traffic jams. Roller coasters, ferris wheels, and merry-go-rounds were erected in the parking lot. A high-diver risked a broken neck to jump – backwards – ninety feet into a six-foot tank of water. Square dances, with costumed hillbilly bands, encouraged crowds to enjoy spending their money. And a gigantic prize contest, giving away cars, refrigerators, and washing machines, drew more than one million ballots.

The boom was full of Dick Whittington stories – reports of sudden riches stuffing the wallets of poor boys who invested the equivalent of a cat. *Liberty* magazine in 1955 told of the rags-to-riches saga of Max Tanenbaum, a Polish immigrant who began in Toronto as a horse-and-wagon scrap-iron peddler. In 1949 he bought for peanuts 1,100 acres of cow pasture in the northerly suburbs; five years later each acre was worth $6,000.

The magazine also told of an Italian immigrant who made three attempts to build himself a small spaghetti factory. Each time, half way through construction, he was persuaded to sell his unfinished building for a fantastic profit. After the third time, the thwarted fellow decided to forget about spaghetti. He invested profitably instead in real estate.

Koffler was not interested in the pasta-making profession, but he was excited by the prospect of making money from the great suburbia land bubble. He foresaw the importance of a drugstore to the young families leaving the downtown core for the city's rapidly expanding suburbs, which were replicating like amoebas. "Fertility Valley" and "The Rabbit Hutch" were among the nicknames given to what the sociologists were then calling "baby-boom-breeding incubator communities," inhabited by the ambitious "Organization Man" and the bored "Lonely Crowd." Main Street was said to be moving with them to those new consumer wonderlands, the shopping centres, which were reshaping before his eyes the character of the urban landscape.

Koffler was already an avid reader of the United States trade magazine *Chain Store Age*, and he soon subscribed to *Shopping Centre News* to keep up with trends. The shopping mall, whether enclosed or outdoor, was being proclaimed the consumer Disneyland of the future. For suburbanites, it was the place where the action was: the one-stop marketplace where the good life was on sale; the hangout for kids; the oasis for seniors; the pleasure dome for people-watchers; the modern town square and village green combined in a squeaky-clean environment blending the plash of fountains and the lilt of Muzak with the smells and sights and sounds of the ancient bazaar.

It was a magical place of drama and constant movement, and most exciting to Koffler was its vast consumer traffic potential. He could envision drugstores some day sharing with supermarkets and department stores a primary "anchor" or "customer destination" role in catering to the needs of this fast proliferating new mass market.

But it took money to capitalize on the opportunities beckoning so alluringly to the dreamer. How could a young pharmacist with only one drugstore and a skimpy knowledge of financing hope to break into this uncharted realm? Koffler referred to it as "my greatest adventure," and he set out to explore boldly.

In more ways than one, the Dominion store adjoining his Bathurst Street store served as his stepping stone to adventure. "It had long frustrated me that every time customers asked for something you wasted an awful lot of time searching and then handing it to them," he recalls. "So I began to pay special attention to our neighbouring Dominion store when it switched from conventional behind-the-counter clerk service to self-service. I saw how customers could walk around the well-lit broad aisles with their baskets, help themselves, and queue up to pay for the goods to a cashier stationed at the front of the store. I thought, 'If a grocery store can do that with such efficiency, why can't we?'"

He kept that unformulated idea tucked in the back of his mind. Meanwhile, opportunity came knocking one day in the form of the landlord who owned the adjoining 2,000 square feet of space. It turned out that the Dominion store, following the current trend, was scheduled to move to a larger space in one of the new shopping plazas.

"I'd like to retire," said the landlord. "Would you be interested in buying the building and expanding your store into the empty space?"

"I'll think it over," said Koffler. "I'm interested. But I have another purpose in mind for the empty store."

Koffler, a firm believer in the idea that originality is often plagiarism undetected, was then intrigued by an article he had just read in *Time* magazine. A Californian named Wolinow had made a quick fortune out of the post-war housing shortage by converting old houses into furnished bachelor apartments. His transient clientele provided an extra bonanza. By demanding both first and last month's rent from each successive tenant, Wolinow took in thirteen months' income every twelve months.

Koffler flew down to Los Angeles to check out Wolinow's operation. "Jeez, what a super idea!" he remembers thinking.

On his return, he sold the small apartment building on Connaught Circle he had inherited from his father. With that cash he bought the Bathurst Street property. Then he arranged with a builder for the construction of three extra storeys extending on top of both his store and the vacated Dominion store. The result was a thirty-two-unit apartment building, with the empty store serving as a lobby and rental office. The Sheridan Apartments, as he called them, consisted of thirty-two single rooms; each contained a kitchenette, a washroom, and a tastefully furnished bedroom.

"People were clamouring to get in, and we earned a terrific revenue," he says. The Sheridan Apartments netted him $50,000 a year; this was four times what he had netted from either of his drugstores. The contractor was Max Sharp, who along with his son, Issy Sharp, and son-in-law, Eddie Creed, joined Koffler in establishing the Four Seasons hotel chain. But we shall hear more of that adventure in a later chapter.

Koffler, meanwhile, kept exploring means of getting even more capital so he could gain a foothold in one of the shopping centres. He had been eager to get into Toronto's first mall, which the Bennett brothers were planning to open at Lawrence and Bathurst. But even though Archie Bennett, the senior partner of Principal Investments, was his godfather and a good family friend, Koffler's application was turned down.

Bennett explained to the dejected young pharmacist the hard economic facts of life that governed the leasing in a shopping plaza. Tamblyn's had been chosen to be the anchor drugstore on the plaza, because the pharmacy chain's signature had been required for the covenant on the lease. It meant the chain guaranteed to pay a minimum rental fee per square foot plus a percentage of gross sales. That covenant, signed by a large, reputable corporation like Tamblyn's, enabled the Bennetts to finance the building of their shopping centres.

"It made me realize that to really get ahead in the pharmacy business and build a chain of self-service stores," Koffler now says, "I'd have to have more credibility and I'd have to have more backing."

In desperation, he recalls paying a call to Max Tanenbaum, also a family friend and a granitic financier noted for driving a hard bargain. Tanenbaum lived up to his reputation. He refused to be a silent partner in a potential drugstore chain. And when Koffler asked him pointblank, rather naively perhaps, to co-sign a covenant on a lease for a store in a future shopping mall, Tanenbaum demanded, "What will I get out of it?"

"You're my friend!" said Koffler.

"Sorry," said Tanenbaum, and bowed him out of his office.

Koffler was disappointed by these setbacks, but undeterred. Through the grapevine he heard that a new shopping plaza was being planned for the most northerly limits of the city at York Mills and Bayview by Don Mills Development Limited. He remembers phoning the company's leasing agent, an executive named Jim Harris, about the possibility of becoming a tenant.

"I can't do anything for you," said Harris. "The selection of tenants for this plaza is being done entirely by the land owner himself."

"Can I see the land owner and present my case personally?"

"Well, I don't think so. You see, the man handling both the land and the plaza is a very busy man. He's Mr. E.P. Taylor. And you know who he is."

Koffler did indeed know and he hung up in dismay.

Edward Plunket Taylor, who was to exert a profound influence on the course of Koffler's career, was then acknowledged to be Canada's most powerful financier. He was a titan with a reputation as formidably awesome as John D. Rockefeller or John Pierpont Morgan in the United States. He had parlayed his grandfather's Brading Brewery in Ottawa into a multibillion-dollar empire with tendrils reaching into every corner of Canada and beyond. Through his holding company, Argus Corporation, he controlled Canadian Breweries, Dominion

Stores, Massey-Ferguson, Dominion Tar & Chemical, B.C. Forest Products, Acadia Atlantic Sugar, H.R. MacMillan Export, and the St. Lawrence Corporation.

He was both feared and revered. Radicals branded him "the crushing Croesus of big business"' and "E(xcess) P(rofits) Taylor – the mad miser of millions." Righteous advocates of temperance vilified him as the devil incarnate of beer barons, the horned Beelzebub of Booze himself, responsible for every sodden drunkard in Canada. Sports fans knew him as the portly, pink-jowled racehorse breeder in pearl-grey top hat with spats to match, whose Northern Dancer was the first Canadian-bred prize winner of both the Kentucky Derby and the Preakness. His friends knew him as "Overhead Eddie," so nicknamed because of his entrepreneurial zeal. And on Bay Street, according to Peter C. Newman, the Boswell of business potentates, they said admiringly of him in the 1950s, "Eddie can read a balance sheet like a poem, and tell you where it doesn't scan."

He also had an unerring eye for pinning down will-o'-the-wisp trends in the world of commerce. In 1946 he had assembled about 3,000 acres in northeast Toronto as the site of a new brewery. Then, with his usual keen prescience, he changed his mind and decided instead to build Canada's first fully planned suburb. His Don Mills Development Limited started building in 1952 a $200 million satellite community to house 22,000 people and seventy industries on 2,200 acres about nine miles from downtown Toronto.

In its heyday Don Mills was the darling of city planners throughout North America. It was a radical departure from the prevailing system whereby small individual contractors built and then sold a few houses at a time, without creating all the necessary community infrastructure. Furthermore, it departed from the cookie-cutter process of making each prefabricated house an identical clone of the other. Don Mills was to be a model community; its single-family, three-bedroom, brick bungalows, selling at $14,500 each, were designed by a variety of architects in different shapes and colours and styles. The community, along with the accompanying shopping plazas that Taylor built, ultimately won a well-merited Massey Award for architectural excellence.

Koffler was itching to get involved but was intimidated by Taylor's towering reputation as a mogul. Eddie Creed recalls vividly how agitated his chum felt. Creed then lived in an apartment on Bathurst Street, around the corner from Koffler's home on Rosemary Road and a few blocks north of his drugstore. On most evenings, when he wasn't working the night shift, Koffler would join his boyhood buddy in taking Creed's two purebred, Kerry-blue terriers, Butch and Boda, for a walk around the block.

"I remember it as clear as a bell," says Creed. "Murray would groan, 'I don't want to be just selling chewing gum for the rest of my life. If I could just talk to Mr. Taylor, I bet I could convince him I could put in a self-serve drugstore that would be perfect for his York Mills Plaza."

Creed told him: "I know E.P. Taylor. His wife's a regular customer at my store. I could easily call him for you and set up an appointment."

"Well, I don't know," said Koffler. "It sounds presumptuous."

"Call him up yourself then. What's the worst thing a bigshot industrialist can do to you? So he won't talk to you? You've got nothing to lose."

"Eddie, you think it'll work?"

"Try it."

Koffler, who until this day refers to the industrialist respectfully as *Mr.* Taylor, finally plucked up the courage to try it. "I was bold enough to pick up the phone and introduce myself to Mr. Taylor and I asked for an appointment," he says. "There I was, a simple pharmacist who was a stranger to him, and he didn't refuse, which shows the bigness of the man."

The appointment for this momentous turning point in Koffler's life was for ten o'clock on a Sunday morning. Taylor had granted him fifteen minutes of his time in the small office he maintained in a pavilion outside his big house on his 600-acre farm off Bayview Avenue.

The magnate proved to be a genial, moon-faced, blue-eyed man, relaxed behind a simple oaken table that served as a desk in a room cluttered with copies of the *Daily Racing Form*, as well as *Debrett's Peerage* guide to British gentry and English hunting prints. He became so engrossed in Koffler's heartfelt sales presentation that the appointment lasted for an hour and a half.

"Mr. Taylor," he remembers telling him, "I have projected figures here that'll show you I can do a better job than Tamblyn's in your new plaza. True, I'm just an individual pharmacist, but that's an asset. Tamblyn's is a chain operated by managers. But I'll own the store and make it more personalized. Besides, I've been in the forefront of new merchandising methods. And I'm going to introduce a spectacular new idea. I'll make it a self-serve pharmacy. The very first of its kind in Canada."

"What do you mean?"

"I plan to model it after your own Dominion Stores. As you know, they're just now switching to a self-service formula."

Taylor heard him out politely, shook his hand, and said noncommittally, "Very interesting. Thank you very much, young man. I appreciate your coming up to see me."

Koffler returned to join Creed in the rite of walking Butch and Boda around the block.

"How did you make out?" asked Creed.

"Well, I got it off my chest with Mr. Taylor," Koffler said, gloomily. "I'll probably never hear from him again."

Eight months later he was elated to hear from one of Taylor's associates: "Mr. Koffler, if you're still interested in having your drugstore in the York Mills Plaza, Mr. Taylor would like to talk business with you."

Koffler was happy to talk business. He immediately began negotiating the sale of his Bathurst Street store, which had been grossing $150,000 a year, and proceeded to open in 1953 his unique supermarket-style pharmacy. The concept was so novel there was no place in Canada where he could buy the proper fixtures. He was compelled to make a trip to a furniture manufacturer in Grand Rapids, Michigan, and returned with green metal shelving for the self-serve islands.

He experimented with a good many other innovations for his 2,400-square-foot store. He was impressed by the exteriors of the chain of Laura Secord candy shops, which featured a chalk-white against a stark black background. Under dazzling lighting, the front of each store stood out as though it were a picture in a frame. He borrowed the same blinding-white-against-black motif for his dispensary, thus imparting a feeling of streamlined hygienic modernity.

He threw out the glass-enclosed showcases and adapted from Dominion Stores a number of mass-merchandising devices. His shelves became deeper. The number of open bins multiplied. And to encourage impulse-buying, he stocked bargain specials at the ends of each aisle. "Pile 'em high and watch 'em buy" became his slogan.

Alas, there wasn't much buying at first. York Mills was still isolated in the sparsely settled boondocks, and the entire shopping plaza consisted initially of his store, a Dominion store, Bailey's hardware store, and the Royal Bank. Koffler remembers morosely standing behind the counter on a bleak spring Tuesday morning the day after the opening.

"There wasn't a soul in the shopping centre, not a car in the parking lot," he says. "I'm standing in an empty store, not a penny in the cash register, and I gaze out the window. All I can see gazing back at me are the mournful eyes of a black Angus cow. It's one of Mr. Taylor's herd of cattle grazing on his Windfields Farm, which was located right across the road. This cow keeps looking at me and I stare back and I say to myself, 'What the hell am I doing here in the wilderness? What sort of business acumen do I have?'"

Koffler now acknowledges that the first couple of years in this pastoral environment were lean. But then business improved markedly, thanks to his own acumen and the encouragement of E.P. Taylor, who turned out to be a most approachable and democratic fellow entrepreneur.

"Every week Mr. Taylor would come into the store and ask, 'How are you doing, young man? What are you doing to improve business, Murray?' We got on beautifully.

"I got to know him over a period of time. He was always so friendly and helpful. When I had about sixteen or seventeen drugstores in our chain, I once asked him for advice. 'Should I stay a private family company?' I ask him. 'Or should I become a public company? Or, because your own Dominion Stores want to buy me out and get into the pharmacy business, should I sell out to them?'

"Mr. Taylor says, 'Murray, you don't need partners. You don't need Dominion Stores. You don't need anybody. Go public. Go to McLeod Young Weir, the stockbrokers, and let me buy some shares.'

"That's the sort of entrepreneur Mr. Taylor was. Absolutely no airs about him."

Barry Haberman, who became co-manager of the York Mills store in the 1950s, uses the same phrase to describe Koffler's lack of ostentatiousness. "One day I saw Murray and E.P. Taylor talk business for quite a while at the store," Haberman recalls with amusement. "As soon as Taylor left, Murray took off his jacket, grabbed a pail of water, and began scrubbing shelves. He cleaned and rearranged stock for two or three hours. Then he stepped back and said, 'There! That's how this section should look!'

"Here he'd just negotiated a leasing deal with the most important big businessman in Canada. Yet he didn't think it was beneath him right after to scrub like a washerwoman. Funny how Murray didn't see any ironic contradiction in those two roles at all."

Koffler, however, was able to see an element of humour in his vain attempt to establish a gift department in the store. He and his wife Marvelle put up elaborate glass shelves on one entire wall and filled them with quaint but expensive gimcracks and gewgaws that caught their fancy on shopping expeditions to gift shows. Most expensive were two exquisite white porcelain Heuchinreuther horses imported from Germany. Priced at $100 each, the nags remained on the shelf for what seemed like an eternity.

Then one day a farmer walked into the spotless gift department, dishevelled in his raincoat and overalls and manured boots. With grubby hands, he picked up the pair of horses.

"I could have killed him!" recalls Koffler. "I was about to tell him, 'Don't touch! Get out of my store! You're dirtying it up with your manure-caked boots.'"

But the farmer said: "What'll you charge me for this pair of horses?"

"Two for one hundred and ninety-five dollars," said Koffler. "So you'd better put them down."

"I'll take 'em," the man said.

He turned out to be Taylor's stable manager, who was buying a gift for his boss.

Koffler says the episode taught him two lessons: "First, I learned that you should never judge a book by its cover. Second, never buy retail items for your personal taste, but instead have an expert select them to satisfy the needs of the market."

He soon scrapped the gift department. Similarly, he jettisoned other peripheral sidelines of the business that seemed irrelevant in a drugstore and, more important, were not money-makers. He was determined to streamline the operation and get back to the basics that formed what he considered the four traditional pillars of the business. In order of importance, they consisted of: 1) the prescription department; 2) the cosmetics department; 3) the health and beauty aids department; and 4) the sundries department, which included tobacco and confections.

"My concept was to fill a niche, because no drugstore was focusing on these four fundamentals," he says. "I decided you can't be all things to everybody."

In line with that philosophy, he discarded the hardware department. He got out of the field of testing and selling television tubes, leaving that specialty to the TV repair shops then springing up. He even closed his camera department, although it was one of the busiest in the city. In order to sell new cameras, he had to take old equipment on trade-ins, and found he was losing rather than making money from photography buffs.

On the other hand, he was among the first to adopt the latest U.S. merchandising techniques to drum up new trade.

He co-operated with Fabergé, then the newest house in fragrances, in handing out and inserting in customers' packages blotters scented with Tigress and Woodhue. He also worked with Fabergé in the development of an automatic perfume dispenser that emitted a pungent whiff of the fragrance each time a customer opened the front door.

"Gee, what's *that*?" he recalls women saying ecstatically as they entered.

"Aphrodisiac!" he would purr. "Why not try it?"

Inevitably, some of his newfangled policies provoked a strong reaction among the old guard of diehard druggists. "Some purists claimed that mass merchandising was beneath the dignity of professional pharmacists," he says. "Others maintained that self-service was absolutely contrary to the principles of drugstore sales psychology. In those days we were taught, 'When you sell a tube of toothpaste, suggest a toothbrush.' Now they argued with me, 'If we switch to self-serve, we're not going to make any companion sales.' Well, exactly the opposite happened. Not only did we make companion sales, but people picked up things on display we'd never have considered suggesting to them."

Koffler regarded Dominion Stores as the masters of mass-merchandising, far ahead of the Loblaws chain, and borrowed heavily from their techniques. But in the mid-1950s, a battle raged as Dominion started to invade the retail domain of drugstores – the beginning of a war that continues until this day.

It began with Pablum, the renowned baby food formulated by Dr. Alan Brown, the pediatrician who donated all proceeds resulting from the sale of the product to Toronto's Hospital for Sick Children. Traditionally, the cereal had been sold only in drugstores. But suddenly the manufacturer, Mead Johnson Canada, began distributing the product to Dominion Stores, thus infringing on a valuable monopoly. At the same time, Dominion and other grocery chains started selling drugstore toiletries, such as toothpaste and shaving cream.

The pharmacists were up in arms. At an emergency meeting they expressed their indignation at this arrant poaching on their preserves. Some even went so far as to advocate a "de-emphasizing" boycott. Any of the name-brand toiletries being sold at supermarkets would be hidden under the counter along with Pablum. Instead, they agreed to push exclusively Rexall, Nyal, and other house brands.

"I went along with the proposal for one week," says Koffler. "I saw our business go down – zoom! – like that."

At the next meeting called by his colleagues in the pharmacy community, Koffler stood up and denounced their strategy as so much folly. "What you're doing is baloney," he said. "Don't *de*-emphasize. Instead try to *emphasize*. I propose we all attempt to out-merchandise and out-display Dominion. I suggest we display *more* sizes of Colgate tubes than the super-markets do, *plus* the other non-advertised brands. Give customers greater variety than the supermarkets and in the end your bulk sales will give you greater profits."

In the end, so it was. "Whereas we used to sell a dozen tubes of Colgate toothpaste in a week, we now sold three dozen," he says. "So rather than being our competitor, Dominion became a catalyst and pushed us to better and better sales."

Koffler's stance was far more belligerent – uncharacteristical-ly so – at the next industry confrontation. He was then planning to open two more self-serve drugstores in E.P. Taylor's shopping plazas. Consequently, in retrospect, he thinks he may have felt too big for his britches when the perfume manufacturers, too, started to distribute their fragrances to supermarkets.

At a pre-Christmas banquet held by Drug Trading Co. Ltd., the industry's wholesalers, he stood up before 200 pharmacists and directed his ire at Mike Johnson, the red-cheeked and ordinarily amiable president of Shulton Canada Inc. Koffler was incensed because Johnson's firm had sanctioned the distri-bution of Old Spice, the fragrance for men and women, to food supermarkets.

In Koffler's speech – the most caustic he has ever deliv-ered – he reminded Johnson that Canadian drugstores were the backbone of Shulton's perfume trade, responsible for 95 per cent of its business. They had gone all out to help him introduce Old Spice to the Canadian market and had sold hundreds of thousands of dollars' worth across the country. Now Shulton was showing its gratitude by supplying the fragrance to the pharmacists' arch enemy, the grocery chains.

"Mike Johnson," said Koffler, pointing an accusatory finger at him and watching his face flame redder and redder, "if you continue to help our competition that way, do you know what I propose we of the pharmacy industry do? As of tomorrow morning, I propose that we send all our Old Spice stock back to you by truck and let you eat it. Does everybody here agree?"

All the pharmacists shot up their hands. Johnson broke down in tears.

"I walked out of that banquet hall a hero," Koffler now recalls in anguish. "But for years I suffered remorse. I phoned him up to apologize soon after. But I continue to regret my unpardonable act. It was the cruellest thing I've ever done in my life. I devastated that man. I remember saying afterwards to Marvelle that I'd never again try to build a business on another guy's back."

It was a prophetic statement. Koffler was preparing to launch the Shoppers Drug Mart franchising system with a philosophy based on sharing the rewards of the business.

CHAPTER EIGHT

The Crazy System That Works

Tom Roe remembers his father saying back in 1955, "It's crazy and it'll never work." He remembers his bank manager at the Royal Bank of Canada calling it "a bastard partnership." And he remembers his lawyer, now a Supreme Court judge, throwing up his hands and warning him about the lunatic arrangement, "You'll wind up owning nothing at all."

Tom Roe disregarded the advice of all three men. He persisted in his madness and thus became the first associate pharmacist to sign a two-page franchising contract with Murray Koffler. At sixty-five, he is now reputed to be a millionaire. He acknowledges that before giving his annual bonuses to his staff of forty people, he earns close to $200,000 a year as the associate who runs the 8,000-square-foot, $6-million-a-year Shoppers Drug Mart in the Don Mills Shopping Centre at Don Mills Road and Lawrence Avenue.

Needless to say, Roe thinks his contract with Koffler has worked out rather nicely. But he justly considers the word "franchise" a misnomer as it applies to their historic agreement. In modern usage, the term "franchise" means the right or licence granted to a person to market a company's goods in a particular territory. The scope of Koffler's pioneering is all the more impressive when one considers that the participative franchising system he introduced in the mid-1950s preceded the North American franchise phenomenon, which only gained force in the 1960s.

Unquestionably, the two best-known household names to emerge from that franchising boom are both mass-merchandised, fast-food products. Both are licensed in ways markedly different from Koffler's. And both were marketed in Canada long after Koffler had initiated his franchise-like operation.

One is finger-lickin'-good Kentucky Fried Chicken. Franchise rights were hustled by Colonel Harland Sanders himself, a former hillbilly insurance salesman who developed a secret blend of eleven spices and herbs for the pan-fried chicken he served in a small roadside restaurant in Corbin, Kentucky. The colonel, who eventually set up residence in Toronto, made his first sales pitch there in 1960, carrying two chickens and a pot under his arm. He was concerned only with selling his secret gravy mix, which he had already franchised to 400 owners of conventional restaurants in the U.S. who added the spicy chicken to their menus. And in 1962, Scott's Chicken Villa, located at the corner of Lawrence Avenue and Victoria Park Avenue, became North America's first take-out restaurant devoted exclusively to selling Kentucky Fried Chicken.

Today the Toronto-based Colonel Sanders Kentucky Fried Chicken Ltd. grosses more than $400 million a year from 765 outlets franchised across Canada. It still follows the "licensee" policy set by the late colonel and collects "a nickel royalty for every chicken sold."

Quite different is the franchise formula used by George Cohon, president of McDonald's Restaurants of Canada Limited and, incidentally, a close friend of Koffler's. He is a one-time Fuller Brush salesman and lawyer from Chicago who in 1968 opened in Canada his first McDonald's on Oxford Street in London, Ontario. Cohon has since become a McMillionaire (owning McDonald's stocks worth $50 million) and his franchised operation has become a McMint (grossing well over $1 billion annually via 525 outlets across Canada).

Cohon's franchise policy adheres to the pattern formulated in the late 1950s by his late burgermeister, Ray Kroc. It was then that Kroc, a former saloon piano player and salesman of Tulip Straws to drugstore soda fountains, launched his global empire with a humble hamburger stand in Des Plaines, Illinois, named McDonald's. ("With a name like Kroc," the Czech Bohemian later explained, "what else could I do?")

The waiting list of applicants for the some twenty-five Canadian franchises available each year is amazingly extensive, considering that the start-up cost is quite stiff. The fee for a twenty-year licence is on average $500,000, half of it a down-payment in cash. The company provides the site, the land, the building, but the "licensee" must foot the bill for all the equipment. In addition, he must pay the company 16 per cent of his gross sales – 9 per cent for rent, 4 per cent to participate in national advertising, and 3 per cent as a service fee. According to Kroc's autobiography, *Grinding It Out*, the sales slogan that powered his Big Mac franchising attack exclaimed, "In business *for* yourself, but not *by* yourself!"

With certain modifications, the McDonald formula was pretty well followed by the thousands of franchisors who jumped on the bandwagon in the 1960s, appealing to get-rich-quick small business entrepreneurs. They peddled licences for everything from Mom and Pop Dunkin' Donut stands to a Pacific International franchised system to combat bedwetting among adults and children.

At the peak of the franchise craze in 1967, according to *Big Mac: The Unauthorized Story of McDonald's* by Max Boas and Steve Chain, the North American franchise industry recorded sales of $90 billion. The franchise fever raged with a frenzy reminiscent of the post-war land boom. "We're dealing with an emotion second only to Hugh Hefner's – to open your own business," Al Lapin, a catering truck operator turned successful franchisor of the International House of Pancakes, told *Newsweek* in 1969. "And if I can find out how to franchise sex, I'll really have it made."

When Koffler initiated his managerial profit-sharing plan, the word "franchise" had not yet become part of the language.

He calls it a participation system based on a network of "associates" rather than franchisees or licensees. Each associate is a graduate pharmacist who becomes an autonomous owner-operator. He runs his own store and shares a fraction of his revenue with the company behind him. In return, it assumes all financial risks and provides an umbrella of advertising and marketing expertise needed to build customer traffic.

It is an original concept, which still remains unique in North America as the franchise system for a pharmacy chain. But Koffler, characteristically, doesn't claim to have been a financial wizard when he formulated the plan. The one thing he borrowed was the "KISS" credo of Colonel Harland Sanders: "Keep It Simple, Stupid." The rest, he maintains, was all the result of happy circumstance.

"My lack of formal business training probably was an asset," he now says. "If I'd been a Harvard Business School graduate, perhaps I wouldn't have had the *chutzpah* to be so adventuresome. My banker said my franchise concept was impossible, my accountant said it was impossible, and my lawyer said it would never stand up legally.

"Really, though, my experimenting was a case of necessity being the mother of invention. I needed a well-motivated pharmacist to operate each store, while I leap-frogged on to the next one. At the outset, we were so naive and simple! Just a couple of pharmacists, one on one, agreeing to get together on a handshake and a lot of good faith in each other."

It began with Koffler taking a walk down Bloor Street in midtown Toronto one summer afternoon in 1955 with Tom Roe. A former high school and college classmate of Koffler's and the son of a well-known Toronto druggist named Samuel George Roe, he was a lanky, bespectacled pharmacist with grasshopper legs and a low-key manner. And he was seeking a change from his job as a sales representative for the G.B. Searle pharmaceutical manufacturing firm.

"I'd heard that Murray had just got a lease from E.P. Taylor to open a new store at the Don Mills Shopping Centre," he recalls. "I told him, 'I don't want a job working for you. I want to be my own boss. Do you know of another store that might be available?'"

"No, I don't," said Koffler. "But I do have a proposition that may interest you."

Koffler proposed that Roe become boss of the Don Mills store. He said it was to be a turnkey operation. "This means I lease the store," he explained. "I put fixtures in the store. I put a full inventory of merchandise in the store. Then I turn it over to you. It becomes Tom Roe Drugs Limited.

"You operate the store as an associate. And you take absolutely no risks. I guarantee you'll receive a drugstore manager's normal salary, no matter what happens. In return, you pay me an associate's fee of 10 per cent of your gross sales. Whatever is left after you cover your costs and overhead belongs to you. The more money you make, the happier we'll both be. How does it grab you?"

Roe was stunned. He was even more taken aback after Koffler asked him, "How much money would you like to make from the arrangement?"

Roe was then earning $6,000 a year from the pharmaceutical firm, which included a car allowance. "So I took an astronomical figure," Roe recalls. "And I was pretty sure he'd blanch when I said, '$20,000.'"

Koffler predicted confidently, "Oh, you'll have no trouble at all making that."

Koffler was likewise buoyantly optimistic when he made the same proposal to Barry Haberman, his new associate at the York Mills store. Haberman is also the son of a well-known druggist, Maurice (Moe) Haberman, who had been a crony of Koffler's father. He remembers how nervous he was when being interviewed by the ebullient Koffler in 1957.

"Murray envisioned having a chain of fifty drugstores in the future," Haberman now says in recollection of their conversation. "Murray asked me: 'How much do you hope to earn twenty-five years from now?'

"I'd been making seventy-five dollars a week as a graduate pharmacist. So I thought I was talking big when I said, 'With luck, I hope to make $25,000 a year.'"

Koffler's response to that seemingly grandiose figure was comforting to his nerves. Haberman, who now pays graduate pharmacists a minimum of $40,000 to $50,000 a year at his York Mills store, which grosses $6 million a year, recalls, "Murray just laughed and laughed."

Initially, the associates were asked to pay an advance sum of $5,000 as a kind of warranty. But that fee has long since been dropped from the associates' agreement that Koffler and Roe drafted together in longhand. The original two-page contract has since been refined and fattened into a ten-page document. But the basic formula has remained unchanged over the years.

Essentially, Koffler's company put into their own business more than 400 pharmacists who have not had to put up any money. The associates' fee, which is renegotiated every year, now ranges from one per cent of gross sales until the store becomes profitable to as much as 14 per cent in certain cases. It averages out between 6 and 8 per cent.

The most remarkable thing about the contract is the no-risk factor for associates. If the associate is unhappy, a clause enables him to bow out of the relationship within thirty days and cash in on his equity and earnings. If initially the store shows a loss, he is assured that the company will pick it up. There is not even a risk involved in the bank loan he signs to get a line of credit to pay off the stock inventory. The loan is co-signed and guaranteed by the company, and the company alone is held responsible if something goes wrong with the business. Furthermore, because the various wholesalers provide sixty to ninety days of credit for stock inventory, the associate is assured of a cash flow being generated from day one, when he turns the key in the lock and opens the store.

"Sure, there was a big risk on my part," Koffler now says in a reminiscent mood. "But business *is* a risk, and that's part of the adventure. I had to take that risk in order to keep building, one at a time, the number of Koffler stores I could lease in shopping centres.

"The associate was the 'inside' man. I was the 'outside' man. While each associate I kept adding spent his time minding his individual store, I devoted my time to buying, advertising, and looking for new locations. At the end of the year, Tom and Barry and I would sit around a table and go over, line by line, the expenses and profits of their stores. In the very early years, they made their salary plus maybe $5,000 or $10,000 profit. But later they did fantastically well and I got a good return on my money, too."

Roe attested to that in a speech he made recently to an assembly of his fellow associates. Though he is not Jewish, Roe teasingly cited what he called an old Jewish proverb that expressed why he had prospered so well from Koffler: "If you follow a loaded cart, something's bound to fall off for you."

In 1959, the Kofflerian cart took another rewarding turn. Koffler had placed a third associate in another E.P. Taylor mall in the northern suburbs, and, ever alert to new merchandising trends, he read in a U.S. trade magazine about the launching in Detroit of a unique discount department store. It was called GEM, short for Government Employees' Mart, which meant that nearly 25 per cent of the work force were entitled to discounts on all goods, provided they paid two dollars for a membership card. The article so excited him that he flew to Detroit to examine the GEM store and then invested 10 per cent in a Canadian branch – about $10,000 – to encourage the developers to open a store in suburban Toronto and sublet the drug department.

Four thousand customers queued up for the opening of the first GEM store, located at Yonge and Steeles on the most northerly outskirts of Toronto. "We were overwhelmed," recalls Koffler. "The opening year our GEM drug department did about one million dollars. And we'd been thinking we were doing beautifully in Don Mills with a $300,000 volume and in York Mills with $250,000. It was absolutely unbelievable. So, naturally, we were one of the first to participate when Canada's second GEM store opened in Ottawa."

The GEM stores remained popular until the late 1960s when they were superseded by the price-slashing Towers and Sayvettes and Woolco and K Mart department stores. Meanwhile, primarily responsible for Koffler's successful adventure in the discounting field was the franchise associate he chose to handle the pharmacy concession at the Yonge Street GEM. Harry Kalb had worked as a pharmacy graduate managing the original College Street store for Leon Koffler in the 1930s and was wily in the ways of canny merchandising. When a perfume manufacturer was switching from glass to plastic containers, he got the glass bottles at an extra low price as a reward for suggesting a catchy slogan for the plastic ones: "No bottles to break—just hearts." When the Buckley's cough remedy manufacturers were getting rid of little plastic-topped vials, Kalb bought the whole supply of them at a penny apiece and sold them to a local Chinese restaurant as plum sauce and mustard containers for delivery orders.

Kalb, in his seventies and still active as a broker of odds-and-ends-of-line merchandise, liked telling Murray Koffler the story of how he had learned price-cutting from his father Leon at the College Street store. In 1935, Kalb had bought 100 alarm clocks for about $3 each, which he vainly tried to retail for $4.95.

Leon Koffler would drop around from the Bathurst Street store and invariably ask: "How are you doing with the alarm clocks?"

"Not so hot," Kalb replied despondently. "Didn't sell a single one this week."

"Why don't you consider clearing them at $3.99?"

"Isn't that an awfully brutal price slash of profits?"

"No, it isn't. Because it's better to make one dollar than *not* to make two dollars."

Kalb sold them all at $3.99 within three weeks. He never forgot the lesson.

In his reminiscinces today Kalb says he also learned several valuable lessons in salesmanship from Murray Koffler. He lists them as follows:

"(1) Never chew gum when serving a customer. It's rude. Chewing, whether it's a stick of gum, or a cud, or a wad of tobacco, should be restricted to kids or cows or Popeye.

"(2) Cashiers should never ask customers, 'Is there anything else?' It's a ludicrous, time-wasting question—especially if the customer is lined up at the head of a queue during the rush hour—and it invites a negative response.

"(3) Cashiers should never say 'Thank you' and then look at the cash register. Instead, they should say 'Thank you' and smile while looking the customer square in the eye.

"(4) Never use the numeral 5 or a 0 in a GEM selling price. Instead, to heighten the impression of a discount, favour the figures 8 or 9.

"(5) Avoid using the word 'discount.' It has lost its impact from overuse. Instead, make it a 'special price' or 'weekend special' or 'holiday bargain.'"

Whether it was called a "discount" or a "bargain," the GEM cut-rate, mass-merchandise concept was still luring cost-conscious crowds in 1962. It was then that Koffler devised the name Shoppers Drug Mart for his fledgling chain of Koffler's drugstores. He heard of a store lease that was available in a new plaza called Shoppers World opening on Danforth Avenue at Victoria Park in the east end of Toronto. Koffler signed the lease and put in charge as associate a young pharmacist who was to play a key role in helping build his drugstore empire. Jack Gwartz, then twenty-eight, had been working as assistant manager for Tom Roe at the Don Mills Koffler's store. "I was the idea man, the chief conceptualizer," says Koffler. "Jack was the detail man, the implementer of our ideas. For years we were a great team together."

Characteristically, Gwartz was receptive when Koffler suggested a fresh concept for the Shoppers World drugstore. "We've already become Canada's first drugstore in a discount department store," said Koffler. "So let's take a gamble, Jack. Why not make our new outlet Canada's first free-standing drugstore featuring the GEM policy of both lower prices and mass merchandising?"

As opening day drew near, Koffler was racking his brain increasingly for a name. He felt it was necessary to come up with one. By operating a discount drugstore, he would be competing against his own associates – though the nearest of the three traditional-price Koffler Drug Stores was located in the northerly suburbs at least five miles away from the Danforth area.

He remembers going to sleep and tossing and turning while trying to figure out a new name. The idea came to him at about four o'clock. "I woke up with a start in the middle of the night, bright as a tack," he has since recalled. "I thought, 'I know exactly the name for that store. We're in a place called Shoppers World. So let's name the thing Shoppers Drug Mart.'"

Still not quite sure, he phoned Gwartz the next day to explain the rationale for his name coinage: "Shoppers" suggested value; "Drug" spelled out their business; "Mart" signified a supermarket. Gwartz remembers that Koffler, after tossing the three words around, as well as other alternatives, was still not entirely satisfied. "It's too long," said Koffler. "Too hard to pronounce. Doesn't sound professional enough. Let's keep thinking."

Koffler hung up. Two hours later he phoned back. "You know, I wrote the name down," he said with mounting excitement. "I keep staring at it. And it looks damned good! Let's go with it."

Gwartz now says with bemusement, "It *was* a fairly long name. If we knew then what the cost would be to put the name in lights, we probably would have shortened it."

And Koffler now says with his usual enthusiasm, "It took off like a bomb! Again in our first year, using the same low prices as in our two GEM stores in Toronto and Ottawa, we did $1 million in volume."

Soon all three Koffler Drug Stores, plus a new one he opened at Eglinton Square Shopping Plaza, were operating under the same formula and bearing the name Shoppers Drug Mart. By this time, Koffler was feeling his oats and hitting his stride as a junior mercantile magnate. "I truly believe that entrepreneurs are at their peak from between the ages of thirty-three and fifty," he says. And so when he was midway between those two benchmarks, he embarked on his next adventure: to build the biggest drugstore in North America.

He made that dramatic decision after reading in *Chain Store Age* of a so-called super drugstore that had opened in Abilene, Texas. Its spectacular size appealed to his sense of showmanship. And when he learned that it had grossed a phenomenal $300,000 in a single day, that especially appealed to him.

Not one to wait, Koffler instantly phoned Gwartz and his other associates to meet him at the airport the next morning. They flew down to Abilene, were mightily impressed by its vastness, took photographs of its advanced warehouse style of displaying merchandise, got tips on its pricing structure, and flew back the next morning to Toronto.

Koffler was thus prepared to negotiate the next time that E.P. Taylor's Don Mills Developments Limited offered him a deal. At the corner of Dufferin Street and Lawrence, it proposed to lease sites for a number of small retail stores on an enormously wide, seventy-foot-long tract of land located between a brewery and what was to be the largest Dominion store in the supermarket chain.

Koffler told the leasing agent to forget about dinky little stores. He intended to put up a Shoppers Drug Mart every bit as huge as – if not huger than – the Dominion store. His aim was to build from scratch a colossus of approximately 15,000 square feet.

"It'll be the biggest, free-standing, mass-merchandising, megadrugstore on the continent," he said.

"Impossible," said the leasing agent. "You won't be able to pay the rent."

"You're right," said Koffler.

He agreed that he wouldn't be able to pay it if the rent was calculated on the same percentage basis as his previous drug-stores in E.P. Taylor shopping centres. But this was to be a different situation. It was to be a giant, free-standing store, stocked with a variety of goods not ordinarily carried by a pharmacist, and would do triple the volume of his other stores. Hence the leasing arrangement ought to be different.

A deal was struck and Koffler undertook his newest adventure with his usual *élan*. A great merchant is not merely a forecaster who tries to anticipate the whims of millions; he is the imaginative man who says, "This excites me, and I'll make it excite them." Koffler had this faculty of getting excited and selling his excitement to the public.

His innovations were considered daring in the 1960s; in effect, he was creating the precursor for the warehouse-style megadrugstores à la Howie's of the 1980s. A hotshot merchandising master named Butch Cohen was brought in to operate a separate hardware and toy department. A noted architect, Peter Webb, designed the interior to give it an open, airy, factory warehouse effect: a combination of elegant steel columns and colourful fixtures soaring high into the ceiling.

Koffler introduced several novel touches. He set up a row of twenty showcases displaying fragrances, lipsticks, and other beauty products, making it Canada's biggest cosmetics department at that period. Paper products were not put on shelves but instead cases were cut on one side and piled high on flats. Canadians, who were not yet conditioned to purchasing caseloads of goods, were urged by signs: "Buy 'em by the case, folks! It's cheaper by the dozen!" And hanging from the ceiling were enormous red plastic banners proclaiming boldly: "Save, Save, Save," "Specials, Specials, Specials," "Value, Value, Value."

Koffler selected as the store's associate a fellow pharmacy college classmate, Arthur Resnick, who had exhibited a showman's flair by staging with him the annual black-tie charity ball for their Pi Lambda Phi fraternity. Now in his sixties, Resnick continued to run the Dufferin Street store until his retirement in 1987, proud of the fact that it had reached a yearly sales volume of more than $5 million long before the other Shoppers outlets.

The store required a good year of planning, and Resnick remembers examining it hypercritically with Koffler one evening before the official opening. "Look, Murray," he said, "you can't really see the Shoppers Drug Mart sign over the front doorway. Why not flash a sign right across the whole roof of the store a good fifty feet long?" And so they did.

The grand opening on April 23, 1966, was an extravaganza. The celebration was capped with Latin American music played by the popular Cuban bandleader Chicho Valle and his orchestra. "Some of our loyal customers, who come to our store's twice-annual Seniors' Day, keep reminding me of that gala opening," says Resnick. "They never forget that night when they danced the cha-cha in the aisles."

Likewise unforgettable was Koffler's promotional campaign to make people aware of what Shoppers Drug Mart meant. Koffler's principles of advertising are founded on two adages: "Doing business without advertising is like winking at a pretty girl in the dark–you know what you're doing, but nobody else does"; and "Truth is the safest lie."

His campaign began with a series of ten personalized handbills called "Let's Talk Facts." Koffler wrote the advertising copy, chose the typeface, and, initially, supervised delivery of the pamphlets in his car. Each flier contained a single message he typed out on a sheet of paper and then had blown up to a large, bold typeface. His first message read:

"Something new is happening in your neighbourhood. It's a fact that a new kind of drugstore has opened called Shoppers Drug Mart. It features supermarket selection of all your drugstore needs with every item priced as low as possible every single day . . ."

Other fliers explained, in chatty style, "Come to our store. We buy more products in volume and therefore we get better deals and we pass the lower prices for medicines on to you . . . It's self-serve and therefore we don't have as many clerks and we pass the savings on to you . . . We don't deliver and have no charge accounts and we pass on our reduced costs to you . . ."

Koffler intentionally decided to deliver ten handbills in a row, one every two weeks. He figured the first couple of messages would be thrown away. But by the third flier, he assumed that people would have their curiosity aroused and begin to pay attention. "The consistency–and maybe the annoyance–was such that we got our story across," he says. "The result was that we tripled the volume of our best store in the first year."

He did not overlook the potency of newspaper advertising, but his approach was singularly Kofflerian. When he was first approached to advertise in the *Don Mills Mirror* for his Don Mills store, he asked the publishers of the new community newspaper, Russ Eastcott and Ken Larone, "What's your circulation?"

"About 800."

"What good is that?" said Koffler. "I'll tell you what I'll do. If you give away your paper to the 2,500 people in the Don Mills area, I'll pay you one dollar a year per subscription. You'll then have 100 per cent saturation and on that basis be able to solicit advertising from Eaton's and all the other big stores. In return, you let me have a store ad and a medical column."

At the end of each year, Koffler was also allowed to enclose a personalized card reminding readers: "You've been receiving this newspaper with our compliments. If you'd like to continue getting your free copy, please fill in this card and drop it into our store."

That device increased customer traffic enormously. Its value was heightened when customers deposited the cards into a suggestion box, which further requested: "Please include your comments, criticisms, and recommendations for our store."

Eventually the newspaper became such a money-maker it was acquired by *The Toronto Star*. And under its new title as the *Metro Mirror*, with a circulation of more than 20,000, the scheme became too unwieldy for Koffler. But by then he was off on another promotion that helped popularize both his stores and the Royal Canadian Air Force 5BX exercise plan. One day, when Koffler was feeling sluggish, a friend had recommended the 5BX plan as an excellent health booster. Koffler wrote away for a copy, available through the Queen's Printer in Ottawa for thirty-five cents. After a month's workout routine, he felt so reinvigorated that he dispatched a testimonial letter to people in the neighbourhood.

"Dear Friends," it began. "I should be writing to you as your pharmacist selling you vitamins to maintain your health . . ." However, he had found the RCAF plan such an exhilarating pick-me-up that he was offering customers a copy at cost if they would come to the store to pick up the booklets. More than 1,000 people responded in person and he was gratified to receive hundreds of "Dear Murray" letters of thanks.

It must be said that not all of his selling ideas have been winners. Tom Roe remembers one instance in particular.

Before becoming his associate at the Don Mills store, Roe took the precaution of phoning Koffler's assistant at the York Mills store.

"What's Murray really like to work with?" Roe asked.

"He's all right, I guess, but I'll tell you the big problem," the assistant warned him. "Murray's always reading those U.S. magazines for ideas. Some of the ideas are okay. But others are just damn-fool crazy."

"Oh, oh," Roe remembers thinking. "I better keep an eye out for the real crazy ones."

Today he giggles at the recollection of Koffler's now legendary Crazy Canary Caper. Koffler came into the Don Mills store one day and asked, "Have the canaries come in yet?"

"I beg your pardon?" said the somewhat startled Roe.

"You know, canaries!" said Koffler a bit brusquely.

"What canaries?" said Roe, by now utterly flummoxed.

"I mean the canaries from the Hartz Mountain Pet Supply Company. I made a deal with them to send us 100 of their songbirds. Since Don Mills is a new suburban community filled with young families, I figure every one of them would love to have a white canary twittering away merrily in their homes. And look at all the pet supplies we'll sell."

"Well, okay, if you say so," said Roe dubiously.

He felt even more sceptical when the songbirds arrived in a muted state in a large omnibus flight cage, which he was instructed to keep in the basement. Every morning Roe had to send a girl down to feed the birds and put a few in their individual cages and bring them upstairs in the hope of making a sale.

Months dragged by and he managed to sell half of them. Most of the others got a chill and died during the night. The remaining few birds drooped songless in smelly, messy, rusting cages the Hartz Mountain people angrily refused to take back. "As the months passed by and the cages became more soiled, I became more fearful that the Humane Society inspectors would come around and lock me up," says Roe.

To this day, whenever he thinks Koffler is toying with an idea that won't work, he provokes a giggle or two by parroting the question, "Have the canaries come in yet?"

CHAPTER NINE

"I Never Was an Octopus"

Years later Murray Koffler said of the beginning of his company's national expansion that he never was an octopus. His company was called the Koffler Associated Drug Company, and by 1966 it consisted of seventeen Shoppers Drug Mart outlets. The stores were all bunched in southern Ontario and predominantly ringed around the prosperous Toronto region like a prim, bright, white-and-black daisy chain.

His most recent acquisition had been the takeover of five poorly managed drugstores. All were housed under the roof of the small Sentry chain of discount department stores centred in Sarnia, Kingston, Belleville, and Sault Ste. Marie. The seemingly magical way he transmuted these dross money-losers into golden Shoppers Drug Marts was heavily publicized in the international trade press. He was hailed as a pharmaceutical alchemist with a Midas touch. The publicity was heady stuff, and Koffler was eager to acquire more stores where he could perform more magic.

The impetuous Koffler, though, controlled his headlong impatience and made it a policy to proceed cautiously. "I was able to expand because I never came on strong," he now says. "I never was like an octopus. You never saw me trying to buy up independents just to squeeze them."

He maintains he simply said, "Look, we're just a bunch of druggists helping others take charge of their own destiny. You fellows run your own business. We supply the promotional expertise and financial management. It's a matter of a group volunteering to get together. If you'd like to join us, it could be good for you and good for us. If not, that's fine, too."

One day Koffler felt he had reached the point where he couldn't progress further unless he got more risk capital. He followed the advice of E.P. Taylor that the best way of raising funds was to sell shares in a public stock offering.

With that objective in mind, Koffler first approached Ward Pitfield, a prominent Bay Street investment dealer, to write a prospectus. He drove Pitfield to his giant store at Dufferin and Lawrence. En route, he proudly recounted the volume of business done by his seventeen stores. He was particularly proud of having achieved this success by working economically out of a little office at the back of the Dufferin Street store.

On their arrival Pitfield examined the premises. He noticed it was equipped with corkboard walls and two desks shoved close together to accommodate Koffler and his right-hand man, Jack Gwartz. The only other amenity was a tiny anteroom with just enough space for a stenographer and his bookkeeper, Jules Solomon.

Despite Koffler's enthusiasm, Pitfield was not impressed. The Bay Streeter explained it was not enough for a company to achieve efficiencies; it also needed a certain style. What Koffler had attained here was a corporation with princely aspirations functioning out of minuscule quarters. Koffler further remembers Pitfield looking around and saying: "What happens if you get hit by a truck? You've got seventeen stores, but no head office, no personnel, no backup. Come back and see me when you've built an organization."

Pitfield, now the sixty-one-year-old president of Canadian General Investments Ltd., has no recollection of what he said to Koffler. But he does recall putting together a glowing report on Koffler's business potential and being impressed by his business acumen. "I suggested he wait a bit before going public, but Murray was champing at the bit to get on with it," says Pitfield.

Pretty well the same advice was given to Koffler by the illustrious high finance expert who has since piloted him through the shoals of all his stock transactions. He is Leonard Watt, now sixty-eight, the rubicund and somewhat saturnine "Foxy Grandpa of Bay Street," who then headed Fiscal Consultants, Ltd. "Some days I hate Murray," says Watt in his dry-humoured fashion, a blend of the cherubic and the satanic. "I'm a terrible tease and some people think I ought to have my block knocked off. But not Murray. I'm jealous of him for being so nice. No matter how much I tease him, he's always been an absolute gentleman."

Watt has long teased Koffler for being so naive about the protocol in conducting important Bay Street deals. With wry amusement, he remembers how Koffler originally invited him to lunch at the then rather seedy coffee shop of the King Edward Hotel. There, over a paltry cheese sandwich, Koffler tried to persuade Watt to help him bring Koffler Associated Drug into the public marketplace.

Not long after, he remembers Koffler returning excitedly with a set of figures and a proposal. "How would it shape up if I merged with the Plaza drugstore chain?" said Koffler.

Watt scanned the numbers and gave a beatific smile. "Well, yes," he said. "If you people can get together, I'll agree to play the role of Solomon in judging how you can slice up the pie. Then, yes, you would be ready to go public."

It was easier said than done. Plaza Drug Stores Limited was a chain of thirty-three traditional Ontario stores co-owned equally by seven highly independent pharmacists. As Koffler and Watt saw it, the company had a number of weaknesses, but these were dwarfed by its one great overriding strength, a triple A rating that meant the prime location of most of its stores in shopping centres.

Its chief deficit was its shaky financial structure. To compete for prize mall locations with Tamblyn's chain of 200 drugstores, Plaza had to pay in rental fees an excessive 5 per cent of its annual gross sales. Consequently, it was a top-heavy young company. Its financial position was so precarious it had secretly put out feelers about the possibility of becoming a branch of either the Walgreen drugstore chain in the United States or Dominion Stores in Canada.

Another major flaw was Plaza's chaotic management structure; it was as volatile and prima donna-ridden as the boardroom of a Hollywood studio. The ringmaster of what somebody called the Plaza circus was a remarkable man named Philip Goldman. He died in 1980 at the age of sixty-nine, widely mourned as the "golden-tongued orator" of his profession. The son of an immigrant butcher from Minsk, he was a short, handsome, theatrical pharmacist, with the wavy white locks of a prophet and the sensitive face of a frustrated poet. He was a self-educated showman who spent his spare time reading *Webster's Dictionary* and *Bartlett's Familiar Quotations*, singing Hebrew cantorial melodies at synagogues and Al Jolson black Mammy songs at social functions. He was also the first Jewish pharmacist to serve as president of the Canadian Pharmaceutical Association and later proved to be a superb public relations man for the drugstore chain.

Koffler encountered Goldman at a memorable meeting of the city's pharmacists. They had assembled to debate the issue of cutthroat prescription price-slashing. In his customary style of seizing leadership, Koffler stepped forward to make a breakaway announcement. "Gentlemen, you can do whatever you want, but I don't intend to get involved in this rat race," he said. "As of tomorrow morning, we are *raising* our prescription prices. You can undercut us if you want. But we're going to establish that we are professionals. We deserve an appropriate fee for our services and an appropriate return on our investment."

Flushed with the applause given to him by his fellow pharmacists, Koffler then took Goldman aside. "Phil, your stores have the right locations," he said. "Our stores have the right merchandising formula that can double your sales volume. How about us getting together to form a public company?"

Goldman was intrigued. He conferred with his six partners. "Okay, let's do it," he said when he next saw Koffler. "There's only one problem. How do we slice up the pie?"

Koffler suggested that the two companies submit their profit-and-loss statements and balance sheets to that objective financial analyst, Leonard Watt, and abide by his recommendations for dividing the shares. The partners all met with Watt and agreed.

However, they agreed only in their unanimous, vehement disagreement when he issued his Solomonic judgement. Watt acknowledged that Koffler's seventeen stores amounted to about half of the thirty-three Plaza stores. But he pointed out that if the chains merged, the Shoppers outlets would create two-thirds of the total sales volume and two-thirds of the profits. Hence, he argued, the shares should be split accordingly.

"The hassling back and forth among the Plaza partners was somewhat considerable," Watt recalls in an ironic understatement. Ultimately, though, after consulting a second financial expert, they grudgingly agreed to accept Watt's formula that gave the Plaza group 30 per cent and the Koffler group 70 per cent.

"I convinced them that if they all united to keep the baby alive, it would be healthier than if I dismembered it," Watt now says. "Furthermore, I handed down this bit of wisdom: 'The one thing I'm sure of is that the sum total of the two companies will be worth more than what you people think.' That really wowed them. Something more than they each possessed would now be very marketable."

The next step was to hire a firm of underwriters to market the shares to the public. Koffler still relishes the memory of turning down the offer made to him by the top executive of a very prestigious firm. The executive frowned with frosty disapproval when Koffler mentioned that the accountancy firm of Wm. Eisenberg & Co. and the law firm of Goodman and Carr would serve as his representatives in the stock undertaking.

The executive hemmed and hawed. "I don't mean to cast aspersions on either of these two Jewish firms," he said. "But if you really want to make a good impression on the financial community, I suggest you use instead two firms I recommend with solid, Anglo-Saxon names."

Koffler flared up in a rare outburst of temper. "Listen here," he said, "I'm proud of what my company is doing. I don't need the mantle of anybody to cloak us in respectability."

"But if you use these two companies," the executive said, "it'll enhance your credibility, perhaps even get you more cash for your stocks."

"Thank you, we'll stand on our own good reputation," Koffler said crisply. "So this firm you recommend is not going to be my lawyer. And that firm you recommend is not going to be my accountant. And *your* firm, dear sir, is not going to be my underwriter."

Beaming in retrospect, Koffler says, "I really took umbrage and discounted the fellow entirely. I remember enjoying it so much – rejecting his form of polite discrimination. The guy was so *shocked* he couldn't believe it when I ushered him out."

Watt thoroughly endorsed what Koffler had done. "You don't have to put up with that outmoded Bay Street prejudice," he said. "You've got perfectly competent people handling your auditing and legal functions. You stick with them."

As E.P. Taylor had previously suggested, Watt recommended the Bay Street firm of McLeod Young Weir Limited to handle the underwriting, which Koffler accepted. More as a joke than anything, Watt then suggested, tongue-in-cheek, it might be a good idea to have a WASP sit on the board of directors of the amalgamated firm.

"Why a WASP?" he said teasingly to Koffler. "That's so the public will know you don't go into the synagogue on Saturday to conspire against the rest of us."

Koffler laughed. "That's a super idea," he said. "And I can't think of a better WASP spy than you. So, Leonard, why don't you take it on?"

The butt of his own joke, Watt gracefully accepted. "I avoid like the devil sitting on boards or committees of any kind," he said with a sigh. "But I'll make an exception in this case – as long as it's only for a short period of a year or so."

The merger and public stock issue were held simultaneously on June 20, 1968. It was a date Koffler sentimentally had inscribed on fountain pens and gave as gifts to his new partners. It meant that a total of fifty-two stores – thirty-three from Plaza Drug Stores Limited, seventeen from Koffler Associated Drug, and two franchised stores operated by Jack Gwartz also

BUILDING THE BUSINESS

Murray Koffler at twenty-two outside his Bathurst Street store resolved to remove "sodas" from the sign above.

After eliminating bicycle delivery service of soda pop and sundries, Koffler points to van used only for delivering prescriptions.

Like his father, Murray loved window-display promotions. This one in 1951 was a match-the-twins contest at his Bathurst Street store conducted in tandem with the *Toronto Telegram*.

Pioneer Shoppers "franchise associates" (from left) are: Jack Gwartz, Barry Haberman, Harry Kalb, John Kramer, Koffler, Jules Slater, and Tom Roe, 1961.

On June 20, 1968, Koffler and Philip Goldman, who represented the Plaza Drug chain, officially announced a merger as well as a public stock issue for a total of fifty-two Shoppers Drug Mart stores.

Koffler and his financial adviser Leonard Watt celebrate with Ralph
Cunningham (centre) the 1971 acquisition of eighty-seven
Cunningham drugstores in western Canada for $10 million.

Kicking up their heels to celebrate Shoppers' growth in Alberta are
Koffler with three cowboy-hatted models and his executives, Jack
Gwartz (left), Fred Van Laare, and David MacDonald, 1975.

Koffler takes time out to scribble notes for a speech at that annual wingding and whoop-de-do, the combined Conference of Shoppers Associates and Buying Show, where $40 million worth of business is transacted.

Hamming it up at a Shoppers buying show, Koffler poses with pretty models. The Retail Council of Canada calls these get-togethers of 400 merchandise suppliers and 800 druggists Canada's biggest pharmaceutical trade show.

Koffler, with Jack Gwartz, performs a
light-hearted Indian dance at a Montreal party
for Shoppers' Quebec Pharmaprix associates in
1978. Seven years later he took seriously the
plight of Indians and organized the Canadian
Council for Native Business. In bottom photo,
Koffler rolls his eyes devilishly at the
photographer.

Koffler with actress Farrah Fawcett, then spokeswoman for
Fabergé, at a 1978 cosmetics promotion. Shoppers has since
cornered 18 per cent of the Canadian cosmetics market, grossing
from it more than $150 million in 1986.

Murray and Marvelle with their son Leon (left) and Toronto Rabbi
Jordan Pearlson at opening of first Super-Pharm drugstore in
Herzlia, Israel, in 1977. Leon operates a chain of ten Israeli
Super-Pharms, in 1987.

LET'S TALK FACTS:

There is a new kind of drug store that you must know about. It is called Shoppers Drug Mart and is the latest development in the drug business in Canada and the U.S. It is situated right here in your neighbourhood at the Fairview Mall, Lansdowne Avenue, only a few minutes away from your home.

You shop for your drug store needs the same way you have shopped for years in your supermarket for food. Shoppers Drug Mart gives the same benefits through modern merchandising that changed the corner grocery store into the supermarket. We have changed the small drug store into a super drug store and can now save you money on every item day in and day out. This was never possible before. The people in Moncton found this out last year, and now we've come to Saint John.

Shoppers Drug Mart—Fairview Mall—definitely lowers the cost of drug, health and beauty needs.

Open every day, Monday to Friday from 9:30 a.m. to 9:30 p.m., Saturday from 9:30 a.m. to 6 p.m., and every Sunday from 12 noon to 6 p.m.

Koffler wrote and helped deliver his first ads – personalized handbills explaining in chatty style his supermarket drugstore concept.

Billed as The Shoppers Three, a trio of comely models—Dorothy
Goulah, Cindy Girling, Christine Cattell—helped "glitz up" ads for
beauty products.

Comedienne Bea Arthur, star of TV's *Maude* and *The Golden Girls*, in her role as Shoppers' spokeswoman, performs in commercials as boss of chauffeur Maurice and as a mouthy Mrs. Santa Claus who nags "Nicky."

Client _____ SHOPPERS DRUG MART _____ Product Pick, Pack, Tote _____ Date Aug. 22/85

Length _____ Title _____ 70-1600 _____ Rev. 2 ___ RTO _____ Page No ___ 1 ___ No. of Words _____

Promise _____

Video		Audio

1. OPEN ON SHOT OF BEA WALKING QUICKLY DOWN AISLE WITH CHAUFFEUR BEHIND TRYING TO KEEP UP.

MUSIC: INSTRUMENTAL B.G.
BEA VOC: Quickly,
Maurice.

2. CUT TO MCU OF CHAUFFEUR.

MAURICE VOC: But Madame, we'll miss the wrestling finals!

3. CUT BACK TO BEA AS SHE TURNS TO RESPOND.

BEA VOC: Well I didn't come to Shoppers Drug Mart to miss pick, pack and tote.

4. CHAUFFEUR RESPONDS AS BEA ROLLS HER EYES.

MAURICE VOC: Friends of yours Madame?

5. BEA CONTINUES WALKING DOWN AISLE. AS SHE WALKS SHE POINTS OUT VARIOUS PRODUCTS.
6. CU DISPLAY OF REVLON, MAX FACTOR & L'OREAL PRODUCTS.

BEA VOC: Oh shift out of neutral, Maurice! With a minimum purchase of $10.00 worth of selected cosmetics.

Kert Advertising commercial storyboard depicts Bea Arthur heckling her French-Canadian chauffeur Maurice. He's played by Canadian character actor Derek McGrath, known for TV comedy parts in *Mary Tyler Moore* and *Cheers* series.

On construction site of the first Four Seasons Hotel, on Toronto's Jarvis Street in 1961 (from left): Koffler, Max Sharp, Eddie Creed, Issy Sharp, and Fred Eisen.

Koffler presents a plaque to artists at 1977 Toronto Outdoor Art Exhibition, which he founded. Smiling at his quips are then Mayor David Crombie (right) and Secretary of State John Roberts.

Murray and Marvelle at Shoppers' 1983 "Thanks a Billion" promotional extravaganza with Audrey and Paul Paré, Chairman of the Board of Imasco Limited.

Koffler with his disciple, dynamic David Bloom, who was groomed to take over as chairman, president, and chief executive officer of the Shoppers Drug Mart empire, in 1985.

thrown into the pot – were now amalgamated under the banner of Koffler Stores Limited. It meant the birth of a public company then currently doing an annual sales volume of close to $28 million.

More than 600,000 shares were issued, of which 160,000 were being sold to the public at $10 a share. By the afternoon of June 20, they were trading at $25. For years thereafter it was regarded as a hot glamour stock, splitting at least six times. If one had kept 100 of the original $10 shares, that investment, in terms of accumulated dividends and share appreciation, now would be worth $33,148.

The shares earned a tidy bundle for all sorts of players. Harry Talbot, now a sales director of McLeod Young Weir, remembers that June 20th date vividly. He was broke, having just acquired a $50,000 home at a 9 per cent mortgage interest rate. His wife phoned him at the office, saying she was shopping for accessories for a powder room in their new home. Could they afford a marble sink top and a pair of brass faucets she had spotted?

"Hold off for a while until I phone you later," Talbot cautioned her. "I'm going to break my rule and gamble for a fast profit on the market."

Talbot had been following closely his company's underwriting of the Koffler stock. At eleven o'clock in the morning, he noticed that the shares had already zoomed to $17.50. Talbot had a secret cache of $3,000 tucked away for emergencies; he decided to plunge most of it in the purchase of 200 shares. At two o'clock, when the bidding had reached $25, he sold his shares and phoned his wife.

"Sweetie, you can buy those fancy items for the powder room," he said. "We've just cleared for ourselves a sweet profit of $1,500." Today, he says, the powder room in his abode bears the commemorative title, The Koffler Room.

Leonard Watt remembers breaking one of his rules at that period, too. For years, he was accustomed to escaping from the pressures of Bay Street for a quiet lunch at the Royal York Hotel's Imperial Room. (The cuisine there, he dryly observes, is somewhat more Lucullan than the mingy cheese sandwiches they used to serve at the old King Eddy's dingy coffee shop.) At this posh room, he had watched Louis Jannetta, the one-time humble bus boy, become the city's most celebrated maitre d'.

The day before the Koffler stock issue, Jannetta approached him with more than his usual deference.

"Mr. Watt, I've never bothered you before about your business, have I?" he asked.

"That's right, Louie. You haven't."

"Well, forgive me if I pester you now. I'm tired of being given tips on the market by my other Bay Street customers, with me winding up taken to the cleaners. Everybody tells me Mr. Watt is the only one with the smarts about what's really happening in the market. So today I'm asking you for the first and last time. I've got a nest egg of $5,000. So please, Mr. Watt, can you suggest what I might do with it on the market?"

Perhaps because he was so relieved at having concluded the Koffler deal, Watt made an exception to his inflexible rule of refraining from being a market tipster. He suggested that Jannetta might consider – at his own risk – taking a flier in the stock to be issued the next day. "I think Murray Koffler will go places with his new company," he said. "It might be worth your while buying 500 shares."

"Thank you, Mr. Watt," said Jannetta, pumping his hand with Rotarian fervour. "I'll never bother you again."

Jannetta kept his word for four years, never once mentioning to Watt his investment of 500 shares. Then one day, when the stock had hit $60 and was being split again, Jannetta came over to his table. "Mr. Watt, don't you think Mr. Koffler's stock has done well enough?" he asked. "When are you going to tell me to sell it?"

Watt restrained himself from laughing. He remembers saying gravely to Jannetta in his best deadpan style, "As a matter of fact, Louie, it has done pretty well. I guess you could sell it anytime." According to his calculation, Jannetta must have made about $50,000 on the deal.

(When asked about the matter today, Jannetta, who is noted for never divulging anything about tips, whether monetary or verbal, replies in *his* poker-faced style: "What 500 shares? A maitre d' like me never has $5,000 stashed away to play the market.")

The seven original Plaza partners indulged in no such poor-mouthing. Today most of them admit that the Koffler take-over – for, bluntly, that's what it was – made them almost in-stant millionaires. But their sudden cushion of wealth did not soothe these adamantine individualists. They were a dis-putatious bunch, unaccustomed to taking orders from any-body, and evidently they wrangled among themselves with a ferocity that even ruffled the equanimity of the peace-loving, positive-thinking Koffler.

"Even before the Koffler takeover, the seven fought like cats and dogs," says Stan Glazer, the son of one of the original seven Plaza partners, Max Glazer. "I mean, there wasn't a day that my father wouldn't come home threatening to kill either himself or one of his partners. They were always at each other's throats. It was like a zoo, a soap opera, an ongoing three-ring circus."

Stan Glazer's father Max is the first to concede that he was among the bellowers, and admits he struck up sparks in his relationship with Jack Gwartz, who constantly deferred to Koffler and whose indecisiveness won him the sobriquet, "the master of the definite maybe." Unlike Gwartz, he was often at loggerheads with Koffler. "Murray is a prince of a fellow," Max Glazer says. "But I guess we locked horns because we're kin-dred spirits, both strong in our convictions. I suppose we also clashed because I'm a contemporary of his father's. I'm a guy used to being my own boss, and I found it hard to account to somebody younger."

Max Glazer resigned from Shoppers in 1970, a disgruntled millionaire. He holds no resentment against Koffler, whom he regards as "a brilliant visionary – both he and his father could see tomorrow before we could see today." Like some of the older co-founders, he resented being sidelined with diminished authority. "The attitude toward us seemed to be: 'Who needs these guys from Plaza Drugs anyway? They just came with the package.' We felt we had lost our self-respect and that we were relegated to just sitting around the office and picking our nails."

Bernard Glazier, one of the two Plaza partners who were asked by Gwartz if they wished to take early retirement in the early 1980s, feels more regretful than disgruntled. However, he says that he and several other partners became disenchanted because they were left out of the overall operation of the company. "If you don't participate, you lose interest," he says. "They could have made use of our talents better." Looking back, he criticizes Koffler for being "overly domineering" at board meetings. "Murray would ask questions and then would be too impatient to wait for an answer." But Glazier forgives him for being overbearing at times. "That Murray, he could charm you out of your shoes!" Besides, it would be churlish to knock a Santa Claus who helped him attain a Florida condominium where he can play tennis and golf five months of the year.

The same sort of ambivalence is voiced by Jack Kirk, who also took early retirement. The son of a Polish pantsmaker, he is a short, baldish, moon-faced sixty-four-year-old retiree who tootles around in a Mercedes Benz and enjoys a similar sunny outdoor life during winters at his Florida condo. He rejoices in his present patrician lifestyle, because he can remember being paid at his first pharmacy apprenticeship job three dollars for a seventy-two-hour week, which he figures came to about four cents an hour. Four months after the Koffler takeover, he sold some of his shares and he still savours the thrill of "how tickled pink I was when I fondled my first check for $70,000."

Kirk looks back with satisfaction at his Shoppers post, which made him responsible for locating new sites. "I'd get a terrific high every time we opened a new store," he says. "Because I signed the lease and made the deal, I felt those were *my* stores." Nevertheless, he admits he sometimes found Koffler's tendency to dominate board meetings nettlesome. "You couldn't get your opinion on the table, much less listened to or considered," he recalls. "If you were trying to get two words in, he could talk right over your head. His strength of character is such that he can drown you out. And, of course, we had to accept the fact that Murray was the majority share-holder and his opinions would carry more weight."

But Kirk ends his short recital of sins with a shrug. "You know, you can't argue with success," he says. "Murray'll always be Mr. Terrific in my book, because we swam in the current of his success."

The oldest living original partner is eighty-eight-year-old Wilfred Isaacson. Once known for his fiery temper, which induced him to fling drawers down on the drugstore floor in a rage, the one-time red-haired Irishman from Belfast mellowed with age. He was respected as the elder statesman of his profession because so many pharmacists had apprenticed at "Isaacson's at College and Grace." As secretary-treasurer of the amalgamated company, he would open board meetings with a prayer, which he would intone in Gaelic, and at parties he was famous for reciting poems and songs in Gaelic. From his Florida condo in Venice, where he now does landscape paintings, he said recently that all past controversies were forgotten and he had no fault to find whatsoever with his former colleagues.

The very last of "the last Mohicans," for so the original seven from Plaza called themselves, is Irving Bain, a gifted merchandiser who currently is Shoppers' executive vice-president in charge of retail development. The sixty-year-old Bain takes pride in being a pharmacist with a seven-figure income, and readily confesses: "I loved Max Glazer. But there wasn't a day in our business life that I didn't have a fight with him."

All of them pay tribute to the two Mohicans who did not survive. One was the late Samuel Mandel, a tall, gaunt, sometimes short-tempered pharmacist of strong character. He served as an able vice-president in charge of store planning and was compelled to resign early due to poor health. The other, of course, was the late Philip Goldman. He seems to have been loved by everybody for his sweet, gentle, somewhat cautious personality. As one of the "triumvirate" who administered the amalgamated companies, he was a moderating force, tempering and balancing the effervescent Koffler and his compliant lieutenant Gwartz. Bernard Glazier describes Goldman's influence this way: "If there was a really important disagreement with Murray, we'd talk to Phil and say, '*You* speak to him on our behalf.'"

Despite their jealousies and jostlings, they all looked up to Koffler. Their respect was not merely based on the good fortune he brought them. They genuinely liked him for "being a square-shooter" and for adhering to the cliché that his word was indeed his bond. Or, as one of them phrased it un-grammatically but felicitously: "With a handshake from Murray, you can go to the bank with."

Koffler today disputes the notion that he was domineering at board meetings. He acknowledges that some of the partners may not have spoken up because they were not aggressive enough and possibly overwhelmed by "a person like me, pulsating all the time." But he asks rather wistfully, "How can they say I dominated them? Our company has always been democratic. From day one, our policy has been that no decisions are made singularly. Absolutely everything is decided around a table."

Leonard Watt describes Koffler's boardroom demeanour from the viewpoint of a financial analyst who has been trained to be a sharp-eyed observer. "Murray is the only guy I know who can turn his ears off," he says. "When Murray wants to make a point at a meeting, Murray focuses on what's on Murray's mind. He simply doesn't hear anything else. Other people at a meeting can be talking about other things, but the moment they stop, Murray pops up and drives home the subject close to his heart."

Stan Glazer, a pharmacist with an MBA degree, has been trained to become a professional manager with a sceptical eye. "The first thing you learn at business school is that there's no such thing as democracy in business," he says. "You've got to have a president who says, 'The buck stops here,' or the business can't function. Murray deserves a lot of credit for trying to practise management by consensus. But often, by the sheer strength of his presence, he'd railroad things through a committee without realizing it. Basically, what Murray wanted Murray got. Period."

The consensus is that Koffler did his best to unite his disparate partners as democratically as he could, improvising a form of collective management. The first thing he did was to assemble them around a table at Plaza's headquarters office-cum-warehouse in north Toronto. "Gentlemen," he said, "we've got to decide who's going to do what?"

Since Koffler had put the deal together, he requested that he be named chief executive officer and president of the company for the first year. Then he went around the table, asking each partner, "What would you like to do?" Positions were thus temporarily allocated. Each accepted the idea that at the end of the year they would evaluate themselves and each other and, if necessary, reallocate their functions. All was to be decided with a democratic vote.

"Everything was to be out on the table except our assessments of how the others were performing," Koffler recalls. "All criticisms were to be written down privately on our position papers. I felt it would be harmful to have an open forum on that. It would be too much like we used to do at boys' camp bull sessions, pointing fingers of accusation at each other around the camp fire. I prefer instead to accentuate the positive. And so, ad-libbing as we went, I think our method of assigning responsibilities worked out pretty well."

In a somewhat similar fashion, all thirty-three Plaza managers were to be offered the opportunity to become Shoppers associates, pending a trial period. Almost all passed the test. Admittedly, though, it took time for many of them to adjust to Koffler's drastic revamping of their traditional drugstores. He eliminated the dowdy green interior design, replacing it with bright lighting and stark white decor. He explained that the pure, antiseptic colour scheme would show off the merchandise more advantageously. And he personally went through each store like a hurricane, leaving in his wake the debris of outmoded services, from bicycle delivery to charge accounts, to be scrapped.

Another major shakeup by Koffler was the shutdown of the Plaza warehouse. He explained that he was taking this step for two reasons: the cost of maintaining a fleet of trucks and a stockroom of "dead merchandise" was wasteful and could be handled more economically by professionals in the business of distributing wholesale goods; also, by calling for tenders from the wholesalers, he was able to negotiate a mutually profitable deal with National Drug Limited, which won in the bidding. In one fell swoop, the wholesaler garnered the business of all fifty-two amalgamated stores. In turn, the stores got merchandise at a percentage above cost, which was less than what could have been provided by the Plaza warehouse system.

One wholesaler who did not have to submit a tender was Irving Frisch, president of Kohl & Frisch Ltd., specialists in supplying tobacco and confectionery. His late partner, Moses Kohl, launched the wholesale business more than seventy years ago by delivering on a bicycle and five years later began supplying tobacco and sundries to Leon Koffler's original College Street store. When Murray Koffler initiated his expansion into shopping plazas, Frisch remembers meeting him one day outside the Royal Bank on College Street.

"Why haven't you approached me, like the other wholesalers, to handle our tobacco business?" asked Koffler.

"Tenders, tenders. With the trust between old friends that we've established, who needs that stuff. Let's just continue."

"You're right," said Koffler, with a laugh.

And Frisch remembers, "We shook hands. But it was a hello handshake. Not a business handshake. We didn't even need that."

After the Plaza takeover, Koffler recalls that Frisch continued to service the expanded chain, giving unusually long credit terms. In fact, Koffler got angry with him for being so generous. "Why don't you collect your bills on time?" Koffler scolded him.

"Murray, that's my problem," said Frisch.

Koffler now says, "He knew he was going to get paid, but he felt that was the way he could best maintain the faith we had in each other. He went out of his way to get us the best tobacco and confectionery deals that would help our chain grow. On our part, we played a role in adding a lot of volume to his business, which helped his company develop."

Frisch verifies that statement: "Loyalty still means a lot between old friends, even in today's fiercely competitive marketplace." He points out that his specialty wholesale firm now grosses $200 million a year, having become the largest of its kind in Ontario. And his staff of ninety, he observes, no longer has to resort to delivery via bicycle.

When the Plaza warehouse was closed, Koffler leased out the vacated space, which took care of the rental of his head-quarters office space. He then made a subtle yet significant change. He abolished the term "head office" and decided that henceforth it would be called "central office." Psychologically anyway, he thus helped combat the impression that the associates in the field—the autonomous "presidents of their individual stores," as he called them—were being ruled by an autocrat calling the shots from an aloof, Kremlin-like headquarters.

That sensitivity to semantics reflected the change in the psyche of Koffler himself. Just as he had attempted to change his pharmacists into professional managers, so had Koffler changed from a small businessman into a captain of industry. It was not a calculated change; he improvised constantly, steering his ship by hunch and by guess and by God. In the process, Koffler established a set of useful guidelines that helped him govern a rapidly growing corporate empire. Some of his key principles can be summarized:

• Strive to make the company a horizontal rather than a vertical operation. In a horizontal structure, you build up motivation—and profits—by encouraging each associate to be his own self-starter. In a vertical operation, where orders come from the top, you tend to stultify new ideas. That tendency was once caricatured nicely in a jingle by a Unilever executive:

> Along this tree
> From root to crown

Ideas flow up
And vetoes down

- Always be open to fresh ideas, no matter how half-baked they may seem at first.
- Don't try to get big for the sake of bigness alone. Keep an eye on the action and not on the size.
- Don't set out to make a million by hook or by crook; you're bound to fail. But if you bring together a group of dedicated fellow achievers, the business will follow, and you're bound to make more than a million.
- Delegate whenever you can. Chances are he can do it better than you, because he's concentrating on one thing, while you as an administrative executive are concentrating on many things. Or, as Andrew Carnegie once put it: "The great manager is the one who knows how to surround himself with men smarter than himself."
- Mistakes are building blocks, the price you pay for improvement. The executive who never makes mistakes lives in a vacuum, and that's the worst mistake of all.
- After you've delegated authority, don't breathe down the fellow's neck.
- When dealing with customers, a good merchant always exercises the elastic-band principle. Offer them special qualities and services unique to your establishment, and you'll keep pulling them back to the store.
- Make it a rule to invest in people rather than in a business. If you get the right people, the business will follow.
- Avoid nay-sayers who carry their caution to an extreme. To be sure, brakes may be necessary, but they don't run a car.
- Likewise, sidestep yes-men, if you want to acquire accurate information about your company. One of the hardest things to do is to listen to the sound of other drummers when the one you want to hear beats loudly in your own ears. And one of the easiest ways to ruin a company is to perpetuate a boardroom where the chairman is a monarch and the directors his fawning courtiers.

- Success comes in cans, not can'ts. Always challenge in personal terms those who negate your positive suggestions with a generalized "You can't do it." Use the strategy of taking them at their word and retaliating: "Well, if you tell me you can't do it, you're probably right. I'll find someone who *can* do it."
- You don't need to build a business by climbing over the next guy's body. Hitting the other fellow in public can be deleterious. The more times Coke mentions Pepsi, the more times Pepsi gets recognized.
- Try to be a sunshine-spreader rather than a gloom-and-doomer. It's good business–and good for the soul–to compliment and stroke employees who deserve the praise. It's bad for business–and bad for your character–to be a character assassin of others. To cite one of Koffler's favourite maxims: "What Peter says about Paul tells me a lot more about Peter than it tells me about Paul."
- Never try to put on the dog and say you know something when you don't. The dogcatcher will catch up with you.
- Try to be honest with yourself and recognize your limitations and your strengths. Koffler considers his number-one weakness as an executive his "lack of stick-to-it-iveness." Once he has initiated a project and delegated its management to others, his mind tends to be preoccupied with the next undertaking. His chief asset, he believes, is his ability to "zero in on the essence of a meeting, sum up the problem, and present a strategy for its solution."
- Finally, Koffler puts great faith in the adage, "He who rules must humour fully as much as he commands." Indeed, of all the qualities needed for a corporation president, he has found that a paramount requisite is humour to help leaven the solemnity of the problems that pile up. This playful sense of the absurd is vital, he believes, if you hope to retain your sanity.

The pranks that Koffler plays in his executive role are inclined to be fey and fanciful and sometimes downright cornball, according to Jack Gwartz, who has withstood many of them over the years. Two stand out in his memory. The most outrageous piece of tomfoolery was staged by Koffler after he had acquired his Jokers Hill Farm near Toronto. If he wanted to cut short one of his marathon think-tank meetings at the office, Koffler would put on a battered old farmer's straw hat. "Gol durn an' by heck," he would say, assuming a country bumpkin accent. "I better mosey home to the farm an' milk them cows. If I don't milk 'em purty soon, those pesky critters, instead of saying' 'Moo' they'll be groanin' 'Oo-oo-oo-oo-oo!'"

After another interminable think tank, Koffler invited twenty of his executives and associates to a late-night dinner at the fancy Café de L'Auberge at the Inn on the Park. There he pulled off his most charming escapade. While all were seated around the table about to have their coffee and cognac, Chicho Valle, the Cuban orchestra leader, began rattling his maracas and singing a Latin American tune. Though exhausted like the others, Koffler instantly sprang to his feet, bowed to Gwartz, and said straight-faced, "May I have this dance?"

"Delighted," said Gwartz and they twirled on the dance floor.

The others followed their cue. Soon all twenty were wiggling and shimmying to a cha-cha beat, their exhaustion forgotten, and Chicho Valle laughing so hard he was unable to shake his gourds.

Koffler and his company cohorts deserved all the fun they got. Shoppers was preparing to expand from coast to coast, and though no octopus tentacles were necessary to grapple with the problems ahead – including a vicious strike – they needed all the wit and wisdom at their command.

CHAPTER TEN

Growing Pains and Profits

The 1970s was an era of enormous expansion for the fledgling Shoppers Drug Mart chain. "From coast to coast," in the electric phrase of Murray Koffler, "we went hell-bent for acquisitions." His executive vice-president, Jack Gwartz, normally a man of subdued vocabulary, uses equally lurid language when recalling the excitement of the period. "The company kept rolling right along," says Gwartz, "like a juggernaut."

Exactly how Koffler speeded on ahead as an acquisitor is a matter of debate. He himself has denied that he behaved like an octopus. Rather, he maintains that he did not invade the turf of rival drugstore chains but simply bought whatever seemed like a good opportunity for himself and others – and hang the metaphors. However, he can't resist adding, with a nice histrionic touch, that there was a battle when he took over a major West Coast chain and was compelled to fight off "a plague of union problems."

A former British Columbia trade unionist, who used to be a foe of Koffler's and has since come to admire him, has contributed his own vivid imagery in recollection of that turbulent period. In his analogy, the two types of takeover acquisitors can be likened to the two varieties of owls, whose differing styles were thus once described by Senator Huey Long, the cracker-barrel yarn-spinner from Louisiana. "President Herbert Hoover was a hoot owl and President Franklin D.

Roosevelt was a scrootch owl," Long used to say. "A hoot owl bangs into the nest and knocks the hen clean off and catches her while she's falling. But a scrootch owl slips into the roost and scrootches up to the hen and talks softly to her. And the hen just falls in love with him, and the next thing you know, there ain't no hen."

The one-time labour propagandist, who prefers to remain anonymous, says that Koffler is more like a scrootch owl – but a scrootch owl with a conscience: "If the hen has laid any golden eggs, he shares them with his fellow owls."

The man most instrumental in helping Koffler build an empire across Canada has the ensnaring charm of the most seductive of scrootch owls. He is David MacDonald, the former president of Shoppers Atlantic Canada and for the past fifteen years the president of Shoppers Drug Mart West. Born in Campbellton, New Brunswick, he is a lean, rumpled, pipe-smoking storyteller of fifty-three, with a droll wit he filters through a trace of a Scottish accent and the deceptive air of a hick Jimmy Stewart pawing the pavements of the big city of Vancouver. In fact, he is an engaging sophisticate, with a pharmacist's degree from Dalhousie University in Halifax, who was urbane enough to be elected president of the Canadian Pharmaceutical Association and remains smart enough to cherish his small-town roots.

MacDonald met Koffler through Philip Goldman, the Shoppers vice-president who also had served as president of the Canadian Pharmaceutical Association. Goldman persuaded MacDonald to sell one of his three drugstores in Moncton to Shoppers and become a franchised associate as well as the head of their Maritime division.

"I literally did business with Murray on a handshake," says MacDonald. He remembers bringing along an accountant to help negotiate the terms for selling his store to the chain. As the accountant reached over to open his briefcase, Koffler asked, "What are you looking for?"

"Some figures to substantiate what Mr. MacDonald is saying."

"Look," said Koffler, launching into an argument he has used with many others who have become life-long colleagues.

"We are going to be doing business for years and years together. If I can't believe what David is saying to me now, then we might as well end the discussion."

MacDonald now says, "Murray never did look at those figures." MacDonald sold the lease to Shoppers for $75,000 in 1969. With the money, he bought 2,000 shares in Shoppers, then selling at $37.50, and still retains the shares, now worth well over $800,000. He later sold his two other Moncton stores to Shoppers for $125,000 each. He says simply, "I'm a millionaire today and happy as a clam about my years with Shoppers."

In the early 1970s he and Koffler made a Maritime-wide expedition, which was sparked by a phone call from National Drug Limited. The wholesale firm was worried about the considerable debt owed to it by Lord's Supervalue Pharmacies, a chain of twenty-six traditional stores (seven in Ontario and nineteen in the Atlantic Provinces) that had gone into receivership. Would Koffler do a favour to National Drug? Would he examine the properties with the possibility of taking them over and thus assuming their debts?

Koffler agreed to do so with his Maritime specialist, MacDonald. They hired a two-engine Cessna and spent three adventuresome days with the tangy smell of the sea in their nostrils and the delicious taste of cod tongues and lobster tails in their palates as they went "puddle-hopping," as Koffler called it, to communities stretching from Prince Edward Island to Cape Breton Island. Some were so isolated they had primitive grass strips rather than paved runways. Others were so bogged down in mud after a spell of rain that the pilot couldn't land.

Nevertheless, the pair had fun visiting the quaint little towns. "We got it down to a science," says MacDonald. "We'd have the pilot wait for us at each landing at one of these crazy airfields. Whenever we got in the air, we'd have him radio a cab to meet us in the next town. Then we'd go hit a town and in an hour or so we'd be back in the plane."

Most of the stores were poorly managed. "This was in midsummer, and I'll never forget that in a few of the stores there were racks of winter parkas on sale," Koffler recalls. "As for drug products, the stock was very thin. Packages were face up, to create the illusion of more inventory than they had. Everything was helter-skelter."

But their saving grace was that most stores were in prime locations. Koffler remembers looking at a store on a main street and thinking, "Gosh, this town is starving for a good drugstore and this store, if operated right, has the potential of doing a million dollars of business a year. Yet right now it's doing a mere $250,000."

Shoppers bought the Lord's chain for $2.4 million, and Koffler was delighted when that particular store did indeed reach the $1 million mark within a year. The store managers were not backward, he says, but they had poor inventory, insufficient financing, and lacklustre guidance. But recognizing Shoppers as their lifeline, the Maritimers got into the spirit of things and were zestfully eager to change. The majority of the revamped, mass-merchandise stores (which grew to number eighty-six by the beginning of 1988) easily doubled their volume within one year.

Koffler's thrust into western Canada in 1971 was not accomplished that easily. But despite all the problems that bedeviled the acquisition, his successful takeover of a chain of drugstores larger than Shoppers was an extraordinary feat. It began with a phone call one morning from a West Coast stockbroker. He chanced to pass on information about Cunningham Drug Stores Ltd. It was a Vancouver-based chain of eighty-seven traditional stores – seventy-eight of them in British Columbia, eight in Alberta, and one in Whitehorse in the Yukon Territory. The scuttlebutt was that the company had fallen on hard times and was desperately looking for buyers.

Koffler flew west with Jack Gwartz to assess the possibility of a takeover. He found that the chain had been founded sixty years previously by the late George Cunningham, a widely respected pharmacist of the old school. His son, Ralph Cunningham, a refined socialite with an aristocratic bearing who had attended all the right private schools, was the major shareholder. But he wasn't really interested in running the public company.

"What had been a very successful business was sliding badly downhill," Koffler sized it up. It reminded him of the similar erosion of the once strong Tamblyn empire in Ontario. That chain had been forged into a network of 200 drugstores by the fastidious entrepreneur, Gordon Tamblyn, who would fly into a rage if his finger in a white glove left a mark when he rubbed it across a glass showcase. After Tamblyn's death, his heirs supervising the chain did not keep up with the times; neither had the custodians of George Cunningham's estate.

"After visiting as many stores as I could, I recognized that this was a great opportunity," he recalls. "First, they had practically no cosmetic business at all. Two, they were still delivering orders and doing all that old stuff that smacked of the 1950s."

He could detect that it couldn't compete with London Drugs, a newcomer chain of large, well-merchandised stores just starting to have an impact on British Columbia. Still, Cunningham's had a lot going for it. "It had a good name and good locations," he concluded. "I felt it was a good way for us to get a foothold in the West."

Consequently, in February, 1971, Shoppers paid $10 million for the chain, whose annual gross sales had dipped to a low of $25 million. By the spring of 1972, seventy of the stores had been converted into Shoppers-style outlets and were in the process of being franchised. And by 1975, the western division had tripled its retail sales base to a handsome $75 million.

The changeover was achieved by several of Koffler's hand-picked viceroys, the top one being MacDonald. "Murray is the master of the con," MacDonald now says in a joshing manner, chuckling at the memory of being summoned to the Toronto central office and urged to pack his bags and go to British Columbia bearing the formidable title of vice-president of corporate integration.

"You've got to be crazy!" he told Koffler. "I'm happy doing my thing in the Maritimes. How can you send a relatively green kid like me out West to tackle all those corporate responsibilities?" But Koffler, he says in retrospect, "saw something in me I didn't see – and he was perceptive enough to sell the corporate posting to me as one hell of a great adventure."

He recalls Koffler overriding his qualms by telling him breezily, "David, you'll be doing me and the company a personal favour. Go to Vancouver for one year. Teach the Cunningham management team out there our Shoppers system. Then you can walk away."

That promised one year in the West, says MacDonald, stretched out to the rest of his business career. On his arrival, though, he was sorely tempted to pack his bags again and fly right back home. "When I got there," he remembers dolefully, "I found that we appeared to have bought a bag of sawdust."

The most immediate problem was to find a means of transforming rigidly conservative store managers into resilient decision-makers. MacDonald got a taste of what he was up against after conducting his first meeting with them. A Cunningham old-timer, conditioned to going by the book, approached him timidly. "I'd like to know what the new company's policy will be on an important point of procedure," the manager said. "I mean, when should I put my store awning down?"

At first, MacDonald remembers thinking, "This guy must be kidding." When it was clear the fellow was sincere, MacDonald told him in profane exasperation: "Put the f---ing thing *down* when the sun comes out. Then put the f---ing thing *up* when the sun goes in."

They were not all such wimpish Caspar Milquetoasts. But they were understandably apprehensive about losing their jobs. And many were suspicious of the promises made by these city slickers from the Mystic East. To "illuminate the people out there," as Koffler phrases it, he and the golden-tongued Philip Goldman delivered soothing speeches before a crowd of more than 500 Cunningham employees gathered at Vancouver's Bayshore Inn. Their honeyed words allayed the fears of a good many in the audience.

"I was enthralled," recalls John Parker, sixty-year-old Vancouver associate. Parker remembers that Koffler spoke for almost an hour to the overflow audience but was so eloquent that his speech seemed on the short side. "Murray has a way of making his cause your cause," he says. "I liked him right smack off the bat and I jumped in with both feet." Parker, who quotes from T.S. Eliot as well as the ancient philosophers, has no regrets about becoming one of the first ten Cunningham managers· to sign up as a franchise associate. He respects Koffler as a businessman who showed him how he could double his sales volume in a year to $1 million and then in another year double that to $2 million.

Not all the managers were that compliant. Jim Charles confesses that he was initially one of the doubting Thomases. Now forty-seven, he's a commanding, big-shouldered man who holds the title of vice-president of administration for Shoppers West. At one point he worked his way up from thirty-three-cents-an-hour Cunningham delivery boy in Langley, British Columbia, to a most unpopular executive position. He was elevated to that ticklish spot rather like Gilbert and Sullivan's Ko-Ko in *The Mikado*, the humble tailor who became Lord High Executioner.

As Charles tells the story, the chain was in such dire financial straits that Cunningham appointed him to spend six months managing each money-losing store. Then he was to render a verdict, deciding whether the property ought to be shut down or not. "As you can imagine," says Charles, displaying an edge of flinty humour, "whenever I arrived to manage a new store, my coming was not exactly good news. My image was what you might call dubious. They shivered and quaked and privately nicknamed me The Closer."

Charles doesn't blame the personnel for being so edgy when he appeared on the scene wielding his Ko-Koesque snickersee. "The atmosphere in a Cunningham store was awfully stifling," he says. "Supervisors didn't encourage you to use your own initiative. Controls were tough and tight."

The red tape was particularly stifling: it put managers into a straitjacket and lowered the already shaky morale of all personnel. "If you felt an employee should be rewarded for extra effort, you had to go through a long process of filling out forms justifying why you wanted to increase his pay," says Charles. "It might take three months for the raise to come through. By then, the pay boost was no longer a positive incentive. The employee's reaction was, 'It's about time!' instead of 'I deserve it.'"

It is little wonder that Charles was more than a little sceptical when he first met Koffler at the Bayshore Inn meeting. Charles was the ringleader of a dozen similarly wary managers who elected him president of the Cunningham Employees Pharmacist Association. "We didn't altogether trust Murray," he says. "He was trying to get us to sign franchise agreements with a company dedicated to entrepreneurial excellence. But we didn't understand what those words meant. We'd come from a paternalistic organization that told you what to do. Murray was offering us the freedom to be our own boss."

Some diehards couldn't handle that freedom and fell by the wayside. Others expressed a willingness to change, yet bullheadedly resisted signing franchise contracts.

"My lawyer couldn't recommend that I sign the document," Charles recalls. "He said it was heavily loaded toward the corporation. And because the company owned the lease, he said you had very little protection. You could make a supreme effort for a number of years, build up a business, and then they'd have every right to turf you out."

Charles and his band of sceptics were flown to Toronto for several days to examine for themselves the Shoppers stores and talk to associates. Six of the dozen signed on their return and the other six signed sporadically over the next six months.

By that time, Shoppers was embroiled in an ugly strike. It lasted four months. It gave rise to union picketing and harassment of thirteen stores, and was one of the reasons for the permanent shutdown of Cunningham's vast 100-employee, 85,000-square-foot distribution warehouse. And the company wound up with a loss of more than $2 million because of the strike.

The hapless affair sprang from the sad mistakes and lack of human understanding on both sides, according to Stan Glazer, who was appointed western operations director by Koffler and asked to serve as MacDonald's number-two man. Glazer believes the trouble started with an inadvertent mistake made by Philip Goldman in a speech delivered before the West Coast managers on the issue of employee wage increases. Until the company got a handle of things, Goldman asked each manager to review the needs of his own staff. They were to assume the responsibility for giving salary increases as they saw fit.

"These were managers who had never made a decision in their entire life," says Glazer. "So instead of going ahead and hiking salaries what they did was to do nothing." As the months slipped by without any raises, says Glazer, resentment festered into a "we-they" attitude of ill will directed against the company. And so the disgruntled employees in thirteen stores – all in the Vancouver area – voted to be certified by the Retail Clerks' Union. It was considered the most militant of British Columbia's very tough trade unions.

The company's unwitting error was compounded by another one even more serious, according to Glazer. "We got good legal counsel, but we didn't go out and get good industrial relations counsel," he says. "We were druggists from Ontario, where there was no such thing as retail unions except in supermarkets. We knew how to run drugstores; we knew nothing about labour relations. So we accepted the advice of our lawyers. They said we must deal from strength and take a strike."

Koffler felt two ways about the delicate situation. In general terms, he assumes a liberal attitude toward trade unionism. "In the old days, when labour was exploited, unions were very necessary," he says. "For instance, in my father's time during the Depression, people in the Toronto garment trade worked in sweat shops on Spadina Avenue sewing garments at a nickel a piece. Because labour flexed its muscles through unions, management was forced to recognize the rights of the worker." But since then, he believes management has become more socially conscious, and labour has overstepped its bounds. "Though unions do have their place, I think the pendulum has swung too far," he says. "Nowadays labour is managing management."

At the time of the strike, he acknowledges he was naive to ignore the unique strength of trade unionism in certain British Columbia communities. "There mother and father, sister and brother – all are devoted union members," he says. "It's their social club and their bargaining agent, a place to go to parties, as much a lifestyle thing as a monetary thing."

Nevertheless, he balked against unions in drugstores. He argued that Shoppers was a chain of independently owned franchised stores rather than a monolithic corporation with hundreds of employees on the payroll. He maintained that each associate should have the right to negotiate with his dozen or so employees on a one-to-one basis without the interference of a union bargaining agent. Psychologically, Koffler also seems to have regarded the union's intrusion as a personal affront. "It was like a slap in the face to Murray," Glazer believes. "Like somebody saying, 'Hey! You haven't treated us well. So we've had to bring in a third party in order to get a fair shake.'"

The conflict between managers and store clerks was further aggravated by the some 100 stock keepers, truck drivers, and other employees of the Cunningham-owned distribution warehouse called Western Wholesale Limited. All certified by the Retail Wholesale Department Store Union, they walked out in a sympathy strike.

"It was sheer hell for all of us having to cross the picket line," recalls Fred Van Laare, Shoppers' present executive vice-president of operational services. When the strike broke, he was manning a blackboard in the company's offices adjoining the warehouse. "We were converting two or three Cunningham stores a week into Shoppers-style stores, and it was a real logistical and organizational nightmare," Van Laare recalls. But it was nothing like the chaos that erupted at the outbreak of the strike. Van Laare was among the management executives who instantly pitched in at the warehouse. He was responsible for safeguarding the narcotics vault and driving the forklifts.

To supply stores throughout the province and Alberta, the company hired scab truck drivers and stock keepers. Most of them were high school students seeking summertime jobs. Their jobs lasted for precisely one day. That evening after work, Van Laare saw the strikers chase a pack of the students over the back wall of the building and through back alleys. "Some of the union guys beat the s--- out of the kids and broke one kid's arm," says Glazer. "I saw it with my own eyes."

The company then hired hefty truck drivers who specialized in working for outfits on strike. "They were very big guys," says Glazer. "Looked as though they weighed about 400 pounds each. And they were guys willing to risk being hurt. They gave the impression that if attacked by the union guys they'd break a few arms and legs before going down."

The unions brought in their own goons from Seattle, and the violence escalated. They jammed big spikes against employees' cars being driven into the warehouse grounds and scratched the paint off. Just before closing time, they scattered heavy-headed tacks around the parking lot, so that employees' cars would come out with tires punctured. They phoned office management people in the middle of the night, threatening, "Your family's going to get hurt if the company doesn't give in."

Picketers devised a campaign of terror tactics to harass the thirteen strike-bound stores. They blocked the store entrances. They engaged in shoving and yelling matches with customers, urging them not to shop. In several cases, according to Charles, "they put defecation – and I do mean human excrement – in front of stores and homes of their owners." Other trade unions joined in the pressure and advised their members to boycott Shoppers. It was all bad public relations, and it doubtlessly wasn't helped when MacDonald and other management people, in their naiveté, tried to fight back on radio phone-in shows.

The company's reputation was most damaged, Glazer believes, by an ill-advised pharmacist who was a rabid anti-unionist. He feared for the safety of his family after picketers made threatening phone calls, hurled pop bottles at his house, and rattled him by putting a prank ad in the newspapers claiming his house was up for sale. In his anger, he stood in front of his store screaming obscenities at the picketers. He finally took the step of hiring his own burly bodyguard from a detective agency who walked up and down in front of his store holding on a leash a fiercesome German shepherd dog.

"He wasn't using his noodle, because the picketers saw this as a beautiful opportunity to make propaganda hay," says Glazer. A wily picketer rolled up a newspaper, stuck it in front of the German shepherd, and the dog, of course, feeling threatened, promptly bit it. The union summoned the police, the press, and Rosemary Brown, the local labour-supporting New Democratic Party member of the provincial parliament. Newspaper photographers took a picture of the picketer clutching his hand and moaning he had been bitten by this ravening guard dog. Rosemary Brown delivered a tirade bewailing the use of such union-busting tactics and asking why the company couldn't settle the strike in a civilized fashion.

The company took the hint, which was buttressed by a labour arbitrator from the province's then NDP government who told management, in effect: "If you want to survive as a business entity here, you'll have to learn how to live with unions." Once Shoppers accepted that reality and signed a collective bargaining agreement, the strike was over within a few days.

All stores, whether unionized or not, granted the same increase in wages. Charles, who shortly thereafter became Shoppers' West Coast personnel director in charge of union negotiations ("I was scared witless by my first seven negotiations"), recollects that the identical parity formula has prevailed ever since. As of the beginning of 1988, all fifty of British Columbia's non-unionized stores were continuing to pay clerks the same wage scale as the sixteen stores then unionized. The rate for a clerk who had worked at a store for a period of twelve months was then $10.96 an hour. "That is higher than in any other province in Canada," Charles reported to an inquiring journalist.

Koffler today deplores the wage differential. Shaking his head in dismay, he maintains that "wages in B.C. are among the highest in North America" and that the overly tough stance of unions has tended to drive industry from the province. In retrospect, he thinks one of the wisest things he did was to get rid of the Cunningham warehouse, which was sold to National Drug Company. By disposing of that labour-intensive property, he figures the company saved 5 per cent of the cost price of merchandise, a saving passed on to the consumer. Though some Cunningham customers complained of the "cold sterility" of the stark white decor and protested that the glare of bright lights hurt their eyes, they gradually accepted Shoppers' modernity. Koffler estimates that the majority of revamped British Columbia stores followed a pattern that became common in the West: doubling their sales volume within a year.

Van Laare was the catalyst responsible for the similar boost in business for Shoppers in Alberta. As operations director for that province, he turned around the money-losing stores and transformed them into what he calls "healthy bottom-liners." Koffler goes further than that. Thanks in good measure to Van Laare's early efforts, he says the forty stores in Alberta, as of the beginning of 1988, have become among the "major profit centres" of Shoppers' western division.

The man responsible for giving Shoppers its toehold in Manitoba is perhaps the most beloved pharmacist in the Prairie provinces today. At seventy, still as lively as a gopher and bearing a resemblance to one, he is a bustling immigrant from the village of Ost in Poland. His name is David Stern, but practically everybody in the profession knows him as "Little Davey." Stern eventually built his own 2,400-square-foot Economy Discount Drugstore, at Main and Redwood in Winnipeg, into a thriving business. It maintained a separate hospital supply business in the basement and grossed $2.7 million a year. His rapport with physicians and customers was unparalleled in Winnipeg. "We had a lot of charge accounts on the books, and if the man of the house died, we'd cancel the bill out. Didn't matter a hoot how much he owed me. These people weren't customers. They were family. I *knew* them – by first name yet – from the grandpa down."

Koffler first sought him out in 1973 because he had heard it was Manitoba's largest volume drugstore. According to Stern's recollection, after prolonged negotiations in a hotel room, Koffler sweet-talked him into selling the store, and in return appointed him Shoppers' co-ordinator for the province.

Koffler remembers being enamoured of "that sweetheart of a charmer, Davey," who, like a coquette being courted, resisted his advances at first with the pragmatic argument: "We're doing so well already. So what do we need you for?"

Koffler replied: "I think you could do better with us. Instead of competing, we'll put our advertising dollars together. We'll spend money on you and change your store. We'll take your nursing home business out of the basement and create a beautiful facility for you."

His blandishments worked. Within a year, his store was grossing $5 million. Today, with Stern's former apprentice Harry Kaplan functioning as associate, the 10,000-square-foot Shoppers Economy Discount Store grosses more than $7 million a year and is one of the chain's frontrunners in the prescription business. The store is still the flagship of the seventeen shoppers outlets in Manitoba.

Koffler's liaisons in the province of Quebec, though ultimately fruitful, were less harmonious and, for a long stretch, painful. The experience involved two separate courtships that began promisingly in the year 1972.

Koffler was first pursued by a pair of personable young Montreal pharmacists, Ralph Young and Charles (Chuck) Retter. "We think your operation is fantastic," he remembers Young saying enthusiastically to him at Shoppers' central office in Toronto. "And we're confident it'll work in Quebec. Let us know when you decide to make the move. We're willing to change our two shopping-centre pharmacies into trial Shoppers stores and get the ball rolling."

"Fine," said Koffler, who was acquainted with Young's family though unfamiliar with Retter. "You're just the kind of people we're looking for. We'll need bilingual pharmacists and we'll need functioning stores if we hope to break into the Quebec market. Sounds like a super idea. We're interested."

In the next scene of the Quebec scenario, Koffler was the suitor. By this time he was a high-profile company president of forty-eight much in demand on the speakers' circuit. Consequently, he was asked to be the keynote speaker at the

Canadian conference of the International Council of Shopping Centres held in Montreal. By coincidence, he shared the platform with Arnold Steinberg, executive vice-president of Steinberg's Limited. He in turn was the nephew of Sam Steinberg, who had taken over a tiny Montreal shop originally stocked with $200 worth of groceries by his immigrant mother. With his four brothers, Sam had parlayed it into Quebec's biggest privately owned supermarket chain.

In his speech, Arnold Steinberg let drop the news that the family company was hoping to expand into the pharmacy business and later to expand into Ontario. Koffler's ears perked up; he took Steinberg aside. "Look, Arnold," he said, "we want to come into the province of Quebec. You want to come into the province of Ontario. We know the drug business. You know the Quebec shopping-centre business and the legalities of opening stores here. I think there's the makings of an excellent union here. Let's go fifty-fifty in a Quebec drugstore chain. Then we'll look into the prospects for Ontario later."

The offspring of Koffler's corporate matchmaking was a joint venture formed in late 1972 and named Pharmaprix Limitée. It was the closest French equivalent he could dream up for Shoppers Drug Mart—a fusion of "pharmacy" and "price." Steinberg was to find new locations in malls and smooth out administrative problems. Shoppers was to promote and operate stores acquired via Young and Retter. Indeed, that pair, functioning alternately as president and vice-president of the Shoppers Quebec division, had speedily transformed their traditional stores into sleek Shoppers mass-merchandised outlets. Both were thrilled when their sales volume had doubled in one year, as Koffler had predicted. Altogether, things looked rosy for the *ménage à quatre*.

Alas, as Shakespeare remarked in another context, troubles come swarming not in single spies but in battalions. The Quebec College of Pharmacy barraged them with archaic regulations. One ruling specified that chain ownership of more than three drugstores was prohibited. Pharmaprix got around it by calling itself a service organization rather than a chain; it charged its independently owned store "subscribers" a "service fee" instead of a "franchise fee." Another ancient regulation banned dispensaries in stores which sold cosmetics and other non-medicinal products. Koffler circumvented that taboo by using his flair for imaginative design; he created a metal frame that isolated the dispensary from the rest of the store. This device satisfied the college inspectors while visually enhancing the interior.

However, the licensing board was mulishly stubborn about another restriction. It refused to budge from a bureaucratic ruling that a pharmacy department was forbidden in a supermarket. That stumbling block left Steinberg's mightily frustrated.

On his part, as Koffler phrases it delicately, he felt frustrated over his "sad experiences" with Steinberg's as a location-finder. "They did find a lot of good locations," he says. "But they were good for food markets and not all good for drugstores." What's more, they selected too many locations in rural communities with populations too small for a mass-merchandised Shoppers outlet. In addition, they often leased poorly located stores inside the shopping malls themselves. Koffler blames himself and his own Toronto-based central office for not conducting sufficient marketing studies and for sending out a management team unfamiliar with an alien environment.

His saddest experience, though, was with his supposedly on-the-spot management team of Young and Retter. "We never did get a clear indication from that pair about their individual responsibilities," he says. "They never did clarify who was president and who was vice-president. So for a couple of years it was very difficult knowing who undertook the authority."

To top it all, Koffler was shocked to discover that Young and Retter, while supposedly administering the Quebec division, were seeking locations for themselves. "We disassociated ourselves from them immediately," says Koffler, sourly recalling their falling out. He considered their act both a conflict of interest and a breach of trust. "After all, they came to us," he says. "They brought their stores into our system. They learned all our ways. Then they went off on their own."

The upshot of these troubles was that Pharmaprix lost money for eight years. In 1980, Steinberg's, wearied of the incessant money drain, bowed out of the joint venture. "There were no bad feelings between us," Koffler insists. Since then, Shoppers has streamlined the management of its Quebec division, and as of the beginning of 1988 the total of forty-six Pharmaprix and their allied Pharmaprix Carnaval stores had been showing a steady profit over the past couple of years.

Koffler concluded that decade of expansion with the historic opening of a drugstore in Winnipeg at the beginning of the year 1980. It was the latest link in a chain of 400 Shoppers outlets stretching not only across the ten provinces of Canada but down to Florida.

In retrospect now, he believes he was lucky to have learned a profoundly important lesson early on during his adventures in the 1970s. He became aware that an empire builder needs the help of myriad experts in specialized fields of knowledge – if he hoped to expand nationally without wasteful duplication of effort, he would require some form of in-house training facility.

That realization dawned one night in 1972. High over the Rockies, while flying to Vancouver, he began wondering aloud how he could train Cunningham employees to become Shoppers personnel. He turned to his seatmate, a bespectacled, owlish intellectual named Alexander (Ubby) Krakauer – a former associate managing a store in Brampton, Ontario, who had joined the Shoppers Toronto central office as an operations executive.

"You know, Ubby, I've been thinking of growth," he mused. "How do we teach new people the basics of operating a Shoppers store as we grow larger and larger, not only in B.C. but elsewhere? Cashiers won't know how to handle cash registers according to our system. Cosmeticians won't know how to do a proper selling job with beauty aids. Pharmacists wanting to be franchised associates won't have a grasp of running a business, from advertising to financial management. Even stock boys will have to be taught merchandising. So that each region won't have to rediscover the wheel over and over again, we'll obviously need our own school."

After due discussion over their drinks, Krakauer suggested, "Why not call it the Koffler Academy?"

"Super idea," said Koffler. "And since you, Ubby, have an academic mind, I herewith anoint and appoint you dean of the academy."

Looking back now, Koffler says it was the smartest decision ever made at 32,000 feet. The brain trust of consultants he appointed also taught the empire builder one or two things.

CHAPTER ELEVEN

On Dr. Freud's Marketing Couch

L ike many self-made businessmen, Murray Koffler was inclined to be suspicious of professional consultants. He
secretly suspected that many of these so-called experts
had lost their jobs or their bankrupt companies and then had
the nerve to assume the mantle of know-it-alls. They were the
business equivalents of the professors of creative writing once
lampooned by George Bernard Shaw. "Those who can, do."
said Shaw. "Those who can't, teach."

A superb doer himself, Koffler more than smiled when he
happened to read a mock definition of a consultant in *The Globe
and Mail's* "Your Morning Smile" column. Koffler laughed so
heartily that he clipped the debunking witticism and then
passed it around to his colleagues. It read: "A consultant is
someone who would if he could but he can't, so he tells those
who already can how they should."

So it was understandable that Koffler was more than a mite
sceptical when he arranged to meet one day in 1972 with a
professional consultant named Covell Brown. Brown, a professional marketing and retail consultant, is board chairman of a
Toronto firm named Veritas Consultants Limited. Initially,
Koffler sought out Brown for just one aspect of marketing. He
had heard that Brown had devised a training program for the
national association of dealers who operated the Canadian Tire
chain of stores.

"You've done all this work for Canadian Tire," said Koffler at their meeting at Inn on the Park. "How would you like to develop a similar program for our Koffler Academy? We're setting it up so we can have a structured way of teaching our people."

"Before I can help you teach people what to do, I've got to know who you are," said Brown. "So my first step is to make a research study of what you do and how well you do it."

"What will it cost?"

"In round figures? Twenty thousand dollars."

Koffler gasped. "My gawd, that's a lot!"

Koffler then looked him straight in the eye and, according to Brown, said, "Okay. Every dog deserves one bite."

Brown now recalls with a laugh, "It was Murray's way of making the point: 'I'm giving you this one shot at it. But mess it up, fella, and it'll be the last one you'll get from me.'"

It was the beginning of a business relationship that has lasted until this day, firmly based on the mutual admiration of two virtuoso marketers. Brown admires Koffler for accepting Brown's grandiose concept that "marketing is the heart of any corporation – the very foundation of the temple." As a consequence, Brown maintains that Koffler has built "one of the truly great marketing and retailing achievements, not only in Canada but anywhere."

Koffler returns the compliment. He says that Veritas, as a result of its marketing studies for Shoppers, has consistently been "one of the foundation stones of our company." As for the Koffler Academy, thanks in part to Brown's input, it has developed into "the most sophisticated business training course for pharmacy personnel on the continent."

Despite a rather flamboyant character, Brown retains many of the earthy characteristics of a farmboy whose parents brewed their own beer and plowed their land behind horses in bush country in the state of Washington. Later, at fifteen, he left home in Anchorage, Alaska, to work at everything from being a building construction painter to a short-order cook. He capped his wanderings by attaining an MBA from Harvard University and the equivalent of degrees in literature and political science from the University of California in Santa Barbara. In addition, he has a keen, extracurricular grasp of psychiatric literature.

Brown by no means considers Koffler a flawless paragon. "In the early years, Murray was inclined to be short-tempered and hard-driving, and at times it could be exquisitely uncomfortable for anyone to be within shrapnel distance," Brown recalls. "But you can't say that Murray is *inclined* to be egocentric. He *is* egocentric – and, because of it, a lot of fun to work with. I'm reminded of Frank Lloyd Wright, the great architect, who once said early in his career: 'I'll have to make a choice. Am I going to be hypocritically humble? Or honestly arrogant?'"

Indeed, Koffler's sometimes overwhelming personality was noted even before their deal was struck by Brown's long-time marketing colleague, Stan Thomas, who recently was hired by Shoppers' Toronto central office as the company's senior vice-president in charge of marketing. Like Brown, he favours snappy maxims on office signs, one of them reading: "Think and surprise us all." And like the sophisticated Brown, he comes from a humble background.

Thomas picked up the basics of marketing and retailing at the age of twelve. He then began working as a dishwasher and bus boy at the Tasty Barbecue Cafe on Wyandotte Street in Windsor, Ontario, which was owned by his father, a Macedonian immigrant. At the University of Windsor, he was a brilliant student specializing in psychology, mathematics, and business. At Toronto's York University, while studying for his MBA, he and some fellow students approached Koffler in 1970; they wanted permission to conduct a research study analysing the management of Shoppers.

At first Koffler rejected their proposal. "Things are really rolling for us and we're at a high," he said. "Why do I need a bunch of students to come in and evaluate how we're doing?"

"The very fact that everything's going right for you is a *very* good reason you ought to take a second look at the operation," Thomas argued.

Koffler sat back and reflected a moment. "You're right," he agreed. "Sure, we're doing okay. But maybe we *can* do better."

Thomas, then an impressionable twenty-one-year-old student, was much impressed by Koffler's open-minded attitude, and even more so by his reaction to their report's blunt recommendation. "We suggested that he was going to have an awful lot of difficulty achieving his goals given his style as a company president," recalls Thomas. "Why? Because he was too dominant."

Thomas remembers that Koffler appeared to take their recommendations seriously. "The bottom line was he felt we were right," Thomas says now. He believes the report may well have been the springboard that prompted Koffler to dive wholeheartedly into his famous Shoppers think tanks designed to generate creative ideas.

The research study won an A mark for Thomas at York University and, two years later, helped him win a marketer's job at Veritas. Thomas helped Brown conduct a thorough productivity analysis of seventy-seven Shoppers outlets, examining how much each store was earning per square foot. "We took a hard look at every aspect that was contributing to the company's growth," he says. "Equally important, we identified the road blocks that would prevent the company from achieving their objectives."

Thomas helped Brown make a full-scale presentation of their findings at a meeting room at Inn on the Park. Brown remembers that Koffler seemed extremely supportive of the report. But as they neared the end of the long meeting, he recalls Koffler saying in a semi-amused tone, "You know, all this time, all this money, and you *still* haven't told us what to do with the Koffler Academy."

Brown demurred. "We have, in fact, pointed out a number of directions that are relevant," he said. "Now we're ready to get at it and put together a training program for your associates. In the process, we'll also put together a psychological profile of their motives, their fears, their perceptions of their roles."

Koffler wanted to know, "What will this one cost?"

"Quite a bit more than the last one. One hundred thousand dollars."

Brown recalls that Koffler sat bolt upright *"You* have *chutzpah!"* he said, arching his brows.

Brown, who takes pride in being as close to Jewish as a born Baptist can be, puffed on his Partagas Corona and smiled. "I don't think I'm a *chutzpahnik*," he said nonchalantly. "In fact, given the circumstances, I think a hundred grand is a very modest fee for putting Shoppers on the couch and giving you a detailed analysis of its psyche."

"I never bargain fees," Koffler remembers saying. "If you bargain for a fee, you get half a job done. Let's go for it."

In his role as the Sigmund Freud of marketing, Brown, working in tandem with Thomas and a team of interviewers, elicited some fascinating revelations. For one of their "psychological report cards," they tested store managers who were deemed to be successful and matched their performance against those who were doing poorly. They discovered, among other things, that a good many pharmacists felt uncomfortable outside of the dispensary.

"They'd been taught to think of themselves as members of a healing team—as sanctified clinicians rather than just re-tailers." says Brown. "So they felt guilty about selling things like toilet paper and toothpaste. It was unworthy of them." Consequently, one of the first steps in the training program was to help them come to grips with these masked feelings. "In a psychological sense," says Brown, "we had to help give themselves permission to become successful associates."

In his in-depth studies, Thomas found that once they stepped out of the dispensary, a good many felt dreadfully insecure. As he puts it, they felt as though they were abandoning a protective fortress and facing territory that was uncharted and vaguely threatening. "There was a whole front store which represented some 75 to 80 per cent of the total sales that these guys weren't concentrating on," says Thomas. "They had delegated total authority over it to the merchandise manager, who in that period in the early 1970s was a glorified stock boy. He was usually a chap just out of high school and had worked in a drugstore as a kid. Then he's kind of grown up and knows a little bit about the business, and having es-

tablished a beachhead in the front of the store, that was it."
They discovered, in short, that both the pharmacist turned
businessman and the stock boy turned merchandise manager
were often ill-equipped in their skills for communicating with
each other and the public.

Another finding was a jolting eye-opener. After a trip to the
West Coast, Brown reported to Koffler: "You're pretty happy,
aren't you, because sales from the Cunningham drugstores
you've bought have rocketed from $25 million to $60 million,
right?"

"Right," agreed Koffler.

"Well, don't look now, but I'm sorry to say you're not making money on the takeover."

Koffler stood up, astounded. "For heaven's sake, why?"

"Don't blame heaven – blame the bloody British Columbia
education system," said Brown. "According to our diagnosis,
the guys and gals in the stores out there haven't the faintest
idea of retail mathematics."

"What do you mean?"

"Our tests show that the overwhelming majority of them
can't do percentages to figure out their real profit margin," he
said, adding dryly, "And an inability to do a percentage calculation in a retail pricing situation is not exactly an asset."

He explained that those tested had the illusion that if the store
bought an item at a wholesale price of one dollar, for example,
and sold it for one dollar and thirty cents, it had made a clear profit
of 30 per cent. Actually, they had made a profit of 23 per cent.
They also had not taken into account the many expenses
involved for the store or the Shoppers chain in the process of
purchasing, merchandising, advertising, and selling goods.

Veritas was assigned to conduct seminars teaching West
Coast store managers the ABCs of retail pricing. Brown recalls
that the westerners initially were as hostile as bristling porcu-
pines. "They thought of us as those smart-ass guys from the
East who'd come to tell them how to run their business," he
says. "But there was no sense pussyfooting around and hiding
behind our regional barriers."

He recalls striding into a classroom, turning to confront them, and beginning abrasively: "You guys all look at me as an eastern asshole. Well, I want to tell you that *you* guys are easterners to me! Because I'm from Alaska and I won't take s--- from nobody."

Brown now says, laughing, "They probably said to each other, 'Not only is he a city slicker from elsewhere, but he's a *foul-mouthed* city slicker!' But I had to use that shock technique. They weren't just losing money; they weren't making money. Yet there was money to be made. Murray wanted it for them, and he got it."

Koffler himself was extremely forthright at the "bear pit" confrontations that Veritas staged across Canada. At one of these sessions, Thomas recalls seating him in the centre of a U-shaped arrangement of tables in a hotel meeting room. One associate who had been complaining bitterly all morning about his earnings was instantly subdued. Koffler pulled out a sheaf of papers, glanced at the figures, and said, "Last year you made $85,000."

"The guy was absolutely floored and stopped his silly harangues," says Thomas. "The way he'd been grumbling you'd have thought he was making something like $18,000."

Thomas believes the other associates appreciated Koffler's candour. "It's rare for a corporation president to be so upfront," he says. "Other top executives would maybe have dealt with the matter privately. But Murray felt it was important to get the facts on the table and deal with it, instead of letting it lay hidden like a skeleton in a closet."

Out of these freewheeling get-togethers emerged innovations that have since been imitated by pharmacy chains throughout North America. Most dramatic perhaps was the step-down dispensary devised by Koffler. Originally, he had specified that all Shoppers dispensaries were to feature a raised platform; this lofty perch allowed the pharmacist to keep an eye on activities in front of the store. But the Veritas studies indicated that this elevation was a barrier cutting him off from customers.

Consequently, Koffler designed a well at the centre of the counters, enabling the pharmacist to step down to floor level and communicate with people in a democratic, eyeball-to-eyeball level. Though some pharmacists grumbled in jest that the hopping up and down might lead to a hernia, it in fact helped restore in part their old-fashioned role as the friendly neighbourhood druggist.

Other consumer surveys paid off in more ways than one. Studies of unplanned, impulse purchases, for example, showed that sales increased as much as 400 per cent by mass display of goods either in strategically placed dump bins or stacked in their cardboard cases at the ends of aisles. With rewarding results, consumers were videotaped for classroom analysis or were invited to appear live on panels. Typical were these insights from senior citizens who volunteered to speak up at Vancouver and Toronto panel sessions:

"Because I'm over sixty-five, I have lots of time to read your advertising – and your competitors' too"; "Chairs would be a nice touch in your stores"; "I can never get cosmetics for black people"; "Old people bruise easily and I keep bumping into your poorly placed dump bins."

Most profitable of all were the Veritas training films, manuals, and marketing research materials gradually integrated into the curriculum of the Koffler Academy. Ubby Krakauer, the first dean of the academy, used it all to develop courses in conjunction with Humber and Seneca community colleges in the Toronto area. It resulted in what Krakauer termed a vital "reservoir of knowledge" for the continuing education of all Shoppers personnel.

Today, academy diplomas hang prominently on the walls of dispensaries in a place of honour beside parchment degrees from pharmacy colleges. Koffler recalls how the former president of the Tamblyn's chain (since acquired by Boots) once phoned to say a job applicant had submitted as credentials his Koffler Academy diploma. "It made such an impact on the president that he hired the fellow," says Koffler. "He knew the man had received good training." The academy has no equal in the United States. The American Association of Retail Pharmacists failed in an attempt to develop an equivalent management school in Brooklyn. And the academy, of course, is the basic model for the $6 million Koffler Institute of Pharmacy Management, whose facilities will be available to the pharmacists of every drugstore in Canada when it is completed.

Shoppers' present vice-president in charge of human resources and the Koffler Academy is Ray Hallett. He considers Koffler and Krakauer the " fathers" of the academy, and the academy itself the "national training arm" of the chain. Each of the four regional central offices – in Toronto, Vancouver, Montreal, and Moncton – maintains a staff of "facilitators" (a term preferred to "teachers"). In remote regions the training is done via correspondence courses. More generally, though, it's done in a classroom setting, either in a hotel meeting room or at a regional central office.

A staff of six facilitators does the training in classrooms on the first floor of the four-storey Shoppers Drug Mart Building erected in 1980 at 225 Yorkland Boulevard in north Toronto. In accordance with Koffler's specifications to designer Leslie Rebanks, the glass-and-concrete structure is sparkling white inside and outside. It reminds visitors of an ice palace, with forest-green carpeting and colour photos of Canadian landscapes providing glimmers of warmth for its some 250 corporate staff people.

Employees may borrow the more than 300 books and periodicals in the academy library; they range from *Drugstore News* and *Human Banking* to *Management: Analysis, Concepts and Cases*. They may make use of a lending library of twenty do-it-yourself audiotape cassettes by experts in various disciplines. Also available are fourteen audio-video training films.

One recent morning at nine o'clock twenty students enrolled at the Koffler Academy for a two-day course devoted to improving their store supervisory skills. They were uniformly exuberant and ranged in age from twenty to twenty-five. They worked as assistant store managers, head beauty advisers, head cashiers, and merchandise managers. And they seemed extremely bright, alert, and enthusiastic in their responses to their training facilitator, Steve Purse. The Koffler Academy –

which is big on titles–also calls him its co-ordinator for the Ontario central region. He is a tall, bespectacled thirty-three-year-old with a sandy beard and a passion for teaching. While at high school, Purse worked part-time for the Shoppers store in Toronto's Fairview Shopping Centre as a two-dollar-an-hour "receiver"–the title for a stock boy, who receives goods from the suppliers, prices them, and shelves them. With encouragement from Shoppers, he went on to get a BA from York University and an MBA from the University of Windsor. Now, he says, his vocation as a teacher has become "the most enjoyable period of my life."

His enjoyment was reflected in his amiability as he paced in front of the students seated around a U-shaped arrangement of wooden tables in the classroom. He was equipped with flip charts, a lectern, and all the latest audio-visual paraphernalia, including an overhead projector. But apart from showing a hilarious film titled *Unorganized Manager*, he shunned high-tech gimmickry.

He was particularly good in a session devoted to effective communication. "Speak to express–not impress." he said. As an example, he read aloud a true-life memo from a corporate executive prating on in bureaucratic bafflegab about "system analysis." Then, amid groans from the class, he asked them to write down what the message meant.

The students responded with their own store experiences to illustrate another one of his maxims: "Nature gave us two ears and one mouth so we could listen twice as much as we speak." They all listened sympathetically to a merchandise manager relate what is evidently a common problem, followed by a lively discussion of the dilemma: "There's this little old lady who's got nothing else to do every morning but drop around to our store and then talk my ear off with her prattle," he said. "How can I escape from her daily attack of verbal diarrhea without seeming to be rude to a regular customer?"

That situation is one of the rare contingencies not covered in the two textbook manuals considered the bibles of the academy. Both are in looseleaf binder form, thus allowing for new pages of guidelines to be inserted. One, bound in a black-

and-white cover, is the 300-page, prosaically titled *Shoppers Drug Mart Policy and Procedures Manual*. The other, inside a blue-and-white cover with more than 400 pages, bears the equally humdrum title, *Shoppers Drug Mart Store Operations Manual*.

Yet both brim with wonderfully arcane lore about the marketing of a drugstore. Among other exotica, a neophyte in the business can learn about the potency of the "power wall." It's located on the right-hand side of the store closest to the turnstile entrance and the shopping-cart corral. Veritas studies of consumer shopping habits indicated it's the number-one traffic area. Consequently, it's stocked with the best-selling staples, hair shampoos and sprays, deodorants, soaps and denture products. A "morgue," it turns out, is not for corpses; it's a series of bins set up alphabetically in the basement stockroom for damaged goods to be returned to suppliers. "Facing" means pulling products forward on a shelf to create a tidy, well-stocked image. "OTCs" are over-the-counter medications; merchandise managers are advised to display them on shelves in front of the dispensary with high-gross next to low-gross items and complementary sellers next to each other. And, demonstrating that pharmacy is as jargon-ridden as any other profession, one learns from the personnel management section that to be "dehired" is a polite way of saying you've been fired.

Manual guidelines instruct employees on the handling of every conceivable situation. Pharmacists are advised to answer the phone "with a pleasant, modulated voice, using the phrase, 'Shoppers Drug Mart, (Herbert) speaking.'" Herbert is told to respond to customers' requests on a positive rather than a negative note, with this example given: "I can direct you to the shopping mall washroom, which is very close" rather than "I can't let you use our washrooms, it's against policy." And if Herbert happens to be interviewed on radio or TV, he is cautioned: "Look your interviewer in the eye. Never argue. If you can't answer a question, say so. Try to say 'Shoppers Drug Mart' at least once."

The Veritas marketing studies have shown that 80 per cent of Shoppers sales transactions are conducted by women (with customers predominantly aged between twenty-five and forty-five). Consequently, the manuals offer many tips on promoting the "beauty island," which is prominently located at the front of each store. Among other things, the head beauty adviser is urged to set up an indexed card system of the hair colouring and skin tone of regular customers and alert them by mail or phone for special sales. She is told to organize in-store cosmetic clinics and make-up workshops for community groups; the "before" and "after" photos taken invariably win steady customers. And she is encouraged to sponsor contestants in local beauty pageants, using girls who work part-time in the cosmetics department. The manual adds: " Photo coverage is great!"

True-or-false quizzes in the manuals stress repeatedly the Shoppers slogan "CARE" – "Customers Are Really Everything." It takes no mental giant to catch on quickly that the correct answer is "true" for every statement in the quiz. Typical statements read: " We are dependent on the customer; they are *not* dependent on us"; " The customer is not a statistic or an interruption; she/he is a human being"; and " It is often the *way* a customer is handled that creates complaints, rather than the content of the problem."

That last statement is bolstered by evidence in Veritas research indicating that 65 per cent of customer complaints concern service and courtesy and only 25 per cent price and product. The manuals point out that arguing with a customer is a no-win piece of folly: "You may win the argument, but you lose the customer." Furthermore, a customer who walks out of a store feeling disgruntled becomes a negative walking billboard bad-mouthing to friends never to shop at Shoppers.

The inspirational guidelines on employee relations sound as if they had been dictated by Koffler himself. "For psychological success, people need to feel good about themselves," reads one philosophical dissertation in the manuals. "For this to happen in the store, they need to feel that they are an accepted member of the team and that their individual contribution is recognized and rewarded." To stimulate self-worth means to motivate, and the manual goes on to define motivation this way: "Motivating . . . is getting people to do those things that make them and the store successful, and also reinforces the fact that they are terrific human beings." And to scold yet encourage an employee, the manual offers an ingenious double whammy of a phrase: "I get angry with you because you are one of my best people and I know you can do the job."

But the most Kofflerian thing in the manuals is an old-fashioned scolding administered to the associates on their lack of communication. "Never, ever, under any conditions, assume that anyone knows anything about anything," the admonition begins.

"*Don't assume* that your employees are a happy lot, contentedly slaving away for you, if you haven't been paying them much attention. Find out . . . by asking them questions. Discuss.

"*Don't assume* that your customer will understand that you don't have time to talk with him at length on a particular day because you are extremely busy. Tell him so and gain his understanding.

"*Don't assume* that because you are a nice guy, doing your part in the community, offering your store as a base for various fund-raising collections, that everyone knows and appreciates it. Tell the newspaper about it.

"*Don't assume* that help will be forthcoming from Central Office if they don't know you have a problem. Tell them.

"Communication is a two-way street. Make sure you are both sending and receiving."

This exhortation – not to make assumptions, not to take anything for granted – reflects a paradoxical aspect of Koffler's character. While he is a positive-thinking optimist about most matters, he is sufficiently practical to retain a healthy scepticism about statements that fly in the face of his own experiences. And while he is a confirmed marketing man, he challenges market research surveys if their findings conflict with his own instincts, unscientific though they may be.

"The astonishing thing about Murray is that his feelings for the pulse of the marketplace were often so far ahead of market research," says Covell Brown. "He'd scratch his head and come up with brilliant campaign slogans without research. In fact, Murray mistrusted the alleged supporting evidence of some research projects. The astonishing thing was that his gut feelings and fine instincts proved more often right than wrong."

The point is illustrated with a story Koffler tells dating back to the time he was appointed to the board of directors of Rothmans of Pall Mall Limited. One day an ad agency presented to the board a slick advertising campaign for Peter Stuyvesant cigarettes. It was based on the slogan, "You will enjoy P.S. 100's," which was supposed to signify you wanted to smoke the cigarette that was 100 millimetres in length.

"Board members are not supposed to get involved in advertising decisions," recalls Koffler. "They're supposed to listen. But this proposal bothered me so much that I just had to express a dissenting opinion."

He thereupon challenged the agency account executive: "I don't think your ad campaign will work. Why do you assume people will make the thought connection linking P.S. 100's with the name Peter Stuyvesant?"

"Because our marketing surveys tell us so," said the executive, and that was good enough for him.

But because it didn't jibe with his own common sense, Koffler took his dogmatic statement with a stalactite of salt. So he proceeded to undertake his own survey. He dropped into five Shoppers stores and asked, "Let me have a pack of P.S. 100's."

Each cashier checked and then answered in effect: "Sorry, sir. We don't sell P.S. 100's."

At the sixth store, Koffler simply asked, "Let me have a pack of Peter Stuyvesants." The cashier knew instantly what he wanted.

At the next board meeting, Koffler told his fellow directors of his personal survey. "With due respect, I think we're off on the wrong track here," he said. "You're advertising one thing and the product has a totally different name on the package."

Alas, they didn't listen. The campaign flopped, showing little market penetration.

"Needless to say," says Koffler, "they don't try to sell Peter Stuyvesants that way anymore."

Koffler had better luck with his advertising campaigns for Shoppers. But there it was Koffler who had the last say. Besides, as he readily acknowledges, his consultants happened to be smart professionals who can and could do what they told him he should do.

CHAPTER TWELVE

Wow! Gung Ho!
Let's Go Advertise!

Closeup of Santa Claus: he is seated in his living room in front of the TV set. Beneath his suspenders, he is wearing his favourite T-shirt, the one that says "Hawaii," and he is watching a hockey game.

Enter Mrs. Claus: she looks very much like Bea Arthur, the brassy TV sitcom comedienne of *Maude* and *The Golden Girls* (mainly because she *is* Bea Arthur of *Maude* and *The Golden Girls*).

"Nicky, go warm up the sled," she says. "I want you to take me to the Shoppers Drug Mart Christmas Money Saver Sale."

Santa, engrossed in the game, shrugs off her demand. "Just tell me what you want and I'll have the elves make it up in the morning."

Mrs. Claus wags a finger at him. "Those bozos couldn't possibly make it as cheap."

Santa laughs sarcastically: "Ho, ho, ho!"

Mrs. Claus: "You want ho, ho? Look . . ."

Cut to products, as Mrs. Claus recites the bargain prices voice over.

Santa, impressed: "Does the world know about this?"

Mrs. Claus, beaming: "It does now, sweet patootie!"

Cut to Shoppers' mortar-and-pestle logo. Off camera, voices carol the jingle, "You're gonna be happy at Shoppers Drug Mart."

Close with shot of Santa dipping Mrs. Claus backward and kissing her. They turn in an embrace to wish viewers "Happy Christmas."

When variations of this saucy commercial were first shown during the Christmas season of 1984, neither Murray Koffler nor his advertising team expected it to raise the rumpus it did. People either loved or hated the concept and expressed themselves vociferously.

"The script is clever and adult," culture critic Peter Goddard lauded in *The Toronto Star*. "The entire pitch for Shoppers Drug Mart is an instant survival guide for a season determined to smother you in *schmaltz*." Many consumers echoed his praise in an unprecedented barrage of phone calls and letters to Shoppers' central offices across Canada. "I used to zap out commercials, but not this hilarious one," said one admirer. "It's the best Christmas ad I've ever seen." Another fan found it "hysterically funny, especially when she kisses Santa and gets hair in her mouth."

The detractors were equally clamorous. A letter writer to *The Globe and Mail* protested that cherished Christmas symbols were being violated and replaced "with sophisticated, very haughty and simply crude characters." Mr. and Mrs. Claus, she went on to say, were being depicted as "vulgar and obnoxious and give a child a twisted perspective." Others claimed it was sacrilege, an obscene presentation of Santa's private sex life. "As a grandmother," one woman reprimanded Shoppers in an acrid letter, "I wouldn't want my grandchildren viewing it." Still others phoned to denounce Shoppers for taking "the magic" out of Christmas. "You've done a horrible thing," fumed a mother. "You've shown Mrs. Claus as a fat, dumpy slob who swears. My three-year-old son now calls elves bozos! Unless you cancel these Santa put-downs, you can be sure my son will *never* be allowed to go into a Shoppers Drug Mart again."

Shoppers held firm. To be sure, the hugging and kissing have been toned down from the libidinous to the more wholesomely amorous. But Nicky and Mrs. Claus have continued to exchange their domestic Yuletide banter ever since.

The adman responsible for this provocative manner of beating the drum and banging the cymbal on behalf of Shoppers has been a consultant to Koffler for two decades. When he began doing it in 1966, Koffler was about to open his fifth store and was struggling along with an annual advertising budget of $25,000. In 1987, the Shoppers chain embraced more than 575 stores, and to stimulate public awareness of its goods and services it spent $35 million on media advertising; another $8 million was budgeted under the catch-all heading of "promotion." The chief adman involved is Norman Kert; he is president of Kert Advertising Limited. And besides producing fifteen pieces of advertising for Shoppers, which have won awards both nationally and internationally, he has achieved something of a record. For an advertising agency to represent a client for more than twenty years is considered phenomenal in the fickle and too often cutthroat world of advertising.

But then Norman Kert is something of a phenomenon. He appears perfectly suited to play the role of the jaunty, persuasive, carnation-lapelled hero of the Broadway musical, *The Music Man*. Now fifty-three, he is six feet three and lean as a soda straw, a former radio announcer from Ottawa who wears sporty clothes and a button pinned in his lapel that proclaims: "RESULTS." In a similar fashion, a single word is emblazoned on the huge billboard on the northeast corner of Yonge Street and Eglinton Avenue diagonally opposite his fifty-employee offices in the Canada Square skyscraper building. Towering on top of the name and address of his firm in hot-pink letters ten feet tall is the single word: "SIZZLE." It's an attention-getter that refers to the well-known advertising axiom: "Don't sell the steak; sell the sizzle." Kert sells the sizzle *and* the steak and does it with pizzazz. He refers to Koffler as a "wower," and he explains what that term means this way: "When Murray expounds a good idea, he fires you up and you feel wowed by him. And when you present a good advertising idea to Murray, he wows right back: 'Wow! I'm all gung ho for that! Let's go for it!'"

The two wowers hit it off beautifully at their first meeting. Kert had left Ottawa in 1966 determined to launch his own advertising agency in big-time Toronto. He believed in the personal approach. He wrote no letters. But for five months, with a directory of national advertisers under his arm, he knocked on doors, introduced himself, and tried to sell himself.

One blustery day in February, when he was feeling low, he was bucked up by a phone call from Koffler. "Stuart Brandy, the station manager of CKEY, suggested you for an assignment," said Koffler. "I called 'EY for some radio time to promote the opening of our fifth drugstore – a giant one at Dufferin and Lawrence. Stu advised me not to do it myself, but instead to get this young hotshot Kert just starting up his own agency. Can you get together with me for a talk?"

"You bet," said Kert, aflame with hope.

"Look, I'm very busy at the store. Any chance you can come over to my home at half past nine tonight?"

"Believe me, I can!"

Kert arrived punctually at Koffler's splendid ranch-style house at 23 Beechwood Avenue in north Toronto. "I had never heard of him before, but even then I was struck by the aura he conveys of being a man of substance," recalls Kert. "It's a beautifully decorated spread, and I remember him pointing at various mementoes and paintings in his den, and I thought, 'This man is going to be, or already is, *extremely* successful.'"

Koffler, in turn, was impressed by the samples of Kert's ads and the personality of the man. He now sums him up in three phrases: "Very personable. Very original. A very *decent* guy. He still is."

Their interview ended with Koffler saying, "Your stuff looks very good. So we'll hire you on a one-shot basis to do the radio campaign for the store opening."

Kert astounded him by raising his hand in protest. "No, I can't do that. To do a good job, I have to understand your business. And I have to work for a *total* company."

Koffler arched his brows. "Let me think it over," he said.

Kert remembers thinking as he left, "My gawd! What have I done? Here's my chance for a big Toronto account. Did I blow it?"

He spent a sleepless night, climaxed by a phone call from Koffler at half past eight next morning.

"You know, you're absolutely right," said Koffler. "You have to do the whole thing. You're hired."

And so began a relationship that is not, as Kert puts it, "the kind of master-slave liaison you often get in the advertising game." It has been a very intimate collaboration. At the outset, it consisted of Kert, running a "one-man shop," preparing ads single-handedly for Koffler's "two-man shop" – namely, the two desks side by side in the cubicle of an office that Koffler shared with his administrative lieutenant, Jack Gwartz, in back of the drugstore on Dufferin at Lawrence.

It was there that Kert and Koffler put their heads together and produced the copy for the first Shoppers' radio commercial. It was folksy. It stressed the variety of merchandise selling at low prices. And its frenetic introduction, to use the Madison Avenue phrase, came over like *Gangbusters*:

"Fantastic! Great! Just terrific! Wow! These are just some of the reactions you'll hear from people who visit Shoppers Drug Mart. Reason: it's really something. Rows and rows of drugs, vitamins, health and beauty aids . . . Every type of cosmetics and records and toys. Thousands of things packed to the rafters . . . Because we're the largest drugstore in Canada, we buy more at lower prices and save you more every day . . . Our prescription counter is big enough to give you fast and expert service . . . Bring the whole family, even if you're just sight-seeing! Shoppers Drug Mart, Dufferin and Lawrence."

Kert and Koffler got along so nicely because they agreed on most aspects of advertising. The philosophy of both is straightforward. When making a presentation to a client, Kert asserts: "We're in the business of helping your business grow." He maintains that advertising is not a science, but a persuasion, and that the most persuasive advertising is a good product.

Koffler justly declares: "I've always had an instinctive feel for advertising. I'm down to earth enough to have a grasp of what information the public wants to know about a product." He adds, "With all my soul, I detest the word 'hype.' It connotes that you're trying to put something over on the public. And that corner-cutting is something that any retailer of integrity would never, ever do. I put the word 'hype' in the same category as 'There's a sucker born every minute.' Sure, there are some people who are gullible. But it takes a crook to make suckers out of the gullible."

Koffler took pride of authorship in creating on his own the original print ads for Shoppers. These were the series of "Let's Talk Facts" fliers he wrote to explain why his stores in the Don Mills area were unique.

"What do you think of them?" asked Koffler when Kert first joined him.

"They're terrific," said Kert. "I wouldn't change a word. That personal touch is what makes them so credible. Let's keep running them."

Kert added an additional personalized touch later when Koffler contributed an editorial to Shoppers' four-page circulars containing straight price information. To lace it with an extra dash of authenticity, Kert suggested that the editorials ought to be accompanied by a photo of Koffler.

"You really think so?" asked Koffler.

"Why not? Since you invented the Shoppers concept, they're entitled to know who you are."

"It so happens I have a photo engraving of myself at home," said Koffler, running out of the office. "I'll drive there and be back in a jiffy with the photo plate."

Kert recalls with amusement, "Murray was in such a hurry, he got a ticket for speeding."

But Kert recalls with amazement how thorough-going Koffler was as an editor of the advertising copy that Kert had written. "Murray was meticulous about the most finite of details," says Kert. "He'd sit and rewrite and make sure every single word in the ad was exactly the word he wanted. And in those early days it never mattered how long it took to do it. You never had a sense that he had some place else to go."

Kert remembers one Friday night when they were both seated at Koffler's desk in the cubbyhole behind the store working for more than an hour to find the *mot juste* for a newspaper ad. Suddenly Koffler glanced at his watch and said, "Jeez, I just remembered! We're supposed to be driving north for the weekend. And Marvelle and the kids are waiting for me outside in the station wagon."

Koffler's editing of advertising layout and design was equally painstaking. For Gordon Stromberg, vice-president of advertising for Shoppers and Kert's long-time liaison with the company, Koffler's guidance was like a second education in commercial art. Stromberg is the merry-andrew of Shoppers, a forty-seven-year-old irreverent wit, known to everybody as "Baldy" because of his tumbleweed spiral of unruly brown hair and scimitar moustache. A graduate of the Ontario College of Art, he was advertising manager for Plaza drugstores when the chain was taken over by Koffler in 1968.

"Advertising means putting your company's best foot forward in the marketplace, and Murray knew exactly what foot that was," recalls Stromberg. For the first six months Koffler discussed with him daily how to switch from the old-fashioned format for fliers favoured by the Plaza chain and adopt Koffler's formula: "Simplicity. Simplicity. Simplicity. No frou-frou. No clutter of prices bursting out of exploding balloons. Put figures in clean boxes and words in type that's clearly legible. Remember, a straight line and simplicity of design are things of beauty."

Right from the outset, Koffler, Stromberg, and Kert agreed on the strategy of positioning Shoppers as a leader in offering low prices. Mitch Leigh, composer of the Broadway musical *Man of La Mancha*, was hired to write a musical theme that pointed up the radio commercial message, "At Shoppers Drug Mart, we're the one that saves you money." Newspaper ads featured a thermometer, the most recent total number of prescriptions sold by all Shoppers stores, and the slogan, "At Shoppers, we've learned how to mix good medicine at low prices on everything." With the opening of the one hundredth store, linking the chain from Saint John, New Brunswick, to Burnaby, British Columbia, photos of all 100 were displayed in magazine ads, and billboards near the site of each store alerted motorists: "Can you afford to pass by our everyday low prices?"

Curiously, Kert had a difficult time persuading Koffler to advertise on television. The adman felt it was an ideal medium for selling a Shoppers store as the product itself. Kert painted tantalizing visions of how the wide aisles, sparkling white dispensaries, and serried rows of elixirs, potions, and confections would be exhibited invitingly for a coast-to-coast audience for the first time. Yet Koffler, usually responsive to another's word-painting, stubbornly resisted the new medium until 1970.

Even then, according to Kert's dramatic recounting of events, Koffler was adamant to the bitter end, imploring the adman to ditch plans for spending the seemingly outrageous sum of $250,000 for a year of sixty-second commercials. Kert, requiring signed approval to buy television time for the launching of the national campaign, was told to consult Koffler at his Beechwood Avenue home.

The adman arrived at six o'clock that evening to find his client flat on his back in bed. It turned out that Koffler was recuperating from a back injury, the result of a nasty tumble from one of his horses at Jokers Hill Farm. While his wife Marvelle served him dinner in bed, Koffler read over the documents and, after a long deliberation, finally signed them.

"I was just about to leave, when Murray pulled a reverse Colombo on me," recalls Kert. "You know how they used to show Colombo, the TV series detective, about to go out the door, his raincoat swaying. Then he turns around to face the suspect of the crime and says accusingly, 'Oh, just one more thing . . .'

"Well, this was a reversal of that tactic. I had just gotten to the door to make my exit when Murray said, 'Oh, just a minute. I have one more thing to say . . .'"

Kert looked at him in puzzlement.

"Are you *really* sure we ought to go ahead with this enormous TV outlay?" asked Koffler.

"Absolutely," said Kert. "I'm positive it'll change the whole sales picture for Shoppers."

"Well, just a moment."

Then, to Kert's aghast bewilderment, he saw the pajamaed Koffler crawl painfully out of bed. "Somehow Murray managed to crawl over to a dresser," recalls Kert. "He pulled out a newspaper clipping. He handed it to me. And he groaned, 'Read this!'"

Kert obeyed. It was an article from the op-ed page of the *New York Times* and it questioned the use of television as an advertising medium.

"See!" said Koffler. "How can you ask me to go against the judgement of the mighty *New York Times*?"

"Don't worry, Murray," said Kert, helping his client clamber back into bed. "What the *Times* says may be true for the U.S., but not for Canada."

Recalling the event, Kert now says, "I then got the hell out of his bedroom fast before he could change his mind."

Television swiftly transformed Shoppers Drug Mart into a household name across Canada. The first two commercials established separate themes. One opened with a camera shot of a pharmacist smartly jacketed behind a prescription counter. Viewers saw fingers typing a label to be put on a vial. They heard a bouncy little Mitch Leigh musical theme blend in with the chattering sound of the typewriter keys and serve as counterpoint to the message: "Shoppers Drug Mart is first and foremost a drugstore . . . *Dee-dee-dum!*" The camera slowly panned from the dispensary at the back of the store to the activity in front. It ended with a female shopper getting change from the cashier and depositing the money in her change purse.

A second commercial was likewise strikingly visual in a pharmaceutical setting. A pair of twenty-five-cent coins were dumped into a glass of water and began fizzing like Alka Seltzer. But unlike Alka Seltzer, the two quarters land on the bottom of the glass and remain standing upright and intact on their rims. The voice of CBC news announcer Rex Loring delivered the message that ended with the line, "Shoppers Drug Mart is your prescription to fight inflation."

But as price-slashing discounters crowded into the market, it became clear to Kert that Shoppers could no longer honestly profess to be the low-price leader across the board, proclaiming, "We're the one that saves you money." Consequently, there was a gradual change in emphasis. While "everyday low prices" were still an attraction, they were not the *only* attraction. Over the years, the advertising campaigns veered into a variety of directions. As the number of stores increased nationally, the slogans switched to convenience of location ("Near enough to save you money"), patriotic flag-waving ("Shoppers Drug Mart, Canada's drugstore"), the broad selection of merchandise ("Everything you want in a drugstore"), and a pleasant environment offering a multitude of services ("You're gonna be happy shopping at Shoppers").

The personalities delivering the advertising messages also changed over the years. Karen Magnussen, Canada's Olympics and world figure-skating champion, although a little shaky at first, became an effective spokesperson for Shoppers' Life brand products. "I love Life!" she exclaimed when extolling the virtues of its "multiple vitamins with minerals as a daily part of my skater's personal fitness plan." While she pirouetted around the ice rink, a chorus sang the jingle:

This is the Life for me,
This is the Life, feeling free!
Life, Life makes it easy to be
What you want to be
This is the Life and I love it!

She was followed by a trio of comely actress-models billed as The Shoppers Three. Wearing red, white, and blue blazers, the basic colours of the drugstore chain, Dorothy Goulah, Cindy Girling, and Christine Cattell were deemed appropriately sexy to "glitz up" commercials for beauty products.

When the Pillsbury Dough Boy and the Man from Glad were in their heyday, Kert created a gimmicky spokesperson named Little SDM. He was actually an apple-cheeked, athletic-looking Canadian actor named David Ferry. Clad in a sweatsuit and reduced by a camera process to a midget-sized nine inches, he was shown leaping nimbly from shelf to shelf selling products at a giant Shoppers sale. An off-camera voice boomed: "Shoppers Drug Mart gives you more . . . Our biggest sale of the year . . . It's big, really big . . . It's huge . . ."

Without question, Shoppers' most hugely successful spokesperson has been that peppery wisecracker, Bea Arthur. The script writer who feeds her those acerbic lines is Allen Schopp, associate creative director for Kert's advertising agency, a droll, self-effacing fellow who looks and talks like a pipe-smoking Woody Allen. He and his colleagues set out in 1984 looking for a name performer with a personality strong enough to combat the "zap syndrome" – the growing tendency of viewers to flick off commercials with an electronic zapper device. "Bea Arthur, with her mouthy *Maude* image, seemed ideal," he recalls. When she flew to Toronto to do the commercials, she turned out to be surprisingly shy, with no prima-donna airs whatsoever. "She'd do a take," he recalls, "and then come over to me and ask, 'Was that okay? Are you sure? If you're not happy, I'd be glad to do it again.'"

As a foil, Schopp created an offbeat character named Maurice, a French-Canadian chauffeur who submits cheerfully to her bullying. Hired for that sidekick role was Derek McGrath, a Canadian character actor with credits on such series as *The Mary Tyler Moore Show* and *Cheers*. "With his chauffeur's cap, his moustachio, and cute accent, Maurice has become a cult figure," says Schopp. "Together, they took off like *Gangbusters*."

The Bea Arthur commercials were indeed an instant hit. They won six of the "Bessies" awarded at the advertising industry's 1985 Canadian Television Commercial Festival. More important, they won her immediate identification as Shoppers' official spokesperson. Schopp once drove to the Toronto airport to pick her up and was pleased to hear that the immigration officer had greeted her, "Oh, you're Bea Arthur, the Shoppers Drug Mart lady." He was delighted because her name was bracketed with the commercial rather than her prominence as the star of either *Maude or The Golden Girls*.

That recognition factor was verified by "focus groups," trade jargon for the Veritas consumer research service, which carried a lot of weight in influencing the advertising decisions of Koffler and his management team. The focus groups each consisted of twelve consumers in Toronto and Vancouver, chosen according to age, income, and other demographic criteria. They are each paid $50 to respond to in-depth questions by a moderator; meanwhile, the ad agency observers eavesdrop unseen behind a one-way-view glass wall. Remarkably, every person in the focus groups identified Bea Arthur as the Shoppers Drug Mart lady. In contrast, when asked about Robert Young, they weren't sure whether he was the spokesman for IDA, Guardian, or other drugstore chains.

However, the groups did offer two criticisms of Bea Arthur. Some were miffed because she was an American rather than a Canadian; others were put off because she was too caustic. The agency was quick to respond. Pam Hyatt, a Canadian comedienne, was hired to play the role of Arthur's young homemaker friend named Brenda. Schopp then deliberately softened Arthur's hard-edged public persona. She came across in new commercials as a witty yet kindly aunt figure escorting Brenda around and demonstrating that Shoppers offered "everything you want in a drugstore."

Some of Murray Koffler's most innovative concepts have been in a peripheral but vital area of advertising. They have been designed to bolster the role of the drugstore in the community. Koffler genuinely believes in promoting public health, which embraces not only medicine and pharmacy but also nutrition, fitness, sports, and even beauty in the cosmetic sense. True, some of this concern has proved to be good business in that it has promoted public goodwill toward Shoppers. But at the same time his projects have provided a worthy public service; or, as Koffler puts it proudly, "They take you beyond just making a buck." Here are just a handful of the pace-setting promotions launched by Koffler on behalf of Shoppers, which led to his winning in 1986 the Distinguished Retailer of the Year Award presented by the Retail Council of Canada:

• Shoppers was the first to promote the use of tamper-proof caps on prescription containers. Since then patent medicine bottles and some household products are similarly safe-guarded from misuse by children.

- It was the first Canadian corporate sponsor of the Jerry Lewis muscular dystrophy telethon. Following Koffler's lead, Loblaws' supermarkets and McDonald's hamburger restaurants co-sponsored the telecasts, which previously were strictly U.S. events.
- It was the first to display prophylactics openly on self-serve shelves and to disseminate birth control literature as well. It took that bold stand in 1971 on the urging of public health nurses who were worried about the increasing number of young unwed mothers. And it courageously continued to do so, despite protests from pressure groups claiming that Shoppers was condoning promiscuity.
- It was the first to set up Consumer Health Education Centres (called CHECs) in drugstores. Free pamphlets are provided on subjects ranging from cancer to healthy nutrition.
- It was the first to sponsor free blood-pressure checkup clinics. Its booth at Toronto's Canadian National Exhibition, manned by medical personnel from seventeen hospitals, attracted as many as 60,000 people who had free tests.
- It was the first to establish Salute to Senior Citizen Day in drugstores. Twice yearly, seniors are invited to store parties, where they are fed coffee and baked goodies, are allowed 15 per cent off all merchandise purchased, and participate in festivities that may include grandparent beauty pageants, bingo games, Newfoundland fiddlers, gay nineties saloon dancers, seniors' choirs, free straw hats and fresh carnations, and holiday trips to Florida as raffle prizes.
- It was the first pharmacy chain to become a national support-er of youth amateur sports. Under supervision of a national sports director, each store provides free Shoppers Drug Mart sweaters, advertising, and coaching for local teams compet-ing in athletic events that run the gamut from hockey to soc-cer, from broomball to baseball.

Koffler has long recognized that cosmetics must be adver-tised and promoted differently than the other commodities mass-merchandised in drugstores, and Shoppers now has cornered 18 per cent of the Canadian cosmetic market. It grosses more than $150 million a year from the products sold in its elegant beauty departments, with their smoked-glass, art-deco decor, and photo blowups of chic models. Currently, cosmetics account for 10 per cent of the chain's business (with a high profit margin second only to prescriptions). And with the beauty departments fast expanding into fashion pantyhose, jewelry, and other fashion accessories, they are expected to be responsible eventually for 20 per cent of the company's total sales.

Koffler realized, with cosmetics, that a feeling of excitement, fun, and fantasy must be sold. In the 1970s, he began by publishing a glossy Shoppers Drug Mart *Beauty* magazine. It has since become an even glossier, four-colour bimonthly called *Images*; more than 300,000 copies are given away free with beauty product purchases. The articles offer tips on everything from jogging to hair tinting, including advice on how to shave one's legs gracefully and on wearing adhesive, disposable bras.

Koffler remembers vividly when he decided to make a major entry into the perfumed world of cosmetics; he continues to treasure two souvenirs that remind him of that decision. One is a gold pen that bears the inscription: "To Murray B. Koffler, Fabergé-Shoppers Olympics Promotion, 1976." It was presented to him by Basil (Baz) Weedon, who in 1976 was the debonair and promotion-conscious president of Fabergé of Canada Limited. Koffler was then board chairman of Shoppers and wasn't too much involved in buying for the chain. Nevertheless, he was immediately interested when Weedon approached him one day with a promotional deal. To commemorate the 1976 Olympics, Weedon was packaging a special Olympics kit consisting of Brut toiletries for men and Tigress fragrances for women. It would be promoted as the kit used by Canadian Olympic team members and would retail for $9.95. Would Shoppers Drug Mart like to purchase perhaps $100,000 worth, which would bring Shoppers a handsome profit margin of 40 per cent?

"A super promotion," said Koffler. "It's so terrific we'd like to have it as an exclusive for Shoppers."

"Well, we don't give exclusives," said Weedon. "We intend asking department stores across Canada to participate in the promotion, too."

"How many kits do you have?" asked Koffler.

"A million dollars' worth."

"What if we buy the whole million dollars' worth?"

"Then you'll have an exclusive."

"But if we handled it exclusively, we'd be saving you money," Koffler negotiated with him. "You wouldn't have to ship the product to all those other companies. Neither would you have to spend money on co-op advertising with anybody else. Right?"

"True," Weedon agreed.

"Well then, we would want to pass along that saving to our customers. That means we'd want a much better buy than the 40 per cent off your proposed retail price. What's the best deal you can offer us, so we can sell it at a cheaper price of $6.95?"

"I'd have to work that out with our accountancy bean counters."

"If you can, it's a deal," said Koffler, shaking his hand.

Weedon returned a week later with the appropriate numbers nicely worked out. Now the New York-based international president of Fabergé, Weedon recalls that Koffler's fellow executives objected to him negotiating the deal without consulting them. But Koffler was obdurate. Weedon recalls how Koffler walked out of the boardroom, telling the others, "The decision has already been made. We shook hands on it."

"I could have kissed Murray," Weedon now says. "It was the biggest promotion ever made in Canada with a single cosmetic company. Murray literally signed a check for $1 million. So that's why I presented him with a gold pen as a memento of the historic occasion."

Today reactions differ on the question of whether the historic promotional deal was a success. Despite an adroit advertising campaign orchestrated by Koffler and Kert, only $700,000 of the Olympic kits were sold. Over a period of a year, the Shoppers associates gradually got rid of the remainder of the stock, selling some at bargain rates and returning others to Fabergé.

Koffler smiles now as he fondles the second memento of the cosmetic promotion, a scroll from all of his associates that reads: "Dear Murray. Please remain chairman of the board and let *us* do the buying."

Was the promotion a failure? Koffler doesn't think so. "It's true that $300,000 worth of merchandise was cleared at break-even prices," he says. "But we did sell $700,000 worth at a profit. Equally important, we became a significant force in the cosmetics world. It was our first step toward making the industry accept us as a major player competing with the department stores. Furthermore, it initiated an important change in the attitude of pharmacists. They realized we were big enough to go to cosmetic companies and get special deals. And they woke up to the fact that we were pharmacists and yet at the same time truly in the beauty products business."

Was the advertising campaign a failure? Naturally, Kert, the razzle-dazzle adman, doesn't think so either. Kert likes citing the sagacious remark of John Wanamaker, the illustrious New York department store retailer. When asked, "How successful is your ongoing advertising campaign?", Wanamaker replied: "I figure that 50 per cent of all my advertising works and 50 per cent doesn't. My problem is that I don't know which 50 per cent does the trick."

CHAPTER THIRTEEN

Shoplifters, Pilferers, and Other Pests

O f the many roles he played when building the Shoppers Drug Mart empire, Murray Koffler secretly used to take enormous pride in considering himself a born store detective. In his Walter Mitty fantasy life, he imagined himself to be the Dick Tracy of pharmacy, the demon nemesis of shoplifters. There was nothing scientific about his sleuthing. His built-in detecting talent, as he saw it, was based on personal hunch, intuition, and the hairs on the back of his neck.

"Those hairs, I'd swear, would stiffen up and curl," he now says. "And if I saw somebody walking up and down the aisles, picking up an item, putting it down, and looking around furtively, I was certain of my hunch. I knew instinctively, *'That's going to be a shoplifter!'"*

He was disabused of this certitude one memorable day in 1966 when he observed a youth loitering in his newly opened store at Dufferin and Lawrence. Not only did the hairs on the back of his neck bristle their telltale signal. His suspicion was alerted as well by a vast lump bulging under the youth's coat. "I watch him, and I watch him, and I watch him," recalls Koffler. "His shifty eyes are darting – here, there, everywhere. All of a sudden he turns and sees me watching him. He begins to sprint out."

Koffler lunged forward and grabbed at the bulge and cried out triumphantly, "I gotcha!"

The youth in turn uttered a blood-curdling scream: "Ou-ou-oo-oo-oo-ch!" Then, in an injured tone, he moaned, "Mister, what's the big idea?"

To Koffler's dismay, the suspected culprit exhibited a broken arm that was bandaged and tucked under his coat. "I could see myself being sued for causing injury and false arrest," says Koffler. "I apologized. I presented him with a box of chocolates I snatched from the candy counter. I shook his good left arm. 'Sorry I was so clumsy,' I said. 'I meant to congratulate you. Please forgive my haste. You're the winner of our store-opening contest.'"

Later, mopping the sweat off his brow, Koffler muttered to Arthur Resnick, the associate who operated the store, "I hope this'll be a lesson to all of us. Let's never play amateur detective. And let us never, ever, accost a customer as a shoplifter if we don't have the proper evidence. To stay out of trouble, we'll need trained experts to handle store security."

Not long after this embarrassment, he realized that his chain of self-serve Shoppers stores would provide a shoplifters' paradise. And so, in characteristic Kofflerian style, he became the pharmacy industry's leader in pioneering security safeguards. He invited lawyers, private investigators, members of the police force, and the top security officers from Dominion Stores and Simpsons-Sears to Toronto's Inn on the Park for a one-day, round-table think tank. It was devoted to improving store security procedures. But Koffler didn't call it that. An incorrigible positive thinker, even in matters of crime, he preferred to think in terms of prevention, rather than the apprehension, of thieves. So he called it instead a conference dedicated to constructing a workable "loss prevention" program.

The result was, as he puts it, that "we practically wrote the rule book for crime prevention in the pharmacy industry." He was the first to appoint top executives concerned with nothing but loss prevention. He was also the first to hire and train his chain's own corp of "store detectives." A battalion of more than 300 men and women currently function as the Sherlocks of Shoppers, designated as "in-store investigators."

Their generalissimo, Max Giesbrecht, national director of loss prevention for Shoppers, is a self-effacing man. He refers to the investigators under his command as the "company's silent force." With equal modesty, he refers to himself as "a nondescript-looking fellow." Both understatements are open to question.

Giesbrecht is hardly a colourless fellow. Born in Killarney, Manitoba, the son of an innkeeper, he is a husky, bullnecked, square-jawed ex-Mountie in his fifties and has the commanding presence of a chief of police and the ingratiating manner of a diplomat. Though he protests, "I'm no James Bond," the fact is that he has the unassailable credentials that would enable him to play the role of a master spy. For twenty years he headed the RCMP's Intelligence Service, which meant he was literally in charge of Canada's security. From there he moved to the post of corporate head of security for Dominion Stores Ltd., and then was hired by Shoppers Drug Mart.

He likewise conveys a false impression when he implies that he heads a force of invisible mutes. To be sure, they wear no uniforms and carry no guns and sometimes use disguises to mask their identity. Nevertheless, they are the chief combatants in a loss-prevention program that costs the company $4.8 million a year. They are paid to wage a war against an army of shoplifters, dope addicts, rubbydubs, prescription forgers, embezzlers, and various other slippery-fingered pilferers on both sides of the counter who help account for Shoppers' annual loss of a whopping $18 million–1 per cent of sales–due to "inventory shrinkage."

Thirty per cent of that shrinkage–$5.4 million–is the handiwork of shoplifters. The most publicized of store crooks, they are known in the trade as miscreants who help themselves to "five-finger discounts." They walk out of the store concealing merchandise in shopping bags, maternity clothes, oversize bloomers, double girdles with kangaroo pouches, and cleverly designed packages with false bottoms.

At least 50 per cent of the shrinkage–well over $12.6 million–is caused by internal theft. As Giesbrecht phrases it in his speeches to associates, "It means your employees are putting

KOFFLER GETS AROUND

Busy-as-a-bee Koffler hired a jet plane to fly 3,000 miles to three Shoppers store openings in Winnipeg, Windsor, and Toronto on August 12, 1970.

Skipper Koffler at the helm of his ocean-going, fifty-three-feet-long yacht, *Age Of Aquarius*, sailing in the Mediterranean in 1975.

Koffler atop a tank in the Sinai Desert, at the head of a United Jewish Appeal emergency mission, following Israel's 1967 Six Day War.

Koffler (left) rides with the hounds as a member of the Toronto and North York Hunt, North America's second oldest fox-hunting club, with Master Michael Sifton and Galen Weston at Jokers Hill, 1983.

Koffler with Captain Mark Phillips, then fiancé of Princess Anne, inspecting Jokers Hill horse trials course in 1973.

Prince Philip was Koffler's weekend guest at Jokers Hill in August, 1973, when officiating at the international equestrian competition known as the Three Day Event.

Marvelle and Murray play host to Princess Alexandra at 1970
opening of London Inn on the Park.

Murray, in a rented
morning coat and silk
topper, and Marvelle,
in a spiffy new outfit,
leave the London Inn
on the Park for the
wedding of Princess
Anne and Captain
Mark Phillips.

On November 14, 1973, standing amid the nobility of Europe, in the second row, eighth and ninth from the left, are Marvelle and Murray at the wedding of Princess Anne and Mark Phillips. They were also invited by the Queen to the wedding party at Buckingham Palace.

Koffler, with his back to camera on extreme right, in company with a Canadian mission, meets Prime Minister David Ben-Gurion in his Negev den in Israel, 1968.

Koffler has a tête-à-tête with Israeli Prime Minister Golda Meir and Chancellor Meyer Weisgal of the Weizmann Institute, 1976.

Koffler is greeted by Israeli Prime Minister
Menachem Begin during the Lebanese War in
June, 1982, before departure for Beirut.

As a long-time supporter of the Holy Land and its leaders, Koffler
is received warmly by Israeli President Ephraim Katzir.

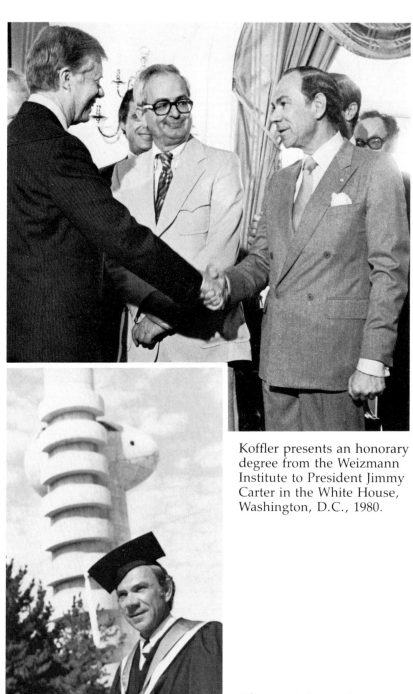

Koffler presents an honorary degree from the Weizmann Institute to President Jimmy Carter in the White House, Washington, D.C., 1980.

After receiving an honorary degree from the Weizmann Institute, Koffler stands near the $8 million Koffler Accelerator in Rehovot, Israel, 1976.

Chatting with John Diefenbaker at the 1973 Toronto Negev Dinner, where the Canadian Prime Minister was the evening's honoured guest.

With his friend, Lord Marcus Sieff, of Britain, long-time board chairman of the Weizmann Institute of Science. Koffler took over that globetrotting post in 1987.

Governor General Jules Leger confers the
nation's highest honour, the Order of Canada,
on Koffler at an investiture ceremony in
Rideau Hall, Ottawa, in 1977.

Entertainer Harry Belafonte, accompanied by his wife, is presented
with the Israel Medal by Koffler at a 1973 Israel Bonds Rally.

Koffler escorted Canadian Prime Minister
Lester Pearson to the Weizmann Institute in
Rehovot for the 1968 establishment of a Lester
Pearson Chair in Protein Sciences.

Escorting renowned painter Marc Chagall for an honorary degree
at Weizmann Institute, 1979.

With Henry Kissinger at the Aspen Conference on
Science for Peace in West Berlin in 1982.

Koffler with British Prime Minister Harold Wilson when Wilson
received an honorary degree at the Weizmann, 1971.

Koffler has a friendly match with tennis champion
Vitas Gueralitis in 1978.

Koffler entertains Isaac Stern and the violinist's son at a 1976
Canada-Israel Cultural Foundation dinner.

While Toronto Mayor Phil Givens looks on, Koffler presents a Weizmann Institute Award in Sciences and Humanities to comedian Danny Kaye.

Murray and Marvelle, while in Paris for a 1978 World United Jewish Appeal Conference, are guests of Baron and Baroness Guy de Rothschild.

Koffler, shown with imposing University of Toronto mace, was awarded an honorary Doctor of Laws degree by his alma mater in 1985. It recognized his philanthropy, especially the forthcoming $6 million Koffler Institute of Pharmacy Management, his legacy to the profession.

At the 1986 Koffler tribute dinner, his five children presented him with this portrait by photographer Yousuf Karsh of Ottawa. It will hang in the foyer of the Koffler Institute of Pharmacy Management, "to inspire all pharmacists of the future who enter its doors."

their hands into your pockets and walking out with your profits." Most often the culprits are cashiers. They squirrel away their swag in commodious panties and longjohns, shoes, sleeves, socks, match flaps, ingeniously contrived money belts, and, until Shoppers banned them, pockets in their uniforms.

The other 20 per cent of shrinkage – $3.6 million – is attributed to pricing and bookkeeping errors (and sometimes calculated embezzling). It may also be due to accidental breakage of stock (and sometimes the scheming of stock boys inside and merchandise salesmen from outside who collaborate in a nimble sleight-of-hand and thus perform a stock vanishing act).

As a rule of thumb, Giesbrecht estimates that if a Shoppers store grosses $2 million annually, the store loses $60,000 from shoplifting alone. His figures show that only 10,000 shoplifters are apprehended annually in what is called a "pinch." It means a minority of approximately one out of every twenty pilferers is actually arrested and charged with theft by an in-store investigator. The majority are merely "stopped and burned": the investigator politely yet firmly makes minor nuisance cases aware that they're being watched. A suspect seen slipping a chocolate bar or a comb into a pocket or a purse is asked in a businesslike manner, "Would you like that item placed in a bag by the cashier on your way out?" Certain exceptional cases – those who seem senile, drunk, or mentally ill or children under the age of twelve – are usually reprimanded and told to take their business elsewhere.

Otherwise, if the shoplifter has been clearly seen in the act and then walks out of the store without having paid for the purloined item, the investigator will make a citizen's arrest. Offenders caught with the stolen item in their possession are escorted courteously to a security office in back of the store. They are informed of their rights to obtain legal counsel. Then the police are summoned and they are charged with theft according to Section 449 of the Criminal Code of Canada.

The case is heard by a judge at a provincial court, whose jurisdiction enables him to rule on alleged theft of property valued at less than $1,000. If it's a first offence, the chances are they will be let off with a discharge and a warning. Frequent offenders may be fined, sometimes jailed, and often assigned to do community work as penance. But the real punishment is the trauma of being guilty of a criminal charge – especially if, as is common in smaller communities, your case is reported in the local newspaper. The stigma as well as the shock of facing family, friends, and business colleagues may alter a person's life.

Almost invariably, every apprehended shoplifter claims it's a first-time theft – even if the investigator has detected him or her in action for a week to establish a pattern. A good many claim kleptomania, which is medically defined as a persistent neurotic impulse to steal without an economic motive. If they submit to the court a letter from a psychiatrist signifying that they are being treated for their mental aberration, judges tend to dismiss their cases.

Self-confessed kleptomaniacs who have been pinched by Shoppers investigators embrace virtually every profession. Some of the more unusual cases include an Ottawa diplomat who stole White Owl cigars; a policeman who casually stuck pens in his uniform; a corporate lawyer who at first claimed huffily that $150 bottles of Opium perfume had accidentally slipped into his briefcase; a professor who pleaded absent-mindedness when purloining a whole box of "Happy Birthday Dear Mother" greeting cards; a brain surgeon who filched girly magazines; a nightclub stripper with a penchant for panty-hose; a nun who pocketed condoms; a priest who secreted packages of cough drops under his collar; and a psychiatrist who had a mania for lifting Estée Lauder blushers and eyeliners and confessed tearfully that he himself treated klep-tomaniacs as patients.

Giesbrecht regards with a sceptical eye psychiatric theories pertaining to kleptomania. A recent study made by a Toronto Freudian, for example, maintains it's a mania triggered by a personal sense of loss. Supposedly the kleptomaniac craves attention and secretly harbours a desire to be caught, thus providing a sense of excitement.

Giesbrecht believes the study is too broadly generalized and its case studies limited. He can think of only one case in his experience that adhered to that traditional pattern. It involved a wealthy dowager, a major shareholder in a well-known corporation, whose husband was president of the company. Their joint annual income totalled $500,000. She had everything to lose by shoplifting. Yet she was caught trying to steal a cheap pair of nylons. "The investigator phoned me because he couldn't handle the situation," recalls Giesbrecht. "Evidently she had stolen thousands of dollars worth of goods and voluntarily wanted to make restitution."

Giesbrecht said to the investigator, "Tell the woman to go home and make a list of everything she could remember having stolen. Then tell her to come see me in the morning."

She arrived in Giesbrecht's office next day with her husband. He seemed pathetically distraught. She, on the other hand, was surprisingly elated. "Suddenly I feel free!" she exclaimed to Giesbrecht. "It's like a load you've lifted off my back."

She turned out to be a woman who had been bored to tears by her staid high-society existence. How did she begin her new life in petty crime? Seeking a thrill while wintering in Palm Springs, she had once shoplifted a trinket from a jewelry store. "I got such a high!" she said, her eyes glowing. "It was like a rush, a drug fix, like being intoxicated on champagne."

After that, she shoplifted every time she entered a store and couldn't seem to stop. Now that she had been caught in the act and absolved, she felt immensely relieved. She could stop playing the game.

"I used to see her quite a bit in public – though never at a Shoppers store," says Giesbrecht. "She always made a point of taking me aside and thanking me again for the help I'd given her."

Giesbrecht acknowledges that many so-called kleptomaniacs seem to get a thrill out of "beating the system," especially if they somehow feel wronged by society or its authority figures. This is reflected in the vindictive gesture made by many confirmed shoplifters. As soon as they get outside, about

200 feet or so from the entrance of a Shoppers store, they take out their plunder from their pockets or shopping bags. Then they look at it and gloat.

By and large, though, he thinks that old-fashioned greed – the desire to get away with something for nothing – is the prime motivation. The gall of retail predators has long ceased to shock him ever since he began policing security for Dominion Stores.

"We had under a surveillance this well-dressed couple who'd come into the store and buy a sandwich," he recalls. "Then they'd wander around with a shopping cart in the fruit department, helping themselves to their dessert. But this time he broke his dental bridge while biting into an apple. You know what he did? He had the nerve to call the manager and threaten to sue. We just put him out of the store and told him to shop down the street, putting Loblaws out of business."

The coolest customers from the upscale social set he ever encountered at Shoppers were a man-and-wife team of shoplifters. He was a senior executive in his late forties and earned well over $140,000 a year travelling around the world for his Montreal-based company. He had married a stylish blonde in her mid-twenties who worked as a fashion buyer and had a taste for high living. He built a large home for her and drove her about in a new Rolls-Royce. But after a year or so of this extravagant tossing around of money like confetti, they went over their accounts and realized they were over their heads in debt.

"So they decided to shoplift in a methodical, business-like manner," says Giesbrecht. "She would steal clothes. He would steal the drugstore and grocery items."

The Shoppers investigator ultimately apprehended the husband after he had walked out of the store with a $70 bottle of cologne hidden in his grocery shopping bag. The man confessed all and pleaded with Giesbrecht to drop charges because of the couple's elite social status. Giesbrecht refused. The resulting police record and $25 fine drastically altered their lavish lifestyle. "Immigration department computers are very quick to pick up our convictions," says Giesbrecht.

"Apparently he had to confess his sins to his superiors and he wasn't able to travel as a jet-setter anymore."

Shoppers investigators use psychological persuasion instead of guns, and armed shoplifters are rare. One of the most fiercesome that Giesbrecht remembers was a muscular fellow who, when frisked by police, proved to be a "regular Rambo" wanted for armed robbery. He had concealed on his person an arsenal that included a revolver, two knives, and a machete strapped to his leg. In the Shoppers security back room, though, he was as tame as a pussycat.

Drug addicts are a different breed of cat. When in need of a fix, they can be a vicious lot, or, as Giesbrecht puts it, "more than a little flaky." In Vancouver, the centre of Canada's illicit narcotics traffic, one resorted to spraying a can of Mace in the eyes of a Shoppers pharmacist. In another instance, when a pharmacist drew out a club from his narcotics safe and tried to beat off a pair of armed drug bandits, they "kneecapped" him – that is, they shot him in the kneecap.

Nevertheless, Vancouver pharmacists continue to be remarkably brave when assaulted. Craig Lum, who is fifty-six, a seemingly gentle pharmacist, takes pride in refusing to kowtow to drug-crazed desperadoes. He works in the dispensary of John Parker's Shoppers store located in the working-class district of North Vancouver; until steel bars were recently installed fronting the door entrance, drug bandits broke in through the plate glass window six times in less than a month.

Lum put up a heroic defence when a bandit, pretending to limp on crutches, brandished an ugly-looking knife one morning and demanded his supply of Dilaudid painkiller tablets, a heroin substitute containing hydromorphine, worth $50 a pill on the streets. Lum retaliated by grabbing a pair of scissors. "If you don't get the hell out of here fast," he said, "I'll come after you."

Startled by this reversal of roles, the bandit threw aside his crutches, bolted down the aisle like a scared rabbit, and dashed straight through the door, smashing the plate glass window. Lum raced after him, gripping the scissors like a dagger, and before the addict roared off in his getaway car, the pharmacist ripped off the tape masking the licence plate and recorded the number. When the bandit was thus traced, Lum was happy to identify him in the police lineup.

Concealed surveillance cameras are used deftly to check up on cashiers suspected of dipping their hands into the till for their own enrichment. They are, of course, the employees with the most convenient access to the company's cash and hence are most vulnerable to temptation. A record embezzlement was made by a sweet, grandmotherly cashier in a Maritimes Shoppers store, who confessed when caught that she had peculated $14,000 over the years; she made restitution for that amount.

Some cashiers indulge in "sweethearting" – not ringing up the immense purchases of friends and relatives. Others develop a "Robin Hood" complex – rationalizing that they are stealing from a rich corporation and then giving away their booty to needy charities, including themselves. The excuses most commonly given by cashiers for their thievery are: (1) a recent divorce; (2) jilted by a boyfriend; (3) beaten up by a husband; (4) going through menopause; (5) in need of money for a child's illness; (6) outwitting a boss felt to be underpaying her. But the real reason, according to Giesbrecht, can be summed up in three words: "It's so easy."

To make it less easy, his investigators play a cat-and-mouse game that involves setting up system monitors in stores being drained of an exorbitant amount of money for no apparent reason. Cashiers are subjected to surprise audits of their cash registers every day and at different times. Mystery sleuths masquerading as shoppers also check out their honesty by making test purchases. If none of these devices reveals wrongdoing, a hidden camera may be trained on a suspected cashier.

But it's an expensive procedure, according to Heino Zylstra, the ex-Mountie who is Shoppers' director of loss prevention for western Canada. Though not up to CIA standards, the necessary camera equipment may cost as much as $22,000 and it's rather tricky to handle. A tiny camera, with a lens no bigger than the head of a nail, can be secreted in a plasterboard hole in the wall or in a crevice in the store's ceiling tile. Or, with an eight-inch wide-angle zoom lens, it can be concealed inside a cigarette carton that has a pin hole poked through it, placed on a shelf over the head of the cashier, and take perfect pictures. Connected with telephone wires, it can then be monitored offsite for hours by an investigator comfortably seated in his own home.

Ken Rey, a former government auditor who is one of Giesbrecht's twelve regional loss prevention managers, demonstrated at a recent conference of Shoppers associates how well the camera equipment works. He showed film footage of a pilfering cashier in action. She later admitted to stealing $2,500 during the five-week period since her ex-boyfriend broke off their wedding engagement. She further confessed how she had avoided being trapped by the usual detecting tactics. She had never tried to steal the money from customers she didn't recognize. Under the eyes of the camera, she failed to register twenty-one sales in the first ninety minutes of her shift. Then, just before going on her break, she removed $80 and deposited the bills in her capacious bra. "At that rate of pilferage," Rey told the assembly of dumbfounded associates, "you're paying dishonest cashiers like her more than $50,000 a year."

Giesbrecht and Zylstra both reject out of hand an image of themselves as Orwellian Big Brothers spying on predatory customers and employees all criminally bent. "We never forget that Shoppers is not in business to assume an adversary role," says Giesbrecht. "We're in business to deal with customers and it's customers who make us great." Zylstra adds: "Nor do we begin with the assumption that everyone who works for Shoppers is a crook. I like to believe that basically everyone is honest. At the same time, it can't be denied, there's a touch of larceny in every one of us. There's an old saying that every policeman could have gone two ways – winding up either an outlaw or a lawman."

Both Giesbrecht and Zylstra are concerted in the belief that investigators must always keep in mind common sense and humanity before pressing charges against anybody. The investigators they hire range in age from twenty to sixty. They may be former policemen, firemen, or lawyers, or young Shop-

pers employees eager to switch to a new career in loss prevention. Zylstra favours women investigators because he thinks
they're "natural shoppers" and blend in well with customers in
the store. Giesbrecht likes recruiting students from community
colleges with a background in psychology or human relations.

Giesbrecht warns new investigators – who are rotated in
different stores to get different kinds of experience – that the
action is most hectic at Shoppers outlets in the downtown core.
"Jimmy," the *nom de crime* alias of an outstanding Toronto in-
store investigator, can vouch for that in spades. For the past
nine years, Jimmy has been the sleuth stationed at the Shoppers store in the Eaton Centre, one of the biggest shopping
complexes in North America, stretching between Queen Street
and Dundas in the pulsating hub of the Yonge Street strip.
Consequently, the 7,000-square-foot store, which grosses well
over $6 million a year for associate Jerry Ziedenberg, boasts an
extraordinarily heavy traffic – and a high crime rate to match.

A sign at the exit warns: "Goods are electronically protect-
ed. Should exit signal sound, please return to checkout counter
for removal of electronic control tag." Ziedenberg's was one of
the first stores in the Shoppers chain to be thus electronically
safeguarded a few years ago. It means the store's more expensive items are tagged with six electromagnetic strips, which
respond to an energy pattern. The item must be deactivated by
the cashier, who drags it over a scanner bar. Otherwise, when
the customer opens the door to leave without having paid, an
alarm sounds in the form of a male voice booming embarrass-
ingly loud that you must return to the cashier.

Another sign warns thieves who are not so easily deterred:
"Shoplifting detection." This means they must contend with
Jimmy. Born in the Dominican Republic, he is a short, skinny
thirty-year-old, with an onion-bald head and docile brown
eyes, who looks superficially like a pushover. However, he is
versed in the martial arts, equipped with an actor's wardrobe
of disguises, has studied psychology at York University, and
often comes to work in a sweatsuit and running shoes in case
he has to chase after ne'er-do-wells.

He averages sixteen citizen arrests a week, which he records in his police court report book as "occurrences." "More than any other Shoppers store in town, I deal with a lot of teen-age hookers, punk rockers, bag ladies, and rubbydub stumble-bums," he says. "When I try to bring the suspects I've pinched into the back security room for questioning, they'll cry, lie, whine, and run. It's an exciting profession. Like being in a movie."

The prostitutes, aged fourteen to seventeen, are the most pathetic offenders. They steal condoms, vaginal douches, lubricants, perfumes, and lipsticks. When caught, they invari-ably try to tempt Jimmy with what they consider a seductive sway of their scrawny juvenile hips and the sexual bribe, "Let me off, Mister, and I'll give you a good time."

Except for the rank gutter smell of their clothes and the cheap ginny reek of their breaths, the bag ladies and rubby-dubs are most harmless. Most colourful are the punk bohemian street people off the Strip: the showoff kooks with their Hallowe'en purple, pink, and green Mohawk hairdos; the gays and sex-change transvestites, who wear gaudy dresses and ask for hormones at the dispensary in bass baritone voices; and the weirdos who startle the cashier in the store's post office booth by buying stamps while pet snakes and mice slither and crawl around their necks.

In line of duty, Jimmy was once stabbed by a pair of ex-Don Jail convicts who made off with cartons of cigarettes. Though he keeps a baseball bat in the security office, he has never had to use it to club an assailant into submission. After calling the bluff of a tattooed holdup bandit, who had a finger outthrust in his pocket pretending it was a gun, he received a police citation for preserving peace and order.

Jimmy is told to exercise his discretion about each "occurrence," and a few of the hard decisions he had to make sometimes haunt him. He remembers once laying charges against a perfume-stealing woman of about twenty who was pregnant when caught. Because she had a long police record, she was imprisoned.

A few weeks later, a roughneck accosted Jimmy in the store and asked belligerently, "Remember that pregnant lady you put the snatch on?"

Jimmy said cautiously, "Maybe. Why?"

"Well, she was my wife, and the baby died while she was in jail. You killed my baby. And some day, Mr. Flatfoot Detective, we'll meet again on a dark street, and I'll kill you."

Nothing came of the threat, and Jimmy says he knows he's not to blame. "But the feeling of guilt is still there," he says, shaking his head. "Did I help kill his baby? It preys on me."

Just about every pharmacist has his personal horror story to relate about meting out justice to shoplifters. David Bloom relates two such tales to illustrate the dilemmas he faced as a neophyte associate running the store in Toronto's Yorkdale Shopping Plaza.

One case involved a vain, grey-haired army captain from the armed forces base located near the plaza. He was scheduled to retire from the army in one week, and in an attempt to make himself look more youthful to women, he had shoplifted a bottle of Grecian Formula hair colouring. "If this gets on my record, I lose my pension," he pleaded with Bloom. "Would you penalize a guy for life because he's made a damn fool of himself just once for an item valued at $9.99?"

Bloom remembers looking at the purloined hair tint and then looking at the shame-faced soldier and thinking, "I can't live with a punishment this harsh. It would be a miscarriage of justice. But I won't let him off the hook completely. I'm going to let him stew for a while."

So he told the captain, "Why don't you go home while I think about it? I'll let you know my decision in a couple of days." When Bloom ultimately phoned him to say he wasn't pressing charges, the soldier blessed him and said he'd suffered mental torture in the last couple of days worse than fighting in the most hellish battle.

The second case was to torment Bloom for eighteen years and provokes twinges of sorrow until this day. He saw a woman put six large packages of Contac-C worth about $20 in her purse. He politely asked her to come into his office and open her purse for examination. When he asked her to explain the hoard of capsules he found there, she said, "You've got me cold. I don't know what gets into me, but I've done this many times before."

He therefore summoned the police and laid charges of theft. But the next day he received a frantic phone call from a former schoolmate of his from William Lyon Mackenzie Collegiate. "Look, you've had my mother arrested," his friend said. "She made a mistake while emotionally ill, and you've got to let her off. When we were at school together, I always thought you were a fair guy. My father's not well with a bad heart condition, and an arrest will kill my mother."

"It's out of my hands," said Bloom. "Hire a lawyer, get a note from her doctor, and let the judge decide about her emotional state."

His former school chum phoned him every three hours over the next few days, begging him to change his mind. But Bloom remained adamant. Eventually, on the basis of her physician's claim that she was a kleptomaniac, she was given a suspended sentence and a reprimand.

"But the hurt remains," says Bloom. "Today, whenever my former friend sees me, he crosses the street."

The associates are not callous; they have been conditioned to steel themselves and be resolute by their normally marshmallow-hearted leader, Murray Koffler. He gets at least twenty phone calls a year from prominent people, urging him to intercede on behalf of a wife, a child, or a friend apprehended for shoplifting. Koffler expresses sympathy for the pain they must be enduring. But then he painstakingly answers, in a carefully thought-out speech, giving three reasons why he can't make an exception to the company policy he originated.

He explains, first of all, that his interference would damage the credibility of the entire loss prevention program he established. "It would pull the rug from under the in-store investigator," he says. "Here's a guy who has this terribly difficult job of watching, then pouncing, with his heart in his throat, his nerves palpitating, on a person he's going to accuse of stealing. Then he brings in the associate. Then the police are brought in. The charges are recorded at the court. The case is in the hands of the crown attorney. If I suddenly step in to withdraw charges, I make fools of everybody all down the line. If I keep asking them to make exceptions, how can we expect the police and the courts to believe us the next time our investigator nabs a shoplifter?"

His second reason is based on principle. "It's wrong to steal and it's wrong to use pull to escape from the consequences of theft," he says. "Our whole business has been built on integrity, and I must stand up for what I believe is right."

Finally, he strives to set a personal example for exemplary behaviour and punishment, even if the shoplifting case has emanated from his own home. He illustrates by citing the case of his housekeeper, Elsa. She was a middle-aged woman who had helped raise all five of the Koffler children at their Beechwood Avenue home. One day, for whatever reason, she went to the beauty department of the Shoppers store at nearby York Mills and Bayview Avenue, and, when nobody seemed to be looking, she popped a couple of Schiaparelli lipsticks worth $15 into her purse. But the investigator, who *was* looking, apprehended her outside. He summoned the police and charges were laid.

"As soon as they found it was our housekeeper," Koffler recalls, "everybody said, 'Oh, Mr. Koffler, we're awfully sorry. We'll withdraw the charge right away.' But I insisted, 'You can't do that. You've got to go through with it on a matter of principle.'"

His wife Marvelle, however, felt that she had to go by her principles. Without informing her husband, she took the housekeeper aside. "I'm sorry, Elsa, you did this," she said. "I'm sure you didn't mean to do it. But Mr. Koffler is very strict about theft. You can't expect the pharmacist who runs the store to hand out forgiveness just because you're our housekeeper. His livelihood is at stake. But, Elsa, you go to court and I'll stand up to give you a good character reference."

And so it was. Marvelle Koffler sat patiently in the courtroom alongside the anxiety-ridden Elsa for two days as the case kept being postponed. Then she stood up to tell the judge, "Your Honour, I'd like to speak on behalf of Elsa. She's been our devoted housekeeper for more than ten years and has been wonderful at bringing up our children. She may have made this mistake. But I can vouch for her excellent character."

The judge looked down at her and the connection suddenly dawned on him. "Madam, are you the wife of the Murray Koffler who's president of Shoppers Drug Mart?"

"Yes."

"Yet you've been waiting here for two days to give a character reference for the woman charged with shoplifting from Shoppers?"

"Yes."

"That's one for the books. Case dismissed."

To this day, says Koffler, Elsa sends them a greeting card each Christmas thanking Marvelle for tempering punishment with compassion.

CHAPTER FOURTEEN

Three Guys Build a Ritzy Hotel

I n the show-business movie *Babes On Broadway*, Mickey Rooney turns to Judy Garland and other members of their gang. "Gee, kids," he says. "This barn would be perfect for putting on our own show." The hotel business, of course, is a branch of show business, and Murray Koffler is a natural showman who loves playing the role of genial host. From all accounts, his entry into the glamour world of innkeeping was announced with a line almost as corny and naive as the Mickey Rooney cliché. It went: "Hey, guys, let's build our own hotel."

It's a matter of debate which of the three guys uttered the line, but it certainly is known who the guys were and where the line was spoken. It was expressed one chill January night in 1958 at a ski lodge in Collingwood, Ontario, near Toronto. And the three guys warming up over hot toddies were an un-likely trio of pretenders to the throne once occupied at the turn of the century by that monarch of luxury hoteliers, César Ritz.

One of the three was Murray Koffler. He was then the thirty-three-year-old owner of a drugstore on Bathurst Street, restlessly casting about for entrepreneurial ventures outside the realm of pharmacy. The second was his close friend Eddie Creed, a thirty-six-year-old furrier helping his parents Jack and Dorothy Creed to run the fashionable Creeds ladies' specialty store on Bloor Street. The third was Eddie's brother-in-law, Isa-dore (Issy) Sharp, who most probably initiated the project. He was a twenty-seven-year-old architect, who with his father

Max, a plasterer-land developer, had recently built for a client a small motel on Highway 27 called Motel 27. Issy had been vainly seeking finances to build his own hotel since 1955.

The trio put their heads – and skimpy finances – together to erect in 1961 a first-class motor hotel in the heart of Toronto's notorious red-light district, the Four Seasons, located on Jarvis Street. Out of it grew the Rolls-Royce of international hotel chains, the Toronto-headquartered, Canadian-controlled Four Seasons Hotels Inc. As of 1988, it grosses $550 million annually by operating twenty-two medium-sized hotels of exceptional quality in principal cities of Canada, the United States, and England.

Its sybaritic hostelries cater to the voluptuaries who adhere to Oscar Wilde's credo: "I have simple tastes; I am easily satisfied by the best." In fact, six of its hotels were chosen among the "world's fifty best" in a 1985 poll of top-level executives from 140 countries conducted by *Institutional Investor* magazine. The Four Seasons Hotel in Washington, D.C., headed the list as number one in North America and the Four Seasons Hotel on Yorkville Avenue in Toronto was selected tops in Canada. Also given top ranking were the Ritz-Carlton, which the chain manages in Chicago, the Pierre in New York, Inn on the Park in London, and the Quatre Saisons in Montreal.

The chain was singled out for accolades in the very first paragraph of the introduction in that best-selling bible of business supremacy, *In Search of Excellence*. The co-authors, Tom Peters and Robert Waterman, were enchanted by the cordial reception they got from the concierge when attempting to book a room late one night without a reservation at the Four Seasons in Washington. "To our astonishment, the concierge looked up, smiled, called us by name, and asked how we were," they wrote. "She remembered our names!" Yet they had only stayed there once before.

Peerless service of that sort is expected by its celebrated guests. The grandees who frequent the Four Seasons hotels include such notables as the Queen Mother and Prince Charles, Prince Albert and Princess Paeola of Belgium, His Highness

Prince Karim Aga Khan, Arabian Prince Abdullah, and His Royal Highness Bandar Sultan of Saudi Arabia. Other notable guests have ranged from Soviet Premier Alexei Kosygin to Israeli Prime Minister Golda Meir, from Henry Kissinger to a whole galaxy of Hollywood stars.

Each hotel records meticulous biographical sketches of its well-heeled clientele via computer, so that on a return visit a guest is automatically greeted by name and gets his favourite view, shampoo, flower arrangement, or type of pillow. They take for granted that their opulent suite will be supplied with such perks as terrycloth robes, Japanese-style disposable slippers, free overnight shoeshines, and, if they are VIPs, a fruit basket, a box of chocolates, or a bottle of Moet & Chandon Dom Perignon.

Staff members have been handpicked, so that they will oblige without blinking at a Texas cattle baron who wanted $10,000 of cigars charged to his bill, an eccentric dowager seeking somebody to take her pet cheetah for a walk, a Kuwaiti oil potentate in need of a chauffeur to drive his two children to a summer camp in north Ontario, and a love-smitten playboy requesting that an orchid be delivered every hour to his girlfriend's suite.

The global prestige of the Four Seasons chain is extraordinary when one considers that it is a fraction the size of its older, more established rivals in the luxury market, such as North America's Hyatt Hotels chain and Britain's Trusthouse Forte. It was former U.S. Secretary of State Dean Acheson who once remarked to Canada's Prime Minister Lester Pearson that he has parlayed a small country into a position of much greater influence than its size would justify. So, too, with the three amateurs who had the quixotic idea of launching a tony hotel. How did the furrier, the architect, and the pharmacist do it?

The "hotel fellowship," as Creed calls them, did so well as a team because they had several things in common. Besides their love for sports, they had a driving need to achieve inherited from their immigrant fathers, innate good taste, and respect for each other's disparate opinions. At the same time, each partner had something distinctive to contribute.

Eddie Creed, the eldest, was probably the most cosmopolitan of the trio. He was a world traveller who had long accompanied his parents to the fashion buying shows of Europe. He
contributed an urbane, yet practical, mercantile sense to their
mutual decision-making. The others nicknamed him "Mr. No,"
not because he was a nay-sayer but a pragmatic sceptic. At
sixty-six, he is a second-generation merchant prince who is
board chairman of Creeds. But for years he was afflicted with a
mammoth inferiority complex, the result of living in the
shadow of a domineering father and being known to every
furrier in the business as "Jack Creed's boy."

His father, who died in 1971 at the age of eighty-six, was a
Napoleonic five-foot-two with a perfectionist's whim of iron.
He was a curious paradox, a Russian-born revolutionary
Communist capitalist. As a youth, he emigrated to Paris to
learn the tailoring trade. He then moved to Winnipeg to set up
a shop at Portage and Main, and in 1916 he moved again, to a
small shop on the first floor of a house on Bloor Street at
Balmuto, and brazenly advertised in a Toronto newspaper:
"Haute Couture Tailor, Just Arrived From Paris!" A prominent
socialite responded and told her friends how skilful he was in
using silver fox and mink to trim custom-designed coats and
suits. His wife Dorothy also gained a reputation for providing
smart handbags, scarves, and jewelry to accessorize their
outfits. Soon their remodelled house was drawing Toronto's
carriage trade, and ultimately their marbled and chandeliered
ladies' specialty emporium was designing furs for Queen Elizabeth's coronation as well as European nobility and an affluent
clientele across Canada.

Eddie, the only son of an exacting father, was educated at
Pickering College, a nearby British-style boys' private school.
After serving as a lieutenant in the Royal Canadian Navy, he
was expected to follow in his bantam-sized father's giant foot-
steps. Somehow, though, he never seemed to measure up to
Jack Creed's towering standards.

"My father held the idea that with the death of the famous
opera singer, Enrico Caruso, the voice of opera would die,
too," says Eddie Creed. "In other words, nobody could ever

perform as well as the master. My father was strong-willed right to the end. I had to learn to understand him and adapt. Otherwise I'd have been in deep trouble."

Koffler recalls that the relationship between father and son was prickly indeed. He first met Eddie at Camp Arowhon, where Koffler played the imperious Mikado opposite Eddie's comic Ko-Ko in the Gilbert and Sullivan operetta. They got to know each other better in the late 1940s, when each served as best man at the other's wedding, and they became inseparable skiing, sailing, and drinking companions.

"Eddie was always a great athlete, and one of my envies was that what came so easily to him, I had to struggle for," says Koffler. "But I didn't envy him living under the difficult regime of his dominating father." He remembers Jack Creed phoning him frequently to ask, "What am I going to do with my no-good son?"

Issy Sharp was also strongly influenced by his father Max, but their relationship was totally different. Max is regarded by everybody as a lovable man. At eighty-five, he is a spry, five-foot-five gnome, and he has always been his son's most ardent booster. He remains so today, as demonstrated by a favourite anecdote the retired builder likes telling about his son. "The nicest compliment I ever heard about Issy came from one of our hotel chain's 8,000 employees," says Max. "This fellow pointed to the twenty-third-floor window at the top of our Inn on the Park in Toronto. Then he said, 'Mr. Sharp, if your son told me to jump out, I'd do it without giving it a second thought. That's how much I trust Issy.'"

Issy returns the compliment. He says of his father: "My fondest childhood memory is this image of me at age six sitting on his lap after he'd come home late from one of his jobs of plastering a building. No matter how exhausted he was, he'd allow me to sit there. I'd pick pieces of plaster out of his hair while he'd tell me stories. He taught me then to have consideration for others and to be a decent person. I've always tried to follow his example in that and other things on my way up in the hotel business."

Issy, now the fifty-five-year-old chairman and chief executive officer of Four Seasons Hotels Inc., is not the gladhander one might expect of Canada's top hotelier. In a gregarious profession, he declines to gregare. He reminds one of Gary Cooper: an ascetic, sinewy, blue-eyed six-footer, quiet, reserved, and laconic. He is an attentive listener, with the courtly manners of a gentleman from a more gracious century.

"Issy was never an operator," says Koffler of his partner's more contained personality. "If he was to see Elizabeth Taylor in the elevator of one of our hotels, he wouldn't think of introducing himself. But my instinct would be to shake her hand and say, 'Welcome to Four Seasons. We're delighted to have you.' I come from a marketing, public, and human relations background, and I love greeting people. But Issy doesn't see it the same way."

Issy says he wouldn't presume to introduce himself to Elizabeth Taylor (who, as it happened, was a guest at the Toronto Four Seasons). "I'd respect her privacy on an elevator," he says. "Besides, what good would it do? It might gratify my ego to meet her. But it wouldn't further the interests of the hotel chain. And *that's* where I get my self-gratification."

He is a doer rather than a talker. Koffler expresses his esteem this way: "Issy has been *the* singular instrument in building the hotel chain. His resolute refusal to compromise quality has been responsible for its fantastic reputation. I admire him as a conceptualizer – especially in architecture and design – as a business manager, as a people organizer, as a hotelier, and as a friend. I've never seen him lose his temper under pressure. He has a positive genius for getting things done in unruffled style."

He acquired his style of doing things superbly from his adventuresome father. Max was a refugee from the pogroms of Auschwitz, Poland, where he was born one of the ten children of a *shoichet* (Yiddish for Orthodox chicken slaughterer). He escaped at eighteen to become a pioneer Zionist, joyfully helping build one of Palestine's first *kibbutzim* at the commune of Degania, where he learned the plasterer's trade. In 1925, he moved to Toronto's Kensington Market area. There he would build a house, his bustling wife Lena would decorate it, and Issy and his three sisters would live in it until a customer would buy it.

By the time he was sixteen, Issy had lived in fifteen houses. As his father prospered in the post-war building boom, the family moved to Forest Hill Village. While studying architecture at Ryerson Polytechnical Institute, he spent summer vacations plastering, bricklaying, and digging ditches for his father. And after he graduated with honours and a silver medal, he joined his father in the firm of Max Sharp & Son Construction Limited, building apartments.

At this point the Koffler, Creed, and Sharp commercial alliance began. Koffler had decided in 1954 to gamble on building the thirty-two-unit Sheridan Apartments atop his Bathurst Street drugstore. Eddie Creed, who had married Issy's oldest sister, Edith, recommended the firm of Max Sharp & Son to contract its construction, and after this success Koffler was eager to invest in other building projects.

Eddie, seeking means of proving his worth in the eyes of his father, was likewise eager. He suggested that Koffler join him in developing a medical building on a tract of land on Bloor Street owned by Jack Creed. Koffler, who was to establish a drugstore on the ground floor, agreed with his usual enthusiasm.

"Just as we were all set to go, my father put a crimp on it," recalls Eddie. "He bowed out. Not only that, he talked his friend, Balmy Cowan, who was prepared to put up the mortgage money, into bowing out, too." His father also "put the kibosh" on their subsequent plan to invest in another apartment building. Undeterred, the pair of young entrepreneurs passed the word along to Max and Issy Sharp about their dreams of making money from real estate.

By coincidence, Issy had been dreaming of building a hotel ever since his marriage to Rosalie Wise. She is the daughter of another Polish immigrant and heads her own interior design firm. Issy remembers how they decided to spend their honeymoon at the newly built Skyline Hotel on Toronto's airport strip just so they could check out the décor. He remembers knocking on doors for five years in the early 1950s, vainly importuning backers for his dream hotel and being rebuffed, "Come back another day, kid."

After their discussion in Collingwood in 1958, the group's vision of building a novel motor hotel slowly began to take shape. Koffler and Issy Sharp drove to Phoenix and Las Vegas on an inspection tour of the latest trends in motels. Creed later joined them on visits to the annual International Hotel Show in New York City. With plans under their arms, they boldly introduced themselves to Tom Lee, interior designer of The Hotel of Tomorrow. "And right there we shook hands and made a deal that he was to be our interior designer." Max and Issy Sharp selected the illustrious Canadian architect, Peter Dickinson, to design the exteriors. Out of their group brainstorming evolved the concept of a motor hotel in the downtown core of the city, with all the amenities of a roadside motel and the convenient location of an urban hotel.

It was to be a leafy oasis, with all rooms facing an inner courtyard of gardens and a large swimming pool, and with all cars and traffic kept away, outside, on the perimeter of the property. The notion of thus controlling the environment in a walled-off haven of urban tranquility was important because the only site they could afford was on Jarvis Street. A popular ribald ditty of the period, according to an essay by David Helwig in *Saturday Night* magazine, went:

Yonge Street for business,
Bay Street for class,
College for shopping,
And Jarvis for ass.

Initially, the plan was to locate the motor hotel on Jarvis at Gerrard, opposite a tawdry hotel reputed to be a brothel. But partly because of Creed's strenuous objections, they eventually chose instead a somewhat less sleazy site one block north of

Gerrard on the northeast corner of Jarvis at Carlton Street, opposite the Canadian Broadcasting Corporation headquarters building.

"Because the CBC was across the road, that gave it a *little* prestige," says Creed dryly. "I'd rather have a drunken actor as a guest than a drunken prostitute."

Koffler recalls that it pioneered several innovations. Out of necessity, it was the first motor hotel in Canada to be built with all the rooms facing inward on a central courtyard. "We could have doubled our profits by having rooms face outside north, south, and east," says Koffler. "But we didn't want windows facing that way out because the surrounding neighbourhood was so terribly poor looking."

It was also the first hotel in Canada not to have dank and dreary beer parlors assigned to each sex with separate entrances for men and women off the main street. It was so designed that guests had to enter through the lobby to be served at the rather swank bar adjoining the dining room. Thus the front-desk clerk could screen the clientele, keeping out what appeared to be ladies of easy virtue and other low-life undesirables.

"We were very, very leery of any soliciting by hookers," says Koffler. "We didn't even allow a woman to check in if she was a single." He remembers how this selective process once led to a *cause célèbre*. Nathan Phillips, the mayor of Toronto, was escorting the nubile Miss Pickle, who had won a beauty contest conducted by a pickle company. "Our security officer wouldn't let them down the hall," he says. "*That's* how cautious we were."

They had reason to take precautions, because they had a devilish time raising money for their proposed million-dollar hotel set in such a squalid environment. Each of the partners personally invested about $100,000. Creed and Sharp used their life insurance as collateral to get a loan from the Bank of Nova Scotia; Koffler sold his Sheridan Apartments to obtain ready cash. Issy pulled off a major financial coup in a deal with Cecil Forsyth, the hard-headed mortgage manager of Great-West Life Assurance Company. Forsyth had rejected him several times over the past few years: "Issy, I'll invest in any apartment building that you and your dad put up," Forsyth chided him. "But what in the hell do you know about hotels?"

This time, though, Forsyth came through with $750,000 in mortgage money. Issy scrounged additional short-term financing from building trade subcontractors. He persuaded the electricians, for example, to deliver $25,000 of work with the promise, "We'll pay you half on completion and the other half six months after the hotel opens."

Creed had the bright idea of approaching G. Allan Burton, head of Simpsons department stores contracting division, to advance financing for their interior furnishings. Now seventy-two and retired as board chairman of Simpsons Limited, Burton, a staid pillar of the Establishment, recalls being invited by Eddie, Issy, and Murray to examine the hotel then under construction.

It was a rainy, slushy night, and his car got stalled in the snow, Burton remembers. Yet somehow he struggled through the miserable storm to the walkway of the construction hut. There he turned to the threesome and said, "Give me a couple of good reasons why you crazies believe you can build a classy hotel in this godforsaken whorehouse section of town."

Burton heard them out, looked at their anxious faces, and then smiled. "All right, boys, I'll back you," he said. "But I'm not doing it because you convinced me. I'm doing it because I've known and trusted your fathers. And I won't let your fathers down."

On March 21, the first day of spring in 1961, the two-storey, 126-room Four Seasons Motor Hotel (its name boldly swiped as the Anglicized version of a German hotel in Munich) opened with a cocktail reception in aid of the Toronto Symphony. It was a gala occasion that came off smoothly because the amateur hoteliers had been astute enough to hire one of the best professional hotel managers in the hospitality trade.

His name was Ian Munro, and he was one of those rarities, a natural-born innkeeper with three key passions in life: a love for good food, good wine, and good conversation. "Ian was the most important ingredient in our partnership," says Koffler. "He set the stage, the tone, the image for our internal

Four Seasons operation." And Issy says, "Everything we know about quality hotel-keeping, we learned from Ian. He had flair."

Born in Glasgow, Munro was a ruddy-faced, 230-pound raconteur with a largesse of spirit and appetites. Guests thought of him as a jolly Charles Laughton with a Scottish brogue. The graduate of a hotel school in London, he went on to manage the famous Treetops Hotel in Kenya and was manager of the Regency Towers Hotel on Avenue Road in Toronto when he took over the Four Seasons. He was noted for his quick wit and *savoir-faire*, two qualities that served him well at the hotel's opening. One of the female guests present, apparently tiddly on champagne, shucked off her evening gown and undies and dived nude into the swimming pool. Munro later recounted its aftermath this way: "I promptly sent two waiters after her, and they came up two abreast."

Another memorable event caused an even greater sensation. Koffler announced to guests that he and his partners were already planning to open a second Toronto hotel. This one was to be a more audacious gamble than the Four Seasons: a resort-style hotel on a stretch of cow pasture overlooking 600 acres of public forested parkland in what was then the lonely boondocks of northeast Toronto on Leslie Street at Eglinton Avenue.

The seemingly mad venture was the result of a fluke. Koffler chanced to be driving on Eglinton to his new drugstore in Don Mills one day and was waiting for a traffic signal to change so he could make a left turn onto Leslie. He then noticed a workman who was literally putting up a sign that read: "Sixteen-Acre Site For Sale. See J.J. Fitzgibbons, Famous Players Ltd., Bloor St., Toronto." Koffler had just read a news item that John J. Fitzgibbons, the president of the Famous Players Canada theatre chain, had lost out in his bid to build a TV station; hence, he was putting up this prime site for sale. Koffler considered it prime because he knew of the grand plans that E.P. Taylor had in mind to develop the entire Don Mills area with an industrial and residential complex.

"I got terribly excited," Koffler recalls. "I could see it as an ideal site for a rustic, in-city hotel that would attract business clientele." He was in such a hurry to drive downtown and negotiate a deal at the Famous Players corporate headquarters that he made a U-turn around the island at Leslie and Eglinton. "The result was I got a traffic ticket."

But he also got to strike up a bargain with Fitzgibbons.

"Sir, will you give me a one-dollar option on the site for just one week?" he asked. "That'll give me time to bring in my partners with a firm proposition."

"What do you intend doing with it?" asked the movie magnate.

Koffler didn't intend to reveal his plans, because he was aware that the theatre chain was also in the hotel business. "So I just sort of hemmed and hawed," he recalls.

"Is it for a shopping centre maybe?" asked Fitzgibbons.

"Maybe," said Koffler, and quickly handed him a dollar bill and left.

Creed, the Mr. No of the partnership, was definitely negative about the primeness of the site. When taken on an inspection tour, he gazed gloomily at the desolate surroundings. He peered at the garbage dump on the corner. He eyed the single building looming in the empty landscape, the pioneering head office of IBM. He turned to Koffler and expressed his "No" succinctly.

"Murray, you've got to be nuts!" he said. "This is way the hell out of I don't know where."

"Where's your imagination?" said Koffler, the visionary, soaring into rhapsodic prophecies. "I predict there'll be a thousand industries blossoming within a five-mile radius of here. Can you visualize a big suburban city in Canada without a decent hotel in the neighbourhood? That's what's going to happen here."

Mr. No was persuaded.

Issy Sharp agreed instantly, "This will be a great opportunity for us." But his wife Rosalie was not so optimistic. She was then pregnant with their fourth child and secretly full of dismay at her first sight of the seeming Siberia. She confided years later to Issy, "I resigned myself then and there to losing our first home and having to hock the silverware."

Despite his public euphoria, Koffler was privately worried about a formidable stumbling block: the site was located in a legally dry area of Toronto. "And to try to run a hotel without a liquor licence was considered either gutsy or stupid," he now says. "Looking back, I guess it was foolhardy. But we had this great confidence that we could somehow get by, serving beer and wine, until we could get the place rezoned."

He justifiably had confidence in the negotiating skills of Max Sharp's other son-in-law, Frederick Eisen. A street-smart diplomat who then worked for the Sharp family's construction firm, Eisen is now a Four Seasons board director. He pulled strings and orchestrated a plebiscite that resulted in the residents of North York voting overwhelmingly for the right to drink what they pleased.

After the group paid Fitzgibbons $10,000 for a year's option on the property, there remained the seemingly insuperable problem of scratching together the some $3 million needed for building the resort hotel. Issy Sharp approached Clifford Ash, general manager of the Bank of Nova Scotia, for financial aid.

"How much are you putting up for this new venture?" asked Ash.

"We're putting up our collective experience and built-up values and a lot of hard planning," said Issy. "We expect you to put up cash."

Ash belied Mark Twain's definition of a banker as a skinflint who will only lend you an umbrella when it's not raining. He produced from his vaults a substantial loan, which is the reason the Four Seasons chain banks with the Bank of Nova Scotia to this day.

Max Sharp recalls with amusement telling his son to try extracting an additional million dollars needed as a loan from the obdurate Cecil Forsyth.

"It's ridiculous to go back to Cecil so soon and ask him to cough up a cool million," he remembers Issy protesting.

"Don't worry," said Max. "Invite him here for lunch. Together, with our combined salesmanship, I'm sure we can get Cecil to cough."

Cecil came and listened and coughed.

Issy persuaded the architect, Peter Dickinson, to design the new hotel for a pittance, "barely enough to pay for his sketch paper." Then in the last throes of cancer, Dickinson took it on as "an interesting little fun project." In the hospital, with a sketch pad on his knee, he outlined brilliantly the skeleton of a six-storey, 200-room (later to become a twenty-three-storey, 568-room) sylvan retreat. Complete with gardens and outdoor pools and lovely paths for bicycling and skating or just rambling, it was perched on the brow of a hill in harmony with its environment.

All the partners – and their wives – pitched in ideas for a possible hotel name. Marvelle Koffler suggested Inn on the Park. After all, it faced Wilket Creek Park and Edwards Gardens. Moreover, she felt the sound had a musical lilt to it, like Manhattan's Tavern on the Green. After rolling it around on their tongues, the others agreed.

The opening itself, on a sunny May day in 1963, was a festive benefit for the Ontario Heart Foundation. It was staged with customary Kofflerian showmanship. A solitary bagpiper, splendid in his scarlet and green tunic and tartan, led his comrades from the 48th Highlanders Band in a march around the lobby. Entertainers such as Carmel Quinn, the Irish singer, flew in every half hour from the Toronto airport to land on a helicopter pad on the hotel's front lawn. The day's events included an art and sculpture show, exhibitions of folk dancing, wrestling, and tennis, a water ballet in the swimming pool, and exotic buffets both indoors and outdoors. Swans gracefully paddled in the garden pool.

The opening night went swimmingly except for two hair-raising mishaps. In the middle of the proceedings, the North York police butted in and tried to end the revelry; they declared that management lacked a banquet permit allowing the serving of hard liquor. In the kitchen, meanwhile, with one last lugubrious gurgle, the electric dishwashing machine broke down.

Munro, the unflappable pro, handled both potential calamities with aplomb. First, he sweet-talked the constabulary out of closing the place down. Then he walked into the kitchen, removed his tuxedo jacket, and plunged his hands into the sinkful of dishes. It was, everybody agreed, a first-class act, and a dramatic example to the staff.

Everybody further agrees that the combined promotional ideas of the three partners succeeded in embossing both hotels with a first-class image. Among other innovations, they are credited with introducing what is believed to have been Canada's first hotel disco club. Koffler was an avid disco dancer from the beginning of the craze in the early 1960s, when Chubby Checker, the Twist, and New York's Peppermint Lounge were in their heyday. In 1964, the Toronto partners imported New York's champion disco dancer, Joe (Killer) Pirrot, as a headliner for the opening of the Café Discotheque at the Inn on the Park. The Café attracted considerable publicity during the ups and downs of the disco rage. It continues to lure people today in its modern guise as Le Club, an Inn night spot where the colours are a blend of hot pink and cool blue and the soft lighting is geared "to make every disco dancer in the room look young and beautiful."

Unquestionably, Koffler's most durable hotel publicity feat was the initiation of Canada's first Johnny Carson-style talk show. His Carson was a folksy radio announcer with a velvety voice who hailed from Moose Jaw, Saskatchewan; he ran a noontime musical-cum-interview show called *Luncheon Date with Elwood Glover* from a CBC studio across the road from the Four Seasons on Jarvis. Koffler crossed the street one day in 1963, introduced himself, and said, "Elwood, why shut yourself up in a studio? Why not come over and set up your mike on a corner table of our restaurant, and literally have a daily luncheon date? Your audience will hear the clatter of dishes and the hum of conversation in the background and it'll add real authenticity to your program."

"A born charmer" is how the Saskatchewaner described Koffler in his memoirs, *Elwood Glover's Luncheon Dates*, and now, at seventy-two, Glover still feels the same way. It began as a half-hour local radio program, with Glover interviewing visiting authors and Hollywood stars, many of them guests at either of the two hotels, the Four Seasons or Inn on the Park. It eventually became a nation-wide network show, with an audience at its peak of one million, telecast live from the dining room of the Four Seasons, and then, from 1970 until Glover retired in 1975, from a 100-seat basement lounge in the hotel called The Studio.

The hotel publicist, Beth Slaney, who was paid by the CBC to serve as producer/program co-ordinator, recalls that "mature women" were among its most fervent fans. They were so infatuated with Glover that many wrote mash letters requesting locks of his hair. Because he was thinning on the top, Slaney is prepared to reveal now that those precious strands the elderly biddies have preserved in lockets over the years are bogus treasures. In fact, she snipped them from her own abundant bouffant.

Koffler was probably the program's most loyal viewer. "He took a proprietary interest in the show," says Slaney. "He was terrific when he appeared on it several times. And he phoned me up constantly to suggest guests who might be entertaining." The luminaries who appeared included Peter Ustinov, Malcolm Muggeridge, Alfred Hitchcock, Glenda Jackson, Helen Hayes, Warren Beatty, Ella Fitzgerald, and Andy Warhol. The two hotels, thus richly publicized every day, soon gained a reputation for being the meeting place of the elite.

The novel ambience of Inn on the Park was used by Issy Sharp as a key selling point to gain a foothold in the plush British hotel market. The quiet Canadian invasion had its genesis one evening in 1963 when Issy stayed at London's famed Dorchester Hotel. "It came to me clear as a bell," he recalls. "*This* is the way to run a stylish hotel. If they can do it, we can do it, and maybe do it better."

A year later, he happened to mention his delight in the Dorchester to a Toronto-based representative of the McAlpine Organization, the venerable British developer of hotels around the world. "Is that so?" said the McAlpine man. "My company owns the Dorchester."

"Well, if you ever want to build a luxury hotel even better than the Dorchester," said Issy rather grandiosely, "my company would be interested."

Issy now says, "My comment was meant to be flippant. I thought I'd hear no more about it."

But the Toronto executive, impressed by the flourishing Inn on the Park, arranged for Issy to meet in London an important director of the McAlpine Group. He was Gerald (later Sir Gerald) Glover, portly, frightfully English, and deucedly stiff-upper-lipped. He was a breeder of thoroughbred horses and leader of a group of British patricians interested in perhaps developing an equivalent inn at the foot of Park Lane overlooking Hyde Park.

Issy assumed the task of negotiating with this uppercrust of milords. It took him five years to soften up the aristocrats during flight-to-London meetings held periodically between 1964 and 1969. Because there were already so many luxury hotels in London in addition to the Dorchester–Claridge's, the Savoy, and the Connaught among them–Glover's group of developers proposed building an inn with 320 moderate-rate, small-sized rooms.

"Their market research indicated that another first-class hotel would fail," recalls Issy. "But we had faith in our judgement rather than in their research. We told the developers we'd pay the full rent they wanted for their 320-room structure. But they'd have to redesign it to meet our standards and build *only* 230 rooms in the same space.

"They were aghast," he remembers. "They called me 'that crazy Canadian.'" But Issy stuck by his guns. Glover phoned him one afternoon from London and casually invited him to fly over and join him for a spot of lunch next day with some of his friends, including the Duke of Westminster.

"Mr. Glover," said Issy. "Do you think it's *really* necessary for me to book an overnight flight just to have a snack with your buddies from the peerage?"

"Well, I say, dear fellow, it might be rather important for you to meet the chaps who are putting up the money."

Issy arrived in London at ten o'clock in the morning, just in time to be seated at noon with the Duke on one side of him at the lunch table and the Duke's titled financial adviser on the other. The English, of course, are never so crass as to discuss money at lunch. Conversation, according to their business protocol, must be restricted to social chitchat. But over their brandy, after completing a six-course lunch, Issy was petrified when the Duke leaned forward and said, "Now, Mr. Sharp. We would like you to tell us what you can about the politics and general economy of Canada and how one should deal with them."

Issy remembers staring at them in astonishment and wondering, "How in the world did I get into this ridiculous predicament?"

He managed to blurt out, "Well, all I can give you is a layman's approach to such lofty matters. But here it is . . ."

Later, as he was being driven to the Dorchester, Issy said, "Mr. Glover, how could you? I'll probably never see your friends from the House of Lords again. But *I* could have embarrassed *you*. Why didn't you forewarn me so I could be prepared?"

"That wouldn't have been cricket," said Glover. "Before signing a contract, they wanted me to present you as you are without any artificial la-de-da. And, my friend, you scored beautifully."

The opening of the London Inn on the Park in 1970 was a regal affair. The Toronto partners (after helping workmen tack down the red carpet a scant hour before the pomp and ceremony began) played host to 1,000 guests, including the stately Princess Alexandra, who acted as the patron of the fund-raising benefit for the Red Cross. The Inn was pronounced by the travel press Europe's posh Hotel of the Year, and it established the Four Seasons as a world-class hotel chain catering to the deluxe market.

However, their reputation for investing in – and managing – moderate-sized luxury hostelries took a beating in the next major Four Seasons expansion. Issy conceived the idea of building a hotel on the south side of Queen Street opposite Toronto's new City Hall. He had an architect draw up the plans, which won the approval of his partners. But Koffler and Creed posed the logical question: Where was the financing to come from?

The answer came to Issy while he was in the sauna at the Toronto Inn on the Park reading *Time* magazine. He noticed a business item reporting that the giant conglomerate, International Telephone and Telegraph Company, had acquired the Sheraton hotel division and was looking for investment opportunities.

"There's our financial backer," Issy said to himself. He immediately picked up the phone, arranged a meeting in New York, and worked out a deal giving the Sheraton Corporation 51 per cent control of the action. The two companies united in an incongruous marriage in 1972 to build for $60 million the Four Seasons-Sheraton, not a minimalist luxury hotel as Issy had planned originally, but a leviathan of a convention hotel. The behemoth contained 1,450 rooms and its forty-three-storey tower loomed so high that it aroused civic antipathy for blocking the City Hall's view of the sun. A financial reporter of the period wrote caustically: "It was like a lady of genteel breeding getting into bed with a brash used car salesman – a union doomed not to last."

Issy, Koffler, and Creed were inclined to agree. In 1976, Four Seasons sold its 49 per cent interest in the mammoth for a lucrative $18.5 million. But it adopted a policy of henceforth restricting its marital couplings to more congenial bedfellows. It was a turning point for the Four Seasons chain in more ways than one.

"It made us realize we couldn't be all things to all people," says Issy. "The Sheraton experience confused people. Instead of building our identity, we were losing it. It meant we had to narrow our focus and specialize in catering exclusively to the high end of the market – not mass but class."

It was also a turning point for Issy personally. "Before the Sheraton episode, Murray and I had a lot to do with getting the hotel company going, co-operating in initiating concepts, and helping to set the tone for it," says Creed. "But from that point on, in his role as corporate president, Issy took on total responsibility. He built up his own management team and deserves credit as the guy who built the Four Seasons into the top-quality company it is today."

Koffler corroborated this accolade in a 1986 article about the hotel chain published in *The Globe and Mail's Report On Business Magazine*. "Issy was the instrument of genius," Koffler told reporter David Olive. "Sophisticated hotel people would never have spent as much on amenities and staffing as we did, but Issy was determined to be classy."

From that point on, Koffler and Creed attended monthly policy meetings and allowed Issy to take full charge of operations. He did so with gusto, exercising a Lorenzo the Magnificent's flair for pampering guests in the upscale lifestyle to which they were accustomed. In 1978, he sold the original Four Seasons Motor Hotel on Jarvis Street because it was getting a bit dingy and didn't meet the high standards now set by the chain. In the same year, he established the new Four Seasons Hotel on Yorkville Avenue, Toronto's chichi shopping district. He acquired the property from Hyatt Hotels, knocking out walls to make the hotel conform to the new Four Seasons look – with a room count down to 379, about 25 per cent less than the original number.

The Four Seasons reputation grew rapidly as he embarked on a campaign to get management contracts for luxury lodgings in ten of the largest cities in the United States. He startled the industry by winning a bidding contest to manage Chicago's opulent Ritz-Carlton. The most stunning coup came in 1981 in New York, where the owners of the Pierre, a fifty-seven-year-old landmark, ousted Trusthouse Forte as manager and installed Four Seasons in its place. He firmly upheld a policy of charging 20 per cent higher but spending 25 per cent more on rooms than the industry average. When serving guests, the chain's staff-to-guest ratio became almost double the industry average: one staff member for every guest. Its key policy is understated elegance provided with that extra touch of personalized service, "so that everyone who stays at a Four

Seasons hotel becomes one of our salesmen." One unpaid salesman is Stanley Marcus, former chairman of the classy Neiman-Marcus stores in Texas. Marcus once told the *Wall Street Journal*: "Four Seasons uses the softest toilet paper I've found anywhere. They pay attention to the smallest details."

Indeed, Sharp is noted for his almost obsessive concern for minute details. Ken Field, president of Bramalea Limited, the Toronto land developers, recalls that when the Four Seasons Hotel was being planned for Yorkville Avenue, Sharp insisted on spending an extra $40,000 for interlocking bricks in the driveway instead of asphalt. "I told Issy, 'You've got to be kidding. Who cares what the driveway is paved with? It's covered with snow half the year anyway!'" Issy's response was that *he* knew – and so would their discriminating clientele.

Another credo coined by Issy is to provide guests with AVPE – an acronym for "A Very Pleasant Experience." The Four Seasons claims to have won the initial battle of the beds among luxury hostelries years ago when it was the first chain to put a shampoo in its bathrooms. Now every hotel has its own personal brand of exotic shampoo, and New York hotel buffs can tell a tourist's hotel by the scent. It was one of the first in North America to introduce a concierge service. And it has been a pacesetter in furnishing the sort of personalized service which, as nicely phrased by another unpaid salesperson, Gloria Vanderbilt, "gives you the feeling someone knows you're there." It's a service achieved in part thanks to Four Seasons computers.

A computer enables telephone operators to call guests by name whenever the guest answers the phone. It allows the hotel to check a guest card and determine in advance whether a hard Japanese pillow or a soft eiderdown one or Irish linen towels are requested. It reminds the staff to stock the suite minibar with Coke rather than Pepsi when the president of Coca-Cola is a guest. And it informs them that the singer Tony Bennett prefers a room with morning light, because the morning after a nightclub performance he likes to paint.

But the chain's reputation for personalized service is due chiefly to the remarkable dedication of its staff. They are motivated in a number of ways. They enjoy profit-sharing plans, get two "stress breaks" a day, and front-desk clerks are paid two or three times what they might expect because they are elevated to the status of the premier hosts that the public first meets.

Mostly, though, they are motivated by the back-patting heaped on them by Issy's management team in the Toronto headquarters. Issy fervently believes in praising staff members for performing beyond the call of duty, and the reports collected in Toronto headquarters bear him out. In emergencies, Four Seasons staff have provided to guests the shoes off their feet and buttons from their own clothes, have applied the Heimlich Manoeuvre on choking guests, have "just happened" to have a Paris telephone directory when a guest wanted to place a call to the French capital.

The most extraordinary thing about the Four Seasons success story is that it has never been marred by friction among the partners. Koffler considers it something of a record in the annals of business. "For twenty-five years, we never had a contract between us, never had harsh words between us, never had a serious fight. Every crucial decision has been talked out between us, and we never had to use the weight of our shares as clout to make a point."

Initially, the equity was split evenly three ways between Koffler, Creed, and the Sharp family, with the understanding that Max and Issy were also responsible as building contractors. But with Issy assuming a full-time leadership role in operating the company, Koffler and Creed agreed that he be made an equal partner. So, without any transferring of money, the others reduced their holdings to 25 per cent.

Their only important disagreement with Issy arose in February, 1986, when the decision was made to change the Four Seasons from a private into a public company. Sharp objected because it would, he believed, be easier to operate a private company rather than having to satisfy a lot of shareholders. All parties agree now that it was a difference of opinion rather than an acrimonious conflict. They further agree it was settled amicably, especially since Four Seasons shares soon catapulted from $14 to over $20 per share.

A total of 4.3 million subordinate voting shares were sold on the Toronto and Montreal stock exchanges for $60.2 million. Of that total, almost two million shares worth $27 million were sold by members of the Koffler and Creed families. Koffler and Creed remained as board members and major shareholders, owning 7½ per cent each. Issy retained control of the company; indeed, through his multiple-voting shares, he controls 83 per cent of the votes. The reason Koffler and Creed wished to sell some of their shares was to attain liquid capital for their family estate planning. Koffler in particular wanted ready cash available to help finance the King Ranch Health and Fitness Resort being built by his son Adam and his daughter Tiana.

Koffler recalls another disagreement – a minor one – he once had with Issy. It, too, concluded harmoniously, and it resulted in the launching of what was to become North America's largest annual outdoor art exhibition. Since the Four Seasons continues the tradition of decorating its hotels with the finest Kirman rugs on the floor, beautiful sculpture on antique tables, and original paintings on the wall, its founding partners now look back affectionately on their first art show as a cherished link with the chain's birth.

It dates back to a summery Sunday afternoon in 1961, when Murray and Marvelle Koffler were strolling around Washington Square in New York, where Greenwich Village artists were displaying their work. The Kofflers were enchanted with what they saw: they chatted with some of the artists and bought a couple of paintings for their recreation room. Then, on the plane flying home, Koffler read a news story on the front page of *The Toronto Star*. It reported that three policemen had kicked two artists off the stairs of the old City Hall for peddling paintings on city property on a Sunday. "How idiotic for provincial Toronto to do something so backward as that!" Koffler sounded off to Marvelle. "I must do something about it."

By coincidence, Koffler also read a news story about Alan Jarvis, director of the National Gallery of Canada, losing his job in Ottawa for awarding a prize to a controversial abstract painting. It had been done by an artist's cat that had ambled across the canvas and had left its inky paw marks behind in an intriguing design. Koffler figured that Jarvis must be progressive-minded about artistic matters and phoned him for advice on putting together an outdoor art show. Jarvis was glad to oblige, working in tandem with art dealer Jack Pollock and art historian David Silcox. But despite their collective know-how, they got nowhere in their attempts to present the exhibition at such public places as Queen's Park and Allen Gardens.

"We won't let petty officials stop us," said Koffler. He asked Creed and Issy to let him stage the show in the parking lot of the newly opened Four Seasons on Jarvis. Creed enthusiastically accepted the idea, though it meant wangling parking space for their guests across the street. But Issy winced at the prospect of banging nails into their new brickwork. Koffler persuasively helped him to overcome his qualms and, in Tom Sawyer-like style, talked all hands into hammering nails into concrete walls and hanging paintings as well on surrounding fences.

For the opening, Koffler invited a hundred dignitaries and plenty of press people. He ordered huge, fresh strawberries flown in from California and had them served with quaffs of Mumm's champagne. And he talked Tom Kneebone, the noted musical revue comic, into officiating at the opening ceremonies in appropriate artistic style.

Kneebone clumped into the parking lot on top of an ancient, spavined, sway-backed horse minus a saddle. The comedian was fittingly attired in a scarlet, purple, and orange Van Gogh smock, with a white silk Lindbergh aviator scarf strung around his neck and blowing in the breeze. Brandishing aloft a fairy princess wand with a gold-coloured star twinkling at its end, he announced, "I herewith declare this first Toronto Outdoor Art Exhibition to be officially open." Then, amid rousing cheers, Kneebone rode galloping aback his nag off into the Far West of Jarvis Street.

Despite the comedy lowjinks, the show has since become a highly respected annual summer rite. "It was a hell of a good promotion for the Four Seasons," Koffler acknowledges. "But it also has sparked great goodwill for Toronto."

Six years after the opening, the city fathers relented and presented it as the first outdoor activity to be held on an annual basis at the new City Hall's Nathan Phillips Square – a block away from the old City Hall that had once booted out those two artists so ignominiously. It has since served as an early showcase for the talents of such Canadian artists as Ken Danby, Gordon Rayner, and Joe Rosenthal. At a token cost to themselves, about 600 artists exhibit their work each year before more than 50,000 visitors and compete for prizes worth $10,000 as well as cash sales.

Koffler estimates that more than a million dollars' worth of Canadian art has been sold at the show over the past quarter century. Though Four Seasons gives a major prize every year to emphasize the continuity, he prefers to serve as honorary chairman and let others run the show. Beth Slaney, the original Four Seasons publicity director, has been paid to act as the show's co-ordinator since its inception, except for ten years when Hilda Wilson did it.

Slaney believes the operation of the Toronto Outdoor Art Exhibition is typical of Koffler's style as a community do-gooder. "Murray's hobby is organizing on a grand scale," she says. "He sees the need. He acts on it. He involves himself emotionally and financially. Then, after creating the project and helping select an administrator, he backs off and is content to play a lesser role – until he's into his next community involvement."

CHAPTER FIFTEEN

Mr. Involver

One of Murray Koffler's many nicknames is "Mr. Involver." It is a sobriquet he has won because of the way he involves himself in so many community causes. He was first tagged with that nickname in circumstances fraught with drama.

It was noontime on June 6, 1968. Koffler was standing at the podium in the Centennial Ballroom of Toronto's Inn on the Park. He was about to address 500 key executives from Canada's pharmaceutical industry. He had invited them to a formal luncheon to announce the merger of Plaza Drugs Ltd. with the Koffler chain of pharmacies.

A moment before Koffler began his talk, Norman Kert, his advertising representative, approached him and whispered, "Have you heard the news? Robert Kennedy is dead." The night before, in Los Angeles, the U.S. senator and presidential candidate had been gunned down by an assassin. Early rumours reported that the killer was a drug-crazed youth. Kert mentioned this to Koffler, adding that perhaps he should say something about Senator Kennedy's death.

Koffler instantly scrapped the notes he had prepared for his speech. He asked the audience to stand for a minute of silent prayer. Then he improvised an emotional appeal: "We who deal in drugs for the medical betterment of mankind must face our moral responsibility. Somehow we must take steps to combat drug abuse. It feeds the underbelly of our society. It threatens to destroy an entire generation of young Canadians. I'm ready to do something about it on a national scale. Right now! I urge you to join me."

Thus was born CODA, the acronym for Council on Drug Abuse. It is a non-profit, voluntary, national association devoted to educating the public about the dangers of the non-medical use of drugs, from marijuana to cocaine. Over the past two decades, CODA has distributed well over four million pamphlets, conducted school seminars for half a million students and 20,000 teachers, served as a major preventive resource for the Canadian Armed Forces bases, and sponsored various media advertising campaigns. As the founding chairman of CODA and now its honorary chairman, Koffler is especially proud that it inspired the programs of PADA (Pharmacists Against Drug Abuse) across Canada. It meant that hundreds of other drugstores, apart from Shoppers Drug Mart outlets, installed racks of medical care literature, which Koffler originally named Drug Information Centres.

Koffler, however, is more rueful than joyful about the lessons he had to learn the hard way concerning the delicate art of public relations. His experience while orchestrating CODA's educational campaigns taught him that journalists must be treated warily. No matter how virtuous the cause you are championing on behalf of the public weal, you must always keep in mind that a reporter remains a news hound – one who may be ready to bite a hospitable hand if it means a better story.

Koffler's hand was first snapped at ungratefully at the initial press conference he assembled to announce the formation of CODA. Thinking only of being a good host, he served the reporters gathered at the Four Seasons Hotel the conventional drinks along with their canapés. To his consternation, the reporter from the *Toronto Telegram* seized on the ironic twist that the booze his host was feeding him so graciously could be construed as being a drug offering. The news story began: "Amid the tinkle of ice in cocktail glasses, the Council on Drug Abuse was officially launched today . . ."

Koffler's hand was bitten even more savagely by a female reporter from *Time* magazine. In the newspaper trade, a deliberate assault on an interview subject is called a "hatchet job," and this hatchet lady was indeed wickedly after his blood. Her two-column report in the August 31, 1970, Canadian edition of *Time* was so scathing that Koffler refused to clip it and preserve it in his eight file cases of memorabilia in his personal archives. Yet he can't dislodge it from his memory. When Koffler talks about the scurrilous article, he sums it up in a lurid headline: "Millionaire Druggist Fakes Interest In Drug Abuse To Get Government Off His Back." The article was not quite that bad, but it was bad enough. It used the snarky insinuations and snide innuendos commonplace in what was then known as "*Time*-style."

Koffler recalls that it was written by a young, so-called hippie sent from New York to interview him. She clearly considered herself part of the flower-power, pot-smoking counter culture and regarded him as the enemy. Playing up the word "drug" as though it were a scarlet banner, she pictured him as the "well-to-do" forty-six-year-old, conservative druggist whose seventy-two "drug outlets" then grossed $50 million a year as a result of pioneering his concept of a "drug supermarket."

She likewise sniped maliciously at Nicholas Leluk, the thirty-five-year-old assistant registrar from the Ontario College of Pharmacy he had selected as full-time executive director of CODA. As though it were a sin, she said Leluk was a druggist who "unhesitatingly describes himself as a 'square – a member of the Establishment.'" Then, in scalding invective, she condemned them both: "It is that sort of admission, on top of CODA's Moral Rearmament-style campaign, that makes it difficult to reach the young, who rarely respond to a holier-than-thou approach."

She then mocked as sanctimonious what Koffler considered CODA's two most praiseworthy accomplishments. One was Man And His Drugs, an imaginative pavilion that occupied the entire Queen Elizabeth Building at the Canadian National

Exhibition in Toronto. It was the fair's most popular exhibit, drawing a million people, but it left CODA in debt for almost $100,000. Koffler put up $25,000 of his own money and signed a note for the rest because he felt the exhibit was that vital. The *Time* writer used fancy language to dismiss it as a useless "psychedelic phantasmagoria of flashing lights, chung-chung sound tracks and Dadaist displays designed both to simulate and decry the chemical fantasies of the turned-on generation."

Patently a turn-off, she wrote, was the International Symposium on Drug Abuse that CODA was simultaneously sponsoring at the Ontario Science Centre. The first international conference of its kind, it attracted 325 delegates from nine countries; its forums were deemed so important they were televised by the CTV network for eight hours across Canada. But the *Time* sharpshooter took potshots at it because "there were scarcely any under-thirties to be seen among the scientists and social workers who rehashed cases of preteen freakouts."

She was most mean-spirited in her conclusion. Using the *Time*-snidery ploy of citing anonymous sources, she insinuated that the entire project was nothing more than a whitewash: "Because CODA gets heavy support from the Canadian Pharmaceutical Association, a few federal officials even suspect that CODA's concern may not be limited to spreading the word that drug abuse is dangerous. Some in Ottawa think that CODA's backers are worried that any formal attack on drug abuse by the federal government could result in stricter federal controls on drug manufacturers, distributors and retailers."

Koffler was devastated. "It was a dastardly article and I felt terribly hurt," he now says. "It made me realize I was too thin-skinned to ever enter politics. I've been asked by both major political parties to run as a candidate. But I keep turning them down, because I know I can't stand the barbs and darts of political and press attacks."

The *Time* jeremiad by no means diminished Koffler's crusading fervour for involving himself in community affairs. It did, however, have two effects. First, it induced him in 1970 to hire as a youth consultant for CODA a former newspaper court reporter named Norman Panzica, who could relate to young people. Koffler learned about Panzica from his son Leon, who came home from York Mills Collegiate quite excited. "Hey, Dad," he said. "We heard this counsellor on drug abuse give a terrific talk at the school assembly today. You ought to meet the guy."

Panzica, who has since conducted more than half a million student "rap" sessions for CODA and written the popular parents' handbook *Your Teen And Drugs*, is still a provocative personality at fifty-two. He describes himself as a "baggy-eyed, pipe-smoking, burned-out John Cassavetes who looks more like a speed freak than most speed freaks do."

The pipe-smoking adjective is relevant, because he uses it as a springboard for discussion. Invariably, when he enters a high school auditorium, a student will spot the pipe sticking out of his jacket pocket and ask, "Sir, you're a drug addict yourself, hooked on tobacco, right?"

Panzica invariably replies, "Right. The difference between you and me, kid, is that when I started smoking, Frank Sinatra and Abbott and Costello and opera stars and baseball stars and cops and doctors all told me it was okay to smoke. The difference between you and people of your parents' generation is that you know the dangers before you start. We didn't."

Panzica's perceptions of Koffler are similarly provocative. At their first meeting, Koffler struck him as looking like Submariner, the character in a Canadian comic book during World War II who could swim for miles and miles underwater. He believes Koffler's character is reflected in the "innocently astute approach" the pharmacist used when hiring him. "Let's make this simple, Norman," he remembers Koffler saying. "We at CODA will give you whatever we can afford. And you give us whatever time you think is justified."

Panzica now remarks with a smile, "Of course, when you negotiate as openly as that, any rational person gives more time than you're being paid for, because you're being trusted so completely."

And Panzica, who has several degrees in psychology, offers a keen observation about Koffler's speaking style at fund-raising meetings. "What comes across, apart from his sincerity, is the curious blend of supreme self-confidence and approval-seeking both at once. His voice speaks passionately, 'This is what I believe we must do. Let's do it together.' But his facial expression says imploringly, 'Is this okay? Please agree.' Whatever it is, it's a winning combination."

Koffler's early debacles with the press exerted a second effect: they strengthened his appreciation of his long-time public relations consultant, Hilda Wilson. Ordinarily a public relations counsellor can be defined as a press agent with a manicure, or perhaps as a Munchausen proficient at composing hyperbole in press releases. But Hilda Wilson is no ordinary PR lady.

"An inexhaustible dynamo," Koffler says of her admiringly. "Hilda is more than a publicist. She's been my right hand in my community involvements for almost twenty years. She was my Girl Friday in helping build a corporate image. She's a super organizer of fund-raising events."

But she is most indispensable, he says, as the drafter of all his speeches. "I can phone her at ten o'clock at night and say, 'Hilda, this is what I want to say in my talk.' I'll spew out the essence of the points I want to make. By next morning, she has framed the rough draft. Then I rewrite it. Sometimes, if I don't use the written address at all, she gets mad as hell. 'Gee, I'm awfully sorry,' I'll apologize. 'But really I do appreciate you, Hilda.' We've grown together in PR and we work together beautifully. To me, she's still the best PR person in the business."

Wilson smiles when informed of Koffler's bugling on her behalf. "The truth is, I don't think Murray *needs* a public relations consultant, or ever did," she says. "I think he's his own best PR man. He's the perfect client for a PR person because he's a natural at it. Right from the beginning, I thought of myself as his facilitator rather than his publicist."

Now sixty, she is a hard-driving, chain-smoking, seemingly tough yet inwardly tender executive, who built her fifteen-staff firm, The Hilda Wilson Group, from scratch. She met Koffler in 1968, after she had borrowed $3,000 to set up her one-woman firm, specializing in financial public relations. One of her clients was Leon Weinstein, the new president of the Loblaws supermarket chain. Koffler noticed that Weinstein quickly developed a high profile in the media as both a personality and public figure. He and the late Sam Shopsowitz, the rotund hot dog and pastrami tycoon, were frequently photographed at fund-raising charitable events, with Weinstein playing the fiddle and Shopsy the accordion. The duo would raise money with the jocose offer: "For a contribution of $50, we'll perform. And for $100, we *won't* perform."

With Wilson's help, Weinstein also gained a reputation as a champion of the consumer. She remembers Koffler phoning her one day when his drugstore chain was about to take over Plaza Drugs and simultaneously make a public stock offering. "He wanted an image on Bay Street that the investment community could relate to," she says. "And he wanted an image equivalent to Leon Weinstein's as a champion of the consumer."

Before being hired, she met Koffler and agreed there was a good business story to tell. "You understand, though, that to communicate the story, there has to be a name, a face, a personality identified with your corporation," she said. "That spokesperson will have to be you."

As she left his office, she remembers Koffler saying wryly, "I'll do whatever you recommend, Hilda. But *please* don't say I have to play the violin in public like Leon."

In the years since, Koffler has never resorted to fiddle-playing as a means of raising funds for community causes. Neither has he been compelled to twist arms. His technique is much more subtle. According to Wilson, he inspires people to give. "He paints a big picture of a cause, but it's not so big that you can't see yourself in it," she says. "Through his eloquence you're moved to help him finish off the details of the picture. It becomes a noble cause and you feel ennobled by participating."

Just as Koffler's honours have multiplied over the years, so have his community involvements, as he likes calling them. At last count, he has been involved in at least forty humanitarian projects. In 1976, when he was at his peak as a corporate executive, he described to Dean Walker of *Canadian Executive* magazine how he allocated the time in his work week. He said he devoted three and a half days to pharmacy business; about half a day to Four Seasons hotel business; and an entire day to the business of his community involvements. In the biblical spirit of casting one's bread on the waters, he maintained, "My communal activities do more for me than I do for them. They've broadened my perspective in terms of the people I've met and the places I've been. And I've had so much fun doing them!"

When asked point blank what motivates him, Koffler frowns, ponders, and then admits he doesn't know. "I'm either burdened or blessed with this mainspring inside of me of being a problem solver. I see a need, it triggers a response, I get excited. Then I can't rest until I help solve the problem." But he regards himself as a catalyst and strategist of immediate action rather than a long-range planner and administrator. "There's nothing worse than a founding chairman who stays there and stays there and stays there," he argues. "I believe in putting the right people on boards and committees and giving them room to move. With their new ideas and fresh vitality, they can do a better job. It's their time to have a place in the sun. So, when they're off and running, my policy is to bow out and tackle my next project. You might say my philosophy is to keep things percolating all the time on the front burner."

Another tenet of his philosophy is his refusal to serve as a mere figurehead on a fund-raising committee. It's his policy not to accept a post unless he can contribute actively his creative talents. In that sense, he adheres to the gift-giving precept of the ancient Jewish sages: "You must not only give what you *have*; you must also give what you *are*."

Koffler's style as a community activist is illustrated by his involvement in Operation Lifeline. That was the name the Toronto press gave to the rescue mission of the Southeast Asian "boat people" undertaken by Howard Adelman in the summer of 1979. Adelman, an idealistic philosophy professor at York University, was deeply moved by the plight of the thousands of homeless refugees forced to flee from Vietnam,

Laos, and Cambodia. He was instrumental in organizing the sponsorship of fifty families and helped influence the Canadian government to open its doors to 50,000 more.

Adelman was advised by Paul Godfrey, the chairman of Metro Toronto, that it was necessary to assemble a reputable board of prominent doers and shakers for a committee meeting. The philosophy professor was in a fix. He was not acquainted with a single business magnate in the community. Then he remembered he had once been a delivery boy for Murray Koffler's drugstore on College Steet. "I phoned him at home, and though he had no recollection of me at all, Murray listened sympathetically as I explained the situation," recalls Adelman.

Koffler answered without hesitation, "Sure. Count me in. Tell me when and where do we meet?"

"At seven sharp tomorrow morning at my home on Wells Hill Avenue."

Koffler, who hates even the thought of being an early riser, gulped. "It means I'll have to get up at the ungodly hour of five a.m.," he said with a shudder. "But okay. I'll be there."

Adelman, now forty-nine, recalls Koffler as "a gregarious Irish imp" with the vision, the sensitivity, and the savvy to get things done. He added prestige to their sixteen-member committee by persuading Roland Michener, Canada's former Governor-General, to join in the project. More importantly, says Adelman, Koffler single-handedly raised $300,000 for Operation Lifeline. Not only did he donate money of his own, but he sent personal letters to the heads of 1,200 corporations across Canada. And he pulled strings to get the CBC to televise a Boat Peoples' Telethon.

Ultimately the government opened the gates to 100,000 boat people and by 1983 the rescue mission was complete. Koffler looks back on it as "a super experience that helped me understand the people in the Vietnamese and Chinese community. The credit belongs to Howard Adelman. He literally saved the lives of the boat people."

Adelman, an authority on the philosophy of charity-giving, was intrigued by Koffler's remarkable reluctance to take any credit whatsoever. "Murray was self-effacing to an unusual degree," he says. "He sat for hours in the CBC producer's studio making sure everybody involved in the telethon got the proper credit. Yet he didn't want any for himself. In a like manner, he was prepared to sit on our committee and contribute his money and energy and ideas. Yet he wouldn't even accept a title. He seemed to do it all for the sheer joy of doing it and doing it well."

Koffler's philosophy on taking credit is flexible. Whether or not he links the family name with a charitable cause seems to depend on the scope of the contribution made either by the Murray Koffler Foundation or the Marvelle Koffler Foundation. For significant gifts, he advises philanthropists: "Put your name up front; put your name where your activity is." He believes it encourages others to give and instills a sense of philanthropic mission in one's heirs. But he emphasizes that the money should be funnelled into a worthwhile cause. He contends that if you aspire to achieve some form of immortality on earth, you want to be remembered for positive humanitarian reasons. Too many achievers have gone down in history with their names attached to objects unworthy of them. Count Karl Nesselrode, for example, is not remembered today as a noble Russian statesman but rather as a fruit custard pie. The Italian coloratura soprano, Luisa Tetrazzini, is now identified as a chicken-and-spaghetti dish and the Australian opera singer, Nellie Melba, wound up on the menu as a piece of dried toast and a peach dessert.

Koffler says he disagrees with wealthy benefactors who tell him, "I'd like to participate with you in this charitable project, but I don't want my name spread all over the place. I'm afraid I'll become a target for mendicants, like bees drawn to a honeypot." Koffler takes an opposite viewpoint. "I maintain that the more things our family name is on, the more gratification my kids will get out of it, and [they] will follow suit in their time," he says. "I've never found anyone wealthy who's gone broke giving away money." Giving, he concludes, can be a form of investment, a means of sharing in the better welfare of your community. Besides, giving can be fun.

Sidney Liswood is the former chief executive officer of Toronto's Mount Sinai Hospital and, at seventy-one, continues to serve as president of its research centre, the Mount Sinai Institute. He has coined a sweet phrase to explain his friend's generosity: "Murray is paying his rent for living on this earth." To illustrate the pleasure Koffler derives from philanthropy, Liswood likes telling the story of a memorable lunch they had in 1968 at the Inn on the Park. It was not meant to be a fund-raising lunch: Koffler, as co-chairman of a recent financial campaign, had already donated $50,000 for constructing the new Mount Sinai Hospital. Rather, it was a social tête-à-tête enabling Liswood to "weep on a friendly shoulder." He explained to Koffler the troubles he was having raising $2 million to complete the hospital's new fourth-floor ambulatory care centre, previously known as the out-patients' department.

"Surely, Sidney, that should be no problem for you," said Koffler. "You know every source around town it's possible to tap."

"No, I've approached everybody I know and I've run absolutely dry," said Liswood dolefully. "If I could only get one person to give us a million, I know that gesture would be enough of a stimulus so that the other million would drop into our lap."

Liswood remembers how Koffler leaned across the table, put out both hands, and broke into his Irishy smile. "You have it," he said.

"What do you mean?"

"I'm giving you the one million dollars."

Liswood now says, "I started to cry."

Koffler was as good as his word. He stopped by the hospital an hour later and, without saying a single word, handed Liswood a check for $1 million. In gratitude, Liswood named the new facility the Koffler Ambulatory Care Centre. In a similar low-key fashion, as a result of an additional $250,000 donated by Koffler in 1982, Mount Sinai has established a Koffler Chair in Hospital Research.

Koffler is aware, however, that such honorifics, while affording a pleasant massage to one's ego, cut no ice with the general populace. In his turn, he likes telling the gently self-mocking story of what happened when he once went to the Mount Sinai Hospital for his semi-annual checkup. He was mildly exasperated when the receptionist asked, "How do you spell the name Koffler?"

He spelled it out for her and there was still no recognition. "Would you like to see it in print?" he asked.

"Yeah, I suppose it would help," she said, expecting him to show her his credit card.

"In that case, would you please turn your head around?" he said.

She did so, and was able to read in big letters on the wall: KOFFLER AMBULATORY CARE CENTRE.

"Oh," she said. "I never noticed that."

"It was not deflating," Koffler insists amiably. "It just goes to prove once again that fame is as fleeting as yesterday's newspaper used to line today's parrot cage."

Nevertheless, no matter how ephemeral fame may be, giving credit counts. Koffler believes this principle especially applies to corporate patronage of the arts. He is vehemently opposed to the cynical business slogan of the late Canadian press baron, Lord Beaverbrook: "Get on. Get honest. Get honoured." Instead Koffler upholds the two credos: "An enlightened businessman must have a social conscience as well as a counting house" and "A thriving business ought to be a stepping stone to an enriched cultural life."

He has preached those two doctrines in his various roles as an arts patron who, to paraphrase the vulgar saying, puts his money plus his innovative ideas where his mouth is. His exalted titles include: founding chairman and million-dollar-donor of the Koffler Centre of the Arts in Toronto's Jewish Community Centre; founding chairman of the Toronto Outdoor Art Exhibition; governor of Massey Hall; patron of the Canadian Opera Company; and chairman of the public appeal campaign for Roy Thomson Hall, personally donating $125,000 toward its construction.

One of his most enduring contributions is the novel form of corporate arts sponsorship he originated for the Toronto

Symphony. Koffler and his wife Marvelle had been loyal subscription members of the symphony since their marriage in 1950. "Tuesdays were the wonderful night every two weeks when we could get away from our problems and get intoxicated on music," he says. So he felt complimented when asked to join the board.

He remembers being invited one day by Edward Pickering, president of the symphony and former president of Simpsons-Sears, to have lunch at that bastion of the Establishment, the York Club. Over their drinks, Pickering asked, "How would you like to be chairman of the symphony's business sponsorship program?"

"What does that mean?"

"Well, you sell a corporation on the idea of sponsoring a special concert for an evening. They pay us $15,000. We give them 2,600 tickets. They're supposed to fill the house by giving away the tickets to customers and employees."

"What if they can't distribute all the tickets?"

"Well, that often happens and it's a little uncomfortable," said Pickering. "It means the orchestra plays to half a house."

"Ed, I don't think it's too difficult getting a corporate sponsor to put up $15,000. But if I were a sponsor, I'd find it very difficult trying to give away 2,600 tickets. Let me think about it."

At their next meeting, Koffler came up with a proposal. "Instead of having a limited number of big corporations bankroll an *extra* concert, at great expense to all, why not have more of them sponsor *existing* concerts for a lesser fee?" he said. "They get front-row seats for their top brass, corporate publicity in the newspaper ads and programs, and a reception before or after the concert. We retain responsibility for selling the tickets. If we sell the house for twenty concerts, I figure our total net will be five times greater than before."

"Frankly, Murray, I'm doubtful. But if you think the idea will work, why don't you run with it?"

Koffler wrote letters and made follow-up phone calls and sold out the entire season. His innovation was so successful that it was taken up by the Canadian Opera Company, the National Ballet of Canada, the Toronto Mendelssohn Choir, and other arts institutions. And when Walter Homburger, managing director of the Toronto Symphony, reported it to the Association of Symphony Orchestras in the U.S., the technique became the standard format for business sponsorship throughout North America.

One of Koffler's most interesting acts of arts patronage was his backing of what was to become the world's most widely seen art film, dubbed into thirty languages: Harry Rasky's *Homage To Chagall: The Colours Of Love*. Originally produced as a ninety-minute, sixteen-millimetre TV documentary for the CBC, the Chagall film deserved a larger audience. One enthusiast was the impresario who controlled Walter Reade Theatres in New York. "Look," he told Rasky. "If you can make a thirty-five-millimetre blowup of the film and raise the distribution money, I'll guarantee a run at the Little Carnegie Cinema next to Carnegie Hall for three weeks."

But despite Rasky's pleadings, the CBC was definitely not interested. Feeling frustrated, Rasky happened to run into Marvelle Koffler one bitterly cold February night in 1976 as they were entering the Art Gallery of Ontario. He mentioned his Chagall dilemma. When she said she was a long-time Chagall fan, he invited her to a private screening at his CBC office on Bay Street.

She was moved to tears by the film and was prompted to do something she had never done before. She told her husband, "Murray, I'd like you to consider investing in this beautiful masterwork." Koffler saw it and was similarly enthralled, and when his attempt to interest the business community in investing in the film fell through, he underwrote the venture for $120,000 to buy the motion picture rights from the CBC and to edit and exhibit the large-screen movie. The Kofflers' daughter Theo took a small share in the film as well.

The film's opening on June 26, 1977, at the Little Carnegie Cinema was orchestrated like a Hollywood premiere. A glittering crowd of 200, including director Otto Preminger, comedian Zero Mostel, and the Canadian actors Christopher Plummer and Lou Jacobi, attended a champagne reception at the Canadian consulate in Manhattan. Movie critics unanimously acclaimed the film, and it was subsequently nominated for an Oscar.

The film sparked several rewarding spinoffs. Koffler has since used it as a vehicle to raise hundreds of thousands of dollars for the Weizmann Institute of Science in Rehovot, Israel. Indeed, before Marc Chagall's death at ninety-seven, he arranged for the French-speaking Jewish painter to receive an honorary degree at the institute. Koffler delights in telling the story of how he took immersion courses at L'Ecole Berlitz, so that he could communicate with Chagall at the gala affair. "We were having dinner and I was speaking my very best Berlitz French," he recalls. "Chagall turns and looks me square in the eye and says, 'Monsieur Kofflair, you must excuse me. I do not speak English.'"

Koffler's fling in show business was a great boost to Rasky's career. The Academy Award nomination gained the film a global reputation and broadened its audience immensely on foreign TV networks; it also won Rasky both an Emmy and the non-fiction movie award from the Directors' Guild of America. Both he and Koffler have hopes it will be distributed on cassettes to art galleries and schools across Canada and converted into a musical for Broadway.

Looking back on their partnership in the venture, Rasky makes two interesting observations. "Murray was a gentleman every step of the way," he says. "He was always accessible. If I had a problem, I didn't have to go through ten secretaries. And if Murray wants to reach you, he always phones you himself. None of this stuff about a secretary calling up and saying, 'Hold on until I summon the master.'"

Most interesting, though Koffler seemed to have "a certain amount of pleasant ham in him," he was astonishingly reluctant to take kudos for his efforts. Rasky remembers saying, "Murray, I'd like to put your name on the film as a co-producer." Koffler replied: "No, I don't want that. It's your film and I don't merit the credit."

Nevertheless, Rasky persisted in inserting a credit line in newspaper ads for the film that read: "Murray Koffler and Harry Rasky present . . ." Rasky strokes his beard and shrugs in amazement. "I gave him that billing on my own initiative.

Murray never asked for it. Yet he had every right to. A most extraordinary thing to happen in the ego-ridden world of showbiz."

When Koffler does consent to the use of his name, one thing is noteworthy. Credit is never accorded to "Murray Koffler," the person. He insists instead that only the name "Koffler" be acknowledged, so that the honour will be shared by his entire family. "The important thing is to link your family name to something positive, something that will live on in your community long after you've all gone," he says. That concept is illustrated by his personal gift of $1 million toward the $8.7 million needed for the new Koffler Student Services Centre of the University of Toronto.

As a graduate of the university's College of Pharmacy, Koffler was enormously pleased in the 1970s when he was asked to serve as both vice-chairman of the university's funding campaign and a member of its governing council. He remembers listening attentively when students on the council told him how the university had become a complex, spread-out megalopolis. They felt cut off from the community of greater Toronto and cut off from each other within the university. They particularly felt a lack of camaraderie and campus spirit. The key reason was that the various services for the 40,000 students were scattered in all corners of the campus in a jumble of sixteen buildings. When asked to locate a central building, Koffler characteristically said, "Okay, I'll do it."

After examining several possible sites suggested by university president John Evans, Koffler chanced to be driving one morning past the venerable Toronto Central Reference Library. It was a dilapidated relic located on the northwest corner of College Street and St. George on the edge of the campus. Built in 1907, thanks to a grant from the U.S. steel titan, Andrew Carnegie, it had become vacant as a result of the modern Metro Central Library on Yonge Street; it was temporarily housing the Faculty of Engineering after a disastrous fire.

Koffler pulled up to a stop and gazed at the gracefully arched, beaux-arts style building, where he had spent so many hours of study in his undergraduate days in the 1940s. It had been designated an historic site and looked like a stately dowager, still handsome but slightly gone to seed. "What an ideal place!" he said to himself.

Alfred Chapman, the architect son of the original architect of the library, guided the renovation and expansion of the building, and finally, on September 5, 1985, a crowd of more than 1,000 attended the official opening. The CBC's Barbara Frum was present to pay tribute to her friend Koffler's "great vision and great generosity" and spoke of "my sentimental attachment to this dear old pile. It is an historic monument to public education now reborn." She went on to declare unabashedly, "I loved the reference library. Subsequently, I came back, as we all did, to see good theatre here, art exhibitions here. I rented films here. I pored through old, old city newspapers stored here for journalistic assignments. And now these halls will provide a new generation with an abundance of services that we in the 1950s could not have dreamed of."

Brought together under one roof were an abundance of facilities. They included student health and housing services, a career counselling centre, interdenominational pastoral counselling, and, for the general public, a one-stop computer shop, Canada's third largest bookstore, and a jewel box of a theatre.

As a showman, Koffler paid particular attention to what had been called for twenty years simply the Central Library Theatre. It had an honourable tradition of presenting controversial plays, but in practical terms it had been difficult to stage *any* kind of play there, according to the theatre's urbane artistic director, Ronald Bryden. A Jamaica-born graduate of both Cambridge and the University of Toronto, he was a one-time drama critic for Britain's *Observer* and *New Statesman*. On one of Koffler's many visits to the site with his family during the renovations, Bryden told him that the theatre's single, tiny, eight-square-foot dressing room was dismally inadequate. To make a complete costume change, actors had to take turns undressing in the toilet. And to make an entrance from the right-hand side of the stage, performers had to stand outside on the fire escape and step onstage via the fire door. Heaven knows how they fared, Bryden lamented, when it was raining.

The expense of its restoration was not covered in the budget. So to pay for renovations that would cost $180,000,

247

Koffler hit upon the idea of selling each of the theatre's 180 seats for $1,000. Subscribers would have their names engraved permanently on a brass plaque. In addition, each would participate in a raffle and the winner of the draw would have the right to choose a name for the theatre. The winner, Mary Kent, happened to be a member of the university's governing council; she named it the Robert Gill, after the revered former director of the university's Hart House Theatre. The alterations duly provided for two separate dressing rooms, each spacious enough to accommodate ten actors.

Bryden, who is accustomed to sizing up performers, later remarked that Koffler would be a director's ideal if the pharmacist were to assume a stage career. "There's a theatrical quality about Mr. Koffler – you can tell it in the way he wears clothes and conducts himself," Bryden told a journalist. "He'd make a marvellous pro actor. He's totally decisive. He knows who he is and why he's there. And he knows exactly when to make his exit. A likeable performer, with terrific timing and a commanding presence – and, like every great actor, a man of infinite surprises. There's no end to the depths in the man."

In that same year, 1985, Koffler delivered the convocation address to graduating pharmacists at the University of Toronto at the time of his being awarded an honorary Doctor of Laws degree for his many years of public service – including his forthcoming $6 million Koffler Institute of Pharmacy Management. Koffler avoided the customary bromides in his speech. Instead, as founding chairman of the Canadian Council for Native Business, he exhorted the convocation audience to give a helping hand to the deprived Indians and Inuit of Canada.

He dramatized their plight by relating two personal experiences that had heightened his awareness of their misery during a trip to Calgary. While inspecting a building addition to the Four Seasons Hotel there, he had stumbled upon several homeless Indians. They were huddled together, with newspapers drawn about them for warmth, in a corner of the concrete basement where they tried to sleep in the bitter cold. "What a sorry state of affairs to be happening right here in Canada!" he thought. The next day, just as he was entering a

Shoppers Drug Mart, he saw two ragged Indians being hustled out the front door. They had been caught shoplifting an alcohol-based lotion, the favourite anesthetic of destitute natives seeking an escape from their economic woes. "This is terrible!" he recalls thinking. "I must do something about it."

And so, characteristically, he did. He persuaded more than 300 corporate leaders to initiate a unique nation-wide board of trade. It was not a charitable handout he was seeking. Rather, in return for $500 annual membership fees, they would serve as a network, bringing native and non-native entrepreneurs together in mutually profitable joint enterprises, everything from Eskimo-manufactured fibreglass canoes to Indian-harvested and packaged gourmet wild rice.

Koffler concluded his speech to the graduating class with a stirring plea: "Will you take the time to step off the beaten way to help your fellow man? That particular fellow man will be the better for it, and so will we."

Integrating our rejected natives, so they may share the aspirations and expectations of all Canadians, would appear to be an insurmountable task for most people. But Koffler is not most people. Since stepping down as board chairman of Shoppers Drug Mart, he has spent an increasing amount of time and energy fulfilling his function as chairman of the Canadian Council for Native Business. He does not think he can right overnight one of our nation's most complex social injustices. But he isn't discouraged. For one thing, he is one of those voracious achievers who, having scaled many mountains, can't resist climbing a new Everest. For another, he learned two decades ago that trying to unravel knotty problems requires endless patience.

As a result of founding the Council on Drug Abuse, he remembers being asked by those two eminent communications gurus of the 1960s, Marshall McLuhan and Buckminster Fuller, to participate in an international conference on Crises In Our Times to be held in the Bahamas. There he and thirty community leaders stood up to relate how they were coping with what they felt to be the most crucial of society's current crises. A black physician, for example, talked of the racial prejudice held against him by the whites; a nun talked about the disruption in her order caused by the trendy modernization of Roman Catholic reformers.

"We found no easy answers to our individual crises," says Koffler now. "But we all came away much richer in knowledge. We learned there's no substitute for the slow, methodical way. You've got to get people to recognize what the crises are, so you can build a people approach to dealing with the problems together."

That slow, methodical approach is gradually paying dividends for the Canadian Council for Native Business. "For many native people, the big hole in their lives is lack of business skills," says Sydney Schipper, a former furrier and community college teacher, who is executive director of the Council.

That vacuum is being filled by a variety of Council programs. Each year a native youth conference, held in either Winnipeg or Orangeville, Ontario, attracts more than 125 participants for an intensive one-week workshop covering all aspects of business indoctrination. The Council's full-time president, Clifford Boland, the former vice-president of a large oil company, invites top executives to conduct sessions on how to finance, market, and manage native businesses.

The Council also organizes workshops dealing with such subjects as the profitable operation of native arts and crafts companies and the promotion of Indian reservations as unique sites for tourist camps and lodges. Most successful of the programs has been the placement of more than fifty native people who serve a two-year "hands-on, work experience internship" in corporations across Canada.

Koffler sees the Council as a fifty-year project, but he is not disheartened by slow progress. He is inspired to go on because young native people, hired for internship programs, have told him: "This council you started is the first career door we've ever had opened to us."

And he is amused by the non-native people who have asked him: "You're so damned committed to this cause, Murray. Are you sure you don't have any Indian blood in your genetic background?"

CHAPTER SIXTEEN

Pied Piper for Israel

R arely can a Canadian businessman point precisely to a single experience that changed the character of his life profoundly. Murray Koffler can. It happened during a ten-day period in early November of 1957. It enabled him to come to terms with his Jewish heritage. And it was a rite of passage transforming him from a successful Canadian entrepreneur with no particular social mission into a Canadian Pied Piper for Israel.

The voice that helped convert Koffler to Zionism and made him a champion of the Jewish community in Canada belonged to an accountant named Alex Fisher, the campaign co-chairman of Toronto's United Jewish Appeal. Out of the blue, Fisher phoned Koffler one day and asked him to join thirty other Toronto businessmen in the first Canadian Study Mission to Israel. Their pilgrimage was designed to inform donors in the Jewish community how their funds had been spent and to induce them to contribute more.

Koffler was surprised that he had been asked. He had a relaxed attitude about Judaism. He was an impassive member of the Jewish community. He was even more lackadaisical about the Holy Land. As a boy, he dimly remembered bearded supplicants with *pushkes* – Yiddish for tin collection boxes – seeking alms from his parents for a Jewish homeland in Palestine. But as for the newborn state of Israel, created a scant nine years previously, he confessed to being almost totally ignorant of its trials and tribulations. He admitted as much to Fisher. What's more, because he had never been involved in community affairs, Koffler said, "I don't feel I deserve to be part of your group."

Fisher, at seventy-one and now a staunch friend of Koffler's, remembers saying, "You've never been involved, because you've never been exposed to Jewish activities. I have a hunch, though, you'll be stirred if you join the gang."

Koffler, then thirty-three and the youngest member of the group, was profoundly stirred. He encountered a pioneer nation in the making, still as raw and primitive as the shack of an airport terminal where they were welcomed when the propeller-driven Pan American DC-8 landed at Tel Aviv. But for ten sun-drenched days, Koffler was intoxicated by the sights and sounds and smells of this most sensual of Mediterranean countries. He drank in the heady perfume of Jaffa orange blossoms and flowering pomegranates and ripening palm dates. It was the veritable land of milk and honey forecast in the Bible by the prophet Micah: "They shall sit every man under his vine and under his fig tree." It was exhilarating to be in a living museum of biblical monuments and miracles.

Dared to do so by his roommate, Alex Fisher, Koffler got up at six o'clock in the morning to swim in the Sea of Galilee. In the Prime Minister's spartan office in the Knesset–the three-storey apartment house serving as a temporary parliament building–he felt privileged when they were received by David Ben-Gurion, the resolute little romantic with the famed aureole of silvery hair and open-necked shirt, who vowed: "To be a realist in Israel, you must believe in miracles."

The entire group was overwhelmed with an almost mystical emotion at the sight of the Western Wall, the only remnant of King Solomon's Temple. It is more popularly known as the Wailing Wall of Jerusalem, because pious Jews for centuries have come to pray and weep for the destroyed Temple. They kiss the holy limestone, which is always covered with dew at night, said to be the Wailing Wall's own tears.

Koffler was intrigued by the young native Israelis known as Sabras. They were so named after the local cactus fruit, because it is tough on the outside but on the inside sweet to taste. The hardiest of them were the children of the *chalutzim*, the early pioneer Zionists who had come to Palestine to plant cypress trees that helped drain the swamps and to fertilize the stony desert soil of their *kibbutzim*; they came "to rebuild the land and to rebuild ourselves as a people." The new breed of healthy, tawny-skinned *kibbutzniks* wrested tomorrow's breakfast from the citrus, olive, and banana orchards with rifles slung over their shoulders as they harvested.

He was particularly captivated by a beautiful, strawberry-blonde Sabra who proudly wore the army uniform of a first lieutenant and served as the Canadian mission's guide. She was just twenty-three and seemed to represent the dynamic new spirit of Israel. Her name was Shula Legum. Today, three decades later, elevated to the rank of colonel, she has remained a devoted friend of the Koffler family, visiting them in Canada with her husband and four sons and becoming, as Koffler says, "part of our extended family."

Koffler's pilgrimage to Israel had an electrifying effect on him. "I saw a different kind of Jew," he says. "They weren't defeated immigrants fleeing from oppressors. Neither were they second-class citizens. They were a proud and uncompromising people, bowing their heads before nobody. I admired their spunk and strength and their vitality. I identified with the valiant way they were coping with their post-war problems of survival. I felt they were giving Jews the world over a positive image. I came home absolutely flying and enthused and thinking: 'I've got to do something to help them.'" Indeed, one of the first things he did on his return was to spearhead the fund-raising drive of the pharmacy division of the United Jewish Appeal.

Fisher believes the Israel trip was responsible for maturing Koffler into a community-minded leader. "Before, he'd gone through life simply having a good time," says Fisher. "He'd make token contributions to the Jewish community. He really didn't feel his Jewishness. But the mission gave him a genuine sense of responsibility and caring for others."

It must be stressed, however, that Koffler's sense of caring and sharing encompasses both the Jewish and non-Jewish communities. He was once asked by Joan Sutton, a columnist for the *Toronto Sun*, whether there was a conflict of his loyalties between Canada and Israel. Koffler made a nice distinction in his answer. "There is no question of having a dual loyalty," he said. "A dual responsibility, yes. But there is only one loyalty and that is to one's own country."

This is verified by Rabbi Arthur Bielfeld, Koffler's perceptive friend and spiritual mentor for almost twenty years at Toronto's Reform Temple Emanu-El. "Murray has been able to transcend the narrow boundaries of Jewish and Canadian culture gracefully; in a way, he's a wonderful amalgam of the two cultures," says Bielfeld. "He's at home in both worlds, and he's one of the rare influential Jews in Canada able to persuade a number of non-Jews to become involved in Jewish activities. They recognize he's not a parvenu pretender in Gentile society. And he makes them feel comfortable in Jewish circles by virtue of their shared interests."

Why has Koffler become such a dedicated do-gooder in the Jewish community? "It's not because he's religious in a pietistic sense," the rabbi theorizes. "And it's not because he's a synagogue-oriented Jew. Partly, it's because Murray comes from a generation of Jewish humanists who are ambivalent about so-called organized religion. I think he's found a kind of surrogate religion in community social service. Partly, too, it's because his father died when Murray, an only child, was just seventeen. So Murray has extended his sense of *mishpocha* – his sense of family – to embrace not only his immediate family but the entire Jewish community."

For Koffler in his role as communal paterfamilias, it's not enough simply to give a charitable gift. "You don't just sign a cheque and then walk away from it," he says. "The energy component equals the money component. In some of my involvements, I give it as much attention as I would give to my business."

He cites as an example his family's cultural contributions to Toronto's Jewish Community Centre. In 1973, he was approached by its president, Bert Fine, who asked Koffler to contribute to the $7 million expansion of the gym facilities of the Centre, which was then called the Northern Young Men's and Young Women's Hebrew Association located on north

Bathurst Street in Toronto's predominantly Jewish suburbia. Koffler immediately agreed to donate $50,000 toward the general fund-raising campaign.

"But on top of that, I'd like to do something more significant for the community," said Koffler. "Let's build a cultural wing of the Y that would take it *beyond* just being a Y." He suggested that they emulate the Jewish Y on Ninety-Second Street in New York City. More than a physical fitness centre, it was known internationally as a temple for art, theatre, music, and dance. "If you agree," said Koffler, "I'll personally donate one million dollars for a cultural centre and help raise funds for whatever else is needed."

Fine promptly agreed. Thus was born the Koffler Centre for the Arts. Koffler still treasures in his den a miniature golden shovel, dated July, 1975, a memento of its ground-breaking ceremony.

His friend Wilfred Posluns, president of Dylex Limited, the retail clothing chain that bestrides North America, also cherishes a souvenir of the occasion. Posluns was then mourning the death of his mother, Leah. He mentioned to Koffler, "I'd be willing to sponsor a theatre in the Centre, provided it was named after my mother." Koffler was delighted. Thus was built the beautiful, 450-seat bandbox of the performing arts known as the Leah Posluns Theatre. Posluns has set up a substantial endowment fund. Furthermore, he sends out more than 2,000 personally signed letters to patrons, urging them to contribute toward the annual upkeep of the theatre.

Similarly, Koffler has established an endowment fund of $250,000 to help maintain his handsome centrepiece of the visual arts in the Centre, the 10,000-square-foot Koffler Gallery. Its chief components are two art galleries. Exhibitions have featured Israeli and Canadian Judaica, but the art is intentionally non-restrictive. Other shows have included a retrospective of the Canadian abstract artist Jack Bush, an exhibit of prize-winning Campbell soup tureens, as well as Indian, Inuit, Japanese, Finnish, Italian, and American art.

As chairman, Koffler heads the Koffler Gallery's twenty-member board of directors. His wife Marvelle was for many years chairman of its cultural management committee and is now a vice-president of the Jewish Community Centre. Their son Adam perpetuates the family tradition by serving as a board member of the gallery. But Jane Mahut, the curator and director of the Koffler Gallery since its inception, insists it's not a family-dominated institution. "That's not Murray's style as patron of the arts," she says. "He gives financial and moral support, but he doesn't tie strings to his giving. He doesn't believe in playing puppet master. He initiates the concept. He hires top professionals in that particular field. Then he turns them free to carry on their own programs."

That seems to be the pattern in all of his community philanthropies. He doesn't believe in meddling with their internal administration just as he would never interfere with the operation of the $100,000 Leon Koffler Endowment Fund he donated in his father's memory to Toronto's Baycrest Centre for Geriatric Care for its pharmacy laboratory.

It is significant that a 240-page sociological study, sponsored by the Canadian Jewish Congress in 1975, concluded that Koffler was one of the two "most powerful men" in Toronto's Jewish community. The other mover-and-shaker was Ray Wolfe, the supermarket magnate (Food City and IGA) who is chairman of the Oshawa Group Limited.

The two community-minded philanthropists put their heads and purses together on a momentous occasion in 1971. As Koffler remembers it, they were both attending a wedding party and Wolfe took him aside in a corner. "Murray, a serious situation has come up," said Wolfe, a remarkably modest, cultured, and community-spirited entrepreneur. "The *Canadian Jewish News* is going under." The English-language broadsheet newspaper was Toronto's only weekly vehicle for the dissemination of news in the Jewish community. Would Koffler join him in salvaging it?

"Count me in," said Koffler.

He and Wolfe both agreed on proposals for altering its distribution and financial structure. It was to become a nationwide publication, circulated to every household that contributes to the United Jewish Appeal. With this enlarged distribution, it would provide a more attractive medium for advertisers.

Koffler, Wolfe, and three others each contributed sufficient funds to purchase and streamline the publication. It is now a lively tabloid of about fifty-four pages weekly, with a guaranteed circulation of more than 50,000. Since each copy is read by an estimated two or three members of each family, it reaches the majority of Canada's 300,000 Jews. It exercises a considerable influence on Jewish affairs internationally and is regarded as the voice of the Establishment of Canadian Jewry. Besides Wolfe, Koffler's co-publishers today include Charles Bronfman, the Montreal financier of the Bronfman dynasty; George Cohon, president of McDonald's Restaurants of Canada; Donald Carr, senior partner with the Toronto law firm of Goodman and Carr; Rubin Zimmerman, Montreal industrialist; Toronto land developer Albert J. Latner; and Montreal land developer Jack Cummings.

"My relationship with Koffler and the board couldn't be happier," says Maurice Lucow, editor-in-chief of the *Canadian Jewish News* since 1980. "Koffler phones me occasionally with great story ideas. But neither he nor any other of his directors have ever tried to interfere with editorial policy or exert any pressure whatsoever. Rarely do you find newspaper publishers like that."

Koffler made use of his publisher's status only once. In 1982, at the height of Israel's military incursion to root out the strongholds of PLO terrorists in Lebanon, Koffler requested credentials as the newspaper's war correspondent. He was accompanied by his son, Leon, and Wilfred Posluns and his son, David. Together they crossed the Israel-Lebanon border and ventured to the dangerous outskirts of Beirut, five days after the bombing began. There they saw dead Syrians whose corpses were waiting to be picked up. They walked warily by yellow circles marked on the ravaged earth to indicate mines not yet defused. And in a perhaps foolhardy burst of adventure, they dared to climb the staircase of an abandoned building and have their lunch on the roof overlooking the airport, which was under severe bombardment.

It took two previous wars in Israel for Koffler to change drastically his fund-raising methods. Ordinarily he is never so crass as to mention money in his speeches on behalf of worthy

257

causes. Customarily, he employs far more subtle tactics to exact necessary cash from potential donors.

"Psychologically, Murray is like a Damon Runyon gambler calling in his markers," says David Marks, a professional fundraiser for the Toronto United Jewish Appeal for many years. "Usually he doesn't lean on people as heavily as he could. But they know where he's coming from. He sets an example to them all. He gives first and he gives big to just about every community cause. Then, when a crisis comes along, he's in a moral position to persuade others with sweet reason that he's now redeeming his IOUs and he expects them to ante up."

But Koffler was not that gentle in 1967 when Israel was facing the crisis of the Six Day War. Armed to the teeth, the Arabs of Egypt, Syria, and Jordan were threatening to "push Israel into the sea." An Israeli commander acknowledged how desperate the situation was on the eve of battle. "Men, if we don't win," he told his civilian soldiers, "we have nowhere to come back to."

Koffler, chairman of the Toronto UJA campaign that year, didn't hesitate. His friend Irving Bain, now a senior vice-president of Shoppers Drug Mart, recalls hearing him make an extraordinarily impassioned speech. "Help the Israelis," Koffler implored an audience of executives, "even if you have to borrow money from the bank."

Bain now remembers that untold numbers reacted to Koffler's incendiary speech like himself. "We got off our butts," says Bain, "and doubled our donations to UJA."

The need was even more pressing in 1973 during the crisis of Israel's Yom Kippur War. It was so called because Egyptian President Anwar Sadat launched his electric surprise attack across the Suez Canal on the holiest day of the Jewish year. Caught off guard, the Israelis suffered horrendous losses. Though they eventually turned the tables on their aggressors and decimated the Soviet-equipped Egyptian Third Army, the Israelis won a Pyrrhic victory. The eighteen days of fighting cost them the lives of 2,500 soldiers and the suffering of 3,000 wounded.

As chairman of Toronto's UJA emergency campaign, Koffler worked prodigious hours day and night like a man possessed. "Murray was here, there, and everywhere, planning and commanding like a general," says David Marks, the campaign's professional fund-raiser. "He was everywhere where he was needed and he was needed everywhere."

Dr. Gerry Halbert, a Toronto dentist, worked painstakingly by his side as his campaign lieutenant. "For three months, we went practically sleepless," says Halbert. Typically, he recalls sweating it out at a strategy meeting at Koffler's Beechwood Avenue home from seven at night until eleven. "I was no sooner home in bed when the phone rang," he recalls. It was Koffler, of course, urging his adjutant, "Come back. We've got more planning to do." Halbert didn't get back to bed again until half past two in the morning.

"God knows how I managed to get any dentistry done during those hectic months," Halbert now says. "Not that I minded. Murray has a way of inspiring you to do more than you think you're capable of doing. 'Don't tell me it can't be done,' he says. 'Let's just do it.' You do, and you know what? You find some of his nobility of purpose has rubbed off on you. If you get tired, he kids you along, 'It's better to be a do-gooder than a do-badder . . . or worse, a do-nothing-er.'"

The high point of Koffler's do-gooding strategy was a grand reception he planned for two important dignitaries. Pinchas Sapir, Israel's finance minister, and Leon Dulcin, world-wide head of the Jewish Agency, were scheduled to come to Toronto while on a global tour to deliver the campaign's climactic fund-raising speeches. But to Koffler's dismay, he received a cable stating that Sapir and Dulcin would arrive on the Jewish holiday of Simchas Torah and could stay for just a few hours.

Koffler pondered the dilemma. "I knew there was no way we could get the Jewish community to turn out on that holiday day of prayer," he recalls. "What to do? I tossed and turned in the middle of the night until the bright idea dawned on me. If Mohammed won't come to the mountain, I figured, then the mountain must come to Mohammed." He called a meeting of the community's Orthodox, Conservative, and Reform rabbis and outlined a proposal to take over the Skyline Hotel near the airport for the day, using its huge ballroom for joint Simchas Torah services. The rabbis were startled by the unusual procedure, but they agreed because Israel's emergency was so dire. One Conservative rabbi even volunteered to break his sect's taboos. He would drive to the hotel on the holy day, bringing his synagogue's Sefer Torah – the Holy Scroll containing the first five books of the Old Testament.

When Sapir and Dulcin arrived at the airport, Koffler was waiting to whisk them to the Skyline and escort them into the ballroom. Sapir, bald, portly, and dignified, with a heavy accent, blinked with amazement as they entered. "He was so moved by what he saw that he broke down," Koffler remembers. "Here were all these worshippers in the ballroom, wearing their praying shawls and skull caps, and waiting for him. He just couldn't believe that on Simchas Torah more than a thousand of them would come to an airport hotel to conduct their services, so he could speak to them."

One by one, as their names were called, the worshippers stood up to pledge their contributions. More than $12 million was pledged that morning; altogether the campaign raised a record-breaking $26.5 million. Koffler was gratified by the knowledge that Toronto that year raised more money per population than any other city in North America.

"It was a remarkable touching thing for Sapir," says Koffler. "He never forgot what 'Morry' – his version of my name, since he couldn't pronounce 'Murray' – had accomplished in his honour. Years later, when I was being awarded an honorary Doctor of Philosophy degree at the Weizmann Institute of Science in Israel, Sapir was still talking about it.

"Sapir got up before the audience and turned to Golda Meir, the Israeli Prime Minister. He said, 'Golda, let me tell you about my friend, Morry . . .' and then he related the story again. That was my turn to break down and be moved to tears."

Koffler's leadership in bridging communications between the two countries has assumed heroic proportions over the years. Invariably, he has infused fresh ideas as well as largesse into the Canada-Israel organizations he has spearheaded. A good example is the Negev Dinner he chaired for the Canadian branch of the venerable Jewish National Fund. Since 1901, the JNF has collected funds to plant trees and develop land in Israel. Its annual Negev dinners (spelled with a little d) were tedious affairs, characterized by windy eulogies to the person being honoured.

When Koffler took over as chairman in 1971, he changed all that; he transformed the Negev Dinner (spelled with a capital D) into the most scintillating social occasion of the year. The first thing he did was to insist that the speeches be cut and their starchiness leavened with humour. The second thing he did was to introduce as a palatable means of showing respect to the honoured guest a professionally produced biographical film. His third innovation was to tone down the commercialism of the fund-raising program booklet, which ostensibly was supposed to laud the honouree. Koffler scrapped the page after repetitive page of self-serving ads blaring in monster type variations of: "CONGRATULATIONS FROM THE NATIONAL WIDGET COMPANY." Instead, National Widget received a terse but dignified credit line as sponsor at the bottom of the page; the bulk of the space was devoted to a pictorial history of the honoured guest and the JNF's achievements in Israel. These were radical innovations, which have since been adopted by other fund-raising philanthropic organizations and have remained the basic format for the Negev Dinners.

Koffler's most revolutionary departure was to make a non-Jew the evening's honouree. The first one thus chosen was John Bassett, former publisher of the *Toronto Telegram* and now the communications titan of the CTV network. That 1971 Negev Dinner raised more than $1 million to build the Bassett Sports and Cultural Centre; it is a recreational complex, with a swimming pool, basketball courts, and a clubhouse created to service five *kibbutzim* in the heart of the Negev Desert. Bassett now considers himself one of Canada's most ardent Zionists. And he considers Koffler one of Canada's "foremost humanitarians, equally loaded with compassion and fun. He's one hell of a fella, and whenever we meet, I embrace him like a brother."

The same fraternal spirit permeates the Canada-Israel Cultural Foundation, which fosters an interchange of musicians, artists, and actors between the two countries. Joel Slater, a Toronto financier who is its former national president, says that the organization had a blue-ribbon board when it was founded twenty-five years ago. But it had lost its vigour and was suffering from financial malnutrition until he persuaded Koffler to become its chairman in 1974. "Murray Koffler's name listed at the head of your board lends credibility to any organization," says Slater. "And, of course, he's a fountain of ideas."

For example, Maureen Forrester And Friends concerts, featuring the so-called Kosher Nostra of violin virtuosos, Isaac Stern, Itzhak Perlman, and Shlomo Mintz, raised $400,000 for the Foundation's endowment fund. Its 1,000 members in Toronto, Montreal, and Ottawa have repeatedly brought to Canada the Israel Philharmonic Orchestra conducted by Zubin Mehta, and the Foundation has sent to Israel more than a dozen Canadian artists. It proudly upholds the motto coined by Aura Herzog, wife of Israel's President Chaim Herzog: "Culture is Israel's bridge to the world, never permitting us to be isolated."

The slogan of another successful project proclaims: "An impossible dream comes true." Koffler is a director of the Canada-Israel Tennis Centre, which has helped to provide 100 tennis courts and the free services of sixty full-time coaches to more than 60,000 children, both Arabic and Jewish, in ten major centres throughout the Holy Land.

Koffler staged the Fund's first Canadian money-raising function at his Jokers Hill Farm in 1977. Three hundred subscribers paid $250 per person to participate in a barbecue and watch four children and a coach from Israel present an exhibition of their newly won prowess on the farm's tennis courts. "One of the Israeli boys who played in the match was so good," says Koffler, "the kid wound up in the world junior championship league." (Joe Frieberg, the Toronto furniture manufacturer who is national president of the Fund, says of Koffler's own tennis playing: "Murray is a good club player, but too much of a gentleman to be fiercely competitive.")

Koffler acknowledges he had one major disappointment in his role as Pied Piper. It came about in 1960 after he had listened to an address made at a conference by Rabbi Stuart Rosenberg of Toronto. The talk was entitled "A Frank Appraisal of the Bar Mitzvah." The rabbi lamented that there was no longer any religious idealism left in the birthday cere- mony when a Jewish youth reaches the age of manhood at thir- teen. The ritual had degenerated into a common Jewish joke in which the youth mistakenly announces, "Today I am a fountain pen." The point of the joke was that the boy was in- undated with fountain pens and other duplicated gifts at the lavish bar mitzvah party staged by his parents.

Koffler founded the Bar Mitzvah Foundation and thus rewrote the script to read: "Today I am a trip to Israel." Instead of plying bar mitzvah boys or bat mitzvah girls with fountain pens or other trivial gifts, relatives were advised to give them gift certificates issued by the Foundation worth up to five hun- dred dollars. The accumulated money was kept as a trust fund, and at the age of sixteen the boy or girl had enough to finance a supervised tour of Israel and a stay at a special Camp Canada in a kibbutz in the Galilee.

Koffler dispatched three groups of teenagers to Israel. The program was ably administered by Rabbi Reuben Slonim of Toronto, with the co-operation of five major children's camps in Canada. But the Foundation foundered after three years, mainly because parents considered their offspring too young to go traipsing off to the Middle East. "Nevertheless, we did provide many youngsters with a great introduction to Israel and the Israelis and the experience gave a fuller meaning to their bar mitzvahs," says Koffler today. "I feel the concept was too far ahead of its time and has a good chance of succeeding in the 1980s."

Koffler's crowning Israeli involvement was not his own brainchild. The noble concept was spawned and thrust upon him by the most magnetic charmer he ever met. His name was

Meyer Weisgal, a flamboyant character with a fantastical background. The Russian-born son of an immigrant cantor, Weisgal peddled matches as a boy on the slum streets of the Lower East Side of New York. He grew up to become a theatre impresario staging Bible spectaculars with casts of up to 3,000 and bearing such titles as *King of the Jews*. He had a keen eye for the marquee and flair for publicity.

Weisgal eventually took his theatricality to Toronto, hired to be editor of the *Canadian Jewish Standard* by the strong-willed "Czarina" of the Tip Top Tailor family, Rose Dunkelman. He converted it into the leading Zionist publication in North America. Then he left it to become the "promoter extraordinaire" for Chaim Weizmann, the crusading Zionist scientist who was the first president of the newborn state of Israel. Weisgal was probably best known as the globetrotting fundraiser for the Weizmann Institute of Science in Rehovot, first serving as Chaim Weizmann's emissary and ultimately serving as the Institute's president and chancellor.

Indeed, when Koffler first met him in 1965 at a Toronto dinner party, Weisgal struck him as a most seductive spellbinder. He was a showman of the old school, who dressed in expensive velvet-collared vicuna coats and wore Hermes neckties. He was short and stumpy, with a gnarled oak face, a sulphurous voice, a technicolor vocabulary of vituperation, and a wild shock of white hair that made him resemble David Ben-Gurion. (In fact, he portrayed the Israeli Prime Minister in the Otto Preminger movie, *Exodus*, on condition that the million-dollar box office take from all world premieres be donated to the Weizmann Institute.)

Koffler was entranced by his wit and worldliness, as well as his warmth and humanity. They remained dear friends until Weisgal's death in 1977. Koffler learned from him wonderful lore on the art of converting a reticent Midas into a generous Maecenas patron. For example, a frugal tycoon from whom Weisgal had hoped to extract a large gift to the Institute reluctantly took out his chequebook after he had been entertained at lunch and wrote a cheque for $25,000. "Thanks a lot," said

Weisgal, tearing up the cheque. "But the meal has already been paid for." With his *noblesse oblige* thus challenged, the magnate somewhat abashedly ponied up half a million.

In Weisgal's autobiography, *So Far*, which Koffler loves to reread, the past master of fund-raising revealed the secrets of eliciting funds for worthy causes. "Don't raise money to the tune of 'Brother, Can You Spare a Dime?'" Weisgal counselled. "If you ask a man for one hundred thousand dollars, he may squirm out of it with a promise of fifty thousand dollars. Ask him for five thousand dollars, and you may expect one thousand dollars." And his key advice read: "It is more efficient to extract one million dollars from a hundred people with bulging bank accounts than from a million people with small ones."

At their first meeting, Koffler remembers with amusement being told Weisgal's favourite story. "He told me how he travelled around the world telling all sorts of wild tales about what the Weizmann Institute would do," recalls Koffler. "Then he'd go back to the scientists there and say, 'I told the world what you're going to do. Now it's up to you to make my tall tales come true.'"

Weisgal was obviously an adroit persuader. He had come to Toronto to visit his Zionist friends, Sam and Ayala Zacks, the Canadian mining promoter and his art collector wife, who were among Koffler's circle of Israel-supporting friends. "Weisgal apparently was impressed by all the questions this young pup of a druggist asked him about the Weizmann Institute," recalls Koffler. "So he told me casually, 'I'm staying overnight especially to hear an Israel artist who's singing at a nightclub here on Yorkville Avenue. Are you free to join me?'"

As soon as they were relaxed at the table the following evening, he remembers Weisgal shaking his hand and exclaiming jovially, "Congratulations, Murray! I've just appointed you first president of the Canadian Society for the Weizmann Institute."

"But Meyer," said the astonished Koffler, caught off guard. "There *is* no Canadian Society for the Weizmann Institute."

"That," said Weisgal blithely, "is now *your* problem."

Koffler grappled with that challenge in his usual ebullient style. He began with a nucleus of ten co-founders at the dinner party. Then, with the aid of his newly appointed executive director, Dr. Stephen Barber, he built the Canadian Society into a nation-wide organization with eleven chapters and more than 6,000 members. In the process, he became a virtual ambassador commuting at least twice a year between Canada and Israel. His first act of protocol was to invite Abba Eban to attend the Society's inaugural black-tie dinner.

Eban, then president of the Weizmann Institute, was more than equal to the occasion. He was a Cambridge don who had Hebraized his first name Aubrey when enlisting in Israel's diplomatic service. He had served as its ambassador to the United States for ten years, became its foreign minister, and later was the author and host of a six-hour TV series on the history of the Jews that was telecast internationally. Introduced by Koffler at the dinner, Eban symbolized the Voice of Israel, spoken in pure plummy Oxbridgian with august Churchillian flourishes. His presence instantly gave the Society a world-class patina.

Koffler compounded that cachet. He arranged for the Society to sponsor a chair in protein sciences at the Weizmann Institute to be named after the Society's first dinner honouree, Lester Pearson. And he escorted the Canadian Prime Minister and his wife Maryon on a tour of the Institute at Rehovot. He reminded the Israeli press that the Nobel Peace Prize winner had headed the Canadian delegation to the United Nations and that in 1948, as chairman of the UN Security Council, he was the leading supporter of the founding of the state of Israel.

"As soon as the Israelis realized who they had in their mist, they bent over backwards to receive Pearson royally," says Koffler. "Mike," as Pearson was known to his intimates, was the affable son of a Methodist parson from the small Ontario town of Newtonbrook; he impressed Koffler as being "shrewd politically" and "a truly decent person, of deserved great prestige – he remained a great friend of Israel and a great friend of the Jews."

As a result of his association with the Institute, Koffler began to assume greater responsibilities. He became a governor and deputy chairman of its board of governors, which included twelve Nobel laureates, and as chairman of the international co-ordinating committee of the Institute, one of the world's five major research centres, he rubbed shoulders with an elite coterie of jet-setters. He received his honorary degree from the Weizmann Institute in company with Britain's former Prime Minister, Sir Harold Wilson, and Koffler was present when a Weizmann honorary degree was conferred on President Jimmy Carter in the White House.

He especially esteems the lifelong friendship he cemented with Marcus, Lord Sieff of Brimpton, who heads the network of more than 300 Marks & Spencer stores in the United Kingdom, Canada, and Europe. The empire was founded by his great uncle, Michael Marks, a poor Polish peddler who couldn't speak English but could count pennies. When he set up his stall in Leeds, England, a hundred years ago, he asked a fellow peddler to scrawl on a sign: "Don't ask the price. It's a penny." Israel, Lord Sieff, the father of Marcus, founded the Weizmann Institute in 1934; on the suggestion of Chaim Weizmann, he erected a single building on the edge of the desert with six scientists and two laboratories. There were no trees, no flowers, not a single blade of grass; it was just a pinpoint in barren Palestine, where jackals howled at night.

Now in his seventies, his son Marcus carried on the family's Zionist tradition as board chairman of the Institute until Koffler took over the post in November, 1987. It has since bloomed into an oasis of greenery embracing a scientific staff of 1,500 in thirty-five buildings involved in 700 research projects and is internationally known as "Israel's Garden of Science." Marcus is a big, prow-chinned, expansive raconteur, with a healthy ego to match, who, among other accomplishments, persuaded Prime Minister Margaret Thatcher to visit Israel.

Both Marcus and Koffler have taken a strong personal interest in Israel's trade problems. Koffler did so when he attended his first international economic conference there in the 1960s. Koffler was aroused into action by a stirring speech urging capitalists abroad: "Bring us your know-how. Bring us your experience. Invest in our country."

It was like a bugle call to Koffler, and he and his partners Eddie Creed and Issy Sharp, and especially the original Israeli pioneer Max Sharp, built a 130-suite Four Seasons condominium hotel in the resort area of Netanya. The Four Seasons ran the hotel for ten years and then in 1980 turned it over to the local Dan Hotels management company. It now functions as the Seasons Netanya, and the Kofflers occupy their own glass-walled penthouse overlooking the Mediterranean whenever they visit Israel.

Koffler headed Canada's second trade mission to Israel in 1976. On that trip he was inspired to "Canadianize" the Holy Land's archaic little apothecary shops just as his friend Ray Wolfe had done to its antiquated food kiosks. The two revolutionary merchandisers successfully pushed Israeli consumerism into the twentieth century by introducing supermarket-style mass merchandising. But the entrepreneurs did so only after coping with much breast-beating and lamentation from backward merchants of the bazaar school of commerce.

When Wolfe opened the first Food City-style supermarket, which was called Super-Sol, Tel Aviv's smalltime fruit and grocery shops shut down and their owners marched the streets in a protest strike. The reaction from competing pharmacists was almost as drastic when Koffler opened his first Israeli version of a Shoppers Drug Mart in 1977. He launched the half-million-dollar store with much fanfare in the town of Herzlia and called it Super-Pharm. By Canadian standards, it was a moderate-sized store of just 2,400 square feet, which Koffler had constructed by linking under one roof seven small shops. But Israelis, conditioned to tiny English chemist-style apothecaries, considered it a leviathan. Consumers were enchanted by its low prices, variety of merchandise, and what Koffler called its "clean-as-a-whistle, spanking-new décor." It was so different from the small shops with limited service to which they were accustomed. It grossed $1.25 million in its first year, which amounted to a sales return per square foot comparable with any of the Shoppers stores in Canada.

Its success, however, aroused fear and consternation among Israel's some 300 pharmacists. Their association put pressure on the Ministry of Health, which in turn found that Super-Pharm seemed to be breaking most of its archaic laws as well as some not even found in the books. Koffler's eldest son Leon, who elected to try building Super-Pharm into a chain, has been frustrated by the red tape and irrational regulations that have thwarted his progress. Inexplicably, he was required to erect expensive glass partitions to separate his dispensary from the rest of one store. In other Super-Pharms, he has been forbidden to sell a wide range of stock items. Despite this strait-jacketing, by 1987 the chain had grown to ten Super-Pharms with a staff of 350 and gross sales of about $15 million annually. "We haven't made any serious money there yet," says Murray Koffler. But he isn't discouraged; instead, he counts his blessings.

"The local pharmacists, who thought we would overwhelm them, have copied us and some are doing better than ever," he says. "The student pharmacists, who felt originally we were an abortion of the profession, are now attracted to us. We've got a waiting list eager to join us. It's given us an opportunity to offer ten scholarships to the Israel School of Pharmacy. And we've managed to reform a lot of outmoded laws dating back to the British mandate days of Palestine."

He sums it up by saying cheerfully, "Thanks to my son Leon, who has picked up the challenge, Super-Pharm is making a definite contribution to Israel's economy. I'm confident that over a period of time it will do very well." He shrugs and smiles. "I like to look at things optimistically. What's the alternative?"

Koffler's Israeli mentor, Meyer Weisgal, used to call himself The Merchant of Immortality. He did so because he felt he was selling patrons of the Weizmann Institute legacies in science research that would last forever. Koffler believes that his most enduring contribution will be the $8 million Koffler Accelerator Tower, the centrepiece of the Institute's Canada Centre for Nuclear Physics. Koffler was stimulated into sponsoring it by the scientist chosen by Weisgal to take over from him the presidency of the Weizmann Institute: Albert Sabin, the American who discovered the Sabin oral polio vaccine.

Strolling with Koffler one day in 1972 on the campus at Rehovot, Sabin pointed to the long white building on a hill that housed the Nuclear Research Institute. Bearing a painting of Albert Einstein, it had been officially opened in 1958 by the world's greatest nuclear physicists, including J. Robert Oppenheimer, Isidor Rabi, Harold Urey, Niels Bohr, and Felix Bloch. Sabin mentioned that exploring the peaceful use of nuclear energy was the next major frontier for science.

The Institute already had the pelletron accelerator – popularly called an "atom-smasher" – capable of generating 3 million volts of power to break down atomic nuclei for scientific examination. But that was a mere nutcracker. The Institute wanted to be at the leading edge of global state-of-the-art research in the field. For that it needed a vastly more powerful – and expensive – accelerator that would generate 14 million volts. As Chaim Weizmann himself had once said when tackling world-class challenges, "There comes a time when you must get out of the bathtub and swim in the ocean."

Was Koffler, as a patron of science, ready to tackle the challenge? It was equivalent to asking whether a duck could swim. It meant he could play a meaningful role in the continuing drama of advancing both Israel and science. An ancient Israeli proverb states: "Just as a tent cannot stand without pegs and cords, so Israel cannot stand without scholars." For his twentieth-century tent of learning, Koffler set aside 100,000 shares of his Shoppers Drug Mart stock, then worth $1 million. By the time the accelerator was ready for construction, the stock was worth close to $2 million. Koffler headed a campaign to raise another $2 million from the general community and members of the Canadian Society for the Weizmann Institute. The remaining $4 million was matched by the Israeli government and other universities that hoped to share the new facility.

Koffler's aesthetic sense was offended when he first saw the sketches of the accelerator's twin eighteen-storey towers. He shook his head in disapproval of the design by Israeli architect Moshe Harel. "They look like a couple of ugly grain silos," he objected. "We can't impose those monstrosities on the gorgeous Weizmann campus. Let's have an international architectural competition to get a design more pleasing to the eye."

"No, let's show the world what Israelis can do," pleaded Harel. "I'll redesign it into something beautiful."

Indeed, the contingent of more than 250 Canadians who flew to Rehovot for its inaugural ceremony in 1977 were duly impressed by its beauty. They saw twin towers of stone and steel soaring more than 185 feet in the Israeli sky. One tower is slender, with a spiral staircase snaking upwards in and out gracefully. The other, which is attached to it at intervals, is a lofty pillar of concrete curves, topped by an elliptical egg-shaped dome.

The Koffler Tower, as it's usually called, has since become an internationally renowned landmark. It is a familiar haven of joint research for Canadian scientists on exchange visits from their nuclear accelerator located on the Vancouver campus of the University of British Columbia. It is the focus of a scene in a science fiction movie. Its image adorns an Israeli postage stamp, with Koffler being the only living person whose name has thus been honoured.

The latest project of the Canadian Society – under the leadership of Toronto retailer James F. Kay, who has taken over from Koffler as its chairman – is a Canadian Institute for Energy and Applied Science. When eventually completed just west of the Koffler accelerator, it will consist of a $13 million, eight-acre complex. Its main features will be two research buildings on a mammoth fifteen-storey "Spire of Light" Solar Tower looming high over a field of sixty heliostat mirrors. Just as the Koffler Tower is designed to harness the atom, so the new Solar Tower will harness energy from the sun.

Koffler was beaming happily one sunny November afternoon in 1986 as he escorted a Canadian journalist friend around the seventy-five-acre Weizmann campus. Koffler wanted to show him the two giant towers he had helped to plant amid the gardens and orange groves of Rehovot. The sky was a gay Chagall-blue; a warm breeze wafted the sweet smells of golden jasmine, pink oleander, purple bougainvillea, scarlet lantana. It could have been a tranquil college campus in southern California except for two things. Many of the scientists strolling down the boulevard of olive trees wore skull caps. And the sign over the iron entrance gate exhorted them in Hebrew letters: "Work for this Country. Work for Science. Work for Humanity."

Koffler sat with his guest in the observation room inside the massive concrete egg atop the Koffler Tower. He was in a philosophic mood as he gazed at the panoramic view. In the distance he could see the greenish-violet hills of Judea. Closer by, an army of workmen were pouring concrete and scooping out with their earth-moving machines an enormous valley for the Solar Tower complex.

The journalist was reminded of the wise saying of the ancient Hebrew sage, Rashi: "Naked a man comes into the world, and naked he leaves it; after all his toil, he carries away nothing – except the deeds he leaves behind." The journalist asked Koffler, "Do you feel something like that when you look at the Koffler Tower?"

"Yes," he said. "I think it's only human to want to do something that lives beyond you. But my involvement with the Weizmann means something more."

He fell silent for a moment.

"You know why I feel so serene whenever I come here?" he said. "I'm in a state of euphoria because it's strongly impressed on me I'm involved with an *outgoing* expression of Israel. Most of the things we in the Diaspora do for Israel are for an *inward* development of the country. Things like the United Jewish Appeal and the Jewish National Fund are all things for Israel alone.

"But when you're involved with science, it's different. Like art, it knows no ethnic or national boundaries. The Weizmann offers Israel and its supporters a way to make a contribution to all humankind. You get the feeling you're sharing with the world the Weizmann's explorations of everything from harnessing the sun, maybe conquering cancer, probing the mysteries of the brain, to unlocking the secrets of life itself. And that's why I'm so enamoured of the Weizmann."

He continued in a pensive mood after posing for a picture amid the scented pines, so reminiscent of Canada, on the lawn in front of the stately twin tower bearing his family name. "You know," he mused, "I encountered one of the strangest links to my family on one of my early trips to Israel, and I can't forget it."

While visiting an Israeli *mabarot* – a village of tin-roofed huts sheltering immigrant refugees newly arrived from Romania – he met an elderly man who said, "Did your father come from the town of Piatraniamz?"

"Yes."

"Well, how is Leon?"

"He's dead."

"He died? I can't believe it!"

Koffler reflected on that scene that remained indelible in his memory. "Here this old man had fled from Romania, escaped from Hitler, scurried from one camp to another, and managed somehow to come by boat to this makeshift village in the Holy Land," said Koffler. "He couldn't believe that my father had gone to the golden land of North America, had opened two drugstores, and became a rich Canadian. But despite all the benefits of living in the New World, his friend Leon had died in his forties. Yet this refugee had survived all the hardships of the camps and was still alive, having arrived at eighty in Israel. He simply couldn't get over it."

Koffler, who had lived to become a benefactor for Israel, shook his head while pondering the tricks that fate can play and said, "I can't get over it either."

CHAPTER SEVENTEEN

Strictly Personal

Looking back on his life not long ago, Murray Koffler said in wonder, "My life has been one high after another." Some highs, of course, have been higher than others. They relate to the two things he cherishes most in life – his immediate family and his extended family of farflung friends. The highest of the highs has been his lifelong romance with his wife, Marvelle. Friends call it the "perfect marriage, the kind made in heaven." If that is so, their courtship could be called a perfect serio-comic love story, the kind made in Hollywood. Indeed, the melodrama of Koffler's proposal is reminiscent of a movie climax already filmed in Hollywood. It is *The Graduate*, which ends with Dustin Hoffman snatching his bride Katharine Ross away from a rival just as she is about to say "I do" to the other man.

The scenario for the Murray-Marvelle romance opens on a sultry July day in 1944. Koffler, then twenty, was paddling a canoe on Lake Simcoe in the Ontario cottage country north of Toronto near Tent City. Suddenly he saw a beautiful slim girl in a bathing suit. She was fifteen and a half years old, and was reading a book and listening to music on a portable radio while sunning herself on a raft.

Koffler gasped. He turned to his fellow paddler, Oscar (Bosco) Kofman, his boyhood chum, destined to become a distinguished neurologist.

"Bosco, who's that stunner?" he asked.

"Marvelle Seligman. Her family owns a cottage nearby. Our crowd here is having a corn roast tonight. Would you like to invite her to come?"

"I sure would," said Koffler.

The attraction seems to have been mutual. "I was shy and felt terribly self-conscious at first as I watched them circle the raft," says Marvelle. "I recognized Bosco, but I didn't know Murray. But as soon as I got to know him, I fell head over heels in love. Really nobody else ever came close to capturing my heart."

His buddies kidded him that he was robbing the cradle for a summer romance. But Koffler persisted in dating Marvelle off and on for the next few years. She would drop around to Koffler's drugstore on Bathurst Street just to be with him. By the time Marvelle was verging close to the age of twenty and yet remained unmarried, her mother may well have given thought to the Jewish adage, "It is easier to guard a sack of fleas than a girl in love."

Her mother, Eva Seligman, was a true matriarch of the old-fashioned materfamilias school. She was a former five-dollar-a-week seamstress who had escaped from the pogroms that had wiped out most of her family in Kiev in the Soviet Union. She could neither read nor write English and for a period was in the position of having to keep boarders in her home. She was compelled to do so because her husband, Irving, a gentle ex-Talmudic scholar and poet from Rachov, Poland, was trying to support their four children as a dressmaker for Spadina Avenue garment shops while building his own manufacturing business.

It was said of Eva that she had a heart of gold and a will of iron. She looked the way a duchess might *like* to look: a handsome, elegant woman who carried herself with a ramrod-straight bearing and gloried in her long raven-black hair. She never spared the rod when raising her children. Even today, a keen-witted invalid of close to ninety, she doesn't hesitate to "tear a strip" off Marvelle when disapproving of her behaviour.

In 1950, Eva disapproved strongly of Koffler's reluctance to declare his marital intentions with regard to Marvelle. She made that clear in a brusque telephone conversation that Koffler will never forget. "Hello, this is Mrs. Seligman," she said when calling him at his Bathurst Street store. Then she came right to the point: "What're you going to do with my daughter?"

Koffler was taken aback. "What do you mean, what am I going to do with your daughter?"

She repeated with irrefutable bluntness, "I mean, what are you going to do with my daughter?"

Koffler faltered in embarrassment. He happened to be serving one of his most patrician customers, Ayala Zacks, the art collector. He desperately wanted to think. So, playing for time, he asked, "Will you please call me back in ten minutes on the store pay phone?"

When she did so, Koffler entered the little booth and carefully closed the door to shut off eavesdroppers.

"Well," she demanded once again, "what're you going to do with my daughter?"

Koffler equivocated. "Mrs. Seligman, I can't name the day. Maybe next year, about fifteen months from now, I may be in a better position to announce our engagement."

"Is that so? Thank you *very* much!" She banged down the receiver.

The ploy was calculated to make Koffler bite the bullet. Eva encouraged Marvelle to drop her occasional dates with marginal suitors. Her daughter was urged instead to appear to "go steady" with the heir of a well-known family, whom we'll identify here under the name of Herby.

Herby had a heavy crush on her. "He was much more serious about our relationship than I was, because my heart was elsewhere," Marvelle now says. "I was never engaged to him. I never accepted a ring from him. But I did accept his invitation to meet his family in New York." She did so for one reason only – to stimulate Koffler into popping the question.

Koffler got wind of reports that Marvelle had left town with her parents and Herby to arrange for a wedding in New York. He frantically put through fifteen phone calls, but nobody in the Seligman family would reveal her whereabouts. He finally learned from her cousin Jeanette that Marvelle, when last heard from, was staying with her parents at the home of an aunt in the rural wilds of Flatbush, Brooklyn.

Over the years, Koffler has recounted the aftermath scene frequently and *con brio*. His most recent version of the script begins this way:

"I really panicked. I race upstairs to my mother's room, where she's bedridden with her ulcerative colitis. I borrow her cracked yellow diamond ring and put it on my finger. I rush to the airport without even having a reservation. I couldn't get a plane ticket. Five minutes before the Trans-Canada airliner takes off, I grab the no-show seat they've been holding for a Mr. Robinson.

"On my arrival, I take a taxi out to this house in the burbs of Brooklyn. I knock on the door. Marvelle opens it."

According to his recollection, this dialogue then ensued:

"Do you love me? Or do you love him?"

"Of course, I love you."

"Are you really engaged to this guy?"

"No. Not really engaged. But he's been talking about it."

"Okay. You're engaged to me."

Koffler then slipped the cracked yellow diamond ring on her finger and they walked into the living room. Sitting there, he remembers, were Marvelle's parents and the unfortunate Herby.

"I tell them, 'Folks, Marvelle really loves me and we're going to get married.'

"I see a bottle of Scotch on the table. I reach over and pour myself a stiff drink and belt it down.

"Then I grab Marvelle by the wrist and I pull her out of the room. And hand in hand we walk away without another word.

"We went to the St. George Hotel in Brooklyn. Being very proper, I had one room and Marvelle had another room. It was very late at night, and I assure you we both slept soundly."

Koffler heard later that the abject Herby, who was genuinely smitten with Marvelle, took it very hard. "He gulped down quite a few Scotches. And he was so upset that Marvelle's cousin Jerry had to take him back to his hotel in a

277

taxi. The poor guy got over it. Subsequently he married very well. I sometimes wonder what he thinks of that hectic day."

The Koffler wedding, held on a snowy Friday, January 20 in 1950, also had its hectic moments. Regrettably, no photos chronicle the wacky scene that climaxed the festivities of the bridal party at the Seligman home on Ava Road. It was a roistering scene featuring Koffler and his best man, Eddie Creed. "To put it mildly, Eddie and I got into some serious drinking and really tied one on," recalls Koffler, in describing their loopy bacchanalia. "I remember there was a full moon, and it was a beautiful snowy evening, and great big flakes covered the Ava Road hill with a soft downy blanket.

"So I put on my bargain raccoon coat that my mother had bought for me at Creeds for fifty dollars, and Eddie puts on *his* raccoon coat, and we walk into the lovely snow. There we were, with our arms clasped around each other, and we somehow tumbled down. We thought that was so awfully funny that we began rolling, one over the other, like a human snowball. We went rolling all the way down the Ava Road hill and laughing all the way."

Marriage to Marvelle changed Koffler from a heavy-drinking, Saturday night social cutup into a deeply committed family man. Marriage to Koffler similarly changed Marvelle, from an immature, sheltered *naif*, five years younger than himself, into a gracious chatelaine able to converse confidently with the Queen herself in Buckingham Palace.

"The greatest thing I have going for me is Marvelle," says Koffler, examining with loving eyes the many photos of them together. "She's an incredible tower of strength. She has long caught up with me and surpassed me in so many ways."

He admires her diverse interests in the arts, her ability to manage six domiciles, and her consistently sunny outlook on life. "I never complain to anybody – except to Marvelle," he says. "I discuss absolutely everything with her. She's a great listener and puts things in perspective for me." He considers himself a lucky man because theirs has been a love affair that has endured. "Even today I sometimes say to myself, 'I'm to meet Marvelle for dinner tonight, and it's still just like going out on a date.'"

Marvelle acknowledges it wasn't easy adjusting to being catapulted into her husband's cyclonic and rarefied social stratosphere. "I was as bashful and awkward as any innocent young thing could be," she says. "But thanks to Murray, I caught up. He's a kind man, and has room for everyone on his shoulders." Among other qualities, she admires "his absolute honesty, his ability to say he's wrong, his capacity to grow."

She does not consider herself a subjugated, non-liberated wife. "I believe no family can have two leaders," she says. "I'm perfectly content to let Murray be the most dominant person in the family. I opted for a career of keeping up with the *uno numero* guy I married." Perhaps the most telling comment on their relationship is made by their eldest daughter, Theo. "As long as I can remember," says Theo, "my mother has been the rose in my father's lapel."

Koffler's marriage to Marvelle opened his eyes to genuinely homey family life. He was accustomed to the quiet solitude of living with his mother in the otherwise empty home on Rosemary Road. He carried Marvelle over the threshold there, and for a period the bride and groom continued to live with the ailing Tiana Koffler in that sedate household. But from then on, his domestic lifestyle was never the same, because of his introduction to the Seligman family. They were a loyal, boisterous, and openly affectionate clan. Their minds, their hearts, their purses, and their doors were always open. Marvelle's brother, Sam Seligman, now an insurance broker in his sixties, remembers that even when their parents' collective income "ranged from no to low," they stressed to their four children the sovereign blessing of giving charity money to those less fortunate than themselves.

Life was simple for the newlyweds in the early years of their marriage. "Our kitchen table played a big role in our lives together," says Marvelle. "Murray would figure out his accounts there and I'd help him make out our narcotics reports to the government. Later, when we bought our first home, there was little money for furnishings. We had bare carpetless floors, ate on a bridge table, and sat on pillows. But it never occurred to us not to invite people in."

Marvelle helped strengthen his sense of Jewish identity. As she says, "I live and breathe my Judaism." She had been raised in a Conservative Jewish home where religion was important. Her father Irving had been a brilliant *yeshiva bocher* – a scholarship student at an advanced Bible college in the Polish city of Lublin. The captions he wrote for the family albums are lovingly enhanced with quotations from Holy Scriptures and the Talmudic sages. Pictures showing Koffler and Marvelle celebrating Passover or the harvest thanksgiving holiday of Succoth bear such inscriptions as "He who has no pity for humanity surely cannot be a descendant of Abraham."

Nowadays Koffler attends Toronto's Reform Temple Emanu-El during the High Holidays and for special services. He is one of the ten original founders who started it in the basement of the Unitarian Church on St. Clair and Avenue Road in Toronto. They used their own carpentry, built their own ark to contain the Holy Scrolls, and used their own lay leader to conduct services because the congregation was too small to retain a rabbi. Now in a handsome building on Old Colony Road in north Toronto, the congregation consists of more than 300 families. Koffler appreciates the lively, thoughtful sermons delivered by Rabbi Arthur Bielfeld. But he prefers the more intimate form of worship in the Sabbath rites that his family has performed for years every Friday evening whenever they are together.

After prayers over the candles, wine, and bread, Koffler explains, "we all join hands around the table and shut our eyes and whoever feels the need to say a prayer does so. It may be a prayer for somebody ill, or a prayer for somebody getting married, a prayer blessing our home, or a prayer simply rejoicing in how great things are. I call it the family hand prayer. It's the form of Judaism most meaningful to me. The lovely rituals, performed over the years, reinforce who I am, make me comfortable with what I am, and enable me to be positive about what I do."

Each of his five children radiates the same positive spirit. Their personalities differ, of course, but they have certain Kofflerian traits in common. Their uncle, Sam Seligman, believes their most dominant characteristic is the strong, emotional clannishness that binds them together. "They're all weepers," he says. "When the Koffler kids get together, and are called upon to toast each other, they always shed tears of happiness."

Yet they are also strongly independent. They have a family business reunion each year: Koffler has arranged for these annual meetings around a boardroom table in accordance with his family estate planning principles first established in 1978. He then allocated 50 per cent of his net assets to himself and Marvelle; the remaining 50 per cent was to be held by the five children. Thus each child owned 10 per cent of the total family assets in trust, and they were free, provided that the trustees agreed they weren't going off half cocked, to invest in their individual business ventures independent of each other.

Another family trait is that they're all outgoing athletes. The family albums are packed with snapshots of the children at an early age whizzing down mountain slopes in the favourite family sport, skiing. Koffler likes saying there are three basic stages in bringing up a Koffler child. "In the first stage you say, 'Okay, this is how you get on your skis. Now follow me.' In the second stage, a few years later, you say, 'Okay, kid, now keep up with me.' And in the third stage, a few years later, the kid is saying, 'Okay, Dad, *I'll* wait for *you* to catch up with *me*.'"

That evolution is certainly true of Leon, the oldest child, the most adventuresome, and a skier of championship calibre. At thirty-six, he is endowed with his father's easy-going charm, but concedes he lacks his father's demonic drive. "Maybe it's sleeping inside me somewhere," he says, "a bit dormant and waiting for me to reach my potential." Yet he has inherited his father's impulsiveness to conquer the unknown, no matter how unorthodox his actions. In his twenties, he dropped out of school to invest $25,000 in a motorcycle business. The business went bust and he went riding through Europe demonstrating the company's model motorcycle. He has since

steadied down. After a year at Grenoble University in Switzer-
land and graduation from the Ryerson Institute in Toronto, he
has demonstrated that he has a natural aptitude for business.

He maintains he doesn't have any psychological hang-ups
about living in his father's shadow. He has told his father
appreciatively, "Thank goodness, you were born before me."

It wasn't all easy, though. While attending York Mills Collegiate, he was put to work summers at a Toronto Shoppers
Drug Mart stamping prices on 10,000 containers of aspirin.
"They gave me a bit of a hard time because I was the boss's
son. But I took my lumps. I accepted it as part of my apprenticeship. I got a kick out of the excitement of the retailing
game." For ten years, he worked as a full-time merchandise
manager, store planner, and trouble-shooter for the Shoppers
chain. He spent four years opening thirty-four stores in
Florida. Then he volunteered to help his father develop the
Super-Pharm chain in Israel, becoming its president in 1984.
He says it has been a continual uphill battle against government red tape and bizarre regulations.

Despite the stumbling blocks, though, he says he'd never
throw in the towel. When frustrated, he takes solace in his
father's advice, "Son, when things look hairy, don't forget your
sense of humour." Besides, he feels he has a personal investment in the country. He has acquired a handsome home in
Herzliya-by-the-Sea; married Irit Strauss, the daughter of an
illustrious family of dairy owners; and fathered an Israeli son,
Shawn, and infant daughter, Elinor. "If a businessman can
make it in this difficult yet exciting pioneer country," says
Leon, "then you know he can make it anywhere in the world."

His sister, Theo, fourteen months younger than himself
and until recently his partner in the Super-Pharm chain, is
more ambivalent about Israel than he is. She cites the witticism, "To make a small fortune in Israel, you must bring in a
large fortune."

Until 1987, she was a director and vice-president of Super-
Pharm, in charge of marketing, advertising, and public
relations. Among other achievements, she instituted the Koffler Academy Training Centre, the first of its kind in Israel. She
bowed out of her 50 per cent partnership to devote more time

to raising her two sons, an infant named Itimar and a toddler named Omri, in their lovely terracota villa with landscaped gardens in the suburbs of Herzliya-by-the-Sea.

She is the wife of Yoav Stern, a deputy commander and major in the Israeli Air Force and a computer science graduate from University of Tel Aviv. As a result of an article that Koffler read in the *International Herald Tribune*, Stern cottoned to the idea of launching Computer Rental Stores in Toronto, Ottawa, and Montreal. Consequently, the couple commute between the two countries.

Theo minces no words about her ambivalent attitude toward Israel. She feels deeply attached to her circle of Israeli friends, whom she regards as "incredible idealists and incredible doers." Yet it pains her to accept the hard fact that her two children some day will have to serve in the Israeli defence forces. "I can't speak about it," she says. "Just as, when people ask me what it's like to be a fighter pilot's wife, I can't think about it."

She is grateful to her parents for having instilled in her a strong work ethic and the goal of becoming an achiever. "As kids, we all had to shovel snow and rake leaves," she says. At sixteen, she was paid $1.95 an hour to work as a stock room apprentice for a Shoppers outlet. She remembers the merchandising manager, Howard Trifler, namesake of the chain's Howie's stores, goading her, "Pull up your socks and work harder."

"I'm a sort of natural leader," she says without false modesty. She majored in languages at the University of Toronto, in business management at the University of Windsor, in child psychology for a year at Oxford University, and worked as a volunteer with Toronto psychologists to help provide recreational therapy to delinquent teenagers with social problems. As a teenager herself in the 1960s, she was a rebellious radical for a spell. "I rebelled against the fact that my parents were always so important and were always going to various functions," she says. "I rebelled just for the hell of it, and it quickly passed."

She patently adores her father. "When the Me Generation came into vogue, Dad counselled us to be part of the You Generation," she says. "'Be outward-directed and try to help others,' he was always saying. 'Don't contemplate your own bellybutton and drown yourself in the Me, Me, Me's.'" And she feels lucky because she and the other children were showered with affection. "If Dad had a phone call from any one of us, he'd drop everything to talk to us. Even if he was tied up at a board meeting, we were never told, 'Sorry, your father is too busy to speak to you.' To Dad, family always comes first."

Tom, the middle child, is considered the sibling who felt he had to prove himself most and is the most aggressive businessman and the most avid all-around athlete. At thirty-one, he comes across as an exuberant, high-voltage jock, with flashing brown eyes and a pleasantly cocky manner. He says he initially "got burned" investing in plastic and injection moulding businesses. But thanks in part to excellent business courses he studied for three years at Toronto's Seneca Community College, he is now the president of a flourishing chain of twenty-five Ontario greeting-card stores. They are titled Best Wishes and Scribbles & Giggles, have a staff of 240, and gross $8 million annually in revenues. He also pilots single-engine planes, goes helicopter skiing in the British Columbia Bugaboos, and participates in triathlons, which involve, consecutively, one mile of swimming, thirty-two miles of bicycling, and ten miles of running.

Being the son of Murray Koffler has been a mixed blessing to Tom: part crown, part hairshirt. "Sure, it's opened many doors," he says. "But it gets you branded the pampered kid who has everything, the rich man's son who's been handed life on a silver platter."

It especially irks him when he is asked, "Are you in a competitive race with your father? Are you trying to beat him in the number of stores you control?"

Tom answers, "Definitely not. I just might set a name for myself in the greeting-card industry. And I'm doing it on my own. Dad has made it clear that the family pot isn't a bottomless pit, and if you blow your share, that's *it*." He regards his father as a "wonderful resource – of guidance and feedback rather than cash. I bless Dad for allowing me to make my mistakes when I was experimenting in those early businesses."

One senses that Tom has finally learned to accept the fact that he need not prove himself equal or better than a celebrated father. "I've been on my own basically for ten years," he says. "Now I've reached the point in business, where I don't have to justify my decisions to anybody, except my wife and kids." His wife is Anna, a vivacious former magazine writer with two degrees from York University, and they have three children, Dustin, Brandon, and an infant named Corey. Among other community activities, both Tom and Anna are involved in fund-raising for the United Jewish Appeal and the Weizmann Institute of Science in Israel.

Over a Sunday brunch one morning at Inn on the Park, Tom gazed fondly at his little family and said, "Like my dad, I realize we're fortunate to have the comfortable lifestyle we do. I wake up every morning and say, 'Thank you.'"

His kid brother, Adam, sounded like an echo of Tom when asked how he felt about his lifestyle. "I wake up in the morning and reckon that the golden thread that my life hangs on these days is really incredible," Adam exulted. "I sit up and think, 'I'm probably the only twenty-eight-year-old in the world building a $35 million hotel complex.'"

Adam is president of King Ranch Health Spa and Fitness Resort. It will be Canada's first international health spa when it opens in 1989. Designed by Canada's leading architect, Arthur Erickson, it will consist of 120 luxury rooms, located on 177 acres of woodland twenty miles north of Toronto in King Township. Adam will make an ideal host. As he says, "The spa will be fresh, young, new, and sleek – which, I guess, is pretty well how I feel."

He was no great shakes in academic subjects at Upper Canada College and the University of Toronto. He seems, however, to have an instinctive flair for commerce. "In our family, you'd be a black sheep if you didn't," he says good-humouredly, recalling how well he did at the University of Western Ontario. His special aptitude is geared to the hotel business. He apprenticed for two years at the Four Seasons in Ottawa, doing everything as a management trainee from washing the urinals to welcoming guests in the dining room as maitre d'. He followed it with a year at the Hilton Tel Aviv and two years at the CN's L'Hôtel at the Toronto Convention Centre.

Then one day in May, 1985, after returning from a stay at the Canyon Ranch Health and Fitness Resort in Tucson, Arizona, his father said to Adam, "Why don't we do something like that here in Canada?"

"Do you think it'll work?" asked Adam.

"Let's find out," said Koffler.

He picked up the phone and called Mel Zuckerman, president of the Tucson operation, who had converted a rundown dude ranch into a streamlined version of a so-called fat farm for the overfed, overaged, but definitely not underprivileged.

"Mel, do you think a Canyon Ranch-type complex will do well here in the northeast?"

"By all means. It gets so blasted hot here in summer that all our activities during that season are indoors. So your winter weather won't handicap you. I've been looking for a new site myself. Count me in."

With Zuckerman functioning as a highly paid consultant and Koffler as his untitled and unpaid adviser, Adam has been developing the concept ever since, with his sister Tiana serving as his partner. Adam maintains he has no complexes about following in the footsteps of a well-known father. "Why not make use of your father's trailblazing?" he asks sensibly. "I intend to make my own mark, as my father did. But Murray, as I call Dad in business situations, gives me lots of leeway. 'Adam, the ball's in your court,' he said to me. 'If you want my input, I'm there when you need it. But it's up to you to make your own decisions.'"

Adam has adopted for himself one of his father's credos, "A happy family is the foundation of a happy life." Married for five years to Shayla, he makes a point of spending at least an hour and a half daily with his children, Zachary and Logan. Interestingly, there is only one character trait of his father that Adam has not tried to emulate. "Except for my mom, he doesn't let people know when he's depressed," says Adam. "He's so concerned with being upbeat all the time, he just won't let his defences down. Neither will he express emotion on a one-to-one basis. I can sit across the table from him and say openly, 'I love you, Dad.' But he's not too comfortable verbalizing words like 'love.' He seems to think they're too mushy, too sentimental. Maybe I'm harping too much on the external expression of love. The important thing, I guess, is that Dad has shown us by his actions that he has lots of internal love for his children."

Tiana, at twenty-four, is the youngest and most emotional member of the family. When interviewed by reporters, she has sometimes been moved to tears by the very mention of her parents' names. She thinks her father is embarrassed by her outbursts for two reasons. "A show of emotions suggests weakness to him, and he likes strong people," she says. "Also, my emotions touch off his emotions, and he feels he has to compensate. He'll scold me, 'Tiana, I'm going to get tough with you. You must learn to be strong. You've got to control your feelings, especially in business dealings.'"

She says wistfully, "I sometimes wonder whether I can develop the steel guts and iron backbone to be a super-executive." Yet she is by no means a flibbertigibbety empty-head. At the University of Tel Aviv she studied the historical roots of anti-Semitism leading to the Nazi Holocaust. Though she has never suffered from overt religious prejudice, her mother made her aware of it and urged her to be proud of her Jewishness.

At Havergal College, Toronto's private Protestant school for girls, which she attended from the age of three to seventeen, Tiana made it known in grade eleven that she would like to stop attending religion classes. She informed the headmistress she was afraid she might lose her identity as a Jew. The headmistress phoned Marvelle in distress. "If Tiana leaves our religion classes, everyone will walk out with her," she said. "All these years, your daughter has made it one of our most exciting subjects. She's brought her Judaism into the classroom.

JUST A SIMPLE PHARMACIST

She's told us about Jewish holidays. Thanks to Tiana, we've had debates and essays on comparative religion. She's injected a lovely feeling into our classes. Please beg her not to leave."

Tiana continued to make religion a popular subject right through to grade thirteen. At Havergal she was also captain of the volleyball, swimming, and soccer teams, excelled in science and maths, and went on to get an honours BA in political science at the University of Western Ontario. Later she worked in the public relations department of the Vickers & Benson advertising agency and the corporate clientele sales department of Insight Planners, the Toronto convention planning company. She is currently a joint partner with Adam in King Ranch, focusing on marketing, fitness, and relaxation therapy, especially for corporate executives trying to make their way through the peaks and valiums of the fast lane. And recently she married Marc Boyman, a thirty-seven-year-old, Belgium-born co-producer of *The Fly*, the science-fiction film by David Cronenberg that won an Academy Award for makeup in 1987.

Tiana acknowledges there are certain pressures involved in living up to the Koffler name. "In New York, in terms of wealth and status, we're little minnows," she says. "But in Toronto and Canada and extending into Israel, the Koffler name means something. Still, I don't believe in trading on my dad's reputation alone. The Koffler name can get you into the door. But once inside you've got to make it on your own. I can't simply prance in and say, 'Hi. I'm Tiana Koffler. Ta da!' People would say, 'So what? Who cares?' I've been taught by my parents that you've got to earn respect."

Koffler and his wife Marvelle certainly enjoy the comforts that come with wealth, but they shun flash and ostentation. Their six residences are notable for two things. They each have a *mezzuza* affixed to the right-hand side of the front door jamb. Rolled up inside the little oblong container is a parchment scroll testifying in Hebrew: "Hear, O Israel, the Lord our God is one." The other thing they each have in common is nicely phrased by Leon Koffler: "They don't have the smell of money." Besides their Beechwod Avenue home in Toronto, which Koffler bought in 1953 for $39,000, the Kofflers' other residences include Jokers Hill Farm north of Toronto, a ski chalet at Collingwood, Ontario, on Georgian Bay, another ski chalet in Sun Valley, Idaho, the penthouse condominium with a panoramic view of the Mediterranean in Israel, and a posh villa in the Dominican Republic overlooking the Caribbean.

The rustic ski chalet at Collingwood is on a height of land beside the Craigleith Ski Club just above Georgian Bay. Koffler bought the two-acre property from the club for $2,000 with the intention of building permanent quarters for his growing family of junior skiers. Koffler loves recounting the story of how he and its designer, the noted Toronto architect Raymond Moriyama, got together. He was jogging one day in Wilkett Creek Park adjoining Inn on the Park when he was struck by the beauty of the stone-and-timber public washroom. He called Marvelle from a pay phone to exclaim, "I've found the perfect design for our ski cabin. And I've called the Parks Commissioner, Tommy Thompson, to find who did it."

Moriyama, who has since designed such prize-winning structures as the Ontario Science Centre and the Metro Toronto Reference Library, was delighted to duplicate what he calls his "park outhouses." The two-storey cabin features natural fieldstone and local cedar and a balcony that affords a spectacular view of the surrounding area.

Moriyama credits Koffler for inspiring him in the creation of the much-vaunted Ontario Science Centre. While working on the Collingwood chalet, he mentioned to Koffler that the Science Centre had him stymied. "I just can't get a focus on its design," he said. "What exactly is a science centre? What is it supposed to do for us?"

Koffler immediately soared into rhapsodies about the Natural Science Centre that he and Marvelle had just visited in Mexico City. "Murray was so determined that I see it that he drove me to the airport," recalls Moriyama. "As usual, Murray's timing was right. I've always been grateful to him for helping me put things in perspective."

Their most stunning home away from home is the Dominican villa, called Casa de Campo. It was originally part of a hotel tennis-and-golf complex built by Gulf & Western, the movie and land development conglomerate, and was intended to be a guest house for visiting VIPs. Eddie Creed, who had a house on the island, informed him the place was for sale. Koffler picked it up for one million pesos – the equivalent of $300,000 in U.S. funds. Today it is worth well over $1 million.

The Kofflers generously share it with their friends; one guest describes its ambience as a cross between Palm Springs, the south of France, and Tara in *Gone With The Wind*. Roofed with white slate, it consists of six ensuite bedrooms, circling an oval-shaped swimming pool and linked to an airy, white marble-and-glass living and dining-room area. A staff of four, consisting of a cook, gardener, and two maids, look after the needs of guests.

In Canada, Koffler's fantasy home come true is Jokers Hill Farm, an estate of 1,000 acres of jackpine forest and cultivated farmland in King Township, thirty-five miles north of Toronto. It enables Koffler to play the role of country squire. More precisely, he plays the role of an English gentleman farmer. As every member of the British gentry knows, a gentleman farmer's farming really encompasses the four h's: horses, hounds, haberdashery, and horticulture.

Koffler has embraced all four of them joyously. He first became entranced with farm life in the early 1940s when there was a wartime shortage of farm labour. High school students with 66 per cent average grades were encouraged to serve as farm help instead of writing their matriculation exams. "For two summers Murray and I were hired hands at a farm near Whitby," testifies his schoolmate, Oscar (Bosço) Kofman. Shaking his head in awe, Bosco says, "Day and night Murray pitched hay and shoveled manure, like a horny-handed man of the soil, and enjoyed every minute of it."

In 1969, Koffler decided to return to the soil as a gentleman farmer. A real estate agent showed him the rundown, 300-acre estate; it had once been a magnificent, 2,000-acre horse farm developed by General Churchill Mann, a one-time Canadian cavalry officer. His wife, Billie, daughter of Sam McLaughlin, founding president of General Motors of Canada, had named the farm after her horse Joker. Evidently the Manns had moved on and sold off parcels of land piecemeal.

Koffler turned down the $500,000 purchase price asked by the new owner for 300 acres, with its five ramshackle farmhouses and stables and unrepaired fences. Instead, he offered shares in Shoppers Drug Mart worth that amount. It was a good deal for Koffler when one considers he was buying land for paper. He invested a sizable fortune, though, in acquiring 700 more acres and revamping and refurnishing what ultimately became a grand equestrian estate.

Moriyama, who was commissioned to design an exquisite gazebo bridging two new tennis courts and a pond, states without qualification that the Kofflers created a minor miracle. "They built their own distinctive graciousness into a place that had been an architectural hodgepodge," he says. "They made pearls out of mortar and brick."

There are three aspects to Jokers. Probably best known is the horse operation, managed for the past dozen years by John Weir. Koffler turned this entire realm over to Weir, an internationally renowned trainer, who developed Jokers Hill into one of North America's leading equestrian centres. Weir gets all the revenues from stabling and training sixty jumpers and hunters. The horses are boarded and schooled year round in first-class facilities. These include a regulation indoor Olympic training arena that looks like a colossal plane hangar; a racetrack for practice galloping; twenty-two miles of groomed riding trails; and an obstacle course of thirty-six Olympic-standard jumps or hurdles, which, to a lay pedestrian, look formidably horrific and absolutely unjumpable.

Weir pays no rent to Koffler. But in return he maintains the paddocks and stables and services the Koffler family's six horses. Koffler is an accomplished rider. His personal mounts are Beaufort, a black fifteen-year-old horse named after the British Duke of Beaufort, and a high-strung bay named Joker.

"You have to keep in practice form," says Koffler, recalling glumly what happened to him in 1986. "I got off the plane from England the night before and jumped on Joker after not riding for three weeks. Sure enough, I was thrown off and I almost had a concussion because I landed on my head."

Another aspect of Jokers is the farming, which is managed somewhat similarly by the affable Bill Fox, who lives on the farm with his family. With a staff of three, he cultivates 300 acres of hay to supply the horses, as well as a vegetable garden and flower garden to supply Koffler's main house. During the harvest season, Koffler indulges himself in his gentleman hayseed role by cutting hay. "Nothing to it," he says blithely. "I sit on a tractor for a couple of hours and just run up and down the fields."

He participates even less strenuously in tapping the farm's sugar bush during the sugaring off. He restricts himself to sending out jars of Jokers Hill maple syrup as Christmas gifts. "It would be cheaper to give them full sets of the finest sterling silver," he says with a laugh. "I figure our cost of operating the maple syrup production, bottling, and labelling is the highest on the continent."

The third aspect of Jokers can be classified as gracious living at the main farmhouse, with much of the graciousness being maintained by their veteran "house help," Maria and John Arruda, who have served the Kofflers as cook-housekeeper and houseman-gardener for twenty-two years. The farmhouse is a V-shaped assemblage of at least fourteen sizable rooms and spacious hallways spread out on top of a hill around a swimming pool and gardens of peonies, poppies, zinnias, and marigolds. The Kofflers were guided by Napier Simpson, the distinguished Ontario heritage architect, in performing structural work on the original residence. And they have decorated the entire place with the aid of their good friend, Toronto interior designer John North. The wild greens and cool blues of some of Canada's most famous artists appear to brighten up corners everywhere. There are glowing landscapes by Tom Thomson, Lawren Harris, A.Y. Jackson, and Emily Carr. The Kofflers take pride in having selected every piece of furniture themselves, mainly antiques and objets d'art, whose beauty attracted them on their world travels. The pieces include carvings from Africa, sculpture from China, wall hangings from Amsterdam, a foxhunt breakfast table from a castle in

England, and an archaic potbelly stove they spotted on the Left Bank in Paris. "It's the sort of old-fashioned, wood-burning stove they used in French houses without central heating," says Koffler, adding wryly, "I decided to bring it home, in case we ever ride out of Easy Street."

An array of parties at Jokers Hill range from shuck-your-own-corn barbecue picnics to lawn parties of Gatsby-like splendour with musicians performing under the stars. As many as 200 well-heeled and well-tailored guests at these affairs are glad to contribute to Koffler's wide-ranging causes, whether for the Canadian Opera Company or a campaign to clean up the streets of Israel on behalf of the Israeli Foundation for Ecological Action. (Koffler's tidying-up crusade begins in his own backyard. Every morning when he is at the farm, he goes for a brisk jog on the concession road accompanied by his fifteen-year-old golden retriever, Aquarius. The fastidious Koffler stops and carefully picks up empty cigarette packages and beer cans that motorists have carelessly tossed out the window. He piles them neatly in a heap and later sends a truck back to dispose of the litter.)

The pleasures of Koffler's country life have included his involvement not only with the horsey set but also riding with the hounds as a member of the foxy set. For the past dozen years he has worn the "hunting pinks" – the dandified red jacket with a blue collar – of the Toronto and North York Hunt, which is the second oldest continuous fox-hunting club in North America. Oscar Wilde once derided the sport as a snob's pursuit: "The English country gentleman galloping after a fox – the unspeakable in full pursuit of the uneatable." Koffler disagrees. He points out that the Ontario government used to pay bounty hunters $25 to get rid of each bushy-tailed pest. Besides, he claims, the intent here is not to kill a fox; if perchance the hounds have cornered or treed a fox, the Master or the Whip of the hunt will promptly call them off. "I've yet to catch or kill a fox," says Koffler. "You hunt them just for the thrill of the chase."

Unquestionably his greatest thrill arising from the horse world was his cordial acquaintanceship with the royal family. It all happened because of his determination to make Jokers

Hill the Canadian home of a truly world-class staging of the international equestrian competitions known as the Three-Day Event. It's a sporting event in which riders from different countries compete over a period of three days in various phases of horsemanship, from dressage to jumping. Koffler assumed the responsibility of presenting the three-day horse trials in 1971, 1973, and 1975.

In the spring of 1973, he invited Captain Mark Phillips, then the world champion rider, to be his house guest at Jokers and help him design the course for the forthcoming summer Three-Day Event of the Continental Championships of North America. The fiancé of Princess Anne, who was then Britain's number-one woman rider, Phillips proved to be a clubbable chap. "He has a certain amount of British reserve, yet mixes very easily," says Koffler. "He's a lot of fun actually, likes partying, and certainly knows his stuff on equestrian matters."

That summer, Koffler struck up a friendship, too, with Prince Philip, who was his weekend guest during the Three-Day Event. In his capacity as chairman of the Federation Equestrian International, he came to measure the course and officiate at the horse trials. Koffler arranged to have his boyhood friend at summer camp, Barney Danson, Canadian Minister of Defence, drop the prince down via an air force helicopter on Jokers Hill farm pasture.

More than 5,000 horse and royalty fans flocked to witness the action and be served tomato sandwiches along with rivers of champagne. Prince Philip took a lot of snapshots (Tiana, then ten, greeted him chewing gum and saying "Hi") and he turned out to have a royal sense of humour. "He certainly loved caviar," recalls Koffler. "We'd bought a big can of this fantastic Iranian Malossol caviar. He dug into it. 'Oh, my goodness,' he said. 'My favourite caviar! I could make a whole meal of this. You know, I never get enough of it at home.'"

In appreciation of Koffler's hospitality, Prince Philip presented his host with a magnificent ceramic sculpture of himself swinging a polo mallet on horseback. In return, Koffler presented him with a soapstone carving of the jester symbol of Jokers Hill as well as a pair of salt-and-pepper shakers that

Tiana had made in her ceramics class at school. Just as the helicopter was about to take off, Adam Koffler came roaring down the pasture runway in a car containing his majestically unruffled, seventy-five-year-old grandmother, Eva Seligman.

"Hey, Prince!" yelled Adam. "You forgot to say good-bye to *bubey*!"

Whereupon his *bubey* presented Prince Philip with a homemade sponge cake. "Baked especially for your wife," said the queenly Eva.

Queen Elizabeth II was obviously appreciative. Koffler received that November a regal card from St. James's Palace bearing the crowned Elizabeth Rex seal. It stated that the Lord Chamberlain was commanded by Her Majesty and the Duke of Edinburgh to invite Mr. and Mrs. Koffler to attend a party at Buckingham Palace as well as the wedding of Princess Anne to Captain Mark Phillips in Westminster Abbey.

Koffler delights in a photo of himself in a morning suit and silk top hat (which he rented) preparing to go to Westminster Abbey. And both he and Marvelle treasure memories of their reception at Buckingham Palace. It was called a formal "breakfast" affair, which meant guests were supposed to arrive in white ties and tails and evening gowns at ten in the evening and stay until breakfast at three o'clock in the morning. Koffler was alarmed when their chauffeur-driven limousine arrived at ten minutes to ten – all the lights were out at the palace, and there didn't seem to be a soul in the place. He said to Marvelle, "Are you sure this is the right palace?"

But at precisely ten o'clock, all the lights were switched on. And suddenly out of nowhere Rolls-Royces, carrying the crowned heads and pedigreed elite of the world, were lined up outside the gates waiting to get in. They had been circling around the palace during the blackout until the exact minute of protocol when one was supposed to arrive.

Both Koffler and Marvelle agree it was like a royal ball out of a fairytale. Yet it was touched with the universal humanity of all such weddings, as when the Queen, then forty-seven, confided to them with a sigh she didn't feel old enough to have a daughter getting married.

"When Prince Philip introduced us to the Queen," Koffler remembers, "Her Majesty said, 'Oh, I'm so happy to meet you. I have all the pictures that Philip took at your Jokers Hill in my photo album.'" He asks in amazement, "Would you believe? She keeps a family scrapbook!"

He found the Queen Mother just as homey. He recalls her saying, "Oh, I'm *so* glad to meet you. We've heard all about you and your family from Philip. It's so nice of you to come all the way over here just to attend *our* family gathering."

Marvelle was likewise struck by the informality of the royal family. "The Queen looked dazzling in her jewelry and gown," Marvelle remembers. "And we talked together for about fifteen minutes – you'll never guess – about the paper dolls we used to cut out as children. I told her how I'd cut out and save from girls' cut-out books paper dolls of herself and her sister Margaret and her mom and dad. She said, 'I did the same thing!'"

She says the Queen Mother couldn't have been friendlier. "As soon as we told her our names, her eyes lit up. She'd done her homework, and knew all the details about Philip's stay at our farm. She took Murray and myself by the hand and said, 'Come, my children. I want you to meet my friends.'"

She introduced them, among other royalty, to Princess Grace and Prince Rainier of Monaco. "She looked stunning, of course," he says. But he recalls with amusement she couldn't have been less interested in the conversation he had with her husband about real estate. "Prince Rainier was trying to persuade us to build a Four Seasons Hotel in Monte Carlo," he says. "We didn't."

Koffler found piquant, too, the practicality of the bride and groom. Princess Anne and her husband seemed genuinely impressed by the Kofflers' wedding gift – a quilt with a traditional Canadian log cabin pattern especially handcrafted for the royal couple by an antique store in Woodbridge, Ontario. "They must have received a thousand gifts," says Koffler. "But Mark had made note of ours and said without prompting, 'Thank you for the lovely quilt.' Then Anne took off on it. She said, 'Your quilt isn't going to languish in our inventory stockpile of gifts. It's so warm looking. We're definitely going to enjoy using it.'"

Koffler enjoys browsing through photo albums showing other world luminaries he has known, because the pictures evoke such pleasurable memories. Among the grand folk who have stayed at Jokers Hill, he rates Pierre Trudeau as a most stimulating and personable "genius." Several photos reveal Koffler and Marvelle cross-country skiing and just kibitzing around with the former Prime Minister and his former wife, Margaret.

Trudeau was a brilliant intellectual, who was also fun to be with. "They call him arrogant," says Koffler. "But I think that's because he was impatient with reporters and politicians who intruded on him. I found him a marvellous conversationalist. He could talk to you on any topic, from politics to religion. Yet he never made you feel you had a lesser intellect than he had.

"He was tremendously moved by our Sabbath dinner ceremony of joining hands in prayer. He referred to it a year or two later when he was our guest at our ski chalet in Sun Valley. 'Oh, do you remember that wonderful Friday evening at your farm?' he said. 'Though I'm a Catholic, it was the most beautiful religious service conducted by a family I've ever seen.'"

Another leader who won his respect and affection was the late Israel Prime Minister Golda Meir. He acted as her host when she visited Toronto, and they became good friends on a first-name basis through his annual visits to the Weizmann Institute of Science in Israel. He recalls her as an arresting figure: a one-time Milwaukee schoolteacher with the nicotine-stained fingers of a chainsmoker, a homely face of extraordinary softness, and the simple grey bun of a grandmother. Some of her political opponents claimed sourly that "the First Lady of Israel's Labor Party is the only man in the cabinet." But Koffler saw her differently. "She could be a one-woman fortress of strength, like Margaret Thatcher, but she had a real woman's heart," he says. "She was a very emotional woman, but no sentimentalized Yiddish Momma. She was a worrier who could be tough. She was uncompromising about the Arabs.

She couldn't forgive them, she said, for turning Israeli children into warriors forced to kill. Yet she wasn't a gloomy worrywart. She had her own brand of humour that could crack you up. It wasn't loud ha-ha humour. It was chuckle humour."

A good many photos in Koffler's albums provoke chuckle-some responses. And there are many shots of the Kofflers cruising aboard the ocean-going yacht, *Age Of Aquarius*, a fifty-three-foot ketch of white fibreglass with a full-time crew of captain, first mate, and cook and sufficient cabin space to sleep ten. Koffler bought it in partnership with two friends, George Zuckerman and Max Goldhar, in 1968. They sold it twelve years later, but all three yacht mates agree they got their money's worth of luxury living. Goldhar, a land developer in his sixties, recalls: "We'd choose exotic destinations by spinning a globe and calling out, 'Where will we go this time? Yugoslavia? Scandinavia? Corsica? Or Capri?' And as soon as we'd hit port, we'd raise our flag bearing a cocktail glass to signal to people that the party was about to begin."

Eddie Creed, who has been Koffler's guest on many a cruise, recently jotted down on paper what he believes to be the key to the personality of his roving best friend. He wrote:

"What makes Murray run? The answer is simple. It is his quest for life. His desire to experience it all in his lifetime. To not miss anything. Whether it's to dance the frug in Paris or waltz at the Vienna Opera Ball. To sail up the fjords of Norway. To adventure on a camera safari in the jungles of Africa. To go on a cultural tour with a scholarly group from the Royal Ontario Museum to the Great Wall of China. To fish for grayling in the Yukon with his kids or to be the life of the party at the opening of the elegant Four Seasons Hotel on Yorkville. That's Murray."

In other words, as it was phrased succinctly by Henry David Thoreau, his goal is "to suck the marrow of life."

Koffler agrees with both the furrier and the philosopher. At Jokers Hill Farm recently, he sipped a glass of the best Moreau Blanc from his wine cellar, sniffed the fragrance of the pines and blossoming crab apple trees, and gazed at the faroff hazy blue of Lake Simcoe, where he had first fallen in love with

Marvelle sunning on her raft. "What a privilege it is to be alive and living here!" said Koffler, raising his glass. "My life has been one high after another, one happenstance after another. I wonder what the next chapter will be?"

CHAPTER EIGHTEEN

Honorary Chairman

A year had passed since his gala tribute dinner when he had formally announced his retirement as board chairman of Shoppers Drug Mart. Now, on a cold February morning in 1987, Murray Koffler, Shoppers' honorary chairman, was preparing to attend the annual luncheon of retired associates who automatically become members of the Shoppers Alumni Club.

He wore his sixty-three years lightly, but the past year had taken its toll. The smile lines were etched more deeply around his mouth; his glossy brown hair was frosted with new streaks of grey. For despite Koffler's best intentions, it had been a year crowded with activity. He had planned on taking a cue from his friend, the architect Raymond Moriyama. In a well-publicized public lecture entitled "Can Your Life Become a Work of Art?," Moriyama had suggested that successful professionals in their prime might follow the advice of his grandfather. A mining executive in Japan, who was also a philosopher and haiku poet, his grandfather had recommended the therapy of retiring for a year of meditation and doing absolutely nothing.

For Moriyama, it worked. "My grandfather taught me to look at the moon reflected in water cupped in my hands . . . and other lessons in sensitivity and inward perception," he said. Moriyama felt the experience helped him grow as a man, a husband, and father of five children. Among other things, he took a six-month trip to India to retrace Buddha's journey. The other six months were devoted to renewing his friendship with his wife and family at home.

"I really listened to my children," said Moriyama. "I spent time thinking about what they said. I watched squirrels. They do the most crazy things. And I watched raindrops running down the window."

In like style, Koffler vowed he would take a year's sabbatical. "I'll fulfil my lifelong aspiration to be nothing but a bum," he solemnly declared. He yearned to escape the slavery of being tied to a time schedule. He dreamed of perhaps hopping onto a motorcycle for an aimless vagabondage. He had visions of maybe helping a fellow retired pharmacist to run a perfect model neighbourhood drugstore, like his father's, just to see if it could be done. Or possibly he would commune with nature, like the sages of yore in ancient Palestine, by sitting in the sun beneath a fig tree.

Alas, all his dreams of moonbeam-watching or fig-tree-sitting or bike-hoboing came to naught. True, he managed to squeeze in a fishing trip to the Yukon to enjoy himself with his sons and found that satisfying. But while at Expo in Vancouver, he found that bicycling alone in Stanley Park to watch the squirrels was a lonely pastime. "Being alone is no fun and I didn't enjoy it," decided Koffler, the consummate gregarious man. While in Vancouver, he also attended an international conference of philanthropists; for the first time in years, he sat in the audience as an observer rather than at the high table assuming his usual leadership role. He remembers feeling a touch of guilt and a touch of envy.

"It was an unusual feeling, and I don't know if I enjoyed it," he says. "First I thought, 'Have I abandoned my responsibility? Am I letting anybody down?' Then I thought, 'What a letdown! I'm usually the centre of attention at these communal affairs. Gee, maybe I should be back at the head table, playing a bigger role with the others in a leadership position. I don't know if I can cope with just being a passive bum.'"

His most traumatic experience in the past year had been both physical and emotional. For weeks he had experienced a tingling feeling in his fingers and feet. Physicians at Mount Sinai Hospital in Toronto advised him that his right kidney had a tumour that appeared malignant and the kidney was surgically removed. His enforced idleness while convalescing in the hospital jolted Koffler, the extrovert, into a state of unaccustomed introspection. Temporarily anyway he became an introvert reassessing his accepted values.

"I'd always lived by the Dale Carnegie principles of positive thinking," he later recalled. "If I felt depressed, I'd buck myself up with my inspirational phrases. I'd get solace by repeating, 'If you get handed a lemon, make lemonade out of it.' Or I'd say to myself, 'I'm going to be happy today, no matter what comes my way; no matter if it's blue or grey, I'm going to be happy today.' Well, you know what? When it came to the crunch, and things seemed really tough to take, I found the lemon still tasted lemony and it was damned hard to convince myself that the blue and grey would go away." It was a revelation to the incorrigible optimist.

On recovery, though, when he was given a clean bill of good health by his physicians, Koffler reverted to his usual ebullient self. He decided he wasn't the sort of man who can sit underneath that idyllic fig tree.

It is little wonder that Koffler, a congenital latecomer, was delayed making his departure for the luncheon of the Shoppers Alumni Club. As he was finally putting on his coat to leave his office, from where he oversees a multitude of philanthropic and community involvements, his train of thought was interrupted by Joanne Agnelli, his new executive secretary for the past year.

"Mr. Koffler," she said. "I hope you won't mind me saying that I won't *ever* take you as a role model . . ."

He glanced at her sharply, startled out of his reverie.

". . . for my retirement," she said, concluding her sentence.

"What do you mean?" asked Koffler.

"Well, I understand you're supposed to be loafing for a year," she said, reprimanding him in a motherly tongue. "If you call this hectic pace of yours lazying around in retirement, then I say, 'No, thank you' to the Koffler method of retiring."

Koffler laughed. But her observation made him thoughtful as he drove downtown to the luncheon. As he later confided, "It put me in mind of how my father used to work around the clock from eight in the morning until well past midnight. People would say, 'Leon, take it easy! You're working yourself into your early grave.' But my father never paid attention."

The fact that his father died at the early age of forty-seven made Koffler aware of his own possible "shortivity," his slightly ironic term for his potentially abbreviated longevity. "I never had the comfort of thinking I was going to live to a ripe old age," he said. "So after I reached that landmark age of forty-seven, I felt it was all clear sailing. I told myself, 'I'm going to make every day count.' But now I wonder if I've gone overboard, like my father . . ."

Such sombre thoughts were discarded when Koffler arrived at the giant Sheraton Centre on Queen Street for the luncheon of the Shoppers Alumni Club. The luncheon was to be held at one of the hotel's convention dining rooms at the tail end of that semi-annual rite known as the Shoppers Buying Show and Associates' Conference. It was a three-day national rally that was a combination of bazaar and trade fair, carnival and convention, evangelical-style jamboree and pep talk whoop-de-doo. The hoopla was all geared to boosting the morale and profits of Shoppers associates and their suppliers; or, in the lingo of the rally, "to impact our bottom line."

The semi-annual conference had grown over the past two decades into the nation's biggest pharmaceutical buying show. In the high-flown rhetoric of one speaker at the 1987 rally: "We have over one million years of drugstore experience right here in this room." In factual terms, more than $40 million of business is transacted at 150 booths staffed by 400 merchandise suppliers, and in attendance are 800 buyers representing the Shoppers chain.

Koffler wouldn't miss it for anything. He revels in the fun and comradeship, the bustle and hurlyburly, the carny sales spiels, and the smells of samples of everything from Cracker Jack to the most expensive of perfumes. The sights are always festive and sometimes funny. During the meeting coffee breaks, you might well see a clown wearing a King Kong gorilla suit handing out bananas and banana bread with the coffee. You might encounter "Commander" Roman Niemy of the Shoppers Life and Red Saver Private Brands Division and his "strike force soldiers" marching out of a sales meeting. They have just been urged by a battalion leader, made up to look like television's fiercesome Mr. T, to wage an assault on the store front lines and "fight for shelf space for our own house brands." To prepare them for the "war zone offence," each commando wears a tropical camouflage battle cap; a big circular red, white, and blue button reads: "RIGHT ON TARGET."

Speaking quietly, and punctuating his informal address with humour, Koffler reminisced to a luncheon audience of about 300 old-timers how the buying shows began. They started in the mid-sixties as a modest buying program, he recalled, with no frills at all. Koffler then had eight Shoppers outlets, which he guided from a little hutch of an office at the back of the store on Dufferin at Lawrence. Its associate was Arthur Resnick, who, having reached the age of sixty-seven, was among his former colleagues who had decided to retire in 1987.

When the eight outlets showed collective sales of almost $12 million, Koffler suggested to his associates that they had grown to the point where the company had enough buying clout to make joint purchases at a maximum discount. They agreed. But where would the buying be done?

It was Resnick who said, "Why not the Conroy?" It was a cosy family hotel right across the road on Lawrence at Dufferin. "At the beginning, it was almost like an audition," Koffler recalled. "We interviewed the sales representatives one by one. You can imagine how difficult it was for them to come into this room, sit down, and wait and wait their turn to show us samples of their wares."

It has long since evolved into a mammoth get-together so vast it requires the combined convention facilities of the Sheraton Centre and the Hilton Harbour Castle Hotel. It had been described in circusy terms as "Brass's bold, bright, beautiful bastion of breathtaking bigness." That Barnumesque catalogue of alliteration was put into the mouth of the master of ceremonies at the 1986 rally by the Shoppers' publicist-cum-ghostwriter Hilda Wilson. The Brass refers to Goldie Brass, the blonde, super-efficient former payroll secretary, now Shoppers director of marketing communications. She has been orchestrating the rallies for almost twenty years with guidance from Koffler.

Koffler most enjoys recalling the spectacular show in February, 1983, that climaxed the celebration of what he billed as the Shoppers "Thanks A Billion" party. In showmanlike fashion, he transformed an internal company hurrah into an external consumer promotional extravaganza. His feat was hailed in the trade as the most successful national incentive program for employees and customers ever staged in the Canadian retail industry.

The idea originated in early 1982 when Koffler told his colleagues at a think tank, "We expect to gross $1 billion by the end of this fiscal year. So why not go all out and invite everybody to help us celebrate the occasion with a monster bash?"

The party ran for five months and was heralded in billboards, newspapers, radio and TV commercials, fliers, window banners, and skywriting all announcing, "Thanks A Billion." Prizes worth $1 million were offered via raffles and performance-related competitions and ran the gamut from trips to the French Riviera to Tiffany lamps. Special sales were keyed to the billion theme. Cosmetics were sold with the catch phrase "Look Like A Billion," and everyday drugstore items were sold as "One In A Billion" bargains.

All this publicity hoo-ha concluded in February, 1983, with a glitzy "Thanks A Billion" party for which Shoppers took over Toronto's entire O'Keefe Centre. Of the many letters of congratulations that poured in, saluting Shoppers for reaching this milestone, Koffler recalled with greatest pleasure a poem composed by his neighbour, John Devlin, then chairman of Rothmans of Pall Mall Ltd. It led off Zena Cherry's four-column report of the event in *The Globe and Mail* next morning:

A billion seconds ago, man had exploded the first atomic bomb;

A billion minutes ago, Christ was still alive on this earth;
A billion hours ago, man was living in caves;
A billion dollars of spending in Washington was yesterday;
A billion dollars of sales this year is Shoppers Drug Mart.

Heading the list of prominent executives present were two names mentioned in Zena Cherry's social column who both played important roles at the zenith of Koffler's career. One was Paul Paré, chairman of the board of Imasco Limited, which had taken over ownership of Shoppers Drug Mart in 1978. The other was David Ronald Bloom, the newly appointed president of Shoppers Drug Mart. How their lives crossed is a story that also gives Koffler great pleasure when recounting it.

His first encounter with Paré was prefaced by two of Koffler's famous think tanks in 1975. He had passed the age of fifty, and recalled how unprepared he had been as a seventeen-year-old to take charge of the two family drugstores when his father had died at forty-seven. So he and Marvelle assembled their five children for an all-day estate-planning session around a table in a suite at the Quatre Saisons Hotel in Montreal where they had all gathered for a wedding. He laid it on the line and said, "Let's talk about our futures."

Were they and their prospective mates willing to cope with the responsibility – as well as the inevitable divisive tensions – of one day operating the family business, which then consisted of 300 stores? Or would they prefer that he sell the business now to a larger Canadian company and with the capital thus available have the freedom to embark on their independent careers? They debated the issue all day and that night decided in a vote they favoured selling the business and choosing career opportunities of their own.

The following month, Koffler arranged with eighteen key members of his management team to hold a similar freewheeling discussion at Jokers Hill Farm. He presented straightforwardly the prospects that would face them on his death and offered them a choice. Should the company become part of a large international corporation, which would offer all sorts of opportunities for Shoppers' financial development and executive careers? Or should it be forced later to deal with estate trustees whose only concern would be to preserve assets for the Koffler family, who owned more than 50 per cent of the company? They, too, agreed unanimously that to sell Shoppers Drug Mart would be the wisest move.

Koffler was charged with the task of finding an appropriate purchaser. Eventually, on May 1, 1978, after discussing the offers of four other potential buyers, he sold the Shoppers chain of 364 outlets to Imasco Limited for approximately $70 million. Of that total, 60 per cent was in cash and 40 per cent in Imasco shares. The sale put Koffler in the position of being one of the largest individual shareholders as well as a member of the board of directors of what is today a multinational consumer products and financial services conglomerate. It is expected to gross well over $10 billion in 1988.

Koffler selected Imasco for several reasons. First of all, the Montreal-based company had a solid financial foundation. Its major money-earner, the eighty-five-year-old Imperial Tobacco Ltd., produces more than half of all the cigarettes sold in Canada; among them are such name brands as Player's, du Maurier, Peter Jackson, and Matinee. Though 40 per cent owned by Britain's B.A.T. Industries – British American Tobacco, which operates tobacco factories in more than fifty countries – Imasco was solidly Canadian in its outlook and board membership. Koffler liked its sponsorship of worthy Canadian causes; among them are the Imasco Scholarship Fund for Disabled University Students and the du Maurier Council for the Performing Arts, which supports theatre, music, and ballet.

Koffler liked the way it had faced the fact that tobacco was not a growth industry and had taken steps to diversify in the retail field. Its totally owned subsidiaries included the United Cigar Store chain in Canada and the Hardee's fast-food restaurant chain in the United States. To top the icing on the cake, it had acquired the Canadian chain of sixty Top Drug Marts, which could be nicely integrated into the Shoppers family of stores.

Most important of all, Koffler liked the cut of the jib and the managerial style of Imasco's board chairman. He met Paul Paré in a meeting at Imasco's unpretentious Montreal headquarters. With Paré smoking part of his daily allotment of twenty mild Matinee cigarettes and Koffler puffing his ritual morning Player's, they took to each other instantly. Paré was then fifty-six. Though he has a patrician manner, he is given to punctuating his conversation with blunt Anglo-Saxon epithets he picked up while serving as lieutenant-commander in the Royal Canadian Navy during World War II. And despite his accented name, he is an Anglophone, one of the nine children of an Australian mother and a well-to-do French-Canadian engineer who was a pillar of Montreal's Westmount Establishment. Paré graduated from McGill University with a law degree in 1949, then went right to work for the legal department of Imperial Tobacco and climbed the ladder rapidly. He belongs to the right clubs (the Mount Royal, the Forest & Stream, the Montreal Indoor Tennis Club, the Mount Bruno Country Club). He sits on the right boards (Royal Bank of Canada, IBM Canada, Canadian Pacific Limited, Canadian Investment Fund Ltd.).

"He's a gentleman," said Koffler when sizing him up. "He's sensitive to other people's feelings. Yet he's decisive. When Paul has to make a tough decision, he doesn't waver. He bites the bullet and faces the problem head on." Koffler was further impressed by Paré's hands-off policy, which allows Imasco's subsidiaries to make their own day-to-day decisions. "Even though we were bought by Imasco, we wanted the autonomy to do our own thing," Koffler recalls.

Paré immediately agreed. And he now says he would have been foolish to do otherwise. As grand honcho of what is essentially a management company, Paré regards himself as basically a people-picker. "I don't have any expertise in corporate finance or in anything related to a particular product," he says candidly. "I'm a lawyer trained to assess people. So my main job is to identify the right people for the right job and give them a very wide degree of authority." He states his policy in no-nonsense language: "If it's working fine, keep the hell out of it."

Paré made it an obligatory part of their deal that Koffler would stay on for at least three years as chief executive officer. After that, the understanding was that he would continue to stay on as board chairman as long as he was needed, giving advice to his successor. "We felt we were lucky to have him," says Paré. "He'd made a singular impact across the land as an unequalled merchandiser. He was North America's most successful drugstore franchisor. And to top it, he has this marvellous *joie de vivre* and prodigious energy. I've always thought I was blessed with genes that allow me to move damn fast. But Murray outruns me. At the Shoppers buying shows, he's on the go-go all bloody day and all bloody night, playing host to hundreds and hundreds of pharmacists. Amazing man! I know of only one other guy in the business who can bloody well out-marathon him."

Koffler would be the first to identify this *Wunderkind*. He is, of course, Koffler's protégé, David Bloom. "In building an executive team," John Wareham, president of a New York executive-search company, wrote in *Secrets Of A Corporate Headhunter*, "the chief executive officer unconsciously recruits in his own image." Koffler says admiringly of his recruit for the top spot, "David Bloom is a Murray Koffler multiplied by a factor of ten. He's the right man in the right place at the right time."

Characteristically, when Imasco took over Shoppers in 1978, Bloom was holding down not one but two of its top-level managerial posts. He was executive vice-president of operations at the national level; he was as well president of Shoppers' central region, overseeing all its stores in Ontario and Manitoba, and was also one of the architects for the operational direction of the company. Bloom was then thirty-five, the complete corporation man and the consummate professional manager of the pharmacy world. He has superb stamina, sandpaper persistence, a flypaper memory for details, an enormous gusto for accomplishment, and a voracious appetite for long hours and plain hard work. In addition, he is an adept brain picker and a deft people picker, seemingly intuitive about being able to spot a talented comer. He has trained himself to be a speed reader and is an even faster talker, giving a speech with a staccato delivery.

Bloom doesn't profess to be a Koffler clone. "I'm not as daring a risk-taker as Murray," he says. "My risks are more calculated. I measure the payoff, and if it's not big enough, I won't take the gamble."

A key difference between the two is their conflicting attitude toward books on how to achieve success in business management. Koffler, perhaps because he is a self-made success as an entrepreneur, can't abide them. He managed to plow only half way through one business best-seller, *The One Minute Manager*, by Kenneth Blanchard and Spencer Johnson. "Too simplistic," he said, and decided he couldn't waste one more minute on it.

He had even more trouble grappling with *Iacocca*, the autobiography of the auto tycoon who was fired by Ford and became the driving force behind the turnaround of Chrysler. "Lee Iacocca may be an industrial genius, but I don't think the book did him justice," says Koffler. "I think he brought himself down. Maybe it's because I've never been hurt as bad as this guy. He obviously was a very aggressive man. He was elbowing himself on the upward trail and met a lot of resistance. But some of his ways of dealing with management I found very offensive. He was so vindictive in print he turned me off. I couldn't finish it."

In typical Koffler style, he makes a joke of his lack of appetite for guide books that purport to provide the swift uphill glide to success. "I recognize that people just gobble up the how-to books, but I can't swallow them," he says with amusement. "For instance, I've read the how-to-golf books on the market, and they haven't made a bit of difference to my stroke. I've tried reading them in the middle of the night when I can't sleep. Marvelle once woke up to see me gripping my hands in the air and swinging. She asked me in alarm, 'What're you doing?' I said, 'I'm on the seventh hole.'"

Bloom, on the other hand, has great respect for how-to managerial guides. Indeed, he sometimes sounds like a running thesaurus of managementese. Though he lacks a Bachelor of Business Administration degree, he likes saying "I've earned it on the firing line," and his colleagues say he probably could write the authoritative book on the subject from his practical firsthand knowledge. He has extended his experience by taking night courses on managerial negotiating at York University and by participating in management seminars in Britain and the U.S.

His conversation is peppered with three favourite verbs: to "maximize," "synergize," and "energize." His speeches are flavoured with peppy acronyms. One is "MBWA" (Management By Walking Around), which he borrowed from the Tom Peters bible of corporate leaders, *Passion For Excellence.* Another is "CARE" (Customers Are Really Everything), which he adapted from an internal staff training program conducted by Gimbels department stores in the U.S. Bloom points out with amusement, "Both phrases simply verify what Murray Koffler put into practice twenty-five years ago."

Like Koffler, Bloom likes collecting uplifting mottos. He is not, however, an adherent of Dale Carnegie's homilies on improving interpersonal relationships. Bloom prefers maxims related to the business world. A best-seller about the much-vaunted Japanese style of corporate management furnished him with the Oriental proverb: "Give a hungry man a fish and he will eat for a day. Show him how to catch a fish and he will eat for the rest of his life."

Bloom genuinely believes in team spirit and its psychology as a motivating force. "I'm more of a team player than Murray," says Bloom. He readily acknowledges that Koffler is a trailblazing entrepreneur who singlehandedly set out to build his business from scratch. Since Bloom can't claim to have embarked on a similar campaign of empire-building, he sees himself as an "intrepreneur." It's a term he borrowed from another business best-seller, John Naisbitt's *Megatrends,* and it means one who competes aggressively for business within the structure of a corporation.

At the Shoppers buying shows, Bloom makes no bones about assuming a militant stance. "Uncle David Wants You!" is bannered on a poster, in which Bloom, pointing a declamatory finger as in the famous Uncle Sam recruitment pose, exhorts his associate pharmacists to compete for profits more vigorously. In another talk, Bloom referred to his colleagues as the "New Centurions of Retailing" and stimulated them into action with the ringing cry: "The battlefield and the front lines are in your stores."

Bloom admits that some of his campaign slogans may seem corny, but points out that they work. "I'm like a leader charging into a battle with a banner bearing the mortar and pestle insignia," he explains. "I just can't yell out to my troops, 'Guys, I want you to follow me blindly.' A leader needs a vision, a goal, an idea, a motivating thrust. It's got to excite them and give them direction. You've got to package it as a cause, so that *you* don't have to pull *them*. The idea is to get them so fired up with pride that *they* tug *you*."

Bloom is driven not by financial reward, he explains, but by "the feeling of self-accomplishment. I've always had this burning passion to achieve. I just can't accept defeat." He was most influenced by two dynamos on his mother's side of the family. One was his maternal grandfather, Lazer Weinstein, an immigrant from Kiev in the Ukraine. He rose to be president of the Canadian Fruit and Produce Co. He was given the title of Apple King, because his orchards at his farm in Newcastle, Ontario, sold the largest number of apples at the Ontario Food Terminal in Toronto. The other strong influence was Bloom's uncle, Seymour Weinstein. He is still known as the Watermelon King at the Food Terminal, because he was the major Ontario importer of the melons. "Uncle Seymour is in awe of my accomplishments, too," says Bloom. "He keeps saying, 'I can't get over it.'"

Bloom is grateful to his Uncle Seymour for hiring him as a watermelon salesman and truck driver at $1.50 an hour one summer at the Food Terminal. Bloom, then a rather sheltered teenaged suburbanite who had graduated from William Lyon Mackenzie Collegiate, learned about the earthy side of life and picked up a lot of street savvy. He had to get up at four o'clock in the morning to be at the wholesale market by five. The produce had to be sold by 8:30 a.m. and all truck deliveries completed by 3 p.m.

Bloom was intrigued by the camaraderie of the Italian, Polish, and Russian immigrants. They would hug each other in the morning as a greeting. Then they would haggle at the top of their lungs. Bloom now says, "What really impressed me was their entrepreneurship in the purest sense of the word. They spoke in broken English. Yet they had this gutsy yearning to overcome and succeed. Their tenacity must have rubbed off on me. It became part of the fabric of my character. For instance, I'm not a tremendous tennis player. Just average. But if you ask anyone who plays tennis with me, they'll tell you I never give up. I may not be Bjorn Borg, but you'll get a game from me, and you'll say, 'I got a lot of exercise from David Bloom.'"

His meteoric rise in the pharmacy world was fuelled by innate self-confidence plus, as one colleague puts it, "plenty of steam in the boiler." When he was nineteen, his apprenticeship at his Uncle Max Weinstein's drugstore lasted three days. He was being paid a dollar an hour for working as a dispensary assistant all day and then at nights as well had to deliver prescriptions. To gain experience in a drugstore chain, he switched to a Plaza store on the outskirts of town at Jane and Wilson, where he was paid $1.50 an hour. He quickly won a reputation as a diligent worker. His girlfriend, Molly Rosenbloom, who eventually became his wife and mother of their two children, would pick him up at midnight on Saturdays so they could go out on a date. His wife has since become an integral part of his success. Bloom says, "Molly was the ultimate consumer advocate and sounding board for many of the ideas that I conceived in my travels across the country. I wholeheartedly give her credit for her enormous contribution to so many of my achievements."

He graduated from the Ontario College of Pharmacy in 1967, and a year later, after Shoppers had acquired the Plaza chain, he was the associate of the Plaza store in the Yorkdale Shopping Centre. "I gave it my total commitment," he says, recalling how he would work until one o'clock in the morning devising novel merchandising promotions. His zany "Zoo of Value" display was among many store-level promotions that helped boost sales from half a million to $1 million in the very first year.

By 1972, Shoppers offered Bloom the opportunity to work as director of its operations for eastern Canada; it was a vast territory stretching from Winnipeg to New Glasgow in Nova Scotia. He took it on, though it meant working at the Shoppers central office five days a week plus weekends at the Yorkdale

Plaza store, which he owned as an associate. It meant that he was working seventy hours a week, but he was only twenty-eight at the time and loved the double-barrelled action.

In 1983, when Paul Paré of Imasco announced that Bloom had been appointed president of Shoppers, it was clear that the thirty-nine-year-old chief executive officer was a man who had just begun his rocketing career in the corporate strato-sphere. He was also a man who had been cautioned privately by Paré to be a tactful "stickhandler."

Bloom was already aware of the need to tread warily and not trample on egos. "Most of my business life I've had to deal with people twenty years older than myself," he says. "It's es-pecially touchy when I've been overseeing veterans who've been with Shoppers since day one. It's natural to be envious of a much younger guy who's been promoted over your head. So I've leaned over backwards not to seem pushy."

Indeed, Koffler, who has consistently been Bloom's number-one rooter, couldn't resist joshing his disciple a little at his 1986 tribute dinner. In his farewell speech, the retiring board chairman ribbed Bloom about his zeal when reaching for the company's top job.

"I was impressed with this fellow," Koffler had said. "And as a joke, I used to say, 'David, some day you are going to be president.' It was a joke, you know. Who ever promises a presidency? Well, you know, he took me seriously. In the latter years, I started to pale. My ribs started to ache from the el-bowing: 'Move over!' I kept dreaming. I'd wake up in the middle of the night in a cold sweat. But, by unanimous con-sent, David Bloom became the president and deservedly so. He started to build his dream."

Koffler turned to the audience and added, "Please don't get the idea that I'm planning to sail away into the sunset." he reminded them that as honorary chairman he would maintain a strong tie with the company he had founded and nurtured. True, he would play a smaller role in the administration of Shoppers, but he would perform a more significant role in the affairs of its holding company, Imasco. Not only would he con-tinue as an Imasco board director; he would be active as well on its finance, compensation, and executive committees.

CHAPTER NINETEEN

Passing the Baton

Murray Koffler has since called it passing the baton. At the beginning of 1987, when David Bloom assumed his new post as chairman and chief executive officer of the Imasco Drug Retailing Group, he was undertaking a formidable double mandate. He was to continue as president, chairman, and chief executive officer of Shoppers Drug Mart Limited, expected to gross almost $2 billion in annual revenue by the end of 1988. It meant he was the top man guiding the destiny of 550 stores, with 12,000 employees and a 30 per cent share of the Canadian market. At the same time, Imasco put him in charge of its 850 Peoples Drug Stores, with 18,000 employees located in fourteen states of the United States. The Peoples chain, too, was expected to gross close to $2 billion (in Canadian funds) by the end of 1988.

Altogether it meant that Bloom, in effect, was boss of a combined North American pharmacy colossus, with a total of 1,400 stores, a staff of 30,000, and an annual gross of close to $4 billion. This made it the fourth largest drugstore chain in the world (after Walgreen and Rite-Aid, the two U.S. giants, and Boots, the dominant chain in Britain). It has meant further that Bloom has since become an international commuter, as peripatetic as a grasshopper. He must split his time between both countries, putting in a sixty-hour work week. "I could teach time management in the classroom of any North American university," he says, grinning. "I've earned my degree."

When hopping from the Shoppers Toronto headquarters office to the Peoples headquarters office in Alexandria, Virginia, Bloom drives to a private hangar near the Pearson International Airport in the company's telephone-equipped BMW. He takes off at precisely 7:30 a.m., in the company's eight-passenger Westwind jet plane. At 9 a.m., he is in his office in Alexandria, a bedroom community of Washington, D.C. "While other Toronto executives are bogged down in the early morning downtown traffic," he says triumphantly, "I've done a good hour's work on the plane."

Still, sixty hours add up to a long stretch. Other executives less mettlesome might resist shouldering such an onerous double workload. But Bloom, of course, is cheerfully undaunted. In addition to his job, he takes seriously his volunteer duties to "give back to the community what you get out of it – an obligation I learned from Murray." He devotes considerable time to his role as a director of four national organizations: the Canadian Foundation for the Advancement of Pharmacy, the Retail Council of Canada, the Canadian Junior Chamber/ Jaycees, and the Young Presidents Organization, whose elitist membership is limited to international presidents, aged between forty and fifty, of multimillion-dollar corporations. Furthermore, he takes an active interest in numerous public health institutions, and those closest to his heart are the Juvenile Diabetes Foundation of Canada, the Mount Sinai Hospital, and the Toronto Hospital for Sick Children, as well as other children's hospitals right across the country.

Bloom faces the challenge of turning around Peoples Drug Stores Inc. Peoples' profitability had dropped sharply in 1986. The company needed to be repositioned, reorganized, and modernized to compete in the new competitive retailing marketplace. The subsidiary's sixty-three-year-old chairman, president, and chief executive officer, Sheldon Fantle, who had been with the company for forty years, resigned to take an early retirement. Bloom was asked to take charge and become what he prefers to call its catalyst. His "game plan" is to coordinate more closely the working relationship of Shoppers and Peoples. He says the two autonomous chains will retain their individual character and should be regarded as sister companies, not a pair of twins. Another key element was to establish a new strategic plan for the company, which would guide all activities over the next three years.

The Shoppers stores differ from the Peoples outlets in several ways: they are franchised to associate pharmacists; they average 6,500 square feet; and they are what Bloom calls "consumer-driven," meaning they are strong on consumer research and respond quickly to the need of the constantly changing marketplace. The Peoples stores, on the other hand, are closely owned by the corporation; they average 10,000 square feet, with a heavy emphasis on sundries rather than over-the-counter medicines and health and beauty aids; and, until now, they have been "vendor-driven," meaning they responded to what the suppliers brought them to sell.

One of the first changes Bloom made was to introduce an ongoing consumer research program at Peoples. In addition, the two sisters have started sharing their managerial skills in such areas as advertising, marketing, and store planning. Most importantly, he has passed the word along to suppliers that they are now dealing with a North American chain of 1,400 stores and must take into account that the stores' buying power has increased immensely.

"It's all a matter of synergism," says Bloom, using one of his favourite managementese terms. "I mean, it's one plus one equals three. You put two parts together. They react. And the sum total of those parts is greater than the individual efforts. You can call it my way of maximizing our opportunities."

He glories in the "wall-to-wall consumers" offered to him in the hugely populated U.S. market. He acknowledges that the thirty-eight Shoppers outlets that once operated in Florida and Georgia didn't succeed. Mainly it was because they were too widely separated from each other and from the central office in Toronto to be managed efficiently. But with the new synergism at work, Bloom confidently predicts that by the mid-1990s, the two sisters will have combined sales and profits to become the "number-one drugstore chain in the world."

That, in any case, is his goal, and Bloom credits three people with giving him the opportunity to meet that challenge.

One, of course, is Koffler. The second is Paré, who stepped down as Imasco's chairman in May 30, 1987, at the company's mandatory retirement age of sixty-five, to become a board director. The third is a remarkable executive named Purdy Crawford, the president, chief executive officer, and now chairman of Imasco, who was recruited by Paré to be his successor in 1983 and officially assumed his presidential post in 1985. Now in his mid-fifties, he is a coal miner's son from Springhill, Nova Scotia, whose affability reminds one of Dickens's Mr. Pickwick. Despite his disarmingly serene air, Crawford is regarded widely as one of Canada's canniest, toughest, and most brilliant corporate dealmakers. He is a graduate of Harvard Law School and the former senior partner of the prestigious Toronto law form of Osler, Hoskin and Harcourt, where he specialized in corporate mergers and acquisitions. He was the architect of Imasco's audacious 1986 takeover for $2.6 billion of Genstar Corp., a tactic designed to get it the nation's largest trust company, Canada Trustco. Crawford says, "I've acted for both black knights and white knights in takeover fights. It's like being the general in a modern equivalent of civilized war."

Bloom remembers inviting Imasco's new general to accompany him on a trip in the pre-Christmas season of 1985 to inspect the Shoppers troops deployed in their drugstore trenches right across Canada. Crawford instantly accepted. It turned out to be a seven-day-and-night endurance test. They were usually up in the morning at seven for breakfast meetings and got to bed well past midnight. They blitzed through 100 stores in twelve cities, met about 150 pharmacists and regional management teams, and plunged into a wicked blizzard in Newfoundland.

"On Saturday at noon we finally both fell asleep in chairs at the last airport," recalls Bloom. "I felt we passed the test, emotionally and physically, in flying colours. And when Purdy woke up, he told me, 'You can be proud of the wonderful family spirit of your people. Shoppers has won our confidence and you can count on our 100 per cent support. Imasco is prepared to set aside growth capital so Shoppers can achieve the goals

you've set for it. The opportunities are endless and the tomorrows are bright.'"

All three of his executive supporters agree that Bloom
deserves kudos for the innovations he introduced from the
time he assumed the presidency of Shoppers in 1983. One of
his first steps was to boost staff morale. He wanted them to
participate more actively in bolstering the business and to
recognize and reward them for their accomplishments. One
successful morale-booster was called "Catch Someone Doing
Something Right." He invited supervisors to send him special-
ly prepared memos praising colleagues for performing functions beyond the normal call of duty, for which they were duly
commended and awarded.

Bloom also embarked on a plan to broaden the responsibilities of sixteen executives on his management team whose
talents, he felt, had been underutilized. One of them, for example, who has since become Bloom's right-hand man is Herb
Binder, who began at eleven as a bicycle delivery boy for a
Toronto drugstore. Binder became co-owner of the Parlton
Pharmacy, a tiny, 690-square-foot drugstore on the corner of
Parliament Street and Carlton. "If you took one giant step into
the store from Parliament," says Binder, "you'd be right in my
dispensary." It was located in the heart of the then tough
Cabbagetown district and catered to a good many prostitutes,
pimps, rubbydubs, and other raffish characters. Nevertheless,
Binder did a thriving cosmetic and prescription business.
Koffler persuaded him to become an associate in 1969, and
eleven years later Bloom persuaded him to become Shoppers'
vice-president of operations for western Ontario. Bloom has
since promoted Binder to take on his own former role of executive vice-president of operations of Shoppers. It means that
Binder is the company's chief operations officer on a national
level.

Binder, who has worked for both Koffler and Bloom, draws
an interesting distinction between their managerial styles.
"Murray's style is to take a look at the whole picture. He'd say,
'I'm not interested in the detailed mechanics, the specific nuts
and bolts. I'm interested in the overview.' David looks at the

overview, too. But with all that energy of his he just likes to get involved. He's the type of inquisitive guy who wants to know, 'What are the whys and wheres and hows?' David is more a hands-on manager than Murray, and with the tremendous volume of business that our stores now handle, that's a very important factor today."

All three of his executive supporters agree that Bloom merits kudos for anticipating – and meeting – changing consumer needs in the volatile retail field of the 1980s. Bloom began doing so four months before he officially assumed his duties as the new Shoppers president. Paré had frequently mentioned that the company ought to "prepare for its tomorrows." And so, in December, 1982, Bloom presented him with an extraordinarily prescient, eighteen-page position paper entitled "Planning For The Tomorrows," a blueprint that distilled the thinking of ten members of the Shoppers team of senior management. The in-depth consumer research was conducted by Management Horizons, a U.S. firm that Bloom had commissioned. And his strategy for keeping receptive and flexible to new ideas in the marketplace was summed up by Bloom in a speech he gave at a Shoppers buying show at the time. He confessed he had plagiarized his policy from Muhammad Ali, the poet laureate of boxing:

> Float like a butterfly
> Sting like a bee,
> You can't hit
> What you can't see.

Essential to Shoppers' (and Bloom's) strategy is the need to keep the competition guessing. Bloom selected Howard Trifler to spearhead a one-man secret department he created called Retail Development. One of Bloom's protégés whose skills seemed underutilized, Trifler has since been promoted to the post of senior executive vice-president heading the Howie's Division of Shoppers. Now in his early forties, he is a brash and breezy high school dropout who began as a $50-a-week stock boy in a Shoppers store on Danforth Avenue in Toronto's blue-collar east end. He has worked himself up to merchandising expert for Shoppers' Alberta, Saskatchewan, and British Columbia stores when Bloom picked him out of the ranks to head the new department.

"Howie is an exciting, new style of executive, a strong conceptualizer with a great offbeat sense of humour," says Bloom. "I respect his retail savvy and his street sense. But I must admit I got a lot of flak from some of my colleagues when I assigned him to travel throughout the U.S. and identify the significant upcoming trends in retailing. They thought I'd gone off the deep end. They said, 'Shoppers is number one in Canada. So why rock the boat?'"

On the basis of Trifler's shrewd analysis of the situation, consumer research, and input from the Shoppers management team, Bloom was able to isolate three retail trends he felt Shoppers ought to exploit. One was the deep-discount, warehouse-style, jumbo-combo drugstore phenomenon. These were not as big as the mega-combo food-and-drug giants, which were 100,000 square feet, so monstrous that they required their stock boys to whiz around the aisles on roller skates. Instead, Bloom identified modified super drugstores, which also carried a diversity of other retail products. They were warehouse or "box" type stores, running from 25,000 to 40,000 square feet. They emphasized discount "off prices." And they featured a light-hearted, shopping-can-be-fun ambience. They all had breezy, informal names such as Ike's in Memphis, Marc's in Cleveland, Cecille's in Detroit, and Freddy's in Fort Lauderdale.

In the preliminary development stages, the Shoppers modified warehouse-style, off-price emporium was given the secret code name of Antelope. Twenty names were submitted. By ironic coincidence, the research surveys showed that consumers ranked Trifler's first name, Howie, as the most popular title for the new discount emporium. And so the first "Howie's . . . More Than A Drugstore" opened in April, 1984, on Danforth at Coxwell in Toronto's working-class east end. The building was a former supermarket of 12,500 square feet. The lettering for the store sign had a topsy-turvy jazzy look, and the predominant colours were vivid tomato red, canary yellow, and tangerine orange, instead of the conventional Shoppers bone-white.

Inside was a cornucopia of items not normally found in Shoppers outlets. Most were displayed in cut cardboard boxes, a bazaar of wares that included toys, pots and pans, underwear, Seiko watches, appliances, automotive products, household hardware, dog and cat food, and a limited amount of non-perishable food items such as jars of jam, canned vegetables, and snack-pack breakfast cereals. Since the research showed that deep-discount customers were ready to trade off wide selection for price, Bloom introduced the strategy that one expert categorized as: "Thick on the best . . . Hell with the rest." In other words, as Bloom phrases it, "You're either one of the leading national brands, or you're not on the shelf." The advertising for the store was designed to give it a distinctive personality. In the phrase of Gordon Stromberg, vice-president of advertising for Shoppers, the message was "hit-em-over-the-head hard sell, delivered with a good dollop of entertainment."

More than 1,000 customers lined up in a queue extending for three blocks to attend what was billed as "the biggest opening since the Grand Canyon." Circulars joked about the free eats and drinks to be served at Howie's Grand Bash: "Are you a lover of Chateaubriand, Lobster Thermidor, and Beef Wellington? Then eat before you come." Posters in Danforth Avenue bus shelters wisecracked: "If you're waiting for the Howie's limousine, start walking." The radio commercials, announced by a raffish character purporting to be Howie himself, huckstered "rock-bottom prices" with a thesaurus of circus adjectives: "The most fantastic, stupendous, incredible, amazing, phenomenal, unbelievable, extraordinary, mind-boggling . . . grand opening specials I've ever seen."

Print ads after the opening didn't let up. Like a series of firecrackers lit under tin cans, they featured what Allen Schopp, creative director of Kert Advertising, called raucous Howieisms. "They're little comedy *bits*, with a zinger in the tail, always signed in hand-lettered script with the name Howie," he says. Some Howieisms razz the customers: "If you can't see savings at Howie's, get glasses." Others joke around in cornball fashion: "Do we have savings? Are you kidding? Does a tree bark? Does a cow moo?" Still others have an engaging charm, like the ad for a Father's Day sale: "Show your father you don't mind looking like him. Come in and save at Howie's."

The first Howie's on Danforth grossed an extraordinary $7 million in its first year. By the end of 1988, there will be eleven Howie's stores of up to 24,000 square feet purveying their wares in Manitoba and Ontario.

A second concept emerging from the research was to incorporate a convenience food section into a traditional Shoppers drugstore. It would carry a line of products akin to the Seven-Eleven, Becker's, and Mac's chains and would be open from 7 a.m. until 11 p.m., and, where permissible, seven days a week. And it would cater to a new socio-economic consumer group, the two-income family. They crave convenience and have a minimum amount of time to shop. Bloom pictured them as a woman standing in front of her microwave oven cooking a pre-packaged meal while her husband hollers, "Hurry up! I'm going jogging in ten minutes." Given the preliminary secret code name of Kangaroo, the Shoppers version was ultimately named by group decision a Shoppers Drug Mart Food Basket. The first two were established in 1985, one in Halifax and one in Vancouver. There are now approximately fifteen of these mini-combos thriving across Canada.

Consumer research indicated the need for a third hybrid, which was named the Shoppers Drug Mart Home Health Care Centre. These cater to a specialized segment of the market, the growing populace of seniors and invalids who would rather recuperate at home than in a hospital or nursing home. Fifteen of them currently are located in Manitoba, Ontario, and Atlantic Canada. They function as either separate 3,000-square-foot stores or as departments piggybacked onto regular Shoppers drugstores. They sell everything from wheelchairs to colostomy bags, from crutches to trusses. Bloom foresees an increasing number of pharmacists in the future trained to become licensed orthotic fitters, because studies project that by the year 2000 almost 4 million Canadians will be over the age of sixty-five.

What other forecasts can be made for pharmacists over the next two decades? The trend toward "one-stop shopping" and giantism, it seems, will continue unabated. On one end of the spectrum will be super-mega-combos of about 125,000 square feet. These behemoths will sell about fifty classifications of products, everything from fresh haddock to TV sets. They will probably be operated by the supermarket mammoths. On the other end of the spectrum will be specialty chains such as Shoppers. Bloom envisions a number of Shoppers retailing variations. They will include the standard Shoppers Drug Mart drugstores, Howie's, Food Baskets, and Home Health Care Centres. But there could also be other offshoots targeted to health food consumers and other specialized segments of the market. They may be under one roof, bearing the Shoppers banner; or they could be banded together in free-standing stores, side by side with the McDonald's and Canadian Tire chains, united to capture the lion's share of the same consumer's shopping money.

Whatever form the stores take in the future, they will be thoroughly computerized, for the day of the pharmacist pill-roller who did everything by hand is already long gone. Back in the 1940s, when Koffler was starting out as a graduate pharmacist, a customer seeking a repeat of a prescription would bring in the empty bottle and estimate the date when it was originally filled. Koffler would have to drag out and pore through voluminous record cards in old-fashioned bill file folders. He would spend perhaps twenty minutes compounding the pills, ointment, or elixir and then write instructions on the label.

Today, 80 per cent of prescription medications have been prepared in advance by pharmaceutical manufacturers. And in an increasing number of Shoppers stores, when a regular customer wants a repeat of a prescription, the pharmacist simply punches the prescription number on a computer. The machine has been programmed to retrieve a detailed medical history of the patient, which includes the patient's allergies plus information about possible side effects of the medication. The printer prints as well all the salient data and any warnings on a label.

With the newest equipment, the cash register, too, serves as a terminal for inventory control. It automatically records the sale of, say, a particular brand of toothpaste, how many tubes are still in stock, and whether they need to be reordered. A complete computerized system is expensive and may cost $40,000, but it saves up to 25 per cent in accounting. In the future, the bookkeeping and cashier checkout systems will all be automated.

There are no Cassandras predicting that robots will ever take the place of pharmacists. Freed by technology from burdensome counting and pouring and typing, however, the role of pharmacists is expected to change drastically. Bloom and Koffler agree with their colleagues that the pharmacists of tomorrow will be health advisers. They will thus play a more vital role as liaisons between the physician and the patient.

In Florida, the laws were changed recently so that pharmacists can prescribe cortisone creams for skin rashes and evaluate or treat such things as menstrual cramps, fungal problems, and head lice. In Canada, where pharmacists are constantly taking refresher courses (sponsored by the Canadian Society of Hospital Pharmacists), they are often better informed about new drugs on the market than physicians. Consequently, they refer to themselves justifiably as "monitors of drug therapy" who are important members of the "medical discipline."

Some predict that by the year 2000, if you want to get advice from your pharmacist, you'll have to make an appointment and pay a fee for the consultation as you would with a physician. Your future pharmacist is more apt to be a she than a he, and no matter what the gender, you can anticipate a shortage of them. That future situation is simply a continuation of the present trends. Today, 70 per cent of the graduates from Canada's nine colleges of pharmacy are women, who are flocking to the profession for varied reasons: they take to it because they appear to be more detail-oriented than men; they can work as part-time relief in the dispensary if need be while raising a family; and it's a career that offers good remuneration.

After five years of training, graduates in 1988 can expect to be paid a minimum of about $35,000 a year and take their pick of jobs in a store dispensary, for a pharmaceutical manufacturer, or in a hospital (where the status of a pharmacist is generally higher than that of a nurse, physiotherapist, or lab technician, and just below that of a physician in the pecking order). If she becomes a Shoppers associate pharmacist, operating a standard 6,500-square-foot store, with a staff of twenty-five to thirty and grossing the average of close to $4 million in sales, her income will be quite comfortable.

Canada's present labour pool of approximately 15,000 pharmacists can't keep up with the demand, especially in small rural communities. To fill the need for pharmacists in Ontario towns such as Kapuskasing, Brockville, Cornwall, and Timmins, Shoppers has started sending recruiting teams to England.

What about the future of the old-fashioned corner druggist, who lived over the store with its lovely, odd, alchemical flasks in the window and, like Koffler's father, enjoyed an almost shamanistic standing as "Doc," the wonder-working sorcerer of the community? Today he has lost something of his mystique as well as his mystery. Both he and his customers are far more sophisticated than in a bygone era. No longer does he read his prescriptions in Latin black magic. He is more interested in counselling patients in plain English about the danger of taking milk with certain antibiotics and making sure they are not allergic to penicillin.

"Unless they affiliate with a chain similar to Shoppers," predicts Bloom, "many small independent pharmacists will not be economically viable. The strong, efficient independents will survive. But the weaker ones, unable to buy in quantity, won't be able to compete with the food and drugstore chains and will fall by the wayside before the year 2000."

Will their disappearance reflect the growing depersonalization prevalent in our society? Will it result in the loss of a neighbourhood institution that for so many years radiated precious human warmth, a friendly fusion of community centre and free group therapy clinic? "To a certain degree, that's true," concedes Bloom. "If you're a pharmacist in a major urban mall, like the Eaton Centre in Toronto or the alleged world's biggest shopping complex, the West Edmonton Mall, you're bound to lose a sense of intimacy. That's because you're doing business with a transient trade. However, if you operate a Shoppers store at Laureleaf Road and Steeles Avenue, for example, on the northern outskirts of Toronto, you can build a repeat neighbourhood trade. And you can relate to your regulars on a close, first-name basis, like an old-time pharmacist." Nevertheless, even if the big chain stores are getting bigger and the small independent stores are falling by the wayside, the prestige of the pharmacist has never been higher. A recent study showed that pharmacists rank with the clergy as the most trusted and caring professionals in North America.

And, according to Bloom and others, the man most responsible for adding lustre to the profession was Murray Koffler. It's generally acknowledged in the field that he reshaped the image of the twentieth-century North American drugstore. In addition, he strengthened the business acumen of the practitioners in a lopsided profession that was supposed to be half mercantile and half medical. The Koffler Institute of Pharmacy Management will enhance further the managerial skills of all future pharmacists, whether they work for Shoppers or not.

Since taking over his stewardship of Shoppers in 1983, Bloom always takes pains to mention his gratitude to his role model. If an institution is the lengthened shadow of one man, then for Bloom that man is Koffler. "I've simply built on the core legacies of success that Murray passed on to me," says Bloom. "Their momentum has been powerful enough to propel us into the 1990s."

Bloom lists Koffler's three cardinal legacies this way. One is the initial Shoppers Drug Mart franchise concept. The second is a democratic management style that involves the participation of associates in national and regional planning. The third is a network of glittering, highly efficient stores that have built solid customer loyalty across Canada.

A fourth dimension is highlighted by Arthur Konviser, appointed by Bloom to the new position of vice-president of public affairs for Shoppers. The son of an Orthodox rabbi from Rhodesia, Konviser is a perceptive, owlish, fortyish lawyer who was hired by Koffler in 1976 to serve as his executive assistant. "Murray was never just a bottom-liner," says Konviser. "He created a heart and soul for Shoppers. And he bequeathed to the present management team a unique corporate culture. It's a blend of values, rituals, and community involvement – a spirit of good corporate citizenship that will always bear his stamp."

Koffler's response to these hosannas is that he is not as ingenious an empire-builder as others might suggest. Asked by a friend to assess his career not long ago, he said, "I'll take credit for one thing. I knew when to move over. I was smart enough to leave room for the next guy to come along and take the business to the next plateau. Sure, I had enough drive to start with one store and build to 400. But it needs a younger, different type of personality, a corporation man like David Bloom, to take the company from 400 stores to an international company of 1,400 stores."

He has seen too many corporations go downhill because the top manager was reluctant to let go of the reins of power and plan for an orderly succession. "For an intelligent manager, the trick is to build a good team and know when to pass the baton," he says. "One man can't run the race himself. Well, I had a good marathon run, and I knew when to leave on a high, with everybody expressing goodwill. It was a smooth transition."

Yet he refuses to be cast in the role of a relic who has put himself out to pasture, spending his dotage listening to the grass grow and getting under his wife's feet. He was warned off from that fate by the witticism of his friend Maryon Pearson, wife of Canada's former Prime Minister Lester Pearson. When her husband retired from politics to write his autobiography at home, she protested, "I married Mike for better or worse – but not for lunch."

Koffler did not intend to become a drag on Marvelle, or anybody else for that matter. "I don't consider it a retirement," he insisted. "For me, it'll be a change of direction. I'm simply moving on to the next chapter."

His sideline of philanthropy and community involvement, for example, was scheduled to become virtually full-time. But then he was confronted with major surgery, and that gave him considerable pause for thought. "When I was subjected to the CAT-scan at the hospital, and they advised me I had a tumour that looked malignant, believe me, that turns you into a philosopher overnight. You become more reflective about your life and your so-called achievements."

Looking back, and unreeling his memory spools, he is convinced more than ever that he has been a singularly lucky man. He has always maintained that he was just a simple pharmacist, whose career has been one lucky happenstance after another, and today he likes reiterating again and again how "fortunate" and "privileged" and "gratified" he feels.

When counting his blessings, he feels fortunate to have been born Jewish. The Old Testament states that God regarded the children of Israel benignly: "I will make of thee a great nation, and I will bless thee, and make thy name great . . . Ye shall be a peculiar treasure unto me above all people." Koffler adds about his heritage: "I like being Jewish and I like the Jewish ethic that we are supposed to live by. Being born Jewish means you're a member of a clan noted for its qualities, spiritually and culturally. Just think of the Jewish leadership in the arts, sciences, business, and other fields. Because we stand out, we sometimes have to withstand some antagonism. But that's to be expected. If you stick your head above the crowd, you've got to expect the occasional brickbat."

He feels fortunate to have been born a Canadian. "I think Canadian businessmen in particular have two great things going for them," he says. Koffler believes they have inherited some of the aggressive entrepreneurship characteristic of Americans. They have also inherited some of the old-fashioned tradition of politeness from the British. "I like the propriety and stability and respect for the niceties we have in

Canadian business," he says. "While I admire the entrepreneurial zeal of Americans in the business world, I'm not enamoured of their neglect of graciousness. When I have a business meeting in New York, they don't seem to have time to say, 'Hello. How are you? So nice to see you.' They're so intensely competitive, so honed to a sharp edge by their frenetic pace, all they can say is, 'Let's get down to the deal.' I think there's more in life than that."

He feels fortunate to have been a businessman at a period in history when businessmen are highly regarded. With the exception of the British royal family, Koffler contends, the lords and dukes and other plutocrats of the diamond-duster set have taken a back seat in the realm of popular celebrityhood. "The Castros and other revolutionaries of our day get the recognition because they've put an end to the inequities of suppression," he says. "As for warriors, the Caesars of yesterday, who subjugated people, are considered today's tyrants. The true luminaries of our era, I believe, are the business achievers who provide work opportunities for people."

He feels fortunate to have made money without being enslaved by Mammon. He disagrees strongly with those who worship wealth and adhere to the theory that the have-nots automatically envy the haves and the haves envy the have-mores. "I espouse two theories about money," he says. "I believe that making money should be fun, not a religion. And I believe that money ultimately is just a figure on a balance sheet, and its only value is its use."

He feels fortunate that life by and large has been kind to him. He remembers being struck by an observation once made to a *Toronto Life* magazine journalist by Issy Sharp, his Four Seasons partner. Still mourning the loss of a young son who had died of a virulent form of cancer, Sharp remarked that Koffler had gone through life "unscathed" by tragedy.

"That was very intuitive of Issy," Koffler acknowledged. He was not emotionally scarred by the death of his parents. "And though I've made mistakes in business," Koffler says, "my failures have never been backward steps." His friends go further than that and say his failures have always been minor, the successes major.

Curiously, the most unforgettable regret in his life that devastated him had nothing to do with his family or his career. It involved Greta Allen, who for many years worked as his dedicated and devoted executive assistant. He remembers last talking to her at the end of a staff Christmas party she had organized at the office.

"Greta, it's the beginning of the holiday weekend," he recalls saying, while putting on his coat. "When are you going home?"

"I have some work to do."

"But the whole office is closing down."

"Well, I have one little task to do," she said. "Then I'll go." She was found at home next morning, having committed suicide with an overdose of pills.

"I was terribly shocked," Koffler now says. "I had always prided myself on being a handler of people. But it suddenly hit me that I'd never taken her out to lunch, never inquired about her family or background, never done the gracious things a civilized executive should do. I hadn't the faintest idea about her suffering and what caused her to kill herself. I've felt remorse to this day that I'd been so insensitive and so clueless."

On the other hand, he feels gratified that so many admirers have heaped praise on him. Among the kudos that he appreciates is the unexpected note he received from David P. Silcox, the Toronto art critic, who said, "You always make living seem like the miraculous gift it is." Another unsolicited compliment came from the Canadian author Pierre Berton, who singled him out in a broadcast for being "a generous man with his money . . . a Canadian achiever who had a dream and made it work."

He feels gratified that a host of friends are prepared to recommend him to posts of high public office. One of them, John Bassett, has suggested that Koffler would make an ideal Canadian ambassador to Israel. Another, George Zuckerman, maintains that Koffler has the panache and *savoir-faire* to be Canada's first Jewish Governor General or its ambassador to the Court of St. James.

Koffler is understandably flattered but has turned down such notions, just as he has the invitation to run for election extended by the leaders of two of Canada's major political parties. "Thanks, but no thanks," he says. "I don't have enough of a thick skin to assume any of those public positions. I like to be liked by people, and I'd be hurt if they publicly resented something in me."

In November of 1987, however, the mercurial Koffler, after rejecting the offer twice, decided to accept a prestigious high office, which fittingly caps his career. Following in the footsteps of such illustrious leaders as Lord Marcus Sieff, Abba Eban, Meyer Weisgal, and Chaim Weizmann, Koffler agreed to be nominated and was duly elected chairman of the board of governors of the Weizmann Institute of Science in Israel. It means he is the roving global ambassador and chief executive officer of an eminent institution that has twelve Nobel laureates sitting on its 100-member board of governors. It is supported by more than 50,000 active participants in twenty-seven countries, ranging from the American Committee for the Weizmann Institute of Science to the Venezuela Asociacion de Amigos del Instituto Cientifico Weizmann. Its budget exceeds $70 million U.S. annually.

Koffler hastens to explain he did not turn down the post for negative reasons. On the contrary, when he was first approached by the Weizmann's search committee in late 1986, and again in May, 1987, he rejected the office because he thought better people than himself could do justice to the job. Lord Sieff was stepping down after serving two terms as chairman for the past eight years. "I said no, because I felt it might be more useful to select an American," says Koffler. "The chances were he'd have a wider sphere of influence and more powerful contacts than myself."

However, because of his intimacy with the Weizmann, after serving as a deputy chairman of the board for six years and a board member for twenty years, the search committee persisted and ultimately prevailed upon Koffler to accept. "Naturally, I'm gratified to have been chosen," says Koffler. "It looks like I'm having another kick at the can."

Finally, he feels gratified that he has come to terms with his own mortality and what somebody once called the "inescapable lousiness of old age." While convalescing in the hospital after surgery, he was able to contemplate the prospect of death. "I found I don't fear death as much as I fear the possibility of a long, protracted, serious illness, withering away like a vegetable," he says. "My hope always is to live vitally, and when I go, to go quickly." When he does go, he would like his epitaph to read simply: "Here lies Murray Koffler – he was a true friend to a good many friends."

He was that; he is that: a friend of true comity, of civility and courtesy. Murray Koffler is, as well, an idealist of passionate affirmation and gentle innocence, and he has been a pioneer on the frontiers of Canadian business enterprise. But he was not, and certainly is not, "just a simple pharmacist," as he has jokingly insisted. His achievements in creating the Shoppers Drug Mart empire and his immeasurable contributions toward improving the quality of life in Canada and abroad bespeak, rather, a man of great complexity, foresight, and intuition who has managed to retain a simple sweetness.

In this age of ascendancy for enterprise and entrepreneurial risk-taking in Canada, Murray Koffler provides us with a sparkling example of business success tempered by caring and by an understanding of human relations. As he has said himself, "I think I've played a good game, had a great kick at the can, and I'm ready for the next chapter of my life." That chapter will be his to write.

Acknowledgements

For this authorized biography of Murray Koffler, the subject gave me *carte blanche* to print anything negative about him that I might pick up during the course of my research. God knows I did my damndest to do so, for I personally have no taste for hagiography. I interviewed more than 150 people, and the transcripts of my tapes ran to well over a million words. Yet not one of the 150 – not even his competitors – had anything nasty to say about Koffler. This surely must be a record in the world of big business. According to what I read in Peter Newman's *The Canadian Establishment*, the greasy pole leading to the top of commerce was almost invariably drenched with the blood of corporate back-stabbings.

Well, I regret to say you'll find no blood in this book. There's no gore, no greed, no overweening ambition to play king of the castle – the very ingredients supposedly necessary for a best-selling business book. On the contrary, the people I spoke to seemed bent on canonizing Koffler.

As Gordon Stromberg, the long-time vice-president of advertising for Shoppers Drug Mart, jovially told me, the majority of his staff members appear to have elevated him to a saintly status and venerate him as Mahatma Koffler. I ultimately became desperate to show some chinks in his armour – or perhaps I should say ragged patches in his pristine white diaper, or whatever in heaven a Mahatma Koffler is supposed to wear. And so I resorted to pleading with him, "As

334

an old friend, would you please reveal to me an illicit love affair or some other juicy scandal to spice up this book?"

Alas, though he earnestly tried to help me, Koffler could come up with no skeletons or dastardly secrets that had been kept dangling in the dark corners of his family closet. You may not believe all the nice things they say about him, but the truth is, quite simply, he is that sort of fellow: a genuinely decent man.

He has been that way since we were school chums together at Oakwood Collegiate in Toronto. He was different from the rest of us in a singular way. He demonstrated that trait early, in the days when we belonged to a boys' club that would congregate in Koffler's home to play Monopoly. It has long since become my joke that the immensely wealthy Koffler was the only one in our gang who took Monopoly seriously.

I got to know him in a more profoundly intimate way when I started researching this book two years ago. I wish to express my heartfelt thanks to him, because working on the project, whether in Canada or in Israel, has been an unalloyed delight. I'd like to relate here two stories that didn't seem to fit in elsewhere and yet reflect his multifaceted personality. One story gives the lie to the notion that Koffler never loses his aplomb. The episode occurred in 1973 when Koffler and his wife Marvelle were the only two non-Israelis allowed to attend the twenty-fifth anniversary of Israel's air force. The celebration was held in a lean-to quonset hut at the original Israeli military base.

"When the widows of the many airmen who'd lost their lives in the many wars since 1948 got up to speak, the Israelis were dry-eyed," Koffler told me. Then he added, in the curious, old-fashioned, gentlemanly manner that I found so endearing, "You know, I couldn't help myself, and I had to put my sunglasses on, because the tears were just rolling down my face."

During the many hours we spent together, the tears rolling down my face were more apt to be tears of laughter. Though few outsiders are aware of it, he can be a very funny man. This is illustrated in the second story, which will give you an idea of his droll–or sometimes cuckoo–sense of humour. The incident occurred at a black-tie state dinner in Paris, where Koffler was exploring the possibility of opening a Four Seasons Hotel. His host from the French government leaned forward and asked Koffler if he had a preference in wine.

"Yes," replied Koffler, tongue-in-cheek. "I'd like one of those fine imported Canadian wines."

Twenty minutes later, the embarrassed official confessed he had no Canadian vintages in the cellar and would Monsieur Koffler indicate a secondary preference.

"*Eh bien,*" riposted Monsieur Koffler. "In that case, one of your local wines will have to do."

I would like to express thanks to that incomparable hostess Marvelle Koffler for the many glasses of wine, pots of coffee, and snacks she whipped together and served us while her husband shared his reminiscences with me at their Beechwood Avenue home in Toronto.

Most of the people I interviewed are given due credit in my narrative. But some who were most generous with their time are just mentioned briefly and others were squeezed out entirely due to space limitations.

For their insights and recollections, I would therefore like to give special thanks to Joyce Anderson, Gerry Baboushkin, Sonja Bata, Samuel Black, Goldie Brass, Verne Chelin, Zena Cherry, George Cohon, George Connell, David Crombie, Barney Danson, Pipe Major Sandy Dewar, Chuck Doodson, Fred Eisen, Ralph Fisher, Joe Frieberg, Marvin Goldberg, Mike Harrison, Percy Hermant, Dr. Charles Hollenberg, Jules James, Kenneth Jarvis, Blanche Freeman Katz, Roy Kendall, Douglas Kent, Oscar and Joyce Kofman, Arthur Konviser, Mel and Marilyn Lastman, Joe and Florence Lokash, Pauline McGibbon, Alistair B. McInnes, George Michaud, Marcia Munro, Roman Niemy, John Parker, John North, Nicholas Pearce, Bill Powell, Morrie Ryp, Lucy and Lou Samuels, Sam and Fran Seligman, Marcus Lord Sieff, Dr. Harold Siegal, Beth Slaney, Joel Slater, Rabbi Reuben Slonim, Jules Solomon, Robert Stancati, Dr. Ernst Stieb, Joan Sutton, Malcolm Swartz, Howard Trifler, Fred K. Van Laare, Baz Weedon, Morris Weldman, Vicki Williams, Hilda Wilson, Michael Wilson, Jerry Ziedenberg.

I would also like to thank some of the Israelis, especially those at the Weizmann Institute of Science, who were helpful. They include Prof. David Danon, Prof. Israel Dostrovsky, Ricky Freisen, Prof. Gabriel Goldring, Prof. David Lavie, Nechemia Meyers, Molly Orin, Prof. Michael Sela, and Prof. David Samuel, as well as Dr. Cyril Legum and Colonel Shula Legum of Tel Aviv.

Finally, my thanks go to those inspiring idealists who have joined Murray Koffler in leading the Canadian Council for Native Business, notably Jack Beaver, Clifford Boland, Dan Braniff, Doug Cuthand, Joe Dion, and Sydney Schipper.

F.R.
Toronto, Canada

RX: A Prescription List of Murray Koffler's Good Works

Honours and Awards

1969 Distinguished Citizen Award, B'nai B'rith
1972 Distinguished Service Citation, Ontario Society for Crippled Children
1974 Humanitarian Award, Canadian Council of Christians and Jews
1975 Honorary Citizen, City of Winnipeg
1976 Doctor of Philosophy (*honoris causa*), Weizmann Institute of Science, Rehovot, Israel
1976 Gavel of the XXI Olympiad, Montreal
1976 A.H. Robins Bowl of Hygeia for outstanding service to Pharmacy
1977 Member, Order of Canada
1979 Honorary Life Member, Order of St. John of Jerusalem
1980 Distinguished Service Citation, Council on Drug Abuse
1982 Man of the Year Award, Ontario Society of Artists
1982 Diplome d'Honneur, Le Conseil Pasteur, France
1983 Marketer of the Year Award, Sales & Marketing Executives Association
1985 Doctor of Laws (*honoris causa*), University of Toronto
1985 Honorary Life Membership Award, Canadian Pharmaceutical Assoc.
1986 Toronto Jewish Congress, Ben Sadowski Award of Merit
1986 City of Toronto Award of Merit
1986 Distinguished Retailer of the Year, Retail Council of Canada

Corporate Involvement

Hon. Chairman, Shoppers Drug Mart Limited
Director, Imasco Limited
Director, Four Seasons Hotels Limited
Director, The Manufacturers Life Insurance Company
Director, Bank Leumi
Director, The Canadian Jewish News
Director, Native Economic Development Program

Community Involvement

Founder, Chairman, Canadian Council for Native Business
Founder, Chairman, Koffler Centre of the Arts, Toronto
Founder, Honorary Chairman, Toronto Outdoor Art
    Exhibition
Founder, Honorary Chairman, Council on Drug Abuse
Founder, Jokers Hill Horse Trails
Founder, Temple Emanu-El, Toronto
Founder, Director, Tel Aviv Foundation
Patron, Lester B. Pearson College of the Pacific
Chairman, Weizmann Institute of Science, Israel
Governor, Canadian Opera Company
Chairman, Canada-Israel Cultural Foundation
Honorary Chairman, Canadian Society of the Weizmann
    Institute of Science
Chairman, Public Appeal Campaign, Roy Thomson Hall,
    Toronto, 1982-83
Chairman, United Jewish Appeal, 1973
Vice-Chairman, Update Campaign, University of Toronto,
    1976
Co-Chairman, Emergency Fund 1967, United Jewish Appeal
Co-Chairman, Canadian Council of Christians and Jews
Honorary President, Ontario Men's ORT
Honorary Director, Distress Centre Inc.
Director, Koffler Student Services Centre, University of
    Toronto
Director, Koffler Institute of Pharmacy Management,
    University of Toronto
Director, Canadian Council of Christians and Jews
Director, Israel Tennis Centre

Director, Jerusalem Foundation
Director, Jewish Community Centre, Toronto
Director, Jewish National Fund
Director, Mount Sinai Hospital, Toronto
Director, Mount Sinai Institute, Toronto
Director, Olympic Trust of Canada
Director, Canadian Foundation for Refugees
Director, Toronto North York Hunt Club
Director, United Jewish Appeal
Director, United Jewish Welfare Fund of Toronto
Director, World Wildlife Federation

Past Involvement

Co-Chairman, Operation Lifeline
Governor, University of Toronto
Governor, Roy Thomson Hall and Massey Hall
Director, Canada Development Corporation
Director, Canadian Club
Chairman, Camp Canada
Chairman, Bar Mitzvah Foundation
Chairman, Foundation for Ecological Action
Director, Toronto Symphony
Director, Canadian Equestrian Team

Koffler Institute of Pharmacy Management — Financial Contributors

Founders

Apotex Inc.
Bristol-Myers Canada Inc. and its Divisions
Carlton Cards Limited, Rust Craft, Plus Mark
Cosmair Canada Inc.
Drug Trading Company Ltd.
Fabergé of Canada Ltd.
Imasco Limited
Johnson & Johnson
Kimberly Clark of Canada
The Koffler Family
Miles Laboratories, Ltd.
Novopharm Ltd.
Plough Canada Inc., Schering Canada Inc., Scholl (Canada) Inc.
Procter & Gamble Co. of Canada Ltd.
Shoppers Drug Mart Associates

Benefactors

Atlantic Packaging Products
Boots Drug Stores (Canada) Ltd.
Chesebrough-Pond's (Canada) Inc.
Coca-Cola Limited
Gillette Canada Ltd.
S.C. Johnson & Son Ltd.
Kert Advertising Ltd.
Kohl & Frisch Ltd.
Lever Brothers
National Drug & Chemical Company
A.C. Nielson Co. of Canada Ltd.
Noma Industries
Parke-Davis & Co. Ltd.
Revlon International
Sterling Drugs Ltd.
Toy Sales Ltd.

Patrons

Chas. Abel Photo Service Ltd.
American Express Canada Ltd.
Ayerst Laboratories
Irving Bain
Bathurst Sales
Beecham Canada Ltd.
R.D. Belvedere & Associates
Herbert Binder

David R. Bloom
Bonne Bell of Canada Ltd.
Campeau Corporation
CIBA-GEIGY Canada Ltd.
Colgate-Palmolive Canada
Dafoe & Dafoe Inc.
Deloitte Haskins + Sells
Duracell Inc.
Wm. Eisenberg & Co.
Encore Sales Ltd.
Faber-Castell Canada Ltd.
Marvin Goldberg
Hilroy Limited
Hostess Food Products Ltd.
Eli Lilly Canada Ltd.
Marathon Realty Co. Ltd.
Merrell-Dow Pharmaceuticals
(Canada) Inc.
Nabisco Brands Ltd.

Norton Simon Canada Inc.
Noxzema Chemical Co. of
Canada Ltd.
Pannell Kerr Forster
Playtex Ltd.
The Royal Bank of Canada
Julius Schmid of Canada
Scott Paper Ltd.
Smith + Nephew Limited
Soberman, Isenbaum &
Colomby
Stella Pharmaceutical Co.
Malcolm Swartz
3M Canada Inc.
Toronto-Dominion Bank
Tye-Sil
Veritas Consultants Inc.
Web Offset Publications Ltd.
Whitehall Laboratories Ltd.

Sponsors

Alberto Culver Canada Limited
Carvell Antworth
Bank of Montreal
Bank of Nova Scotia
Benson & Hedges
Bic Inc.
Big V Pharmacies Co. Ltd.
Bramalea Ltd.
The Cadillac Fairview Corp.
Ltd.
Cambridge Leaseholds Ltd.
Canadian General Electric
Canadian Imperial Bank of
Commerce
Colourtron Photo Service
Continent-Wide Enterprises
Dale Daley
Doris Hosiery Mills Ltd.
Drugtown Pharmacies Ltd.
Giltex Hosiery Inc.
Glaxo Canada Ltd.
Goodman & Carr
Roy Gosse

Raymond Guyatt
Barry Haberman
Gerald Halbert
Herdt & Charton Inc.
C.E. Jamieson Ltd.
Errol Jamieson
Kent Drugs Ltd.
Kerr Bros. Ltd.
Kodak Canada Ltd.
Albert Krakauer
Lander Co. Canada Ltd.
David H. MacDonald
RJR MacDonald Inc.
Grant MacMellon
Markborough Properties
Martinway Plaza Ltd.
McDonald's Restaurants of
Canada Ltd.
Merck Frosst Laboratories
Nivel Inc.
Oral-B Laboratories Inc.
Parfumerie Versailles Ltd.

Barry Phillips
Realmont Ltd.
Thomas Roe
Rothmans of Pall Mall Canada
  Inc.
Gary Smith
Squibb Canada Inc.

Super X Drugs Ltd.
Tambrands Canada Inc.
Trizec Corporation
Upjohn Company of Canada
Wampole Ltd.
Hilda Wilson Group
Douglas Winsor

Supporters

Derek Abdalla
Air Thermal Systems
James Arthur
Bank Leumi le Israel
Wayne Barton
Alvin Bloom
Aubrey Browne
W.K. Buckley Ltd.
Burnac Corporation
Brian Chute
Carson Collins
Coty Canada
Counsel Management Ltd.
Cathy Crooks
Crown Paper, a division of
  Crown Forest Industries Ltd.
Dell Chemists
Ronald Dort
Susan Essensa
Marcel Fortier
Alex M. Fraser
Gerber Canada Inc.
Louis Goelman
Goodman & Goodman
Oscar Goodman
Robert Greenspoon
Peter Hebert
Derek Hierlihy
Sterling Hubley
James Hutchison
Sidney Kadish
Robert Katz
Dale Kenzie
Jack Kirk
Irving Kraft

Jacques Lafond
Harold Landis
Albert Levy
Lorne Logan
John Lynch
Donald MacDonald
Maclean Hunter (KEY Radio)
Sheldon Manly
Joseph Martin
Henry Mazukiewich
Murray McIntyre
Warren Meek
Gus Miller
Ronald Nadeau
Wm. Neilson Co. Ltd.
NutraSweet Group of G.D.
  Searle
Ontario Pharmacists Association
Paramount Hosiery Ltd.
Pepsi-Cola Canada Ltd.
Ronald Radwick
Regent Tobacco & Confectionery
  Inc.
Brian Relph
Arthur Resnick
Gordon Resnick
Donald Rogers
David Rose
Joseph Rosenkrantz
Denis Rossi
J. Shiffman & Sons Ltd.
Wayne Simmons
David Skidd
David Stern
Ronald Surman

Malcolm Thomas
Thorne Riddell & Co.
Errol Toombs
Raymond Tresidder
Howard Trifler
Lawrence Ura
Fred Van Laare
Charles J. Wambeke

Morris Weldman
Western Inventory Services
John P. Wilson
Wood Gundy Charitable
  Foundation
Wrigley Canada Inc.
York Uniforms Ltd.
Gary Yorston

Donors

Adrem Limited
Eli Ajram
Jean Allaire
Allan Candy
Allard Foundation
Joyce Anderson
Harold Armstrong
Anthony W. Austen
Mabel Au-Yeung
J.J. Barnicke Ltd.
Janet Barrie
Ross M. Baxter
Martin J. Belitz
Bellevue Photographic Ltd.
Floran Benoit
Benwind Industries
Earl M. Biderman
Billben Drug Ltd.
Bryan Bird
Birenbaum, Kauffman &
  Steinberg
Irving Borchiver
Harvey & Ruth Borden
Robert Borek
Michael Borkovich
Goldie Brass
Barbara E. Brocklebank
Mr. & Mrs. C.R. Bronfman
Edward Bronfman
J.C. Brouillette
James Brown
Horst Bruckschwaiger
James Burchell
Lenny Burke

Guy L. Bussiere
CFAC Calgary
CFRB Toronto
CFTO-TV
CHUM Toronto
The CSL Group Inc.
Arnold Cader
David Campbell
Can-Aqua Industries Ltd.
Carolyn Sales Inc.
Julie Lynn Carruthers
Sharon Casey
Joseph Chan
James Charles
Verne Chelin
Sean Cheverie
Peter Chin
Gene L. Chipeniuk
Ronald Chong
Adele Chown
Anthony Chung
Jeffrey Churchman
Harvey Cohen
Russell Cohen
Carl Cole Family Foundation
Colonial Broadcasting
Catherine Conroy
Constellation Hotel
Michael Corey
Bradley Cowden
Creed's Ltd.
Crown Life Insurance Co.
Elaine Culiner
Peter Cummings

Murray Dale
Sultanali Davdani
Jack Davies
Edward T. Demchuk
David Dennis
Tejinder Rah Singh Dhami
Bruce Duncan
Wm. M. Dunne & Assoc.
Dunwoody & Associates
Thong Duong
Dupont Pharmaceuticals
E.B. Eddy Products
Lawrence Erwin
Albert Everson
Evyan Perfumes Canada Ltd.
Joseph Feldt
Wil Filion
Grant Fisher
The Fitness Institute
Kevin Fleming
Walter Fleming
Patrick Fong
Harold Forman
The Friedberg Family
   Foundation
Gerald Friesen
John Frumento
Prakash Gadhia
Tomislav Gagarin
John Gamble
Timothy L.M. Garden
Thomas J. Gibney
Bernard Glazier
Dominic Gniewek
Shirley Gold
Mr. & Mrs. Maxwell Goldhar
Alvin Goldman
Dr. & Mrs. Bernard Goldman,
   Ellie Tesher, David Jolley
Mervin Gollom
Charlotte Goods
Hugh Gorham
Anna Gorski
David Goudie

David Grant
Joseph Greco
Esther Green
Greenwin Property
   Management Ltd.
Colleen Di Gregorio
Murray Grossman
Terry Gudofsky
Bradley Guinn
Gary Guitard
Peter Haines
Raymond Hallett
Fraser Halliwell
Bradley Hargrove
Gregory Harmeson
Frank Hartnett
Robert Hartnett
Raymond Heide
Helene Curtis Ltd.
Jack Hilbert
Jack Holtzman
Harvey Horowitz
Kevin Huang
Charles Hudes
Michael Humphries
Ray Iijima
Inducon Developments Ltd.
Infinity Developments
Charles Ingvaldson
George Irving
Wilfred Isaacson
Glenn Jackson
David Jamieson
JDS Investments Ltd.
L.R. Johnson
Harry Kalb
Thomas Kam
Walter Kane
David Karn
Kassel's Pharmacy
Leonard Katz
Nancy Keays
Kevin Kelly
Valerie Kempthorne

Michael Kennedy
Linda King
Melvin Kochberg
David Kohn
Arthur B. Konviser
Robert Koo
Paul Kwari
Dennis Kwong
Howard Lackie
Terrence W. Landry
Yvon Landry
Darlene La Pointe
Raymond La Rose
Thomas Latimer
Albert Lau
Mark Layton
Pat LeBlanc
Lederle Products
Frank Ledvinka
Douglas Legge
Irving Leitner
Kim Lem
James Leonard
Michel Lesieur
Robert Levy
Alfred Liu
Damion Lo
Earl Lohn
Mr. & Mrs. Joseph Lokash
Richard Longworth
Norman Louie
Lubertex Inc.
Dan Lui
Samuel Lui
Thomas Lynch
William Lysak
Marj & Scott MacKenzie
Douglas MacLeod
Douglas MacLise
Alvin MacNeil
Gary MacPhee
Majestic Industries (Canada)
   Ltd.
Patrick Man
Lillian Mandel

Eddie Maniero
Manufacturers Life Insurance
   Company
Marks & Spencer
Chet Maslanka
Noemi Masson
Vital Mauriello
Joseph W. McAskill
McBee Co. Ltd.
William McConnachie
Raymond McConnell
Clayton McFadden
Robert McFadgen
David McIntyre
MDC Group
Medico Pharmacy
Menkes Development Inc.
Mennen Canada Inc.
Metcalfe Pharmacy
Meyerovitch, Goldstein, Flantz
   & Fishman
George Michaud
Neil Mix
Ben Mizrahi
Aurel Mooney
Donald Moore
Morlee Distributors
Terry Morrison
Elliott Moss
Gary Mulholland
Leon Munoz
Harold Nashman
National Home Products
Jim Netherton
Roman Niemy
Nordic Laboratories Inc.
John North
Michael Nowlan
Olympia & York Developments
Ontario Store Fixtures
Organon Canada Ltd.
Osler, Hoskin & Harcourt
Ottawa Pharmacy
William Pacy
Edward Parker

John Parker
Eric Peach
Leo Perkell
Sheryl Ann Petrie
James Poon
Peter Pridie
Clifford Proceviat
Professional Pharmaceutical
  Corp.
Anna Z. Radecki
Melvin E. Reingold
Kenneth Relph
Boyd Riggs
Robert Robbins
Walter Rochford
Rorer Canada Inc.
Philip Rosenberg
Mark Rosenhek
Rowntree Macintosh Canada
  Ltd.
Murray Rumack
Morley Rypp
Katherine Sage
Spiro Sakell
Samson, Belair
Edward Samworth
Sav-on Drugs Ltd.
S.B.I. Management Ltd.
Elmars Sebrins
Harold Segal
Harold J. Segal
S.J. Seligman Insurance
Seven-Up Canada Inc.
Robert Seymour
Lorne Shapiro
Cecil Sheaves
Marvin Silver
Jack Silverstein
Gary Skanes
Smiles 'N Chuckles
Adele Smith
Eric Smith
Smith Kline & French Canada
  Ltd.
Isadore Snyder

Robert Spevakow
Douglas Spitzig
Arnold Stein
Steinberg Inc.
Bernard Steinberg
Sidney Steinberg
Arthur Steinman
Jack Stephens & David
  Campbell
Norman Stern
Stewart, MacKeen & Covert
Gordon Stromberg
Stuart House Canada Ltd.
Bashir Surani
Ian Sussman
Sutter Hill Development Ltd.
Lawrence Sweig
Raymond Sweig
Jayesh Tailor
Edward Tanaka
Mark Thompson
Hannu Uurainen
Dalton Van Cleave
Edward Vlahov
Maurice Wang
Robert Webster
In Memory of Norman
  Weingarten
Geo. Weston Ltd.
Ken Whiteley
Victoria Williams
Murray Winkler
Winnipeg Photo
Randall Wiser
Bernd Wittke
Robert G. Wright
John Yagi
Kane Yee
Robert Yorston
David Young
Diane Young
Manny Young
Gerald Ziedenberg
Mr. & Mrs. George Zuckerman

Contributors

A.K.L. Pharmacies Ltd.
Linda Abrams
Acco Canadian Co. Ltd.
R.W. Allen Pharmacy Limited
Joyanna Anisio
Christine Argue
Murray Armstrong
Philip Assaf
Tom Axler
Kenneth Baumann
Charles Baumgartner
Beauty Creations
Beiersdorf (Canada) Ltd.
Bennett Jones
Sander Biderman
Lou Blanaru
James Bobb
Mary Booth
Howard Borden
Richard Brennan
Bob Buckham
Edward Bucovy
CAP Communications
CHIN–FM
CHQT Radio
CISN-FM
CJCA Radio
CKND Radio
Cadbury Schweppes Powell
Gary Candy
Cappe Drugs Ltd.
Donald Casey
Centennial Leaseholds Ltd.
Arthur Chin
Cincinatti Time Records
Corson Travel Service
Covent Glen Shopping Centre
Dale Crawford
Milton Davis
Michael Del Grande
Dina Dichek
Bill Dingwall
David Dobko

Wes Doerksen
Dundalk Pharmacy
J. Murray Dykeman
Econo-Malls Ltd.
Edge Properties
Empress Litho Plate Limited
Lloyd Ewing
Fairner Holdings
Farris, Vaughan, Wills, Murphy
Gregory Feld
James Feren
Rose Fitzgerald
Gerrebe Display Ltd.
Max Giesbrecht
Donna Gizbert
Bryna Goldberg
Elizabeth Gould
Louis Greenberg
Daniel Gutkin
Jeff Hanibali
Harding Display Corporation
R.H. Harman
Jack Hoffman
Holiday Sportswear
Orest Hykawy
ICN Canada
Lawrence Israelson
JHF Productions
Richard Jagodzinski
Benson Jarzyna
Jack Johnston
John Johnston
Steven Jonas
Walter Kane
Harry Kaplan
Keele Pharmacy
Darlene Killen
Kirkland Pharmacy Ltd.
Howard Kirsh
Victor Kitamura
Peter Ko
Howard Kopstick
Wayne Kozak

Susan Kriger
Eleanor Kuzmarov
Lapointe, Rosenstein
Ed Lee
David Leith
John E. Little
Edmund K. Lo
James Lococo
Ronald Manson
Richard May
McCall Drug Co.
Paul McKenna
Megatronics Corp.
Mem Co. Canada Ltd.
Mentholatum Co. of Canada
Ramses Messih
Richard Moszynski
Tom Moffatt
Monarch Marking Systems
Linda Morrison
Gail Nickerson
Anne M. Owchar
John Plens
Prestilux Inc.
Purdue Frederick Co.
Richard Rafuse
Pegi L. Rappaport
Barry Ray
Gilbert S. Reilly
Charles Resnick
Kenneth Rey
Richter, Usher, Vineberg
A.H. Robins Canada Inc.
Roussell (Canada) Ltd.
Pinnie Saiger
Murray Salomon
Sazaha Drugs Ltd.

Charles P. Scerbo
Al Schacter
Johan Schenk
Sidney S. Schipper
Pravin Shah
Harry Shapiro
Sheraton Centre of Toronto
William Simpson
Arnold Smith
Jules Solomon
Martin Sone
Margery Spanner
Spence Bros. Drug Stores Ltd.
Patricia Stepkoff
Syntex Ltd.
Heather Tesluck
Jack Thompson
Delbert Thorne
Timex Inc.
Toronto Honda
Toronto Sun
Travel Resources Ltd.
Gillian Turnbull
Universal Electric Products Co.
   Ltd.
Debbie Vidinu
Village Pharmacy
Mel Webb
Webber Inc.
Alan Weingarten
Judy Wells Inc.
Alan Westad
Edie Wilcox
Murray Wiseman
Lap Wu
Vincent Yap
Frank Yip

Index

55; Tincture Nux Vomica, 56;
Buckley's Mixture, 56; Koffler's Fever
Powders For Babies, 56; Koffler's
Cough Syrup, 56; Koffler's Headache
Powders, 56; Koffler's Boracic Acid,
56; Dr. Harold Taube's Stomach
Powder, 56
Mehta, Zubin, 262
Meir, Golda, Israeli Prime Minister, 208,
260, 297–98
Melba, Nellie, 240
Metcalfe, George, 49
Metro Central Library, Toronto, 246, 289
Michener, Roland, Governor-General,
239
Mikado, The, 68, 147, 210
Mintz, Shlomo, 262
Modess, 59
Mom and Pop Dunkin' Donuts, 110
Montreal Indoor Tennis Club, 308
Moriyama, Raymond, 289, 291, 300–01
Morris, Gerry, 93–94
Mostel, Zero, 244
Mount Bruno Country Club, Que., 308
Mount Royal Club, Montreal, 308
Mount Sinai Hospital, Toronto, 241–42,
302
Mulroney, Brian, Canadian Prime
Minister, 10
Munro, Ian, 215–16, 220
Murray Koffler Foundation, 240
Myles, Lou, clothier, 22

Nabisco Brands Ltd., 11
Nathan Phillips Square, Toronto, 230
National Ballet of Canada, 243–44
National Drug Limited, 136, 152
National Gallery of Canada, 228
Neiman Marcus Stores, Texas, 226
Nesselrode, Count Karl, 240
New Jerusalem Colony, Sask., 38
Newman, Peter C., 99
Newspapers: *Globe and Mail*, 10, 159,
175, 305; *Toronto Telegram*, 22, 83, 232;
Toronto Star, 83, 94, 121, 175, 228;
Toronto Sun, 254; *Metro Mirror*,
Toronto, 121; *Don Mills Mirror*,
Toronto, 120–21; *New York Times*,
78–79, 182; *Shopping Centre News*, 95;
Drugstore News, 167; *Northern Miner*,
91; *Financial Post*, 91; *Wall Street
Journal*, 226; *Observer*, London, 247;
International Herald Tribune, 283

Niemy, Roman, 304, 306
Nixon, President Richard, 19
North, John, 292
Northern Dancer, 99

Oakwood Collegiate, Toronto, 63, 70,
75, 91
O'Keefe Centre, Toronto, 305
Old Spice, 106–07
Olive, David, 225
Olympia and York Developments
Limited, 12
One Minute Manager, The, 310
Ontario College of Art, 180
Ontario College of Pharmacy, 52–53, 59,
63, 71–72, 233, 246, 313
Ontario Food Terminal, 312–13
Ontario Science Centre, 234, 289
Operation Lifeline, 238–40
Oppenheimer, J. Robert, 270
Oshawa Group Limited, 256
Osler, Hoskin and Harcourt, Toronto,
318
Oxford University, 283

Pablum, 105
Palais Royal Ballroom, 69
Panzica, Norman, 235–36
Paré, Paul, 17, 306–09, 314, 318
Parke-Davis & Co. Ltd., 11
Parker, John, 146–47, 197
Passion For Excellence, 311
Pearson, Lester, Canadian Prime
Minister, 208, 266, 328
Pearson, Maryon, 266, 328
Peoples Drug Stores, 315–17
Peppermint Lounge, New York, 220
Peres, Shimon, Israeli Prime Minister, 10
Perfumatic (vending machines), 87–88
Perlman, Itzhak, 262
Peters, Tom, 207, 311
Peterson, David, Ontario Premier, 10
Peter Stuyvesant cigarettes, 172–73
Pharmacists Against Drug Abuse (PADA),
232
Pharmacy profession: European history,
41; in Shakespeare, 42; in early North
America, 43–44; folksy 1920s image,
44–45; alternative to medical
profession, 52; ornate store
appearance, 53; drugstore smells,
53–54; Latin prescriptions, 54; early
dispensaries, 54–55; non-prescription